Social
Research
Strategy and Tactics

Bernard S. Phillips

Boston University

Social Research

Strategy and Tactics

Third Edition

Macmillan Publishing Co., Inc.
New York
Collier Macmillan Publishers
London

Macmillan Publishing Co., Inc.
866 Third Avenue, New York, New York 10022

Collier Macmillan Canada, Ltd.

Library of Congress Cataloging in Publication Data

Phillips, Bernard S
  Social research.

  Includes bibliographies and index.
  1. Social science research. I. Title.
H62.P462 1976   300'.7'2   75-4936
ISBN 0-02-395260-1

Printing: 1 2 3 4 5 6 7 8   Year: 6 7 8 9 0 1 2

To Edward A. Suchman,
who helped us learn how to combine
positivism and humanism in
social research

Preface

A central image pervading this third edition is that of the all-too-human scientist, an individual not much different from anyone else, with his or her guilt and hate as well as self-confidence and love, alternately pessimistic and optimistic, conforming and autonomous. Whatever else science is, it is a human endeavor. Science has been cruel because human beings have been cruel, and science has been a powerful force for human welfare because people have been so inclined. Our image of the cold-blooded or mad scientist is a projection of our own separation of intellect and emotions and distrust of the separation, and that image has in turn partly become a self-fulfilling prophecy. However, by shifting our image to a more humanistic one, which is more in accordance with the deepest traditions of science, we can also shift to the fulfillment of a different prophecy. This, then, is a guiding theme of the third edition of *Social Research:* that a humanistic approach to social research is emerging, and that such an image can become the basis for the kind of science of human behavior that can revive our Enlightenment dreams.

As we move toward such a humanistic perspective, we must also reject the sacred cow image of science. In this era of the death of gods, science has been a victim along with other institutions. But the death of science as god also makes room for the birth of science as an institution we can work to improve, that is, as a scientific institution. By being as honest as we can about the way science actually works and discovering its limitations, we can reconstruct it. For example, we can bring to bear on the scientific process the knowledge of the social sciences, examining the social and personality structures involved and placing research within a historical context. As scientific methods come to be seen as fallible, the scientific investigator can gain an increasing sense of freedom and autonomy. No longer the prisoner of a set of unchangeable and infallible rules, he can take increasing responsibility for the further development of the scientific process. All this is no more than the extension of the scientific method back to itself.

When the scientist-as-human-being sees phenomena, he does not see them neatly divided into sociological, psychological, economic, political, historical, and anthropological facets, nor does he focus on only one facet and ignore the rest. In relating to others he must act on the basis of assumptions about personality dynamics as well as social structure, biology as well as physics. And if he must be interdisciplinary in his everyday life, he must also be so when it comes to the research process. His own personality is deeply involved in his investigations, as is the social structure, the physical context of the research situation, and his physiological state at the time. This wider view of the research process that is now emerging represents an extension of disciplinary or subdisciplinary emphases. It means the expansion of the disciplines, so that they can deal effectively with scientific and human problems, and not the abandonment of the disciplines.

Scientific and everyday behavior may be linked from still another perspective. The scientist develops ideas or hypotheses about the nature of the world (context of discovery), and he also tests these ideas against data he collects (context of verification). But this is what we all do all the time, only covertly: we develop ideas about phenomena, and we test those ideas against our experiences. The difference between covert and explicit behavior may appear to be trivial, but it is far from that. By bringing to the surface what would normally be hidden, we have the opportunity to examine it rationally, to put our minds to work. Instead of becoming the victims of blind prejudices about the nature of phenomena, we can test our prejudices and show them up for what they are. In this way, we can move toward an ever deeper understanding of those phenomena.

This emerging humanistic view of social science has been a long time in coming and is in accord with similar trends within the physical science community. Auguste Comte along with most of the founders of sociology had the vision of a discipline that would be both humane and scientific, but the recent history of a world where the sciences of human behavior were no match for accelerating human problems has dimmed that vision. Yet the vision is not dead. The social sciences stand midway between the sciences and the humanities, with the sciences emphasizing the context of verification and the humanities the context of discovery. Perhaps the failures of social science to deal effectively with world problems are due not to the impossibility of constructing a science of human behavior, but rather to the failure of the social sciences to be sufficiently scientific. For if the nature of the scientific method is the continuing interaction between the contexts of discovery and verification, then the world has not yet seen more than a smattering of the scientific method. An effective science of discovery and verification requires a sturdier bridge between the two cultures of the humanities and the sciences than we have yet built.

Such a vision of the scientific method is a very old one. However, it will continue to remain just that—a vision—until we learn to structure its use within the context of day-to-day research. It provides a much broader base for the pyramid of social science than has yet been put to work, yet if we wish to attain heights of effectiveness not yet achieved, we must build over the entire surface of that base. Every aspect of the work of the social researcher is involved here, whether it be his basic philosophical assumptions or his nonverbal communication with the individuals he studies. As we proceed, we shall find that we are learning to do no more than we always thought we were—but in fact were not—achieving.

For example, the scientist is supposed to be open to new ideas, but in fact he remains a prisoner of his own unexamined assumptions or paradigm. By learning to unearth such assumptions, we can subject them to the testing process as well as entertain alternative assumptions. In other words, the scientist can learn to behave ever more scientifically.

Part I consists of a one-chapter introduction to the scientific method. Part II, "Defining the Problem," centers on the context of discovery. If we are to develop more effective ideas about the nature of phenomena, then we must start with those ideas already in existence. What are the assumptions, or paradigms, that set boundaries for viewing phenomena? What tools can uncover these assumptions? What bodies of theory can aid in this process? What theoretical and paradigmatic implications do our research procedures incorporate? How can all these ideas be included within techniques for defining a research problem so as to create a powerful thrust beyond existing knowledge?

Whatever successes we attain within the context of discovery will contribute to the research process only to the degree that they are applied to the context of verification, the subject of Parts III and IV. Part III, "Measurement and Data Construction," is so named because there is a vast difference between the idea of "data construction" and that of "data collection." "Collection" implies a passive role for the scientist: he gathers together pieces of the puzzle that are lying around and puts them together. However, the emerging view is that the investigator participates actively in the "construction" of those pieces. It is his own definition of the problem that sets in motion forces that shape the fate of his inquiry and conclusions. The truths he observes include the truths he creates. This approach opens up a new area of investigation for the social scientist: the research milieu. If there is no way of his avoiding some type of "investigator effect"—as seems to be the case—then a scientific approach demands that these effects be investigated. Of course, there are many other things to be measured as well. One direction for dealing with all this complexity—which matches the complexity within the context of discovery—is that of "triangulating" or integrating a number of different techniques of data construction. This orientation is the same as that behind the parable of the nine blind men and the elephant: each one, by experiencing part of the truth, can add to an understanding of the nature of the elephant.

Part IV, "Analysis and Interpretation of Data," emphasizes the application of mathematical ideas within the context of verification. This approach lies within the grand tradition of the physical sciences, a tradition that has largely produced our image of the scientific method. It is no secret that the effectiveness of the tools discussed in Part IV has been seriously questioned. Yet are their limitations due to our inherent inability to apply mathematical tools to human behavior, or to our failure to become sufficiently sophisticated in the use of mathematics to this end? I take the latter position, since I believe that human behavior is more complex than physical phenomena, and that we have only begun to utilize existing mathematical tools stemming from the physical science tradition. Beyond those tools already in existence lie computer-based models yet to be developed, models which are closer to the complexity of human behavior.

Part V, "Scientific Communication," completes the information feedback loop between discovery and verification: the results of the verification process must be communicated in order to provide the basis for further discoveries. Yet the problem of scientific communication is proving to be no easier to solve than the problem of human communication generally. Whatever the reasons, we all hesitate to move beyond our relatively narrow boundaries. If we can substantially improve scientific communication, we will be replacing Durkheim's "abnormal" division of labor—with its barriers to communication—with a "normal" division of labor. Here, the disciplines are not abandoned, but each enlarges so that it meshes more easily with the others. Such a scientific community would be, in my view, unique to human experience, and its implications are as yet unknown.

I would like to thank those graduate students—David Dillon, Stephanie Hughes, Andrew Plotkin, David Stratman, and Roger Whittaker—who contributed research illustrations to this book, and also the many undergraduate and graduate students in my classes over the past five years who helped me in the development of my ideas. Although it is not possible for me to do justice to the numerous individuals who have made my own ideas possible, I would like to single out one individual whose personal and professional encouragement was essential: Irwin T. Sanders.

B. S. P.

Contents

part I

The Scientific Method

The scientific method has proven to be one of the most powerful forces in human history, and there is reason to believe that its role in the future will increase many fold. Yet how are we to understand the nature of this phenomenon? What patterns of behavior does it encompass? Answers are essential if we are to understand the currents presently shaping modern society. And beyond such understanding lies our ability to direct these currents into channels of our own choosing.

1

Scientific Method: Reflexive, Developmental, Experimental

The scientific method is an extension of the reasoning abilities that we use in everyday situations. For example, if we wish to go somewhere, we must know where we are starting from (reflexive) and where we wish to go (developmental), and we must actually begin to move (experimental). The scientist does the same kinds of things, only he generally goes about his business more systematically, using procedures specifically designed to help him in these tasks. He reviews relevant literature (reflexive), defines a problem for investigation (developmental), and proceeds to set up a research situation bearing on that problem (experimental). This similarity is based on the fact that both everyday and scientific behavior incorporate the three fundamental elements of human behavior: the cognitive or intellectual, the orientation toward goals, and action.

These three elements of human behavior are incorporated within each phase of the research process, although some elements are emphasized in a given phase more than others. For example, reviewing the scientific literature emphasizes the cognitive or reflexive element, but it is also oriented to goals and it is an activity. The definition of a scientific problem is not merely developmental or oriented to goals: it must also incorporate ideas, and it is a kind of action as well. Moreover, the setting up of a research situation does indeed emphasize the active or experimental component of behavior, but an action also stems from ideas and goals. Thus, we can look for these elements of the research process—reflexive, developmental, experimental—in any given stage of that process, no matter how minute. Correspondingly, it is through an understanding of them that we can develop tools for understanding each and every phase of the research process.

1.1 The Scientific Method: Overview

In this section we locate the scientific method in several ways. Some of these convey a view of this method as a process which is never complete. Others locate it in relation to everyday behavior. What emerges is an image of a very human enterprise.

The Research Process

The scientific method may be defined as an effort to achieve increasing understanding of phenomena by (1) defining problems so as to build on available knowledge, (2) obtaining information essential for dealing with these problems, (3) analyzing and interpreting these data in accordance with clearly defined rules, and (4) communicating the results of these efforts to others.

In defining the problem, the researcher delves deeply into what he wants to learn, what is already known about the subject, and how he might move from the known to the unknown. His next step is to obtain whatever data this defined problem calls for, using techniques of investigation that are appropriate to that definition. The rules on which his analysis and interpretation are based—analogous to legal rules of evidence—attempt to take into account all relevant factors that bear on the problem in question. They are also designed to make clear both to the researcher and to others with whom he communicates the information that is the basis for interpretations that are made. By communicating the results of his study, the investigator gives others a chance to arrive at their own interpretations and to repeat or go beyond his study.

The scientific method is, then, a way of collecting, processing, and communicating information, based on activities designed to increase existing information. Such activities take place within social contexts that bring to bear on them a range of personal and societal concerns. These concerns interact with scientific activities, and what emerges differs from the activities as originally conceived.[1]

We are dealing with a method that is defined pragmatically:[2] it is used because of its effectiveness in yielding understandings that are useful to individuals and to society. The method is not fixed, but changes as we learn better ways of obtaining such understandings. We use particular techniques of scientific inquiry because they have proven to be effective in the

---

[1] This emphasis on the social context of scientific methodology is an emerging theme of the sociology of knowledge and has been set forth systematically by Gideon Sjoberg and Roger Nett in *A Methodology for Social Research* (New York: Harper, 1968).

[2] In his *The Conduct of Inquiry: Methodology for Behavioral Science* (San Francisco: Chandler, 1964), Abraham Kaplan applies pragmatism to the range of issues within social research.

past. The method is defined, then, in terms of its consequences, and anything is allowed—within the limits of social and personality constraints
existing at the time—provided that it can yield demonstrably better
understanding.

This view of the research process is a Magna Charta for the investigator.
He is not chained to a set of techniques simply because they have worked
adequately in the past, nor must he defer to the supposedly superior methodological knowledge of other investigators because of their research reputation. It is not necessary for him to continually look back over his shoulder, wondering if others would consider his procedures to be "correct"
or "incorrect." He would be well advised to learn as much as he can about
the techniques others have used in order to produce knowledge, but he
need not adopt them. He is free to invent his own procedures. What counts
is not what others think of those procedures but how well they work. And
if they do work well, then the process of scientific communication is designed to bring home that fact to others and, as a result, to enlarge their
perspectives as to what constitutes effective research methods.

We may note important stages in Western history that led to the methods
we use today. For example, the invention of writing made it possible to
codify existing knowledge far more thoroughly and accurately than previously and, of course, also greatly facilitated the communication process.
There is also the idea of progress, with its foundations both in the Judaic
contrast between a unitary god and mortal man and in the glorification
of human reason and the demonstration of human possibilities characteristic of classical Greece. In more recent times there is the linkage of this
same high aspiration for the individual, as carried forward through the
Renaissance and Reformation, with a delegitimation of religious dogma
as the source of truth. If we call this linkage the spirit of science, then
the union of that spirit with the Protestant work ethic—coupled with many
other factors as well—created the scientific and industrial revolution that
has continued to accelerate to this day. Scientific development was not
simply a resultant of the accumulation of ideas: it was the effectiveness
of those ideas for creating wealth and solving human problems—which
in turn gave further impetus to science—that created the snowballing process which appears to be at the center of social change in the modern
world.

From this perspective, science is rooted in humanism,[3] and it has a pragmatic basis in its ability to produce technologies that can solve human
problems. Then what, we may ask, has gone wrong in the modern era?
Why is science frequently viewed with so much distrust? Why are there
serious splits within the social sciences between those who claim that the

[3] J. Bronowski develops this theme in his *Science and Human Values* (New York:
Harper, 1965), emphasizing such values as truth, independence, originality, dissent,
freedom, and tolerance.

quantitative approach of the physical sciences is the key path to social science knowledge and those who reject mathematics in favor of qualitative and empathic probes of the behavior of individuals and groups? This confrontation—analogous to the war between the two cultures of the sciences and the humanities—may be illustrated by the controversies surrounding the publication of Thomas and Znaniecki's *The Polish Peasant in Europe and America* in 1918. That year divides two periods in the history of American sociology: the earlier period, with its emphasis on social reformism and qualitative research, and the post-World War I period, with its greater concern for scientific rigor and its burgeoning techniques of quantitative research. Was it scientific to incorporate within *The Polish Peasant* personal documents such as letters, autobiographies, and case records, documents that could be easily selected to provide evidence for whatever points the authors wished to make? Or would the omission of such personal documents be unscientific, since the reader would have no first-hand knowledge of the mental and emotional life of the individuals he is attempting to understand?

In the ensuing decades the dominant orientation shifted in a quantitative direction, but now once again sociologists are finding themselves engaged in major methodological controversies. This time, however, it is the quantitative sociologists who are on the defensive. The proliferation of sophisticated quantitative techniques and the enormous growth of quantitative research does not seem to have been accompanied by the expected growth in understanding. Add to this accelerating societal problems and accelerating demands put to social scientists for effective knowledge and you have the present-day situation. At this time we have an opportunity to reconsider all of the fundamental issues on which our research methods are based. Is it possible to incorporate within them both the humanistic and the scientific traditions and, as a result, produce effective knowledge? Can mankind take hold of the juggernaut that is the scientific-industrial revolution and direct it toward more humanistic goals? Or are we helpless, caught in the rush of events, prisoners of the tools we have created?

Both the humanistic and the scientific traditions require a view of scientific research that distinguishes between its myths and its realities. With respect to defining problems, how often is there little continuity between what was done previously and what is being done now? How much awareness is there on the part of the scientist of the relationship between his own thought processes and his social and cultural milieu? As for the collection of data, how often is the investigator so set in the specific techniques he has learned that he fails to open his eyes to new possibilities? What will it take for a sociologist who is a prisoner of participant observation techniques to learn about simulation or survey research? Concerning the analysis of data, to what extent are we actually enlarging our understanding of human behavior with our research, and to what extent are we going around and around in circles? Does the researcher exclude from his analysis the ways in which he participates in constructing the data he observes? And finally—with regard to scientific communication—what are the chances that reports of scientific research will be published; and if published, read; and if read, taken seriously; and if taken seriously, improve the understanding of the reader, so that he will be moved to alter his scientific behavior, do more effective research, and communicate back to the original researcher, as well as to others?

A hopeless situation? Not at all, for somehow, despite all these problems, scientific progress—including that of the social sciences—has been enormous over the years. Yet perhaps that progress is as nothing compared to what might be attained should we address such problems seriously.

Scientific Method and Human Behavior

Let us examine three of the four phases of the research process: (1) definition of the problem, (2) obtaining information, and (3) the analysis and interpretation of this information. Figure 1-1 can help us to see how these phases relate to one another. We see the third phase leading back to the first: our analysis and interpretation of research data gives us the basis for redefining the research problem. In this way, the scientific process becomes a never-ending one, with each research finding becoming the basis for new directions in obtaining knowledge. Implicitly, human knowledge is here seen as potentially infinite: it can continue to expand indefinitely.

The scientist actually goes through these phases quite often. For example, it is common practice for survey researchers to design a pretest, or trial run, of their interview schedules, and to use the results of this effort to improve those instruments for data collection. Also, within each of the above phases the scientist mentally anticipates the other phases any number of times, whether he does this consciously or unconsciously, and his behavior is based on those anticipations. In this way, he mentally goes around the loop any number of times.

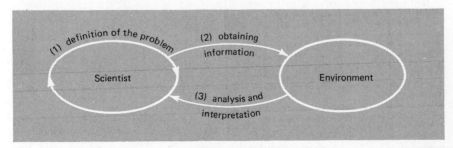

Figure 1-1.
The Scientific Method as a Feedback Process.

This view of the scientific method parallels the social scientist's image of human interaction. Figure 1-2 presents stages of the process of human interaction: (1) "covert rehearsal,"[4] where the individual considers—implicitly or explicitly—a range of possible actions within a given situation, traces through their implications for other stages of the interaction process, and selects a particular course of action, (2) sending messages, and (3) receiving messages. In (2) and (3) the individual obtains a reaction to his chosen course of action from another individual, and the resulting information in turn provides the basis for his next covert rehearsal. Thus, we have a "feedback process" here as well as in the case of the scientific method: the third stage loops back to the first in a never-ending circle.

We are now in a position to examine the fourth stage of the research process: scientific communication. We can see such communication from the perspective of Figure 1-2, where "Individual A" is one scientist and "Individual B" is another. Scientific communication becomes, then, simply an instance of ordinary human communication. However, there are differences as well as similarities. For example, scientific communication is associated with a greater degree of explicitness, more clearly defined rules, and a more systematic approach.

As we proceed to explore the nature of the scientific method, we must examine more thoroughly the various phases of the research process. In particular, it becomes essential to examine the three elements of human behavior which are incorporated within each phase of the research process: the cognitive or intellectual, the orientation toward goals, and action. These are of course also elements of human behavior generally. The ensuing sections explore these elements under headings most appropriate for an understanding of social research: reflexive, developmental, and experimental.

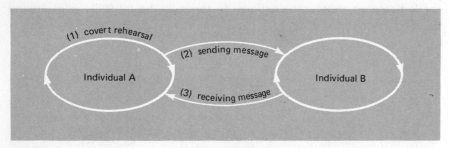

Figure 1-2.
Human Interaction as a Feedback Process.

[4] The concept of "covert rehearsal" and the focus on a cybernetic view of human behavior come from J. Edward Hulett, "A Symbolic Interactionist Model of Human Communication," *AV Communication Review*, **14** (1966), pp. 5–33.

1.2   Reflexive

The reflexive process refers to a process of self-examination, where factors normally hidden are brought into plain view.[5] For example, the scientist learns to probe his own fundamental assumptions, or paradigms, so that these can be opened up to testing, as opposed to setting dogmatic boundaries for investigations. All human behavior is reflexive to the degree that it is based on some understanding of the individual's relation to his environment. For example, within the socialization process we learn to define ourselves as distinct entities via observing the reactions others have to us. Scientific procedures carry the reflexive approach a good deal further. In this section we take up two illustrations of it: the exploration of paradigms and the contrast between logic-in-use and reconstructed logic. These illustrations bear on different phases of the research process.

Paradigms and Scientific Revolutions

Every scientific idea may be seen as resting on a paradigm, or set of explicit and implicit assumptions, that gives the idea meaning and direction. Sociologists in the past have devoted little attention to paradigms, tending to associate such a focus with a philosophical as distinct from a sociological perspective. However, this situation has changed, and a philosophical interest in fundamental assumptions is now more generally viewed as a path to improve theory and more effective research. The book that, more than any other, helped to bring this change about—Thomas S. Kuhn's *The Structure of Scientific Revolutions*—sees changes in paradigms as giving rise to scientific revolutions:

> Political revolutions are inaugurated by a growing sense, often restricted to a segment of the political community, that existing institutions have ceased adequately to meet the problems posed by an environment that they have in part created. In much the same way, scientific revolutions are inaugurated by a growing sense, again often restricted to a narrow subdivision of the scientific community, that an existing paradigm has ceased to function adequately in the exploration of an aspect of nature to which that paradigm itself had previously led the way.[6]

[5] The idea of reflexive analysis is probably as old as mankind, but in recent years it has received increasing attention in social science, as evidenced by works in the sociology of knowledge, the sociology of science, and the sociology of sociology. For an influential and penetrating treatment of the idea, see Alvin W. Gouldner, *The Coming Crisis of Western Sociology* (New York: Basic Books, 1970), especially Chapter 13, "Living as a Sociologist: Toward a Reflexive Sociology," pp. 481–512.

[6] Thomas S. Kuhn, *The Structure of Scientific Revolutions* (Chicago: U. of Chicago, 1962), p. 91.

Kuhn describes a number of major paradigm changes, such as those associated with the work of Copernicus, Newton, and Einstein. In each case, a given paradigm is seen as holding sway for a long period of time until it gives way to a paradigm that has come to be seen as dealing with scientific knowledge more adequately. The key reason for the length of time involved seems to be that paradigms are largely invisible, operating under the surface of scientific literature, and thus cannot easily be confronted by scientific experiments.

A reflexive approach to research aims—among other things—at the uncovering of paradigms so that they too can be tested by the research process. For example, to what extent does the paradigm behind a given theory assume a tendency toward stasis versus one toward change, or a hierarchical versus an equalitarian society? The raising up of these icebergs is a most difficult task, since they are so much a part of the world view of the investigator that he does not see them. The situation is analogous to that of a fish not seeing the water it swims in. To the extent that such difficulties can be overcome, however, a reflexive approach offers the investigator the possibility for much more rapid scientific progress than we have heretofore experienced. In Chapter 2 we shall take up four major paradigms in some detail.

Logic-in-Use and Reconstructed Logic

If we now move to the other end of the research process—the part where the researcher communicates what he has achieved and how he has achieved it—we may make a distinction between what he actually did (logic-in-use) and the way he represents what he actually did (reconstructed logic). This distinction between logic-in-use and reconstructed logic is based on factors more decisive than the honesty of the investigator. Perhaps most important, each individual—including researchers—only has a limited awareness of the nature of his own behavior. In addition, the norms for scientific communication generally do not favor the revelation of all the stupidities, dead ends, bureaucratic impasses, laziness, fears, disorganization, and countless other factors that would interfere with a neat, systematic, and impressive research report.

As a result, there is a great gap between what is reported in the scientific literature and the way things really occurred. In such a situation it is difficult to improve on our methods of research, since our picture of those methods tends to be an idealized one. The situation becomes even worse when we realize that an ability to write effectively is not usually developed in the course of scientific education.

An investigator taking a reflexive approach would begin with an awareness of the existence of this gap. As for narrowing it, here are some possible directions: keeping a daily log of the progress of research and presenting a sequential summary of the log in the final report; an increase in the researcher's awareness of his own behavior; a shift in the norms for communication so that the transmission of inadequacies would be valued and overly systematic reports would be regarded with suspicion; an emphasis on the importance of readable scientific reports.

1.3 Developmental

The idea of progress, or development, has always been central to the scientific method. It has roots in the Judaic-Christian tradition as well as in the glorification of human reason within classical Greece. It is so much a part of modern Western thought that it is difficult for us to imagine a tradition-bound world where the cycles of day and night and of the seasons replace our evolutionary perspective. Within science, the idea of progress constitutes a faith in the ability of the scientific method to yield ever deeper and ever more effective knowledge. In this section we take up two illustrations of the developmental idea: reviewing the literature, and the contexts of discovery and verification.

Reviewing the Literature

In order to define a research problem in such a way that we can go beyond what is known, we must become quite familiar with what is known. Otherwise, the investigator becomes a "new Columbus"—in the words of Pitirim Sorokin—forever rediscovering old truths. Reviewing the literature is essential for maintaining a continuity within science.

The literature review is not simply a passive assessment of the state of knowledge, but an active synthesis of that knowledge within the context of the investigator's particular interests. In this sense, it goes beyond the reflexive idea and becomes developmental. There is no right way in which a given literature review must be done: procedures must vary with the interests of the investigator and the context of the research situation.

The scope of one's literature review reveals one's level of aspiration for a given project. With a narrow perspective, it becomes more difficult to go very far beyond what is known, since that narrowness interfere's with one's ability to locate the fundamental assumptions, or paradigm, within which research is being done. This tends to prevent the investigator from encompassing what is already known as well as from becoming sensitive to the subtleties of the complex forces within the situations he is investigating. Yet is it possible for the researcher to deal with the full range of ideas within his discipline? And even if he is able to do so, how can he possibly go beyond a given discipline in his search for an even more comprehensive framework?

These problems appear to be exceedingly difficult because the paradigm within which most of us do our thinking erects barriers to the integration of vast amounts of human experience, as we shall see in Chapter 2. By being aware of that paradigm, and by taking alternative paradigms into account, the problem becomes manageable. For example, within sociology the researcher can be guided by the various schools of theory, such as structural functionalism, conflict theory, symbolic interactionism, exchange theory, and phenomenological sociology. By defining a problem in relation to these theories, he locates himself relative to a great deal of what has been accomplished within sociology. As he moves to incorporate perspectives from several schools of theory, he simultaneously moves beyond his initial paradigm. For example, a researcher who incorporates a symbolic interactionist perspective is also thereby becoming more sensitive to traditions within the humanities. This approach to reviewing the literature is directly opposed to the idea that if each researcher proceeds within a narrow framework, science as a whole will advance. We build the house of science when each of us sees how his tasks fit within the structure as a whole.

The Contexts of Discovery and Verification

The context of verification deals with knowledge of truth and falsity, with proof, with the construction of evidence for or against a given idea. The context of discovery centers on scientific progress, on the development of improved understandings, better predictions, and a firmer basis for more effective technologies. The two contexts thus deal with different parts of the temporal dimension: discovery focuses on what is not yet, and verification centers on what is. Each implies the importance of the other: to deal with the future, we must know where we are in the present, and an understanding of the present requires visions of the future. If the context of discovery is located largely within the developmental component of the scientific method, then the context of verification encompasses in part the reflexive component. In Figure 1-3 we can see the relationship between these two contexts as a feedback loop, with scientific progress requiring a continuing interaction between the two.

To understand the significance of the context of verification, let us turn

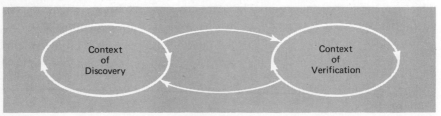

Figure 1-3.
Contexts of Discovery and Verification.

to a passage from the writings of Sir Francis Bacon (1561–1626), one of the originators of the scientific method:

> The human understanding when it has once adopted an opinion either as being the received opinion or as being agreeable to itself draws all things else to support and agree with it. And though there be a greater number and weight of instances to be found on the other side, yet these it either neglects and despises, or else by some distinction sets aside and rejects; in order that by this great and pernicious predetermination the authority of its former conclusions may remain inviolate. And therefore it was a good answer that was made by one who when they showed him hanging in a temple a picture of those who had paid their vows as having escaped shipwreck, and would have him say whether he did not now acknowledge the power of the gods. "Aye," asked he again, "but where are they painted that were drowned, after their vows?"[7]

Bacon is suggesting that our usual methods for collecting and analyzing information tend to favor finding support for our own previous biases, whereas a more scientific approach would emphasize obtaining evidence against as well as for those biases. It is the context of verification which encompasses a variety of procedures designed to deal with this problem. As one illustration within sociology, techniques have been developed for "sampling" which would enable Bacon's seaman to compare the proportion of ships wrecked by those who had "paid their vows" with the proportion of ships wrecked by those who had not.

Most of what we already know about the scientific method has to do with the context of verification. However, we know relatively little about how theories and hypotheses are developed in the first place, about how to define problems in such a way that we can go beyond existing literatures, and about how we can improve our techniques of scientific research. Our scientific methods are far more methods of verification than of discovery.

Dare we hope for a science of discovery as well as verification? Are creative processes themselves fair game for the tools of science? If the history of science is our guide, then this is not an impossible dream, for no limit to the development of human understanding has yet been discovered. However, if we are to move in this direction, it is essential that we define our research problems so that such movement becomes important. Scientific methods can help us to achieve understanding, but it is necessary that they first be harnessed to our goals. And what awaits us is nothing less than the granting of our wish that we can learn to make our future wishes come true.

[7] Francis Bacon, *Novum Organum* (The New Organon) Aphorism XLVI, Book I, ed. by James Spelding, Robert Ellis, and Douglas Heath (Boston: Taggard and Thompson, 1863), Vol. 8, pp. 79–80.

1.4 Experimental

The experimental approach within the scientific method is an active one where the scientist puts his ideas to work in an attempt to develop deeper understandings. By "experimental" I am not referring only to the particular technique of data collection and analysis known as the experiment but, more broadly, to the scientists's active testing of his ideas, using whatever methods of data collection he deems appropriate. His procedures have some impact on the environment, and it is up to the scientist to study that impact and reach some understanding of it. The experimental approach is largely akin to the context of verification. It is not enough to imagine some explanation for phenomena: what is also required is that we do what is necessary to test that explanation. In this section two aspects of the experimental approach are taken up: the phenomenon of investigator effect and the relationship between science and technology.

Investigator Effect

"Investigator effect" refers to the various effects the scientist has on the research process, effects that are rarely planned for and that tend to interfere with this attempts to understand the research situation. In the experiment the scientist deliberately introduces certain phenomena in order to assess their impact, but in most other modes of data collection the scientist attempts to play a passive role so as not to introduce investigator effect. In recent years, however, the pervasiveness of investigator effect has become apparent. Consequently, it appears that all efforts at data collection are at least partly experimental in character. It is up to the researcher to learn to assess these investigator effects so that their occurrence does not distort his conclusions.

A classic illustration of the power of investigator effect is the Hawthorne Experiment,[8] a series of studies by Elton Mayo and his colleagues at Western Electric's Hawthorne Works at Cicero, Illinois, in the late twenties. One of these, conducted in the Relay Assembly Test Room, involved five girls who assembled small telephone parts called relays. Changes were made in the number of rest periods as well as in the length of the working day as part of the routine investigation of the effect these factors had on productivity. The general result was, as expected, that hourly output rose to make up for or exceed any lost time. But when the hours of work were lengthened once again, reverting back to an earlier stage of the experiment, the investigators were surprised to learn that output in the later period was almost 20 per cent higher than it had been in the earlier period. This

---

[8] For a description of this and other Hawthorne studies, see Fritz Roethlisberger and William Dickson, *Management and the Worker* (Cambridge, Mass.: Harvard U. P., 1939).

increased productivity, the investigators hypothesized, was a result of improvements in the social situation for the girls brought about by the experiment itself: they had been isolated from their regular department, were all volunteers, knew that they were being tested, knew the significance of the experiment, and experienced a growing cohesion.

For many years social scientists have been aware of the "Hawthorne effect"—as it had come to be labeled—but it took a series of recent studies by a psychologist, Robert Rosenthal,[9] to raise the issue once again, only now in a way that can no longer be ignored. In a number of experimental studies which were far better controlled than those at the Hawthorne Works, Rosenthal demonstrated the ease by which an experimenter can communicate to his subjects—be they Homo sapiens or rats—his expectations as to how they should behave. Rosenthal concludes that any experimenter may systematically influence his subjects by virtue of his personality and techniques in a given experimental situation. And if these effects have been observed under highly controlled experimental conditions, we have every right to expect them to be of much greater magnitude in situations like the survey, where the interaction between investigator and subjects is so much more extensive. Yet as we become aware of the nature of these effects, we open up opportunities for far more effective social research.

Science and Technology[10]

Figure 1-4 sketches some relationships among scientific theory or ideas, scientific method or procedures for discovery and verification, and scientific technology. The fundamental idea put forward by Figure 1-4 is that these three phenomena all hang together, and that advances or deficiencies in any one of them will affect the others. For example, our techniques of scientific observation will suffer without adequate theory, and our procedures for problem-solving (scientific technology) are dependent on the

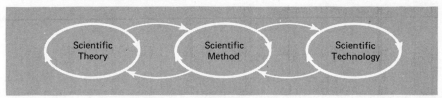

Figure 1-4.
Scientific Theory, Method, and Technology.

[9] Many of these are collected in Robert Rosenthal, *Experimenter Effects in Behavioral Research* (New York: Appleton, 1966).

[10] For a treatment of the philosophical basis for viewing technology as a part of science, see Leonard Goodwin, "The Historical-Philosophical Basis for Uniting Social Science with Social Problem-Solving," *Philosophy of Science*, **29** (1962), pp. 377–92.

state of our theory and methodology. To incorporate scientific technology in the way it appears in Figure 1-4 is to take a position as to the importance of technology within the scientific process. That process moves forward not only in research situations, where basic theory is directly under investigation, but also within applied problem-solving contexts, where the relation to basic theory is somewhat more indirect.

The problem of making the leap from science to technology is portrayed by Hermann Hesse in his novel *The Glass Bead Game* (also published as *Magister Ludi*).[11] The story takes place in the indefinite future and centers around the relationship between Castalia—an autonomous elite institution devoted almost wholly to the mind and the imagination—and the world around it. Joseph Knecht's rise within Castalia to become master of the glass bead game (Magister Ludi)—the game that has become the basis for interrelating all elements of culture, past and present—is followed by his efforts to end Castalia's isolation. He comes to see the glass bead game, for all of its achievements, as doomed to future extinction if that isolation continues.

Hesse seems to be arguing not simply for the utility of uniting science with technology but for its necessity. Writing just prior to World War II, he was undoubtedly deeply influenced by signs of the impending European holocaust. He located the central problem as the establishment in all institutions of glass bead games—actions and ideas that might, on the surface, appear to be noble, intellectual, and humanistic, but that at root are fundamentally irresponsible. To what extent do modern universities play the glass bead game, giving to social technologies merely the crumbs of their intellectual efforts? Hesse does not claim that the glass bead game is useless. Indeed, the excitement of the intellectual syntheses that the game can produce is conveyed throughout the volume. But Hesse does see such efforts as reaching a point of diminishing returns unless they are carried forward into the marketplace. By losing sight of other ends, the glass bead game insures its own eventual destruction.

1.5 Summary

To obtain an understanding of the scientific method, it is useful to see it as an extension of the reasoning processes we employ in everyday situations. Reflexively, science requires that we unearth and test our fundamental assumptions, or paradigms, and also that we report the results of our investigations with a reconstructed logic as close as possible to the logic-in-use employed. Correspondingly, effective behavior in ordinary situations requires a knowledge of our own motivations that is as profound as possible, and enduring relationships with others require a good deal

[11] Hermann Hesse, *Magister Ludi* (New York: Bantam, 1970), pp. 150–51.

of honesty within the communication process. Developmentally, the scientist must start by putting together what is already known within the scientific literature, and he can then continue by successively moving back and forth between the context of verification and the context of discovery. In ordinary situations, each of us can solve problems only to the degree that we have knowledge of the situation, the motivation to invent a solution (discovery), and the ability to test that solution in practice (verification). Experimentally, scientific testing which takes place both in situations invented by the scientist and in other problem-solving situations must be based on the kind of comprehensive knowledge that takes into account the phenomenon of investigator effect.

With this view of science, we need not see it as a dehumanizing force in society. Indeed, it may well be the most powerful humanizing force available to us. If it is an extension of our best efforts in ordinary situations, then it can teach us to improve those efforts. And any learning that occurs in those situations can be a basis for improving the scientific methods available to us, for those methods are merely a human construction and are thus subject to continuing change. Such an approach is in the direction of fulfilling our shattered Enlightenment dream of a society based on reason.

Exercises

1. Take any paper you have written and analyze it with reference to its paradigm, or underlying assumptions. To what degree are they reflexive, developmental, and experimental?

2. Write a short short story about a creature from "Timeland" who visits "Spaceland." Assume that Spaceland is very much our own society, with severe limitations placed on reflexive, developmental, and experimental orientations, and that Timeland is a scientific society.[12]

3. Review Figures 1-1, 1-2, 1-3, and 1-4, all of which deal with feed-

---

[12] Edwin Abbott's *Flatland* (New York: Dover, 1952), originally published in the 1880's, was one of the first science-fiction classics. Abbott described the world of a two-dimensional Flatlander who cannot understand why the zero-dimensional and one-dimensional residents of Pointland and Lineland are completely unaware of their limitations, and who becomes aware of his own limitations via a visit to Spaceland. However, when he attempts to explain this new world of possibilities to his fellow Flatlanders—with the aid of such phrases as "Upward, not Northward"—he is thrown into prison. He describes his situation as follows:

Hence I am absolutely destitute of converts, and for aught that I can see, the millennial Revelation has been made to me for nothing. Prometheus up in Spaceland was bound for bringing down fire for mortals, but I—poor Flatland Prometheus—lie here in prison for bringing down nothing to my countrymen. Yet I exist in the hope that these memoirs, in some manner, I know not how, may find their way to the minds of humanity in Some Dimension, and may stir up a race of rebels who shall refuse to be confined to limited Dimensionality (pp. 150–51).

back loops. Now reread the discussion of the Hawthorne Experiment. Apply the feedback loop idea to that discussion, developing a diagram of any aspect of it.

4. Following the idea of the scientific method as an extension of ordinary processes of reasoning, how would you apply that method to some everyday problem, such as the problem of improving your tennis game?

Annotated References

HESSE, HERMANN. Magister Ludi. New York: Bantam Books, Inc., 1970. Recognized as one of the important novels of this century, Hesse's last work allegorically confronts us with the irresponsibility of our institutions, resulting in large measure from their narrowness. His fundamental question—how to achieve a synethesis of science, art, and technology in the modern world—is posed within a story framework that is sufficiently suggestive to help define this as a problem.

KUHN, THOMAS S. *The Structure of Scientific Revolutions.* Chicago: University of Chicago Press, 1962. If Kuhn's thesis that scientists are prisoners of their own implicit assumptions is correct, then scientific progress is far, far slower than it might be. Kuhn throws light on the process by which such assumptions are altered as well as on the ways in which threats to them are resisted.

POLANYI, MICHAEL. *Personal Knowledge: Towards a Post-Critical Philosophy.* New York: Harper & Row, Publishers, Inc., 1962. Polanyi describes the significance of his work as follows: "The power of science to grow by the originality of individual thought is thus established within a cosmic perspective of steadily emergent meaning. Science, conceived as understanding nature, seamlessly joins with the humanities, bent on the understanding of man and human greatness. Man's ideals, unfolding in action, come into view."

part II

Defining the Problem

The process of defining the research problem is probably the most important, most ignored, and least understood aspect of the scientific method. It is important for the same reason that the Hawthorne effect proved to be so powerful: the researcher exerts a powerful influence over the phenomena he is investigating at every step along the way, and his definition of the problem—whether implicit or explicit—indicates the direction of that influence. This influence was largely ignored in the past, because the social scientist is only now gaining an awareness of his participation in the construction of the data he formerly thought he merely observed, an awareness stimulated by recent developments in sociological theory. Until recently the thrust of sociological attention has been outward, looking at the societal forces that shape human behavior, and that thrust has not been wide enough to include a view of how the individual researcher alters the structures he observes.

There are three levels of analysis which must be taken seriously in defining problems for scientific investigation: the paradigmatic, the theoretical, and the methodological. Chapters 2 and 3 focus on paradigms, Chapter 4 on theory, and Chapter 5 on methods, although each chapter overlaps with the others as well. My heaviest emphasis is on the paradigmatic level of analysis, just because this is the level that is least understood, most ignored, and—I believe—most important. In Chapter 4, my emphasis is on the literature of sociology, although the same approach can be applied to

19

other disciplines as well. Finally, we must be able to climb from these ladders of abstraction and construct the particular techniques necessary to move forward on a problem that has been defined paradigmatically and theoretically. Although research procedures are used for illustrating purposes throughout Part Two, it is in Chapter 5 that we emphasize procedures used to pull paradigms and theories together with research techniques.

chapter 2

Paradigms: Formism, Mechanism, Organicism, Pragmatism

Methods of social research are built on a foundation of social science theory. Such theory is, in turn, constructed on the basis of fundamental assumptions, or paradigms, assumptions that are more often implicit than explicit. In this chapter we center on four world views, or paradigms, whose development may be seen as bearing a rough correspondence to historical events: formism, mechanism, organicism, and pragmatism.[1] A formist view of the world may be derived from the Judaic-Christian tradition as well as from classical Greece. It sees the world as phenomena that fit into inflexible categories that are either the same or different. The mechanistic view, by contrast, integrates phenomena in highly complex and systematic ways, although it is only experience with the nonliving part of the universe that is salient. Organicism, as illustrated by the Hegelian dialectic, is also systematic, only its focus is on the animate aspects of the universe. It differs from pragmatism in that the latter is more change-oriented and more open to complexity.

The approach we shall take to these world views is that they are all useful to the student of social research, and that elements of each one may be found within a given theory or research procedure. This "multiple paradigm" orientation is distinct from the view that the paradigm that has emerged most recently—pragmatism—incorporates the best features of all the others and is sufficient unto itself. Rather than see pragmatism as the furthest point in the evolution of paradigms, we may see it as having much to gain through a continuing interaction with the paradigms that preceded

[1] For a detailed presentation of the philosophies behind each of these, see Stephen C. Pepper, *World Hypotheses* (Berkeley: U. of Calif., 1961). These four are, of course, only one approach to slicing the pie of our paradigms.

it. For example, pragmatism has much to learn from the essence of conflict embodied within formism.

2.1 Formism

Formism is all around us, since it is built into the very structure of our language. However specialized the language of the scientist becomes, it remains like an island in the vast ocean of everyday language and thought. The scientist learns to think in ordinary language, and that thinking process then becomes the basis on which he builds his scientific endeavors. Yet for all this, that ocean remains for him something that is not problematic: he consciously sees only what is located on his island. In Section 2.1 we make a very small beginning in exploring that ocean. A general analysis of formism is followed by an illustration, a format followed in the subsequent sections on mechanism, organicism, and pragmatism.

The Nature of Formism: Same and Different

According to Stephen Pepper, formism—manifested as a "world hypothesis," or comprehensive philosophy—"is associated with Plato, Aristotle, the scholastics, neoscholastics, neorealists, modern Cambridge realists."[2] Its "root metaphor" is similarity, based on the simple common-sense perception of phenomena as either the same or different. This either-or mode of thinking is based on a fundamental assumption made explicit by Aristotle in his law of identity: A is A, B is B, C is C, and so forth. It is an assumption that a thing is itself, an assumption that appears to be completely reasonable: I am I, you are you, society is society, truth is truth. Conversely, I am not you, truth is not falsehood. All phenomena are either the same, or they are different: "A is related to B" is either true, or it is false.

This focus on sameness or difference is implicit in our language. For example, any noun, such as "truth," divides the world into two classes of phenomena, those that are included within this category and those that are excluded. The former are all the same in some sense, and the latter are all different in the same sense. This either-or orientation is not simply manifested throughout everyday language and thought processes: it is also the basis for certain vital measurement procedures in the social sciences. Specifically, nominal measurement, or scaling, procedures—techniques for measuring with reference to such categories as "Democrat" and "Republican" or "employed" and "retired"—derive from this formist approach.

This Aristotelian law of identity—that A is A—has both temporal and spatial implications. Temporally, it structures a static world where A remains A indefinitely. Change becomes something unusual, something to be explained. In sociology, for example, we are taught very early to look

[2] Ibid., p. 141.

for repetitive patterns and to avoid the transitory. In addition, there are narrow spatial implications. The key relationship we consider is that of sameness or difference, inclusion or exclusion. Phenomena are seen as non-overlapping circles, where events take place in one circle or another. As social researchers, we are encouraged to examine very simple relationships, e.g., whether or not a relationship exists between A and B, A and C, and so forth. We qualify our interpretations by stating that we assume all factors not directly considered are unrelated to those we do consider. In everyday life our roles are defined largely in isolation from one another. When we communicate with one another, we generally stereotype the attitudes of others as either agreeing or disagreeing with our own. Such an approach cannot handle complex relationships that are also a matter of degree.

Viewed more positively, however, the Aristotelian law of identity structures a liberating spatiotemporal perspective, one that we might examine in the context of our Judaic-Christian heritage. Temporally, the idea of progress depends on a clear distinction between A and B, if A represents where we are and B where we would like to be. The distinction between man and God creates ideals for man beyond his existing state, ideals which he rarely approaches, yet continues to strive for. In the Old Testament, for example, we have a picture of man continually falling into evil ways, and yet rejecting those ways in search of something better. According to Max Weber, that search—transposed to feudal Europe—gave a powerful impetus, in the guise of the "Protestant ethic," to the development of industrialization.[3] The seemingly simplistic distinction between good and evil is at the same time a most powerful idea, for such simplicity can help the individual to harness his diverse motivational forces. As Tawney puts it, "What is required of the Puritan is not individual meritorious acts, but a holy life—a system in which every element is grouped round a central idea, the service of God, from which all disturbing irrelevancies have been pruned, and to which all minor interests are subordinated."[4] It is this same idea of progress that appears to be such a vital component of the scientific method.

Spatially, let us take A to be man and B to be God. Then all members of A are seen to be the same, that is, there is the idea of a common humanity, of the brotherhood of man. Each individual is seen, in the Judaic-Christian tradition, as embodying the spirit of God and, thus, as being of divine importance. This is a most liberating—as distinct from limiting—idea: man is encouraged to take himself and his own experiences seriously. He is also encouraged to treat others in the same way, to be alert to their worth. Such relationships of men to one another were structured by the idea of

[3] Max Weber, *The Protestant Ethic and the Spirit of Capitalism* (New York: Scribners, 1958).
[4] Richard H. Tawney, *Religion and the Rise of Capitalism* (New York: Mentor, 1963), p. 201.

universal laws to which all men should submit, as illustrated by the Ten Commandments. This submission of A to B—with the law viewed as given by God—is seen as functioning to protect the weak from the strong by requiring all to submit to the same laws. All of this is perhaps as important to the scientific method as the idea of progress: progress must be achieved by individuals who believe in themselves, in the worth of their own experiences, and in the worth of the experiences of others.

Yet how can it be that the Aristotelian law of identity can be at once so limiting and so liberating? Is this not a paradox? If it appears to be a paradox, that appearance is due to a language that structures our thought into neat dichotomies, where an idea is seen simplistically as either limiting or liberating, but not both. It is limiting when we look beyond formism, attempting to transcend its deficiencies. It is liberating when we look backward to preBiblical times, when universal law was less developed. Our problem is to make use of an awareness of its limitations to carry further its liberating forces. We can obtain a clearer view of the nature of formism by means of a detailed illustration.

Formism Illustrated: Aging and Adjustment[5]

Although it is easy enough to illustrate the formist world view with the Old Testament or the writings of Aristotle or present-day language, my major purpose in presenting this paradigm is to enable the student of social research to bring his own fundamental assumptions to the surface so that he can deal with them scientifically. Consequently, I shall present a research illustration—from my own work, because I am familiar with the context—that embodies the ethos of formism. The questions it centered on were: What causes adjustment or maladjustment among aged individuals? Why are some individuals over sixty in excellent mental health and others in a state of retreat from themselves and the world? Is the sociological idea of role change of any value in achieving understanding of this adjustment process? Is the social psychological concept of age-identification—how old a person feels—of any value as well? Is there any truth to the folk saying, "You're as old as you feel"?

Without my being conscious of it, my mode of thinking was most formist. I started with the simple dichotomy between the adjusted and the maladjusted; let us symbolize these two categories as A and B. I then proceeded to think of a series of possible causes of a person's adjustment or maladjustment: role changes like loss of employment ($\bar{K}$, which equals not K), death of spouse ($\bar{L}$, which equals not L), and feeling old ($\bar{M}$, which equals not M). Each of these possible causal factors was paired with its opposite: maintenance of employment (K), living with spouse (L), and feeling middle-aged or young (M). The questions I was posing may

[5] Bernard S. Phillips, "A Role Theory Approach to Adjustment in Old Age," *American Sociological Review,* **22** (April 1957), pp. 212–17.

then be restated as follows: (1) Are people who are A (adjusted) also K (employed), L (living with spouse), and M (feeling middle-aged or young)? (2) Are people who are B (maladjusted) also retired ($\bar{K}$), widows or widowers ($\bar{L}$), and feeling old ($\bar{M}$)? This is a description of two different worlds: that of the adjusted and that of the maladjusted older person. Within each world there is a search for what individuals in that world have in common. Thus, there is the formist emphasis on what is different and what is the same.

An interview survey used to test the above ideas was completed in 1956. Tables 2-1, 2-2, and 2-3 present the relationships between adjustment and employment, adjustment and marital status, and adjustment and age identification, respectively. As may be seen from Tables 2-1, 2-2, and 2-3, phenomena are in fact not as simple as the formist approach suggests. *All* employed individuals are not adjusted, and *all* of the retired are not maladjusted. Neither is it true that *all* married individuals are adjusted and

Table 2-1
Employment and Adjustment

| Employment Status | Personal Adjustment | | | | | |
| | Adjusted (A) | | Maladjusted (B) | | Total | |
	%	(Number)	%	(Number)	%	(Number)
Employed (K)	78	(133)	22	(38)	100	(171)
Retired ($\bar{K}$)	58	(57)	42	(41)	100	(98)

$P < .01$ (*t* test of significance of difference between two percentages)

Table 2-2
Marital Status and Adjustment

| Marital Status | Personal Adjustment | | | | | |
| | Adjusted (A) | | Maladjusted (B) | | Total | |
	%	(Number)	%	(Number)	%	(Number)
Married (L)	73	(126)	27	(47)	100	(173)
Widow or widower ($\bar{L}$)	60	(130)	40	(87)	100	(217)

$P < .01$ (*t* test of significance of difference between two percentages)

Table 2-3
Age Identification and Adjustment

	Personal Adjustment					
	Adjusted (A)		Maladjusted (B)			Total
Age-Identification	%	(Number)	%	(Number)	%	(Number)
Feel young or middle-aged (M)	69	(237)	31	(106)	100	(343)
Feel old (M̄)	42	(50)	58	(68)	100	(118)

$P < .01$ (t test of significance of difference between two percentages)

all widows and widowers are maladjusted, nor is it the case that *all* those who feel young or middle-aged are adjusted and *all* those who feel old are maladjusted.

Despite this, it is possible to focus on the differences between these pairs of categories—between employed and retired, married and widowed, those who feel young and those who feel old—by means of statistical tests (see Chapter 12). We begin by assuming that the percentage differences between these categories could have occurred by chance, and we make use of statistical inference to test whether that assumption (the "null hypothesis") is tenable. Thus, for example, we examine the contrast between the 78% of the employed who are adjusted and the 58% of the retired who are adjusted, and we find the chances to be less than one in a hundred that this 20% spread could have occurred simply on the basis of chance. As a consequence, we reject our null hypothesis of such an occurrence on the basis of chance, and we infer that the difference is "statistically significant."

What have we accomplished by such a procedure? There are two major advances we have made in our understanding, one having to do with the idea that A is not B, and the other relating to the idea that A is A. There definitely is a difference between those employed and those retired, those married and those widowed, and those who feel young and those who feel old: the former groupings tend to be adjusted more than the latter. If A is not B, then our task is cut out for us: we can now seek to discover the conditions under which B can become A, for example, how the maladjusted among the retired or the widowed or those who feel old can become adjusted. We have set a direction implying a path toward further progress.

As for the idea that A is A, we learn from this approach that employed individuals have something in common, and the same for the married and those who feel young: there is a common tendency toward adjustment (A).

Similarly, there is a common tendency toward maladjustment (B) among the retired, the widowed, and those who feel old. Thus, we are able to expand our understanding of the significance of the categories of adjustment and maladjustment. We are able to see something that employed individuals share with married individuals and with those who feel young; and we are also able to see what the retired share with the widowed and those who feel old. This expansion of understanding is also what ordinary language—which is based on the formist world view—helps us to achieve. A given word defines a category of experiences, and as we apply that word to new experiences, the word takes on additional meanings.

Yet for all this, a formist approach is a seriously limited one, temporally and spatially. Temporally, our very success in finding differences between various groups becomes a failure to the degree that we do not follow up this initial understanding with attempts to explore the processes involved: Why do the retired or the widowed or those who feel old become maladjusted? How do individuals in those categories learn to become adjusted? The fault here does not lie with the statistical test, but with the cultural orientations of the users. The achievement—the finding of statistically significant differences—which is one step on the road to understanding, can become an end in itself that blocks further progress.

Spatially, the formist approach produces an overly simplistic view of phenomena, tending to separate phenomena into neat compartments and avoiding complex overlappings. Granting that there is a greater likelihood for a retired person to be maladjusted than an employed individual, the fact remains that 22% of employed individuals are maladjusted. How are we to account for that? And how are we to account for the 58% of retired individuals who are adjusted? To admit that other factors are indeed operative, and to explore some of those factors—as is done in Tables 2-2 and 2-3—is not enough: we must achieve an understanding of how they act in combination, since they do not remain separated in everyday life.

2.2 Mechanism

The mechanistic world view is a very recent phenomenon when we take for our scale of measurement the sweep of human prehistory and history. According to Pepper, it is associated with Democritus, Lucretius, Galileo, Descartes, Hobbes, Locke, Berkeley, Hume, and Reichenbach. We might trace its roots among many ancient civilizations or in the mathematical developments—such as plane geometry—of classical Greece. However, such developments were closely intertwined with a formist mentality as distinct from the mechanistic one that emerged centuries later. By this I mean that the focus was on the dichotomy, on the contrast between truth and falsity, the perfect circle within our imaginations and the imperfect ones we experience. There tended to be little concern with movement, which fits very well with the slow-moving preindustrial world. The student of geometry was concerned with the nature of spatial relationships, relationships that have existed and will continue to exist. The triangles and circles did not move about. And if the world he experienced did move somewhat, he could ignore those experiences, because they were not as perfect as the shapes that concerned him. In the mechanistic perspective, by contrast, the world of motion became salient, and this is a perspective that we can associate with the birth of the industrial revolution and the decline of feudalism.

The Nature of Mechanism: The Continuum and the Machine

The idea of the continuum is implicit in the idea of polar opposites, although it may remain hidden indefinitely. Between the black and the white lie the shades of gray; between man and God lie the varying degrees of sin and righteousness; between the primary group and the secondary group lie other groups that exercise varying degrees of influence over the individual. Language itself, although its fundamental structure is formist, has expanded over the years to incorporate ever more concepts that do not fit easily into the formist mold, concepts like "degree," "continuum," "shades of gray."

But all of this is a very passive way of viewing the continuum. A more active orientation involves a commitment to move from one pole to the other. Such a commitment might begin with a formist dichotomy separating the individual from his environment, but that is only one step along the way. It also requires identifying one's goals with moving toward or dealing with the environment in some way. In this respect, the Judaic-Christian tradition—such as the Protestant ethic described by Max Weber—provides motivational force.

And it is within this context that the machine assumes importance. A machine is a device that enables its user to apply force more effectively to his environment than he might do otherwise. In this way he can achieve greater force than he would otherwise be capable of, or he can change the direction or location of a given force. The lever illustrates the increased force that can be obtained. Archimedes is reputed to have said, "Give me a place to stand and a lever long enough and I will move the world." The pulley and the wheel and axle are other types of levers. The screw is a member of another category of machines—the inclined planes—that also includes the wedge (two inclined planes joined together). Here, too, an enormous mechanical advantage can be achieved, with the user giving up distance or speed in order to achieve force. All complicated machines are built up from these simple types. And by powering the machine with energy released from natural resources and thus creating automatic machinery, man has greatly increased his ability to shape his environment by applying force to it.

The machine incorporates within its structure the idea of the continuum.

With the lever or the inclined plane, as with other machines, there is a definite direction or path along which we are to move if we are to achieve the desired mechanical advantage, that is, the sacrifice of distance moved for force gained. And it is mathematics to which we can turn—the body of knowledge that deals with complex manipulations of the idea of the continuum, especially as embodied within the number system—for understanding a good deal about the relationships involved. For example, the physical law of machines is *The force (F) we apply multiplied by the distance (d) through which the force moves is equal to the resistance or weight (R) multiplied by the distance through which it is moved.* Mathematically, we have

$$F \times d = R \times d.$$

Suppose that we wish to use the lever of Figure 2-1 to lift a weight of 1,000 pounds a height of 3 feet. Then, according to the law of machines (and disregarding friction as well as approximating the actual arcs through which force and resistance move), we can determine how much force we must apply to overcome that resistance:

$$F \times 6 = 1,000 \times 3, \text{ or } 6F = 3,000, \text{ or } F = 500.$$

Thus, we can obtain a mechanical advantage of 1,000/500, or 2, by using the lever in this situation. This gain is obtained at some expense, namely, that we must move the lever arm 6 feet to lift the resistance 3 feet.

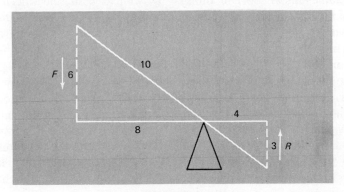

Figure 2-1.
The Law of Machines.

The mechanistic perspective is both limiting and liberating, as is the formist one. Spatially, it places nonliving things in the center of the universe with living things thereby shoved aside. Man emerges as an irrelevant entity, located in some minute corner of the vast universe, transforming his food energy into mechanical energy and heat according to a series of meaningless patterns. Material things become the major reality, and man's focus of attention shifts to attempts to understand and manipulate them. Temporally, mechanism teaches us that gains in energy must be accompanied by corresponding losses, thus conveying the idea of a fixed versus a developing universe. Our problem is that of transforming rather than creating energy, that of distributing a fixed pie of rewards within a deterministic universe where all the laws are fixed. We concern ourselves less with the problem of how to create an expanding pie, or how our own actions can alter the directions of the universe.

Mechanism is also most liberating, as may be inferred from its close association with the industrial revolution and man's associated movements away from a life doomed to ceaseless efforts to achieve mere survival. Spatially, it has widened our horizons many fold by opening up to us macroscopic and microscopic worlds, and correspondingly our understanding of the universe has increased. And since it is man himself who has developed this understanding, we must form a heightened respect for his powers. Temporally, man learns to see his universe as in continual motion. Furthermore, he learns to look for change along definite continua. With the aid of mathematical techniques for dealing with movement along continua— such as the differential and integral calculus—he can understand more thoroughly both the movements of objects near at hand and planetary motion. Also, he is able to put such understanding to work in creating the kinds of motion he desires and the kinds of forces that achieve his ends.

The implications of mechanism for the scientific method are vast. It is through this world view that man learns to appreciate the immense power of his mathematical tools of thinking as well as of a scientific approach to phenomena. Through it, he is able to achieve both a coherent view of the universe that offers a more satisfactory naturalistic interpretation of phenomena than was available to him previously and tools of unprecedented effectiveness for shaping that universe. Yet once again—and this seems to be a major theme in the story of mankind—this very success produces certain tendencies toward failure: means to desirable ends can become ends in themselves that subvert or displace the original ends. Spatially, the success of mechanism teaches us the importance of the material and, by implication, the unimportance of the nonmaterial. As a result, intangible or invisible phenomena are moved outside of the scope of scientific inquiry. Yet—as recent experience has taught us—to ignore such factors is to place severe limits on the extent of scientific progress. Temporally, mechanistic successes were not seen as being associated with an understanding of history or evolution. Thus, the proponents of mechanism—who are now all of us to some degree—cut themselves off from an understanding of the formist roots of mechanism. And by cutting off the past, they ignored the future likewise. The scientific method came to be seen as something perfect, fixed forever in time.

Mechanism Illustrated: Occupational Choice[6]

To illustrate the mechanistic world view, I shall discuss the study of choice of medical specialties that served as a central research illustration in the first and second editions of this book. The study was initiated in the fall of 1956 as a result of concern on the part of members of the American Public Health Association about the dearth of qualified medical students interested in a career in public health. A national study of medical students was undertaken in which the general process by which a student chooses a medical field was investigated. My own particular theoretical interests at the time centered around attempting to go beyond formism. Since in my undergraduate years I had obtained a background in mathematics, physics, and chemistry and had managed to keep alive my earlier interests in the application of mathematics to sociology, it is not surprising that my theoretical perspective was shaped by the mechanistic world view.

Mechanistically, the problem of occupational choice reduces to a problem of relating forces and resistances to motion: What are the magnitudes and directions of the various forces operating on a given individual, what are the resistances, and what is the resultant force and the direction of that resultant? To which medical field does that resultant point? The goals, or values, of medical students are thus analogous to the forces operating on them. And analogous to resistance to these forces is "expected goal deprivation": the student's perception of the obstacles within a given medical field standing in the way of his achieving his goals. As for motion, I was concerned with movement to these medical fields and, in particular, with the direction of that motion: Which field is a student moving toward?

Let us begin with the analysis of forces and resistances before moving to the topic of motion. First, we have the idea that the difference between an initial force (f) and a resistance (r) describes the resultant force that remains (f'):

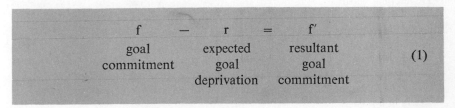

$$f \quad - \quad r \quad = \quad f' \tag{1}$$

| goal commitment | expected goal deprivation | resultant goal commitment |

[6] Bernard S. Phillips, "Expected Value Deprivation and Occupational Preference," *Sociometry,* **27** (June 1964), pp. 151–60.

A student's overall force, or goal commitment, for a medical specialty (F) is based on a number of component forces, or goals, (f_1, f_2 . . .). Similarly, his over-all resistance, or expected goal deprivation, (R) for that specialty is based on his expected deprivations relating to each of those component forces or goals (r_1, r_2 . . .). Finally, the difference between F and R constitutes the student's over-all resultant goal commitment for that specialty (F'). These relationships may be expressed mathematically, in the case where there are ten forces, or goals, under consideration, as follows:

$$F = f_1 + f_2 + f_3 + f_4 + f_5 + f_6 + f_7 + f_8 + f_9 + f_{10}. \qquad (2)$$
$$R = r_1 + r_2 + r_3 + r_4 + r_5 + r_6 + r_7 + r_8 + r_9 + r_{10}. \qquad (3)$$
$$F - R = F'. \qquad (4)$$

The following question was used to measure the magnitude of each of the ten component goals (f_1, f_2, . . . , f_{10}) involved in the goal commitment to a given specialty:

Most people have some idea of·what they would want in an ideal position, that is, if they could dream up a job which had all the elements they like. What importance would each of the following elements have in your ideal job? Put a check in Column A, B, C, D, or E.

	A Indispensable	B Extremely Important	C Very Important	D Fairly Important	E Little or No Importance (or Would Rather Not Have)
In my ideal job I would like an opportunity for: Developing warm personal relationships with patients	___	___	___	___	___
Having prestige among my colleagues in the medical profession	___	___	___	___	___
Being in a position to make a contribution to knowledge	___	___	___	___	___

Seven other values were measured in addition to the above three: learning, involvement with complex problems, opportunity to utilize abilities, helping people, high income, hours not extremely long, and work without great physical exertion.

As for the ten resistances or expected goal deprivations (r_1, r_2, . . . , r_{10}) for a given medical field, these were measured by the following question:

In which of these six fields of medicine in the columns below do you think you have the greatest chance to obtain each of the following things? In which field next? In which field would you have the least chance? Rank the following fields from 1 to 6 according to how they provide opportunities for

	General Practice	Internal Medicine	Pathology	Psychiatry	Public Health	Surgery
Developing warm personal relationships with patients	___	___	___	___	___	___
Having prestige among my colleagues in the medical profession	___	___	___	___	___	___
Being in a position to make a contribution to knowledge	___	___	___	___	___	___

In addition to these three goals, the seven others measured in the preceding question of goal commitment were also measured here.

With these two series of questions providing measures for the set of ten component forces (f_1, f_2, . . . , f_{10}) and ten component resistances (r_1, r_2, . . . , r_{10}), any student's resultant value commitment (F') for any field of medicine can be assessed. To illustrate the general approach without getting lost in the details, let us consider the situation of one student in relation to two of the component forces and resistances (warm personal relationships and contribution to knowledge) and two of the medical fields (general practice and pathology). Suppose that he values highly warm personal relationships and does not value making a contribution to knowledge, and that he perceives general practice as providing the former but not the latter, and that he perceives pathology as providing the latter but not the former. Then his resultant goal commitment ($f - r = f'$) toward general practice is high because he values warm personal relationships, and that goal is not negated by a resistance, since he perceives opportunities in general practice for obtaining warm personal relationships. By contrast, his resultant goal commitment toward pathology would be low, since his expectation that pathology does not provide such opportunities would produce a high resistance. Consequently, these results—if they were supported by similar results with respect to other goals—would tend to produce an over-all resultant goal commitment (F') for general practice that is greater than that for pathology. However, if that student's goal commitments were reversed—no interest in personal relationships, but great interest in contributing to knowledge—and if he perceived general practice and pathology in the same ways, then he would experience a reversal in his resultant goal commitment.

If a student's resultant goal commitment (F') is higher for one field of medicine than another, then we may assume that he will tend to *move* in the direction of the greater force, following the fundamental Newtonian law of motion:

$$F = Ma$$
Force = Mass × Acceleration
Resultant Goal Commitment (F') = Preference for Field of Medicine

In order to test this hypothesis that, for example, a student whose F' is higher for general practice than for pathology will in fact prefer general practice, we must be able to measure both F' and preference. In the preceding pages, questions used to measure F' were presented. As for the measurement of preference, the following question was designed for this purpose:

How would you rank the following fields of medicine according to your interest in working in them? (1 for the specialty you would be most interested in, 2 for the next, 3 to 6 for the ones you are least interested in working in.)

General practice ——— Psychiatry ———
Internal medicine ——— Public health ———
Pathology ——— Surgery ———

We are now ready for the crucial question: how effective is our calculated F' for predicting the preference of a given student for a given medical field? For each student, we can proceed by calculating F' for each of the six fields of medicine, and we can then order these measurements from high to low and test whether students in fact tend to prefer those medical fields for which their F' is high and, conversely, to be unfavorable to those medical fields for which their F' is low. Results are presented in Table 2-4, where data on all six medical fields is combined. Thus, for example,

Table 2-4
Resultant Goal Commitments and Actual Preferences for Fields of Medicine

| | Resultant Goal Commitments (F′)** | | | | | |
| | High | | | | | Low |
	1	2	3	4	5	6
Percentage who give favorable* ratings	86	71	60	44	37	17
Percentage who give unfavorable ratings	14	29	40	56	63	83
Total	100	100	100	100	100	100

* If a medical field was ranked 1, 2, or 3 (versus 4, 5, or 6), the ranking was classified as favorable. No attempt is made here to predict the exact ranking of each medical field, since that is too lofty a goal in the light of existing knowledge.

** Cases where a student had the same F′ for two or more medical fields were omitted. Consequently, percentages are not based on the total sample of 2,674, but each of the six percentages represents a sample of over 1,200.

MECHANICIST TRIES TO PREDICT — FORMIST EXPLAINS

if one student's highest F′ was for general practice and another's for pathology, these were combined to determine whether each tended to prefer the field with his highest F′. These data indicate a rather close relationship—indeed, an unusually close relationship for social science data—between resultant goal commitment for any given medical field and the percentage of students rating that field favorably. For example, 86% of those medical students whose resultant goal commitment for a given medical field is higher than for other fields also rate that field favorably, whereas only 17% of those medical students whose resultant goal commitment is lowest also rate that field favorably.

This illustration conveys both the strong and the weak points of the mechanistic world view. First, we are able to go beyond the formist question of whether or not a relationship between goal commitment and medical preference *exists* to examine the *type* of relationship involved, moving closer to an ability to predict; yet in this mechanistic approach we are only concerned with the motion (or preferences) that forces (goals) produce and not with how forces (goals) are increased or reduced. Second, we succeed in becoming analytical, delving into the component forces (goal commitments) making up any given force, thus increasing our power of prediction; yet we simultaneously neglect the kind of synthetic approach in which, for example, we make use of information on the group as well as the individual. Third, we are able to pull together a large amount of information about each individual by dint of mathematical relationships;

yet at the same time we succeed in ignoring historical context and thus depriving ourselves of a great deal of important information. Finally, we provide a basis for acting on the environment to alter an existing situation to one more favorable to the field of public health; yet we do this within a framework where the gain in one medical field implies a loss in others, and we ignore the possibility of action from which all medical fields can gain, e.g., the opening up of paths toward increasing our knowledge of disease processes generally and of more effective means for distributing medical care.

2.3   Organicism

The fundamental metaphor of the organicist perspective is the organism. This perspective—as it applies to biology—has been stated as follows:

> Since the fundamental character of the living thing is its organization, the customary investigation of the single parts and processes, even the most thorough physico-chemical analysis, cannot provide a complete explanation of the vital phenomena. This investigation gives us no information about the co-ordination of the parts and processes in the complicated system of the living whole which constitutes the essential 'nature' of the organism, and by which the reactions in the organism are distinguished from those in the testtube. But no reason has been brought forward for supposing that the organization of the parts and the mutual adjustments of the vital processes cannot be treated as scientific problems. Thus, the chief task of biology must be to discover the laws of biological systems to which the ingredient parts and processes are subordinate. *We regard this as the fundamental problem for modern biology.*[7]

The organicist is concerned with life, whether manifested in biological organisms or social systems. He attempts to be synthetic as well as analytic, to be historical as well as to focus on a given moment. And far from rejecting the scientific emphasis of mechanism, he aims at establishing the scientific laws governing the behavior of organisms. According to Pepper, organicism is associated with Schelling, Hegel, Green, Bradley, Bosanquet, and Royce.

The Nature of Organicism: Feedback, Adaptation, Growth

All of the substances to be found in organisms are also found in inanimate nature, yet the two are worlds apart. How is this possible? What is the difference between the living and the nonliving if it is something other than the type of matter involved? It appears that what is crucial

[7] Ludwig von Bertalanffy, *Modern Theories of Development: An Introduction to Theoretical Biology* (New York: Harper, Torchbooks, 1962), pp. 64–65.

is the way in which matter is organized, in particular, the organization of matter so as to produce feedback, adaptation, and growth.

The plant, for example, sends its roots through the soil and somehow is able to receive messages from those roots as to the presence or absence of water. Thus, we have a feedback loop: the plant acts on its environment, and it is able to obtain information on the state of that environment. As a result of this information—which transforms the plant's previous store of information—the plant may shift the direction of some of its roots and thus adapt more successfully to its environment. This adaptation, in turn, provides the basis for the continued growth of the plant, a growth that also succeeds in shaping the environment to a degree.

As we move from lower to higher organisms, we find more and more ability on the part of the organism to obtain informational feedback, to alter itself so as to adapt more successfully to its environment, and to act effectively on the environment so as to achieve growth. For example, the vertebrates—in comparison to the insects—are able to resist the force of gravity sufficiently to support a much larger body and, hence, a more complex nervous system. That nervous system—especially as it is manifested in man—provides the basis for information processing that greatly exceeds the capacities of lower forms of life. Man is able to adapt by altering his own personality and social structure without waiting for biological evolution. This capacity for adaptation—and, as a result, for shaping the environment—greatly increases with the continuing development of language.

The foregoing paragraphs deal with the nature of organic processes. Our task now is to examine the nature of organicism as a world view. If mechanism can be most easily associated with the early phases of the industrial revolution, organicism is much more a product of its later phases, that is, of the nineteenth and twentieth centuries. We might refer back to Figure 1-4, which sketches feedback relationships among scientific theory, method, and technology, relationships that represent the continuing acceleration we have experienced as the scientific-industrial revolution. Economic, political, religious, and scientific forces—among others—were released that changed the pace and directions of man's life in ever more dramatic ways. Such experiences tended to contradict the rationalistic view, from mechanism, of an orderly universe, closed and determined, where all phenomena might be explained by the laws of physics. Auguste Comte (1789–1857), for example, argued that a new kind of physics—a social physics, which he called "sociology"—was needed both to explain the apparent chaos of human experience and to provide the basis for solving human problems. He felt that such a science must be built on the sciences that preceded it: mathematics, mechanics, physics, chemistry, and biology.[8]

One of the major characteristics of organicist thought within sociology

[8] Auguste Comte, *The Positive Philosophy*, trans. and condensed by Harriet Martineau (New York: Calvin Blanchard, 1856).

is the emphasis on broad historical movements paralleling the continuing industrial revolution. Such movements are seen as taking place along definite continua, analogous to the continua that the mathematician and the physicist deal with, only the sociological continua are nonmaterial. For example, Sir Henry Maine (1822–1888) saw much of social change as a movement from status to contract, such as the change from the fixed, all-encompassing status of the slave to the changeable and relatively specific contractual relationship between service worker and employer.[9] Ferdinand Tonnies (1855–1936) reversed Maine's view of the new era as representing progress, seeing movement from *Gemeinschaft* (intimate, private, and exclusive living together) to *Gesellschaft* (transitory and superficial patterns of the interaction associated with urban life).[10] Émile Durkheim (1858–1917) conceived of an irreversible historical trend from a society organized on the basis of mechanical solidarity, the fellow feeling based on the kind of homogeneity typical of rural life, to one based on organic solidarity, where individuals are bound to one another by a complex division of labor.[11] But we need not limit ourselves to classical theorists in our search for organicism within sociology. The movement of the discipline as a whole has been in the direction of the power of the group or social structure or society to shape the behavior of the individual.

Looking backward, we may note important advances of organicism over its predecessors. Spatially, we have an extension of concepts into the realm of the animate, and temporally, we have historical and evolutionary perspectives. These concepts begin with formist dichotomies like *Gemeinschaft* and *Gesellschaft*, but there is more of the idea of movement along a continuum. There is also the idea that the achievement of understanding can be—just as in the physical sciences—a powerful tool for helping man to adapt to and shape his rapidly accelerating environment. Yet for all this, there are severe limitations to organicism. The incorporation of the idea of the continuum has been a feeble thing in comparison to the sophistication of available mathematical tools. We have not succeeded in following the advice of Comte in this respect, although progress has indeed been made.

Organicism Illustrated: Community Development and Decay

Organicism has to do not only with feedback, adaptation, and growth but also with inadequate feedback, maladaptation, and decay. Organisms grow ill and die as well as experience birth and life. Indeed, many of the recent efforts to apply sociology to societal problems have to do with ways

[9] Henry Sumner Maine, *Ancient Law* (London: Oxford U. P., 1931).
[10] Ferdinand Tonnies, *Community and Society,* trans. and ed. by Charles P. Loomis (New York: Harper, 1963).
[11] Émile Durkheim, *The Division of Labor in Society* (New York: Free Press, 1964).

COMMUNITY TREATED AS WHOLE (ORGANISM)
WHAT WOULD HAPPEN IF COMMUNITY
DISRUPTED BY OIL REFINARY?

of reducing decay. One particular area of investigation is the impact of changes in the physical environment on the quality of social life. Such phenomena as highways and oil refineries introduce many different types of pollution into the human community along with the benefits that emerge. As an organicist, the sociologist is concerned with directions in which to move for collecting the kinds of information that can help communities either to adapt to such changes with a minimum of decay and a maximum of development or else to avoid deleterious changes in the physical environment by designing more appropriate ones.

Within the United States, for example, there is a legal rationale for the sociologist's role in these efforts.[12] The National Environmental Policy Act of 1969 has resulted in policy and procedures that require the assessment of the "social impact" of contemplated major environmental changes so as to encourage the design of the kinds of changes that are beneficial. The law requires the Council on Environmental Quality "to formulate and recommend national policies to promote the improvement of the quality of the environment." In April 1973 this Council revised the guidelines to the National Environmental Policy Act to include secondary as well as primary consequences for the social environment of physical changes, adopting the idea that secondary effects may often be even more substantial than primary ones.

The following illustration is concerned with a social impact statement for the Environmental Protection Agency in relation to an oil refinery's plans for expansion and modernization in a Middle Atlantic urban community. Such plans were presented along with two alternatives: modernization without expansion and conversion of the existing refinery to a storage facility. Some action by the oil company was essential, since higher standards for the control of pollution were to come into effect within a few years that would make the existing plant obsolete. What an organicist approach to this problem succeeds in doing that mechanism alone fails to do is to deal with nonmaterial as well as material factors, such as patterns of social mobility up or down the stratification ladder, educational changes, optimism or pessimism about the community's future, patterns of communication within the community, and so on. The central question in relation to these intangibles is: What are the forces producing decay and the forces producing growth? How can upward social mobility, educational improvement, optimism about the community's future, and improved patterns of communication within the community be fostered?

A first step in the development of the impact statement was the construction of a "community social profile." This research approach has been described by its originator as "a short-run, easily-administered method which, though lacking in completeness of detail, nevertheless is accurate as far

[12] For details on this rationale, see Pamela Savatsky's letter to the editor, *ASA Footnotes,* **2** (August 1974), p. 9.

as it goes and at the same time penetrating enough to be helpful in program planning."[13] This step was taken in part because of time and budgetary limitations. A small group of sociology graduate students from a nearby university compiled the necessary information by means of interviews with people—with special attention to community leaders—from the community, examination of avilable documents or written materials of all types, and discussions within the group.

The picture of the community that emerged was not an attractive one. The East Europeans who had emigrated during an earlier period had helped to develop an industrial complex while simultaneously securing their own homes and opening paths toward occupational mobility and job security for themselves. But that phase of the industrial revolution did not last indefinitely. While at this earlier time of expansion the community had served as a shopping center for surrounding areas, the central business district had more recently experienced rapid decline. Previously, the community had served also as a recreational center, and individuals with high incomes had resided there. However, pollution of water facilities had been one of a number of factors that destroyed the community's attractiveness in that respect and contributed to the departure of such individuals. And industry itself was no longer expanding in the way it once did, with a resultant tightening of paths toward upward mobility.

It is within this situation that increasing numbers of individuals of Spanish descent began moving into the community, attracted by the lower-paying jobs available, and within a decade they came to comprise almost half of the population. The split between the Hispanic and East European communities is a sharp one, contributing to the community's problems which are not atypical of urban problems in U.S. cities. The first draft of the sociocultural impact statement describes this split along with other kinds of splits in a way that suggests the complexities of the situation.

There are the "have's": generally East European in origin, white collar people in industry, Cubans, a small proportion of Puerto Ricans who are middle class, home owners, concerned about pollution, concerned about taxes, Protestant and Jewish, long term residents who work elsewhere. And there are the "have-not's": some working class East Europeans, blue collar people, most Puerto Ricans, apartment dwellers, illegal immigrants, those concerned about attaining home ownership and better job opportunities, poorly educated, wanting better schools, concerned about crime and drugs and lack of privacy and safety.

Each group lives in a different world, communicating almost completely with others in their own world. But those two worlds are also divided up in many other ways: husbands and wives, parents and children, one family and other families, one neighborhood and other neighborhoods,

[13] Irwin T. Sanders, "The Community Social Profile," *American Sociological Review,* **25** (February 1960), p. 75.

those who are better off and those who are worse off within each world. Thus, each individual finds himself in a limited-information environment, cut off from knowledge about most of his environment. And if that external environment is rapidly changing—as we have every reason to believe—and if that environment affects him in a variety of ways, as we also have every reason to believe, then his ability to cope with his problems is decreasing. He may be conscious of this decreasing ability, but his tendency is to blame it on the world he does not know more than on his failure to understand that world.[14]

This profile indicates that the situation in the community—like all other communities is enormously complex. It is also a situation in rapid flux. And to make matters far more complicated, all of the various forces within the community are in direct or indirect interaction with one another. The modern physicist has difficulty with finding solutions to what he calls "the three-body problem"—the interaction of three bodies of matter in space— but how might he react to this multibodied problem? And all of these forces are in flux. How can we possibly say anything about the impact on the community of expanding and modernizing an oil refinery? And, far more difficult, how might we chart a path toward the development of the community as a whole?

Here, then, is the problem associated with an organicist framework. It enables us to be sensitive to changes and complexity within the community, and it even provides tools for illustrating such phenomena. But this is more or less like telling us that a bridge has many different kinds of weak points, that all of these interact with one another, and that things are rapidly getting worse. What are we to do about the situation? What response can be given to the oil company's request for expansion and modernization? Decisions such as this are being made all the time, yet where is the informational base that would enable us to make such decisions intelligently? To know that expansion and modernization will affect social mobility, education, attitudes about the community's future, and patterns of communication within the community is undoubtedly helpful, but how are we to learn about the complex conditions that will enable such impacts to be helpful rather than harmful? And how do all of these impacts interrelate with changes in air pollution, noise levels, water pollution, changes in traffic patterns, and perhaps several hundred other factors, many of which we are not even aware of?

We are faced here with both the limitations of, and the challenge to, contemporary sociology. The classical organicists provided us with a sensitivity to the complexity and change involved in phenomena, but that sensitivity alone is insufficient for shaping those phenomena. Organicists such as Maine, Tonnies, and Durkheim laid the basis for seeing intangible phe-

[14] Bernard S. Phillips, "Sociocultural Impact of Refinery Modernization," mimeographed, (Boston: Department of Sociology, Boston U., 1973.)

nomena gradationally—with each specifying a particular continuum along which events may be seen to flow—and thus helped make possible the wedding of mechanism with organicism. But it seems that such a wedding has yet to be consummated. And even a serious use of existing mathematics is not sufficient to deal with the complexity and dynamism that sociologists have shown to be involved in human phenomena. Such mathematics was developed to deal with physical phenomena, which are characterized by a much simpler order of complexity and dynamism. What appears to be required is a different paradigm.

2.4 Pragmatism

Many individuals have equated pragmatism with a crass concern for material gain, a willingness to sacrifice principles for the sake of selfish ends, and a shortsightedness in relation to long-range goals, but none of these stereotypes apply to Charles Peirce, William James, George Herbert Mead, John Dewey, or Oliver Wendell Holmes. What, then, is the nature of this paradigm.

The Nature of Pragmatism: The Situation

A pragmatist world view, like the others, is not limited to the pronouncements of a select number of philosophers who may be identified with it, but is shared to a degree by all human beings. That degree, however, depends on a number of orientations. For one thing, the word *pragmatism* derives from a root that means an "act" or "deed." This expresses much of the spirit of pragmatism, which is not action as opposed to ideas but action informed by ideas, that is, ideas seen with reference to their implications for action. Some union of ideas and action takes place continually for all human beings; language and thought embody to some degree the history of human actions, and actions are largely influenced by that same language and thought. Within formism, the union of language and thought takes place within a framework of relatively static and narrow assumptions, thus limiting the degree of openness to changing and complex situations. Within mechanism, there is a greater ability to handle dynamism and complexity via such tools as mathematics, but concern centers on the nonliving universe and there tends to be a deterministic framework. Organicism opens up that framework and applies it to organisms as well as inanimate objects, thus creating a framework of ideas within which still more elements of human situations can be experienced and acted on.

One way in which pragmatism is yet more open to human experience than organicism is its active scientific approach to the environment, as symbolized by the metaphor of the machine. Another way is its respect for the tools of science and scientific thought. Pragmatism is built around a conviction that science and technology are vital for man's development, and that they can be humanized. Yet, historically, pragmatists have tended to go no further than organicists in taking seriously such scientific tools as mathematics. However, the program of pragmatism seems clear: to make use of such tools to deal with man's existential situation.

One important advance of pragmatism over organicism in this respect is its approach to the dichotomy between the individual and his environment—the mind-body problem, as it is called in philosophy—as well as to all dichotomies. For pragmatism, all phenomena are contextual: they take place in a given spatial and temporal situation, and if they are to be understood, that situation must be taken into account. Any dualism is viewed as far too simple a perspective on the complexity of human experience. The individual cannot stand back and passively observe his environment: his observations are active and spring from the particular situation in which he finds himself. Organicism is concerned with systems of phenomena, with the organization of discrete units into larger wholes. Pragmatism carries this idea one step further by including within the system the observer. In this sense at least, pragmatism has the flavor of Eastern philosophy: man is seen as connected with his environment and not as separated from it.

With the rejection of the dualism between the individual and the environment, paths are opened to the investigation of the nature of this interaction. One of the most important contributions made in this area is the work of George Herbert Mead, with his focus on the formation of the personality through symbolic interaction. What is of more recent origin, however, is a deeper view of the individual, reminiscent of the work of Freud and the neo-Freudians, where the question of how the individual changes his environment is posed. There seems to be a convergence of many kinds of theory in sociology and the social sciences around this issue.

Looking at pragmatism in historical perspective, it occurs at a time[15]— the latter part of the industrial revolution—when man has learned to achieve a great deal materially, and when his place in the universe has been undermined by a mechanistic world view that tends to ignore him. Pragmatism asks whether it is possible to make man's role central by using the very tools of science that have helped to develop—through technology—the materialistic perspective. In applying such tools, he cannot afford to be half-hearted: it is much more difficult to apply them than to talk about the importance of applying them. Yet by so doing, the individual builds bridges across the split that has developed historically between mechanism and organicism or, analogously, between physical science and social science. With such a linkage, there is a recapturing of the original

---

[15] Of course, there are elements of pragmatism in all eras, but I refer here to the powerful thrust of pragmatist ideas.

dream of Auguste Comte: to build a science of sociology based on knowledge of mathematics and the physical sciences, a science with the power to solve human problems.

Methodologically, pragmatism involves a return to what is central to the scientific method but has too often been lost sight of: that scientific ideas require testing against human experience, and that their worth depends on their utility in such contexts. If one thinks he has achieved a deeper understanding of some phenomenon, that gain should make a difference in his ability to deal with that phenomenon, whether by prediction or through the solution of problems.

If pragmatism has its strengths, it also has its limitations. For example, how might we communicate with one another in a purely pragmatist way if most of our language and thought processes are based on the dichotomies characteristic of formism? And even if we could somehow manage to communicate completely in shades of gray rather than blacks and whites, would we want to do so? Would we not lose the drama between good and evil, heaven and hell, life and death? How could we motivate ourselves to move from one situation to another if we felt that we were merely moving along some continuum? Could we harness the same kinds of motivational forces that are characteristic of the Judaic-Christian tradition?

Let us move away from weighing pragmatism against formism and see them working together, looking in particular at the research process. A formist approach can give us entree into understanding some of the factors which are related to, say, adjustment, and a pragmatist approach can then help us carry this initial understanding further to uncover some of the complexities involved. We then could shift back to a formist orientation to unearth other factors, continuing back and forth indefinitely. If a mechanistic research orientation was then introduced, mathematical tools could be brought to bear as well. And an organicist approach would help us to unearth some of the changing and subtle social forces involved in the situation.

Just because we have discussed only these four paradigms should not imply that they are the only ones ever involved in the research process. They are meant to illustrate the most important ones which appear to be operative, given existing knowledge. But that knowledge itself is limited. Also, we should be aware that these paradigms are oriented to the Western experience. Eastern thought, for example, carries other paradigms within such world views as Indian Philosophy, Confucianism, Taoism, Buddhism, and Zen.

Pragmatism Illustrated: A Model of the Aging Process

This illustration is taken from a pretest within an ongoing panel study—involving repeated studies of the same individuals—of a relatively healthy and geographically stable population of male veterans participating in the

Normative Aging Study[16] at the Veterans Administration's Outpatient Clinic in Boston. These individuals periodically undergo an elaborate series of health examinations and also respond to questionnaires, gaining free medical care unrelated to any service disabilities in the process. This pretest, or trial study, was based on questionnaires administered to forty-eight individuals coming to the Clinic for medical care during April and May, 1974; its primary purpose was to test the effectiveness of a new questionnaire focusing on employment, which was designed for distribution to all 2,000 participants in the Normative Aging Study.

In order to understand the nature of the pragmatist approach adopted, it is necessary to return to its formist roots, that is, to the aging and adjustment study described in Section 2.1. In that study, it will be recalled, adjustment of older people was found to be related to employment status, marital status, and age-identification. Age-identification was seen as getting at the individual's personality structure, employment status and marital status measured aspects of the social structure surrounding the individual, and adjustment was a measure of mental health. As for the relationships involved: social structure was seen as a factor affecting both personality structure and mental health, and personality structure was seen as a factor affecting mental health. These relationships are portrayed in Figure 2-2, with the particular measurements associated with each factor located underneath the factor. Let us note that the measurements are separated into

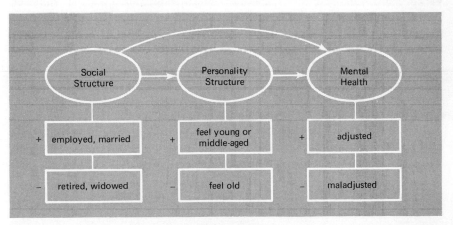

Figure 2-2.
Formist Model of the Aging Process.

[16] For an introduction to the Normative Aging Study, see B. Bell, C. L. Rose, and A. Damon, "The Normative Aging Study: An Interdisciplinary and Longitudinal Study of Health and Aging," *Aging and Human Development,* **3** (February 1972), pp. 1–17. Thanks are due to David J. Ekerdt and Shelley Leavitt for conducting and analyzing the pretest.

"$+$" and "$-$," denoting characteristics associated with adjustment and maladjustment, respectively.

Let us take this movement from the formist to the pragmatist paradigm one step at a time. First, let us conceive of each of the three factors gradationally as distinct from dichotomously. Beginning with the social structure, we must probe the nature of the difference between being employed and being retired as well as between being married and being a widow or a widower. Both of these constitute role changes, but changes in which direction? In order to think gradationally, it is essential to have some continuum in mind. In the typical case, perhaps, the role change from employment to retirement or from being married to being widowed represents a *constriction* of one's social relationships. Following this idea, we might think of the continuum of *role breadth* as the basis for moving from a dichotomous to a gradational view of the social structure.

As for the personality structure, we might follow along with the same kind of approach: to identify oneself as old rather than as middle-aged appears to constitute in general a constriction of one's behavioral possibilities. An old person is not supposed to do this or that, at least in American society. He or she is supposed to dress more conservatively than others, be unable to understand emergent aspects of society, be less interested in sexual behavior, and be generally more dependent on others. Thus, we might think of a continuum of *personality breadth* as paralleling that of role breadth. Finally, let us turn to the factor of health. Instead of centering on the *dichotomy* between adjustment and maladjustment, let us think of a *continuum* of mental health. Here the focus no longer is on adjustment to given conditions but is, at least partially, independent of these conditions. Mental health might continue to improve far beyond the adjustment to given conditions. Within this perspective, mental health is not merely the absence of mental illness: it is a continuum that extends in a positive as well as a negative direction.

Figure 2-3 summarizes this reconceptualization of the formist model so as to convert each dichotomy into a continuum. The arrows around each concept indicate both the existence of a continuum and movement up

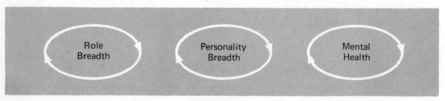

Figure 2-3.
Toward a Pragmatist Model of Aging: Gradational Approach.

or down along the continuum. As a second step in this movement toward a pragmatist model of the aging process, let us take up the question of measurement. Within the formist approach the emphasis was on a relatively static and narrow set of items. On the one hand, there was no reference to change: respondents were asked about their present employment or marital status, about how old they felt presently, about whether they had thoughts of death, and so on. On the other hand, each factor or variable was measured either by a single item or by a few items. The pragmatist approach to measurement is quite different in both respects.

To illustrate this measurement approach concisely, let us limit ourselves to the concept of role breadth. Two sets of seven questions were combined into a single measurement, or scale, of role breadth. The first set begins as follows:

WORK EXPERIENCES: GENERAL

For each of these general aspects of your work experiences, rate your PAST, PRESENT, and EXPECTED FUTURE level of satisfaction (regardless of whether you are retired or plan to retire). For example: for "Your salary," circle either "high," "medium," or "low" in the PAST column according to your preference; then circle your choice in the PRESENT column and your choice in the FUTURE column Do the same for each of the other areas of your work experience ("Your working conditions," etc.)

Do Not Write in This Space

	PAST	PRESENT	EXPECTED FUTURE	
32. Satisfaction with— Your salary.	1. high	1. high	1. high	21
	2. medium	2. medium	2. medium	22
	3. low	3. low	3. low	23
				24
33. Satisfaction with— Your working conditions.	1. high	1. high	1. high	25
	2. medium	2. medium	2. medium	26
	3. low	3. low	3. low	27
				28

These two questions were followed by five others asking about "The feeling that you are solving important problems," "The kind of work you do (did)" "The respect you get (got) because of your job," "The people you work (worked) with," and "Your advancement or chances for advancement." The variety of aspects of the work role that are involved and the orientation to the time dimension are both in keeping with a pragmatist perspective.

The second set of questions begins in this way:

WORK EXPERIENCE: THINGS IN COMMON

	Do Not
These questions deal with the relationships among your work experiences.	Write in
In each question two experiences are named, and you are asked	This
to decide if they have anything in common. For each question:	Space

CIRCLE "NOTHING IN COMMON" if you think they have nothing in common,

CIRCLE "POSSIBLY SOMETHING" if it is possible that they have something in common, and

CIRCLE "DEFINITELY SOMETHING" if you definitely can think of something that they have in common.

40. Your salary *and* The respect you get because of your job.

1. NOTHING IN COMMON	2. POSSIBLY SOMETHING	3. DEFINITELY SOMETHING	54

41. Enjoying the work itself *and* The feeling of independence you get from your work.

1. NOTHING IN COMMON	2. POSSIBLY SOMETHING	3. DEFINITELY SOMETHING	55

The remaining five questions combined other pairs of factors. This set of questions on things in common was designed to assess degree of breadth or narrowness. For example, if factors are seen as having nothing in common, this is taken to be an indication of a narrower view of the work situation that if they are seen to have possibly something in common.

For an understanding of the contrast between this approach to measurement and the formist one, let us contrast Figure 2-4 with the measurement approach depicted in Figure 2-2. Note the limited number of items involved in the latter relative to the former.

As for the results of this pretest, once again, in the interests of conciseness within this context, we shall consider only one aspect, Table 2-5. The relationship here is between work role breadth and personality breadth. The result is a relationship far more striking than any of those in Tables 2-1, 2-2, or 2-3, which convey the results relating to a formist paradigm. One way of assessing tables such as this is to examine the percentage spread, that is, the difference between the percentage in the upper left-hand corner and that in the upper right-hand corner (or, equally, between the percentages in the lower left-hand and lower right-hand corners). For Table 2-5 this difference comes to $89 - 11$, or 78%, as compared with differences of 20%, 13%, and 27% in Tables 2-1, 2-2, and 2-3, respectively. Because of the small number of individuals involved in this pretest, however, we should view these results with caution.

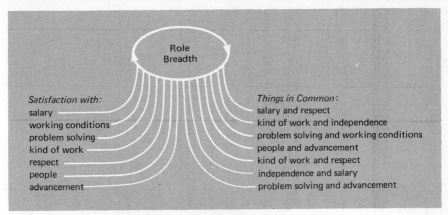

Figure 2-4.

Toward a Pragmatist Model of Aging: Multiple Measurement.

The aspects described so far of a movement from a formist to a pragmatist model of the aging process represent only a beginning. Spatially, we can continue to incorporate more phenomena into the relationships we are studying, since our assumption is that all phenomena are interrelated. Temporally, we have asked individuals about past and future, but the investigation took place at only one point in time. This might be contrasted, for example, with the hundreds of points in time over which aeronautical engineers test airfoils in wind tunnels. Such studies over many points in time are more appropriate for the pragmatist assumption of continuing change. The present illustration is merely the first of a series of studies with the same population.

Table 2-5

Work Role Breadth and Personality Breadth

			Work Role Breadth					
	Low						High	
Personality	1		2		3		4	
Breadth	%	(N)	%	(N)	%	(N)	%	(N)
Low	89	(8)	42	(5)	39	(7)	11	(1)
High	11	(1)	58	(7)	61	(11)	89	(8)
Total	100	(9)	100	(12)	100	(18)	100	(9)

A model of the aging process appropriate to both the spatial and temporal orientations of the pragmatist paradigm is presented in Figure 2-5. Since we have already discussed the gradational and measurement aspects of Figure 2-5, let us focus on the feedback relationships. This might best be done by contrasting this aging process illustration with the medical student illustration of Section 2.2. In that study, the medical students were seen more or less as acting like billiard balls: their goals were forces that propelled them, and their expectations as to the opportunities in the different medical fields corresponded to perceptions as to the location of the desired pockets in the game of pool. Such a metaphor is mechanistic because there is no focus on changes in the forces or in the location of the pockets. Such changes can be produced by the feedback of information, but the formist and mechanistic models do not provide for such feedback. In the pragmatist model of aging, by contrast, role breadth produces changes in personality breadth and mental health, but these latter in turn produce changes in role breadth, with changes continuing back and forth successively. This is like a billiard ball's speed and direction being successively altered, depending on its location and the location of the pockets, which also shift around, depending on where the balls are.

Figure 2-5 is labelled "toward" a pragmatist model because it is only a vague sketch of relationships: it does not specify the nature of these relationships in any precise way but simply indicates their existence. This is much the same as knowing that in the Newtonian laws of gravity there is *some* relationship between the amount of time a body has been falling and the distance it has fallen. Furthermore, the preceding discussion has not indicated how the multiple measurements are put together. Such topics remain to be developed in subsequent chapters, where I hope to clarify both the nature of theoretical models and the nature of the measurement process.

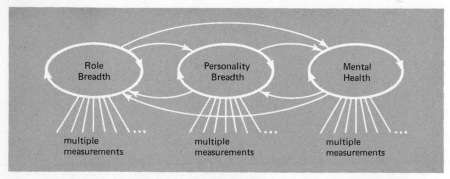

Figure 2-5.
Toward a Pragmatist Model of Aging: Gradation, Multiple Measurement, Feedback.

Table 2-6
A Review of Formism, Mechanism, Organicism and Pragmatism

	Formism	Mechanism	Organicism	Pragmatism
Typical Period	Preindustrial and later	Early industrial and later	Late industrial and later	Postindustrial
Basic Metaphor	Same and different	Continuum and machine	Organism	Situation
Related Ideas	Plato, Aristotle, Scholastics, Neoscholastics, Neo-realists, Modern Cambridge realists	Democritus, Lucretius, Galileo, Descartes, Hobbes, Locke, Berkeley, Hume, Reichenbach	Schelling, Hegel, Green, Bradley, Bosanquet, Royce, Comte, Maine, Tönnies, Durkheim	Peirce, James, Mead, Dewey, Holmes
Research Illustrations	Aging and adjustment study	Occupational choice study	Community development study	A model of the aging process
	Statistical significance	Mathematical model	Community complexity	Comprehensive concepts
	Adjustment vs. maladjustment	Man as machine	Rapid environmental change	Open ended
	Existence of relationships	Type of relationship	Multiple interlocking problems	Problem solving
General Characteristics and Illustrations	Either-or	Gradational	Growth	Man at the center
	Agreement or disagreement	Shades of gray	Feedback	Change and complexity
	Most language	Mathematical	Life	Contextual
	Non-overlapping circles	Billiard-ball universe	Adaptation	Overlapping circles
	Isolated roles	Deterministic	Historical	Spatial and temporal
	Implicit idea of progress	Humans irrelevant	Integrative	Scientific and humanistic
	A is A	Changing the environment	Alters own structure	Ideas and action
	A is not B	Systematic relationships	Changing structures	Change in structure and environment
	Nominal measurement	Materialistic	Social structure	Individual and society

2.5 Summary

Formism, mechanism, organicism and pragmatism refer to fundamental assumptions within the research process, assumptions that are made when a research problem is defined. Table 2-6 presents a review of the ideas associated with these paradigms. By failing to unearth such fundamental assumptions within the research process, the scientist remains a prisoner of assumptions unknown to him. The result is that his activities are scientific only up to a certain point; beyond this point his ideas are held to dogmatically. This is analogous to the great religious barriers to scientific thought that existed prior to the Enlightenment. In modern times, such barriers are contained deep within the personality structure of the scientist and the social structure of his milieu. Social science is structured to create heresies about such matters no less than physical science is structured to create heresies about the physical universe, only the modern heresies represent departures from prevailing ideologies, values, and patterns of interaction rather than from religious dogma. By bringing paradigms to the surface, we can test them scientifically and avoid the diminishing returns that result from a failure to do so. However, the path to such an achievement is no less difficult than the path taken by scientific thinkers in the age of Galileo. In Chapter 3, linguistic and cybernetic tools geared to aiding in this process are presented.

Exercises

1. Select any research article from the social science literature. To what extent, and in what ways, is it formist, mechanistic, organicist, and pragmatist?

2. Analyze a sample of your own writing with respect to evidence of formist, mechanistic, organicist, and pragmatist thought.

3. Construct a number of items for a questionnaire to measure the degree to which an individual is formist, mechanistic, organicist, and pragmatist.

4. Develop a rationale for another paradigm—in addition to those discussed here—which should be taken into account for a fuller understanding of the research process.

Annotated References

KAPLAN, ABRAHAM. *The Conduct of Inquiry*. San Francisco: Chandler Publishing Company, 1964. Kaplan systematically applies his pragmatist perspective to a very wide range of topics bearing on social research. His is the kind of pragmatism that attempts to include the strengths of formism, mechanism, and organicism.

KAPLAN, ABRAHAM. *The New World of Philosophy.* New York: Random House, Inc., Vintage Books, 1961. Kaplan presents nine world views that overlap the ones presented here: pragmatism, analytic philosophy, existentialism, Freudianism, communism, Indian philosophy, Buddhism, Chinese philosophy, and Zen. His treatment of various Eastern perspectives adds a dimension to the predominantly Western focus of this chapter.

PEPPER, STEPHEN C. *World Hypotheses.* Berkeley: University of California Press, 1961. Pepper's book provides an exposition of four world hypotheses: formism, mechanism, organicism, and contextualism, or pragmatism. Pepper's own approach is formist: he see these hypotheses as mutually exclusive, and he does not present them from a historical or evolutionary perspective. It is a difficult book for the student with no background in philosophy. It succeeds in providing an introduction to a great many Western philosophies.

chapter 3

Language and Cybernetics

However profound or far-reaching are the perspectives of the investigator, however well-grounded he is with a sense of history, and however steeped he is in the knowledge produced by the social sciences, he must be in command of effective tools that embody those orientations if he expects to define problems for research. In this chapter I discuss two of these tools: language and cybernetics. It is with the aid of these symbolic systems—products of the humanistic and the scientific tradition—that we are able to pull together available knowledge and define directions for moving beyond existing literatures. The four paradigms presented in Chapter 2 will provide a basis for our discussions here.

3.1   The Language of Science

The language of science is like a chip on the ocean of the scientist's everyday language, and that ocean in turn forms only a portion of the world of his experience. We cannot isolate scientific language from the rest and hope to understand it, just as we cannot isolate any element of culture from its context and do justice to it. Thus, the discussion of the language of science must range widely to include the broader contexts of formist language, mechanistic language, organicist language, and pragmatist language. Some problems that language poses may be illustrated by Fred Hoyle's science fiction classic *The Black Cloud*. The Cloud is an intergalactic creature, much larger than the earth and made up mainly of empty space, that wanders into the solar system in search of solar energy. Communication with the Cloud reveals it to be a superintelligent form of life. After the Cloud learns to decode human language, it (she?) proceeds to give its view of our language:

> Your outstanding oddity is the great similarity of one individual to another. This allows you to use a very crude method of communication. You attach labels to your neurological states—anger, headache, embarrassed, happy, melancholy—these are all labels. If Mr. A. wishes to tell

Mr. B. that he is suffering from a headache he makes no attempt to describe the neurological disruption in his head. Instead he displays his label. He says:

"I have a headache."

When Mr. B. hears this he takes the label "headache" and interprets it in accordance with his own experience. Thus Mr. A. is able to acquaint Mr. B. of his indisposition even though neither party may have the slightest idea what a "headache" really consists of. Such a highly singular method of communication is of course only possible between nearly identical individuals.[1]

How are we to get beyond the inadequacy of formist labels? How can the language of science describe the particulars of neurological phenomena, or of any other phenomena? These are the kinds of questions that can be probed by examining the symbolic implications of formism, mechanism, organicism, and pragmatism.

Formist Language

From the formist perspective, the scientist attempts to draw out scientific truths from the confusing welter of human experience. He is committed to the importance of a division of human communication into truth and falsity. He looks at the history of human thought and tends to be disappointed at the small proportion of that thought that has been definitely confirmed or validated. His aim is to subject existing ideas about phenomena to the hard test of the process of scientific verification, and thus to divide the sheep from the goats, the statements that are true from those that are false.

Within this framework, the three major linguistic tools of the scientist are the *concept,* the *proposition,* and the *theory.* Of the three, the proposition is most central, with the concept seen as a preliminary step to the development of a proposition, and with a theory seen as some system of propositions. Thus, *concepts are abstractions used by the scientist as building blocks for the development of propositions and theories that explain and predict phenomena.* A concept functions to abstract out or select or label certain phenomena—such as those that might go under the heading of "headache"—and thus separates these phenomena from all other phenomena.

Two criteria that are used to evaluate the clarity of concepts are determinacy and uniformity of usage. In the former case, the concern rests with how precisely a concept specifies a particular set of phenomena, and how vague and ambiguous the concept is. How many different meanings does it have, and how clearly is one particular meaning conveyed? How well defined are the limits or boundaries of the phenomena to which the concept

[1] Fred Hoyle, *The Black Cloud* (New York: Signet, 1962), pp. 150–51.

refers? One approach to conceptualization that embodies a formist orientation is known as "operationism." Faced with the multiple meanings, the vagueness, and the ambiguity of existing concepts, the scientist attempts to greatly increase clarity by limiting the meaning of a concept to the specific operations or techniques used to measure the phenomena to which it refers. Thus, for example, the "meaning" of the concept *intelligence* is to be found in the particular operations used to measure intelligence. More colloquially, intelligence comes to be understood as whatever is measured by an intelligence test.

As for uniformity of usage, this involves gaining widespread agreement as to how words are to be used. Lack of agreement tends to be seen with distrust. Scientists are free to create their own meanings or their own concepts, but they must clearly communicate just what they mean. Their readers are then in a position to understand that meaning, and uniformity of usage may be attained within the particular context of the communication. Others can subsequently proceed with different meanings in other contexts, providing that they communicate clearly enough so that uniformity of usage is attained within those contexts.

Propositions *are statements about the nature of reality and may in principle be evaluated in terms of truth and falsity.* Hypotheses are propositions that have been put forward tentatively for the purpose of developing evidence for or against the proposition in question. We hypothesize that employment status is related to adjustment (Table 2-1), when we are not certain that this is true, and that hypothesis directs our attention to collecting evidence for or against this assertion. Laws—which are rarely referred to in the social sciences but are common enough in the physical sciences—are propositions that are quite firmly established, so that we have a continuum from hypothesis to proposition to law.

The major function concepts serve is in the development of propositions. Efforts to obtain clarity of meaning through determinancy and uniformity of usage enable the scientist to develop measurements that produce evidence bearing on his propositions. The scientist thus collects evidence bearing on the nature of reality that is not merely an aid to his own understanding but that can be demonstrated to others as determining truth or falsity. In this sense, evidence is not merely subjective: it is objective. The procedures used can be repeated by any fellow scientist, and the results—other things being equal—should be identical. Truth is not something to be easily obtained, not the result merely of sophisticated discourse or of the reasoning of the intellect. It is, rather, won in the face of a nature that hides its facts. Ideas, however brilliant, must be continually subjected to nature, and only then can truth emerge.

Certain fundamental assumptions underlie a formist approach to language, assumptions on which any particular proposition is based. These were partially discussed in Section 2.1, in the context of the Aristotelian law of identity and the ideas of "same" and "different." We may summarize them in the form of these three principles:

> The *principle of identity* asserts that: *If any proposition is true, it is true.* The *principle of contradiction* asserts that: *No proposition can be both true and false.* The *principle of excluded middle* states that: *Any proposition must be either true or false.*[2]

In Section 2.1 I discussed both liberating and limiting implications of the law of identity; this applies also to the principles of contradiction and the excluded middle. On the one hand, they help the scientist—by providing a rock on which he can stand—to derive from his amorphous and confusing experiences certain initial facts: let him worry about neither change nor contradictions while he is embarking on the difficult task of wresting truths from nature. On the other hand, however, he may come to believe too much in the solidity of that rock, thus failing—at a later point in his investigations—to question his assumptions about a rather static and simplistic world. As the Cloud indicates, it is naive to assume that a few labels can penetrate very deeply into ongoing phenomena.

Moving from propositions to theories, let us begin with an analogy between a theory and a spatial network:

> A scientific theory might therefore be likened to a complex spatial network: its terms are represented by the knots, while the threads connecting the latter correspond, in part, to the fundamental and derivative hypotheses included in the theory. The whole system floats, as it were, above the plane of observation and is anchored to it by rules of interpretation. These might be viewed as strings which are not part of the network but link certain points of the latter with specific places in the plane of observation.[3]

This analogy is presented graphically in Figure 3-1. Thus, *theories are systems of propositions.* Their validity, or truth, is based on their correspondence with measurements taken in the plane of observation, measurements based on certain rules of interpretation, as facilitated by determinancy and uniformity of usage.

At last we have visual indications of the power and limitations of formism. There is the insubstantial yet vital spatial network hovering above us, carrying the idealist tradition of Parmenides (427 B.C.), Plato (347 B.C.), and Hegel (1770–1831), which represents the thrust toward righ-

[2] Morris R. Cohen and Ernest Nagel, *An Introduction to Logic and Scientific Method* (New York: Harcourt, 1934), pp. 181–82.
[3] Carl G. Hempel, *Fundamentals of Concept Formation in Empirical Science*, Vol. 2, No. 7, International Encyclopedia of Unified Science (Chicago: U. of Chicago, 1952), p. 36.

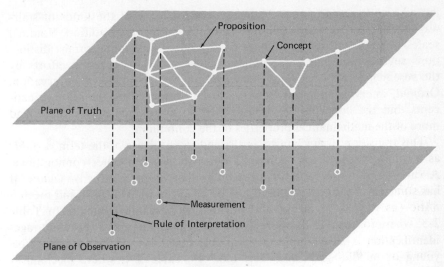

Figure 3-1.
Formist Image of Scientific Theory.

teousness and salvation of the Judeo-Christian tradition and gives the scientist a direction in his search for truth. There are the empirical measurements the scientist can observe, creatures of the world he experiences, carriers of the realistic tradition of Heraclitus (*c*535–*c*475 B.C.), William of Ockham (1300–1349?), Sir Francis Bacon (1561–1626), Thomas Hobbes (1599–1679), and John Locke (1632–1704). And there are the grand efforts of those who attempted to unite these two worlds—Aristotle (384 B.C.–322 B.C.), St. Thomas Aquinas (1225–1274), and Immanuel Kant (1724–1804).[4] The synthesis is both a noble effort and an act of faith, and we are left with a dream that gives us guidance. However, without transcending the limits of formism, it is an impossible dream, for we have no stairway to climb to the heavenly realm of truth: it is an all-or-none leap we are required to make to reach the heavenly city. The process of induction, or the movement from the plane of observation to such truths as the idea of cause and effect, requires—according to David Hume (1711–1776) and much of modern philosophy—leaps, or inferences, that somehow transcend the facts of human experience.

Mechanistic Language

To make a transition from formism to mechanism we must begin to think more of physical scientists and engineers and mathematicians. Start-

[4] For a discussion of these ideas see Joseph F. Rychlak, *A Philosophy of Science of Personality Theory* (Boston: Houghton, 1968), especially Chapter 9, "Dialectical vs. Demonstrative Reasoning in the History of Western Thought."

ing with concepts, Figure 3-2 suggests the existence of the kinds of stairways that are so lacking within the philosophical formist tradition. Nominal scales—as we shall see in Chapter 6—are based on simple formist distinctions such as are found in ordinary language. They represent efforts by the researcher to bring down such concepts to the plane of observation. Ordinal, interval, and ratio scales also constitute efforts to observe concepts, but the concepts are transformed so as to incorporate more and more of the mathematical properties of the continuum.

This transition to mechanism is also indicated by use of the term *variable* as a rough synonym for "concept," but also carrying other connotations. A variable is *a concept that takes on two or more degrees of values*. It has sufficient flexibility so that it can be of aid in both formist and mechanistic (as well as organicist and pragmatist) research contexts. In Table 2-3, where formism is illustrated by a study of aging and adjustment, age-identification is an example of a variable that takes on two values: "feel young or middle-aged" and "feel old." In Table 2-4, where mechanism is illustrated by a study of choice of medical fields, we have the variable of "resultant goal commitments," which ranges from 1 to 6.

We have propositions in the mechanistic as well as the formist approach to science, but the emphasis is different. In the aging study the focus was on establishing whether or not a relationship *exists* between, for example, age-identification and personal adjustment. Using the concept of variable, there was an empirical test of the hypothesis that age-identification (the presumed cause, or the "independent variable") is related to degree of adjustment (the presumed effect, or the "dependent variable"). In the medical study, by contrast, my interest was far more in the degree and the *type* of relationship between resultant goal commitments and medical preference. I felt I would learn very little simply from establishing the existence of a relationship betwen these two variables, for relationships be-

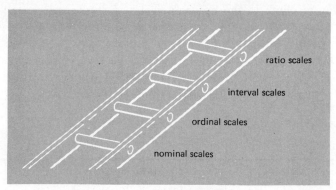

Figure 3-2.
A Conceptual Ladder for Attaining Mathematical Properties.

tween goals and preferences have already been thoroughly documented throughout the social science literature. But if we are interested in attaining more far-reaching knowledge of the type that can yield predictions and provide a basis for problem-solving, then it is vital to explore relationships that are close and also to develop equations for the types of relationships involved. Imagine trying to utilize a law of machines (Figure 2-1) when all we know is that some relationship between force and weight *exists*. It is not even enough to know that the *degree* of relationship, or the correlation between force and resistance, is a close one, analogous to the close relationship between resultant goal commitments and the percentage who give favorable ratings to medical fields in Table 2-4. We must know that $F \times d = R \times d$ so as to be able to act most effectively in shaping our environment.

This difference of focus between formist and mechanistic uses of propositions implies a general difference in the goals of the scientist. In the former case the scientist attempts to *explain* the nature of reality, whereas in the latter he is most concerned with *prediction*. The latter is also a more active emphasis: we predict the forces within the environment in order to be able to control them and thus shape the environment. Also, we may understand how mechanism can build on the basis of formism within this context: explanation is a basis for prediction. The more we understand, the more we are encouraged to attempt prediction, and the better we are equipped to change the environment.

Our final exploration of mechanistic language revolves around the concept of "theory." The difference between formism and mechanism here is illustrated by the difference between the geometric analysis of Figure 3-1 and the mathematical equation specifying the law of machines. Mechanistic theory is concerned primarily with mathematical models, or sets of equations, whereas formist theory deals with formalized systems such as the axiomatic system of plane geometry; it is the difference between an emphasis on logic and an emphasis on the kinds of mathematics (not plane geometry) that emphasize the number system. The mechanistic theorist is less interested in proving the truth of his theory than in putting his mathematical models to work in the solution of problems.

Organicist Language

In moving from mechanistic to organicist usages of language we move from the world of the engineer and the physical scientist to the world of the social scientist. We must not be overawed by the power of mathematics or of the physical laws of the universe, for those ideas generally are oriented to the description of only one kind of universe: a billiard ball, or clock, universe, which is closed rather than open-ended, and which centers on the tangible, or the material, rather than the intangible. It is a world in which human beings are not centrally located within the plane of truth, where they are peripheral observers of the play of the forces of the universe. The world of the social scientist, by contrast, is not a closed one. There are also grand movements, such as from status to contract or from *Gemeinschaft* to *Gesellschaft* or from mechanical solidarity to organic solidarity, but these are open-ended, where the future remains to be decided. It is also a world in which intangible forces are at work—norms, values, social systems, personality systems—and must be dealt with on their own terms. Here, then, are illustrations of organicist language: concepts like status, contract, *gemeinschaft, gesellschaft,* mechanical solidarity, organic solidarity. There is also the idea of the continuum: from status to contract, from *gemeinschaft* to *gesellschaft,* from mechanical solidarity to organic solidarity. Finally, there is an emphasis on social structures, with little attention given to personality structures.

The organicist approach to language might be seen as a hybrid that unites a sensitivity to the diversity of human experience, such as is to be found in formism or in everyday language, with an interest in abstraction or scientific generalization, such as that which accompanies the mechanistic world view. We may illustrate this approach as it relates to concepts with Max Weber's concept of *ideal type:*

> An ideal-type is formed by the one-sided accentuation of one or more points of view and by the synthesis of a great many diffuse, discrete, more or less present and occasionally absent *concrete individual* phenomena, which are arranged according to those one-sidedly emphasized viewpoints into a unified analytical construct. In its conceptual purity, the mental construct cannot be found empirically anywhere in reality. It is a utopia.[5]

The ideal type is not the vague, unanalyzed concept of ordinary usage, with its many different meanings. Nor is it the far more precise and clearly understood concept of the physicist or chemist. It lies somewhere in between, retaining some of the richness of ordinary language and some of the clarity of scientific language; or in a more critical vein, it retains some of the vagueness of ordinary language and some of the narrowness of scientific language.

Perhaps the best-known of Weber's ideal types is that of bureaucracy:

> Modern officialdom functions in the following specific manner:
> I. There is the principle of fixed and official jurisdictional areas, which are generally ordered by rules, that is, by laws or administrative regulations. . . .

---

[5] Max Weber, "Objectivity in Social Science and Social Policy," in *The Methodology of the Social Sciences,* trans. and ed. by Edward A. Shils and Henry A. Finch (New York: Free Press, 1949), p. 90.

II. The principles of office hierarchy and of graded authority mean a firmly ordered system of super- and subordination in which there is a supervision of the lower offices by the higher ones. . . .

III. The management of the modern office is based upon written documents ("the files"), which are preserved in their original or draught form. . . .

IV. Office management, at least all specialized office management—and such management is distinctly modern—usually presupposes thorough and expert training. . . .

V. When the office is fully developed, official activity demands the full working capacity of the official, irrespective of the fact that his obligatory time in the bureau may be firmly delimited. . . .

VI. The management of the office follows general rules, which are more or less stable, more or less exhaustive, and which can be learned. . . .[6]

This concept combines a number of factors: division of labor, hierarchy, written documents, expert training, commitment, and rules. This is a rich mixture—and far richer when we pursue the details of Weber's thinking—yet it is all clearly presented.

Weber makes use of this concept of bureaucratic organization in developing the fundamental thesis that the main trend of history is toward increasing rationalization, illustrated by bureaucratization, a conclusion similar to that of Maine, Tönnies, and Durkheim. This thesis is neither a simple proposition nor a system of propositions in the formist sense: it is too amorphous and not sufficiently systematic. And it is certainly not a theory or model in the mechanistic sense, for it is not mathematical.

Yet despite these limitations, vital elements of both formism and mechanism are included in this organicist approach. First, the richness of ideas is based on freedom from a sole concern with concrete, material phenomena. Both intangible patterns of social organization, such as a division of labor and a hierarchy, and concrete products of that organization, such as written documents, can be included. Such freedom enables the investigator to come to grips with the complexities of industrial society. Second, the focus is on a continuum, as in mechanism. Weber is describing a movement of history along a continuum of degree of rationalization. It is also an open-ended, as distinct from a finite, continuum, in that there is no specific vision of an end point. In this sense, there is a departure from the deterministic features associated with mechanism.

Yet for all this ability of organicism to incorporate vital elements of formism and mechanism, let us not lose sight of its limitations, as suggested by Hoyle's *The Black Cloud*. The Cloud does not merely make use of the idea of the continuum in its communication processes, and it does not merely convey complexity via formist labels similar to those used in human

[6] Max Weber, *From Max Weber: Essays in Sociology,* trans. and ed. by H. H. Gerth and C. Wright Mills (New York: Oxford U. P., 1958), pp. 196–98.

speech: the Cloud somehow is able to communicate the nature of its ever-changing and highly complex neurological states. This seems to require far more than simply the beginnings of mathematics and of language.

Pragmatist Language

Let us begin with an illustration derived from Chapter 2: a comparison between some of the concepts taken from the formist research illustration and from the pragmatist illustration. In particular, let us examine the contrast between the concepts of "employment status" and "marital status," on the one hand, and "role breadth" on the other. One basis for comparison is the either-or nature of the concepts involved. The concepts of employment status and marital status were conceived of as encompassing dichotomous attributes: employment versus retirement, and married versus widowed, respectively. By contrast, the concept of role breadth was seen as very much a matter of degree. Further, there was no arbitrary end-point where role breadth was seen as being achieved: role breadth could continue to increase indefinitely. This gradational perspective and lack of an end point in the "positive" direction also characterized the other pragmatist concepts: personality breadth and mental health.

If the gradational versus dichotomous orientation has to do with the temporal dimension, then the degree of inclusiveness of the concepts has to do with the spatial dimension. We have seen in our discussion of organicist language that it is this degree of inclusiveness which is a distinguishing characteristic of such language, and the same is the case for pragmatist language. In the case of role breadth in Chapter 2, multiple factors were encompassed, just as in the case of Weber's concept of bureaucracy or Maine's concept of status and contract or Tönnies' concepts of *gemeinschaft* and *gesellschaft* or Durkheim's concepts of mechanical solidarity and organic solidarity.

It is easier to distinguish pragmatist language from formist than from organicist language. One difference has to do with the temporal approach: organicist language is not as graditional as is pragmatist language. The *gesellschaft* or a contractual society or organic solidarity have more of the connotation of being end points than does the concept of, say, role breadth. Yet the difference is not a clear-cut one. Since most of language is pervaded by dichotomies, it is very difficult to get away from this orientation when language is used.

Here, it seems, is a paradoxical situation. How are we to employ language in a pragmatist way when language itself is oriented in other ways? The Black Cloud points this problem up in referring to the structure of human language as a device for labeling as distinct from a tool which could reveal the complexity and dynamism and uniqueness of any given phenomenon like a headache that a given individual has at a given time in a given situation.

There appear to be two ways out of this impasse. One is to employ—mentally or through actual recording—the device of the "spatial subscript" and the "temporal superscript."[7] In other words, a series of subscripts can be used to alert us to the idea that cow_1 is not cow_2 is not cow_3. Also, a series of superscripts can remind us that cow^{1975} is not cow^{1976} is not cow^{1977}. By using the subscripts and superscripts in combination, we locate phenomena in space and time and get away from the labeling aspects of language. $Headache_{Joe}^{June\ 3,\ 1976}$ is not $headache_{Joe}^{June\ 4,\ 1976}$. The problem, though, is that it is very difficult for us to learn to think in this way just because our language militates against it.[8]

The other approach is to move to the language of cybernetics, where the very structure of the language involved is an aid to pragmatist thought. Indeed, in the case of mechanism it was necessary to move to the language of mathematics. We can hardly imagine the development of the physical sciences without such a movement. This should not imply that ordinary language must become passé in such an effort. The physical scientist operates with both ordinary and mathematical language, moving back and forth between them. His mathematics sharpens his conceptual tools, and vice-versa. This interplay among languages parallels our overall approach to the paradigms: all of them are important in the difficult enterprise known as the scientific method.

3.2 Cybernetic Thinking

Norbert Wiener, who derived the term *cybernetics* from the Greek word *kubernētēs,* or "steersman," defines it as a science of communication and control. He states its significance as follows:

> Information is a name for the content of what is exchanged with the outer world as we adjust to it, and make our adjustment felt upon it. The process of receiving and of using information is the process of our adjusting to the contingencies of the outer environment, and of our living effectively within that environment. The needs and the complexity of modern life make greater demands on this process of information than ever before, and our press, our museums, our scientific laboratories, our universities, our libraries and textbooks, are obliged to meet the needs of this process or fail in their purpose. To live effectively is to live with adequate information. Thus, communication and control belong to the essence of man's inner life, even as they belong to his life in society.[9]

[7] For a detailed discussion of this approach to language, see Alfred Korzybski, *Science and Sanity* (Lakeville, Conn.: Institute of General Semantics, 1958).

[8] One way of dealing with this problem is developed in my own *Worlds of the Future: Exercises in the Sociological Imagination* (Columbus: Merrill, 1972), especially Chapter 7, "From Pre-Industrial to Post-Industrial Society," pp. 141–63.

[9] Norbert Wiener, *The Human Use of Human Beings* (Garden City, N.Y.: Doubleday, Anchor Press, 1954), pp. 17–18.

Wiener is recapitulating in part our discussion of organicism in Section 2.3, where the emphasis was on feedback, adaptation, and growth. The plant needs information fed back to it as to the existence of water in order to adapt successfully to its environment and achieve growth, just as we need information feedback for our own adaptation and growth. But cybernetics is also formist, mechanistic, and pragmatist. The thermostat—a simple illustration of a cybernetic device—is formist in its sharp differentiation between, on the one hand, environmental temperatures falling outside of its fixed and circumscribed range of what is acceptable and, on the other hand, those environmental temperatures falling within that range. It is mechanistic in its ability to act so as to control that environment, and also in its basis in a mathematical continuum with a demarcation of degrees along that continuum. And if we think of the individual, who continually sets new goals on the basis of both exterior demands and his inner world, who controls his own thermostatic settings, then we see cybernetics from a pragmatist perspective. Thus, cybernetics appears to be the kind of framework within which all four paradigms participate.

Cybernetics provides us with important tools out of the mathematical and physical science tradition for understanding human behavior, both the fundamental assumptions involved and the more concrete behaviors. This section is divided into two parts: "The Beaker Metaphor and System Dynamics" and "The First, Second, and Third Cybernetics." In the first part, we begin with a simple metaphor and use that as a basis for achieving an initial understanding of complex and dynamic tools for building theory. In the second part, three approaches to cybernetics are distinguished, with examples taken from the preceding research illustrations.

The Beaker Metaphor and System Dynamics

The problem to be addressed is a continuation of the one we have just been discussing in the context of ordinary language in Section 3.1: How can tools for pragmatist thinking be developed, tools that can probe deeply into human assumptions and behavior? The idea of a continuum like role breadth, with its temporal and spatial openness, represents an important beginning. But how are we to conceptualize shifts along this continuum? What about rates of change in one direction or another? What of acceleration? How are several continua that affect each other interrelated? Mechanistic tools like the mathematics of the calculus have been applied primarily to changes and relationships among physical phenomena, and they might be applied here as well. But the most serious problem with such tools is that they almost invariably carry with them a mechanistic paradigm, which does not allow for the kinds of feedback characteristic of human phenomena. We move, then, to cybernetics as an approach that incorporates this mathematical heritage yet centers on feedback relationships.

Just as mathematics arrived on the human scene after ordinary language had already been developed, so we shall begin to build an understanding of cybernetics from a simple metaphor out of ordinary language. Let us consider the flow of water from a faucet into a beaker, as depicted in Figure 3-3, and see this phenomenon as a metaphor for the development of mental health. On the left-hand side we have the diagram of the variable of mental health taken from Figure 2-5, where a pragmatist approach to developing a model of the aging process was illustrated. One problem with this simple circle with two arrows is that although it does succeed in indicating that there is a feedback process going on, it fails to show the dynamic nature of the process. Mental health goes up and down, and rates of change vary from one time period to the next, but this is hidden within such a simple diagram.

On the right-hand side of Figure 3-3, we are able to depict the feedback process, the dynamics of that process, and details about the nature of that process. Let us begin with an approach based on our everyday experience of getting water from a tap into a glass. Our aspiration might be the height of the glass: we want to fill it up, but we don't want any overflow. Initially, the gap between the height of the glass and the height of water in the empty glass is great, and we feel free to open up the tap, corresponding to a large force for mental health development and a rapid rate of such development. As the water rises, however, we obtain information feedback as to the height of that water (level of mental health). The gap between the height of the glass and the height of the water is now much less, and we start to turn off the tap and decrease the rate of flow, a process that continues until the glass is full and the tap is shut off completely. If we add the idea that we have a leaky glass (corresponding to the rate of mental health decay), then all aspects of the beaker metaphor have been illustrated.

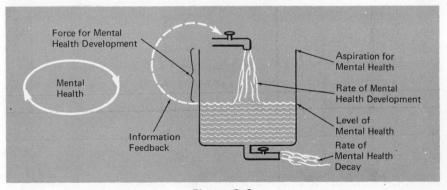

Figure 3-3.
The Beaker Metaphor: Mental Health Development.

But of course life is not as simple as this. The individual is not in complete control of his own destiny. He cannot increase or decrease his mental health at will. Many other factors are involved. Another problem with Figure 3-3 is that it is a picture more than a schematic diagram. As a result, if we applied this approach to a more complex situation, we would have a good deal of difficulty in explaining what is happening. Also, we would have little uniformity of usage: it would be difficult for individuals to communicate with one another.

Figure 3-4 constitutes an attempt to deal with both of these problems. Role breadth is one of the factors related to mental health that was depicted in Figure 2-5; it refers to the degree of openness or constriction in one's relationships to others. We have in Figure 3-4(b) two beaker metaphors, drawn schematically side-by-side, with the left-hand one corresponding to role breadth and the right-hand one corresponding to mental health. Figure 3-4(b) corresponds to the simplified version of the same relationship (taken from Figure 2-5) that appears in Figure 3-4(a).

The "system dynamics"[10] notation used in Figure 3-4(b) constitutes a procedure auxiliary to a method of computer simulation (see Chapter 8) that is structured on the basis of the differential equations, thus carrying

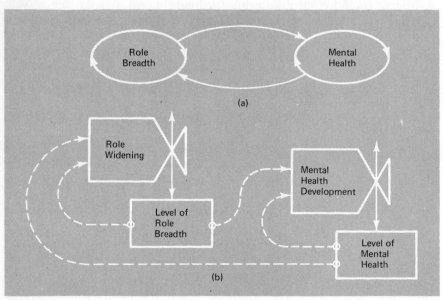

Figure 3-4.
Role Breadth and Mental Health: System Dynamics Notation.

[10] System dynamics is an approach to computer simulation that is discussed in Section 8.2.

forward the tradition of the physical sciences and making that tradition accessible to students with little mathematical background. Differential equations constitute a combination of differential calculus, dealing with rates of flow, and integral calculus, having to do with levels of accumulation. Both of these processes are involved with regard to the two schematized beakers of Figure 3-4(b). The two valves represent faucets governing the rate of flow of role widening and of mental health development, respectively. Flow can be accumulated into the schematized beakers (the two rectangles), indicated by the arrows pointing downward, or flow can be out of the beakers. In Figure 3-3 such outward flow was represented by a drain in the beaker, but here it can more conveniently be depicted by arrows from the valves that go up as well as down. The broken arrows refer to information flows, and they help to form the three loops portrayed: (1) from mental health development to level of mental health and then back again; (2) from role widening to level of role breadth and back again; and (3) from role widening to level of role breadth to mental health development to level of mental health and then back to role widening.

If role breadth affects mental health, mental health in turn can alter role breadth. Such a feedback approach fits well with the existing framework of sociological theory. For example, the structural-functional and conflict theory traditions would focus on ways in which the social system, as illustrated by role breadth, affects the personality system, as illustrated by mental health. In addition, elements of the symbolic interactionist, exchange theory, and ethno-methodological, or phenomenological, traditions would deal with the impact of mental health on role breadth. By working with a model that systematically portrays the interaction between the social system and the personality system, we go beyond either set of these theoretical traditions taken separately. This also implies the utilization of multiple paradigms.

In addition to the spatial breadth attained through such an interactive framework, there are its temporal advantages. In Figure 3-4(a) we can do no more than hint at the rates of change of mental health and role breadth, but when we move to 3-4(b) we have available more tools for examining such change. Even without going into the complexities of computer-based analyses, we can achieve some understanding with this diagram. It alerts us to rates of flow and levels of accumulation. We can see, for example, that a high rate must continue over a period of time before a high level of accumulation can result: we can open up a water tap very widely, but we must wait a bit for the water to accumulate in the glass. Further, it alerts us to more of the complexities involved in human behavior. There are many things going on in Figure 3-4(b). These are no different from what is happening in 3-4(a), but this more simplified diagram hides much of the complexity and dynamism from us.

The First, Second, and Third Cybernetics

In the first part of this section our focus has been on cybernetic structures, namely, on the ways in which phenomena are interrelated. Structure is most important, as any sociologist or psychologist or biologist or physicist will declare. A fundamental reason for its importance is that it helps us to understand and predict the dynamic behavior of systems. In this section our focus shifts from structure to dynamic behavior. With respect to our model of the aging process, for example, mental health might move up or down and then reach equilibrium at a certain level. Alternatively, mental health might continue to accelerate in an upward or downward direction. Another possibility is some complex combination of several of these various possibilities. In this part of the section we shall develop several concepts from cybernetics that can serve as tools for describing various types of dynamic behavior.

We might begin with Magoroh Maruyama's distinction between what he calls the "first cybernetics" and the "second cybernetics":

Since its inception, cybernetics was more or less identified as a science of self-regulating and equilibrating systems. Thermostats, physiological regulation of body temperature, automatic steering devices, economic and political processes were studied under a general mathematical model of deviation-counteracting feedback networks.

By focusing on the deviation-counteracting aspect of the mutual causal relationships however, the cyberneticians paid less attention to the systems in which the mutual causal effects are deviation-amplifying. Such systems are ubiquitous: accumulation of capital in industry, evolution of living organisms, the rise of cultures of various types, interpersonal processes which produce mental illness, international conflicts, and the processes that are loosely termed as "vicious circles" and "compound interests"; in short, all processes of mutual causal relationships that amplify an insignificant or accidental initial kick, build up deviation and diverge from the initial condition. . . .

The deviation-counteracting mutual causal systems and the deviation-amplifying mutual causal systems may appear to be opposite types of systems. But they have one essential feature in common: they are both mutual causal systems, i.e., the elements within a system influence each other either simultaneously or alternatingly. The difference between the two types of systems is that the deviation-counteracting system has mutual negative feedbacks between the elements in it while the deviation-amplifying system has mutual positive feedbacks between the elements in it.[11]

Maruyama is referring to two kinds of dynamic behavior which can result from a given feedback loop. The first cybernetics, which historically

[11] Magoroh Maruyama, "The Second Cybernetics: Deviation-Amplifying Mutual Causal Processes," in Walter Buckley (ed.), *Modern Systems Research for the Behavioral Scientist* (Chicago: Aldine, 1968), p. 304.

has been the dominant approach, deals with *negative loops,* or negative-feedback loops, that is, behavior that moves toward equilibrium at a given level or oscillates around a given level. The beaker metaphor illustrates such a situation when the beaker height is fixed: the water moves toward equilibrium at the height of the beaker. A physical thermostat or the human body's own thermostatic devices illustrate the case of behavior which oscillates around a given level. Such oscillating behavior might also characterize the mental health of an individual, where in spite of ups and downs equilibrium is retained within a given range. Figure 3-5 portrays three kinds of negative loops. The smooth curves *A* and *B* are known as *first-order negative loops,* that is, they are less complex than the oscillating curve *C,* which is a *second-order negative loop.* Curve *A* might correspond to a beaker that drains down to a certain point and then reaches equilibrium, as in the case of an individual drinking his full from a very tall beaker. Curve *B* might refer to the filling of that beaker from a tap and the closing of the tap when the water level nears the top of the beaker. Curve *C* illustrates the operation of a physical or biological thermostat, where forces are generated to bring the temperature down when it gets above a certain level, and forces are developed to raise the temperature when it moves below a given level.

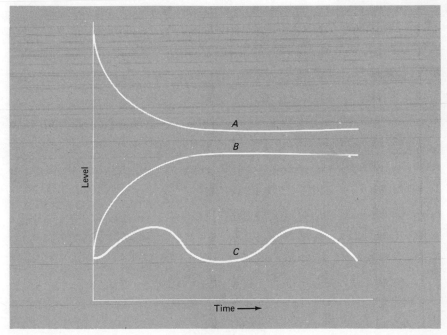

Figure 3-5.
Negative Loops.

According to Maruyama, very little attention has been paid to the second cybernetics, that is, to the kinds of feedback loops that result in the amplification of deviation as distinct from deviation counteraction. Curves *D, E,* and *F* of Figure 3-6 portray various kinds of *positive loops,* or positive-feedback loops. Note that "positive" does not imply "upward": amplification can move downward as well as upward. We might think of the deceleration of confidence in a bank or the deceleration of mental health just as readily as the acceleration of such phenomena. The smooth curves *E* and *F*, corresponding to upward and downward positive loops, are *first-order positive loops,* whereas the more complex curve *D* is a *second-order positive loop.*

All of these cybernetic concepts and more are needed in addressing the complexities and dynamics of human behavior. One central issue they help us to raise is that of how to achieve desirable positive or negative loops and avoid undesirable ones. For example, Gunnar Myrdal portrays an undesirable positive loop in his *An American Dilemma.*[12] He conceived of White prejudice against Blacks as based on such factors as poverty, ignorance, disorderly conduct, and health deficiencies. He saw these factors as interrelated in such a way that a worsening of one of them will tend to

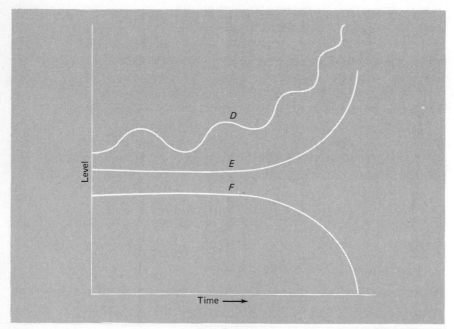

Figure 3-6.
Positive Loops.

[12] New York: Harper, 1944.

move others downward as well, with this vicious circle producing a worse
and worse situation for Blacks. Myrdal also conceived of a desirable positive loop, or an improvement circle. For example, better housing can give
impetus to improvements in education, health, the stability of family relations, and law observance, and these in turn can increase chances for better
housing, and so on.

A recent study that employs cybernetic tools and that also helps us to
pose this problem of the achievement of desirable versus undesirable positive loops is David Dillon's "Toward Cybernetic Understanding in Sociology: A Computer Model of Military Expansion."[13] For pedagogical purposes, I have selected only one small and oversimplified aspect of that
study to illustrate the complexities of actual phenomena. In Figure 3-7
loop A is a positive loop between military expansion and industrial capability. By "positive" I mean that, in a graph of the dynamic behavior of either
one of these variables, we would find it accelerating either upward or downward, like the curves in Figure 3-6. For example, during the period between
the late 1930's and the mid-1940's military expansion and industrial capability within the United States increased hand in hand, with increases in
one stimulating increases in the other. Loop B is "negative," by contrast,
because a military expansion is associated with the kind of international
distrust that produces greater difficulty in importing resources. The result
in terms of dynamic behavior, considering loop B alone, is the kind of
curve we see in Figure 3-5. Note that $+$ indicates a direct relationship
(e.g., the higher military expansion, the higher industrial capability),
whereas $-$ indicates an inverse relationship (e.g., the higher military expansion, the lower resource imports).

What is the dynamic behavior resulting when loops A and B are combined? There is no way of telling from the diagram, since the relative
strengths of the two loops are not indicated. If, for example, loop B were
quite weak relative to A, then we would have an over-all positive loop.
By contrast, if A were weak relative to B, the over-all loop would be nega-

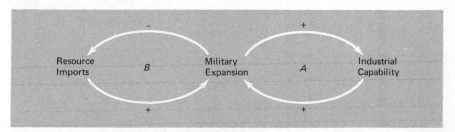

Figure 3-7.
Negative and Positive Loops Combined.

[13] Ph.D. dissertation, Boston University, 1974.

tive. A continuation of this cybernetic approach requires, then, that mathematics be employed to indicate the magnitude of the relationships involved. Furthermore, it is also essential to take into account more and more of the relevant factors as the research proceeds. In the Dillon study, many other variables were involved, including expected economic rewards, actual economic rewards, anticipated social unrest, population size, demanded resources usage, and resource reserves. Finally, if a cybernetic approach is to be scientific, these models must be tested against data. Such models fall within the context of discovery, but they must then be submitted to the context of verification.

The "third cybernetics" refers not to a different kind of loop but, rather, to a way of utilizing both the negative loop and the positive loop ideas. It has to do with a relationship between the model produced and the thinking or intuitive processes within the modeler. Oskar Lange describes cybernetic thinking in this way:

> The importance of cybernetics is twofold. It provides an apparatus for precise analysis which makes the management of economic processes effective, accurate and reliable. In addition to creating the framework for analysis and precise calculation cybernetics develops an appropriate way of thinking—let us call it *cybernetic thinking*—and of approaching and solving problems. This kind of cybernetic thinking has the significance independent of the concrete results of analyses and calculations, similar to that of the mathematical or statistical way of thinking. He who has learned to think in terms of cybernetics can—even without a detailed analysis—see the problem, see the essential links of the situation, the relations among elements and ways to the practical solutions which elude others. The ability to think in cybernetic terms enriches intuition necessary both in economic research and in the practice of management of economic processes.[14]

For Lange, a cybernetic approach involves more than a set of complex tools for analyzing phenomena: it involves a process of thinking and intuition as well. Lange alerts us to avoid thinking of cybernetics only as a tool to be used by the thinker and suggests its broad relationship to the mental processes—indeed, to the personality—of the thinker or scientist. This approach falls within the pragmatist paradigm, where the investigator's orientation is, successively, outward and inward, with each enabling further progress in the other. It also is another illustration of the reflexive aspects of the scientific method.

Dillon's study may be used here for illustrative purposes. We can apply cybernetic concepts like negative and positive loop not only to phenomena associated with military expansion but also to phenomena associated with

---

[14] Oskar Lange, *Introduction to Economic Cybernetics* (Elmsford, N.Y.: Pergamon, 1970), p. 174.

doing research on military expansion. Figure 3-8 portrays three stages of the investigation: (1) economic, (2) international, and (3) conflict theory. In the first phase, Dillon's background in economics provided a basic perspective that produced a detailed version of loop *A* of Figure 3-7. He saw military expansion as leading to a widening of the economic resource base, improved industrial capability, increasing demands for resources, a reduction of resource reserves, and efforts to increase resources through further military expansion. All this corresponds to a growth, or positive loop, aspect of this first theoretical phase, producing improved insights that appeared to account for some available data. This was followed, however, by an expansion of the complexity of the model to the point where the link between Dillon's insights and the model's behavior became extremely loose, corresponding to a negative loop in the development of the model.

The international phase of the model's development was inaugurated by a simplification of its previous complexity—with a retention of essential elements—and an incorporation of factors associated with loop *B* of Figure 3-7. As in the case of the United States' reaction to Japanese military expansion in the post-World War I period, the ability of a nation to import resources following its military expansion can be reduced because of the reactions of other nations to the perceived military and economic threat, and this can in turn produce increased military expansion—as in the case of Japan—in an effort to secure by force what cannot be achieved economically. This second phase of the project parallels the first in the existence of an initial positive loop followed by a negative loop in which the model became quite complex and less sensitive to Dillon's insights.

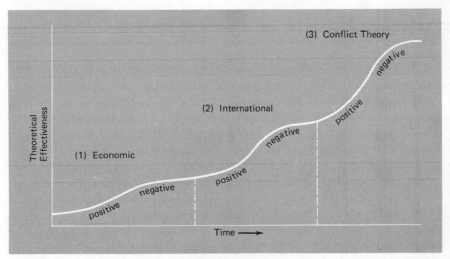

Figure 3-8.
The Third Cybernetics: Second-Order Positive Loop.

Just as the international phase of the research process was shorter than the economic phase, the third, or conflict theory, phase was shorter than the international phase. Here, Dillon dealt with an increasing gap between expected and actual economic rewards resulting from industrial expansion and leading to greater anticipated social unrest. All this, in turn, was seen as producing impetus for further military expansion to provide the resources for satisfying that unrest as well as for being able to deal with the unrest internally. Once again, this phase parallels the others in its component positive and negative loop phases.

It appears that the positive loop portions of the three phases of the project depicted in Figure 3-8 are those best characterized by the third cybernetics, whereas the negative loop aspects are closer to the first and second cybernetics. In the former situations, Dillon was dealing with models that were simpler and closer to the way he could think of the problem intuitively. As a result, the dynamic behavior of the model was more sensitive to his own hunches: he could think of possible changes and obtain the kinds of model behavior that more closely approximated theory and data. In the negative loop situations, by contrast, there was no longer the close relationship between intuition and model behavior: the model was too complex for the insights of the investigator. As the project progressed, the long-term trend was that of a second-order positive loop. This probably resulted from increasing understanding of how to do effective modeling, resulting in a slight shortening in the period for each successive phase of the project and an increasing slope in the successive positive loops. Such an experience helps an investigator to focus on his own behavior.

3.3   Summary

The linguistic and cybernetic tools developed in this chapter are designed to aid the investigator in defining his research problem. These are summarized in Table 3-1. For example, he can learn to recognize his own dichotomous linguistic and thought processes, such as the distinction between the plane of truth and the plane of observation. He can learn to appreciate the importance of ideal types as well as their limitations. He can develop an intuitive grasp of the nature of cybernetics with the aid of the beaker metaphor. He can pose such questions as how positive loops in desirable directions are achieved. He can use such concepts to focus on his own behavior as well as on outer phenomena.

Yet these tools are merely a beginning. Human behavior appears to be incredibly complex and dynamic. The simple distinctions between formist and mechanistic language, between positive loops and negative loops, can only help us partially when we attempt to understand such problems as

Table 3-1
Linguistic and Cybernetic Tools Associated with the Four Paradigms

Formism	Mechanism	Organicism	Pragmatism
Truth and falsity	Mathematical continuum	Language of social scientists	Gradational with no end point
Nominal scales	Ordinal, interval, ratio scales	Ideal types	First, second, third cybernetics
Identity, contradiction, excluded middle	Prediction	Includes formist and mechanistic elements	Contextual: temporal and spatial subscripts
Concepts, propositions, theory	Mathematical models	Concern with the intangible	Computer-based models
Verification of existence of relationship	Degree and type of relationship	Sensitive to diversity of human experience and abstract	Negative and positive loops
Determinacy, uniformity of usage	Language of engineer, physicist	E.g.: from status to contract	Beaker metaphor
Plane of truth and plane of observation	Variable	E.g.: from *gemeinschaft* to *gesellschaft*	System dynamics

military expansion by a given nation during a given period or the forces affecting mental health in a given situation. More complex concepts like second-order negative and positive loops are also helpful. These ideas must be used in conjunction with the wide range of theory that exists in sociology, theory that carries with it the accumulated research of the past. It is in Chapter 4 that we turn to sociological theory. And in addition to theory, ideas within the context of discovery must be subjected to the context of verification, a context which will be emphasized as we move into Parts Three and Four.

Exercises

1. From selections from social science research, and subsequently from pieces of your own writing for a course in the humanities, identify the following phenomena: concept, proposition, theory, variable, explanation,

prediction, existence of a relationship, degree of relationship, type of relationship, ideal type.

2. Locate a negative loop and a positive loop in your own personal behavior. Now do the same for some societal phenomena not discussed in this chapter.

3. As an exercise in the third cybernetics, apply the concepts of negative loop and positive loop to aspects of your own experience a number of times during a given hour, and record the illustrations that emerge from your efforts.

4. Locate illustrations of formist, mechanistic, organicist, and pragmatist language within the journal literature of sociology.

Annotated References

FORRESTER, JAY W. *Principles of Systems.* Cambridge, Mass.: Wright-Allen Press, 1969. In this combined text and workbook, Forrester presents fundamental principles of cybernetics as well as his own methodology of system dynamics. The book moves beyond general principles to specifiic programming techniques and includes many illustrations —from business and economics—of problems and solutions.

KORZYBSKI, ALFRED. *Science and Sanity.* Lakeville, Conn.: Institute of General Semantics, 1958. Korzybski contrasts a non-Aristotelian approach to language with the Aristotelian, or formist, language of our experience, revealing an incredible breadth of knowledge in linguistics, mathematics, physics, biology, and medicine.

SCHON, DONALD A. *Invention and the Evolution of Ideas.* London: Social Science Paperbacks, 1967. Schon's analysis of the evolution of language focuses on metaphor and analogy as central to language. He sees the evolution of concepts as "nothing less than our way of bringing the familiar to bear on the unfamiliar, in such a way as to yield new concepts while at the same time retaining as much as possible of the past."

WIENER, NORBERT. *The Human Use of Human Beings.* Garden City, N.Y.: Doubleday & Company, Inc., Anchor Press, 1954. In nontechnical and eloquent prose, Wiener gives the reader an introduction to the fundamental ideas of cybernetics, emphasizing its many possible roles in society. Throughout, the book is informed by a sense of history as well as by a very broad and humanistic perspective.

chapter 4

Sociological Theory

The theory of a given discipline is a codification of the history of research within that discipline. Unfortunately, theory is too often treated like morality: as something to be placed on a pedestal and worshipped rather than as a guide to actions here and now. If current research is indeed to build on what has been learned previously, then it is essential that theory participate in the research process at every step along the way. This holds true for the definition of a research problem no less than for the interpretation of research results.

Yet what constitutes taking theory seriously? Certainly not the citation of a few important books or theorists, nor even the active use of such a limited range of ideas. The researcher has responsibility for all of the ideas in his discipline relevant to his research and not just a very few he happens to be familiar with. The researcher in the physical sciences tends to have an easier time of it here: theory is codified systematically, and one can get quite far with a specialized approach just because physical phenomena do not interact in as complex ways as human phenomena. But how can the social scientist afford to specialize when all phenomena interact so much?

One direction he can take is to touch base with each of the major theoretical schools of thought within his discipline. In sociology, he can define his research problem in relation to structural functionalism, conflict theory, social exchange theory, symbolic interactionism, and phenomenological sociology. Thus, if he learns anything, he will be able to build on sociology and not bury his work somewhere within sociology. In this chapter we continue with the four studies described in Chapter 2, relating each one of the various schools of sociological thought.

4.1 Aging and Adjustment

Irving Zeitlin classifies contemporary sociological theory into these five categories: structural functionalism (such as the work of Talcott Parsons and Robert Merton), social exchange theory (for example, George Homans and Peter Blau), conflict theory (for example, Lewis Coser, Ralf Dahrendorf, and C. Wright Mills), phenomenology (for example, the ethnomethodology of Harold Garfinkel), and symbolic interactionism (for example, Erving Goffman and Herbert Blumer).[1] Zeitlin questions to what extent these contemporary theorists have gone beyond the classical theorists: Max Weber for structural functionalism and phenomenology, Karl Marx for conflict theory, Edmund Husserl and Alfred Schütz for phenomenology, Sigmund Freud and George Herbert Mead for symbolic interactionism.

Let us begin with the Marxist concept of alienation,[2] which refers most directly to a lack in the worker's sense of self-fulfillment in the work situation because he works for someone else and thus is selling himself to another person. Seeman distinguishes five aspects of alienation: powerlessness, social isolation, meaninglessness, instrumentalization and distrust, and self-estrangement.[3] Suppose we now seek to extend this concept to the situation of the aging individual, equating his assumption of the role of an "aged person" with the worker's assumption of alienating work conditions. Suppose that an individual who identifies himself as old and thus assumes this role is at the same time accepting a sense of powerlessness; that such an individual thereby tends to isolate himself socially from a great portion of the social universe that would prefer not to associate with relatively powerless individuals; that much of the individual's sense of meaningfulness in life is lost through the assumption of a role socially defined as largely useless; that an individual who learns to accept a relatively meaningless role also learns to adopt an instrumental role in relation to others—treating them as means rather than ends—and moves in the direction of self-estrangement.

Here, then, is a path for extending the concept of alienation to include age-related roles, and perhaps other roles as well. Such an extension also suggests a different way of viewing alienation; theory can help in defining a problem, but defining a problem can also help develop theory. An individual who is chronologically old can choose to identify himself as middle-aged, thus escaping from an alienating role. Is it also possible for the worker to refuse to accept an alienating role? Or is he indeed a prisoner of his work situation, as Marx would have it? It is my own belief that he can refuse, just as the aged person can refuse, to accept an alienating role and that he can proceed to reconstruct his role along more developmental lines. To fail to allow for this possibility is a limitation of much of structural-functionalism and conflict theory, with their emphasis on the power of the social structure over the individual. To allow for it is to follow in much of the tradition of phenomenology and symbolic interaction.

[1] Irving M. Zeitlin, *Rethinking Sociology: A Critique of Contemporary Theory* (New York: Appleton, 1973).
[2] Karl Marx, "Alienated Labor," in *Karl Marx: Early Writings,* trans. and ed. by T. B. Bottomore (New York: McGraw-Hill, 1964), pp. 120–34.
[3] Melvin Seeman, *Social Status ond Leadership:* (Columbus: Bureau of Educational Research and Service, Ohio State U., 1960), p. 99.

Let us now proceed from a structural-functional perspective, emphasizing the tendency of individuals to adapt to their situations via conformity to role expectations. Thus, individuals experiencing various role losses—such as death of spouse and retirement—learn to accept this situation of "disengagement," as the gerontological literature designates it. Adjustment, then, is based on an acceptance of the disengagement process, and maladjustment is based on an unrealistic approach. If the aging individual accepts a "realistic" view of his situation, he identifies himself as old and thus adjusts to the inevitable.

Here as before the same limitation of the existing literature emerges: it gives too much weight to the power of the social structure and too little to the power of the individual. It also tends to assume that the individual's conformity to role expectations is functional for the social system within which the role is embedded. But in the study under discussion, such conformity tends *not* to be functional for the individuals involved: those who identify themselves as old tend to be more maladjusted than those who identify themselves as middle-aged. This alternative to conformity points toward the individual's power over the social structure.

Max Weber's concept of "legitimation"[4] also falls within the general tradition of structural-functionalism. This concept generally has been applied in the context of discussions of power and authority. To "legitimize" is to make legitimate, or acceptable, and power that is legitimized is power that has been accepted, or "authority." One advantage of the concept of legitimacy is that it helps us to understand the limits of coercive power in contrast to the power that is in the hands of individuals who are supposedly powerless. For to the degree that power is not legitimized, it becomes limited to the naked force of coercive power. Legitimated power, or authority, however, produces highly effective control without accompanying rebellious feelings.

Suppose we now use this concept of legitimation to focus on the roles of the aged. To what degree do aged individuals legitimate their culturally defined roles, and to what degree do they rebel against those definitions? Their degree of legitimation is also a measure of their acceptance of those roles, leading to their being controlled by those roles without rebellious feelings. By contrast, those who delegitimate these roles free themselves from their power and are in a position to legitimate and adopt alternative roles. But in this context legitimation is not just a question of power: it deeply affects the individual's degree of adjustment. And strangely enough, it is the rebel who turns out to be better adjusted.

Under what conditions do individuals legitimate, or fail to legitimate, political roles, age roles, and other roles? What makes them, in the words of George Herbert Mead, assert their "I" and what impels them to put

---

[4] Max Weber, *From Max Weber: Essays in Sociology,* trans. and ed. by H. H. Gerth and C. Wright Mills (New York: Oxford U. P., 1958), pp. 78–79.

forward their "me"?[5] Or in the language of Herbert Marcuse—based on his attempt to unite Freud with Marx—how can the individual begin to overcome his "surplus repression"?[6] What is involved here is nothing less than the fundamental relation between the individual and society. I am putting forward questions that have been raised before, but answered only partially, in the expectation that this aging context will shed further light on them.

Does the individual who delegitimates his role go through a process of "reflection," in the words of Edmund Husserl, learning to "detach" himself from his immediate situation, suspending belief in that situation, escaping from the "partial" nature of his "external horizon," and transcending the "profile" that his age role transmits by means of a multiprofiled "internal horizon"?[7] Does the individual who legitimates his age role "suspend doubt" in that role, using the words of Alfred Schütz, "bracketing" his own particular interests and problems and learning to adopt in their place the interests and "systems of relevance" emphasized by his age role?[8] Or, escaping from this formist either-or approach, does the individual do each of these to some degree in some contexts and to another degree in other contexts? And when he "suspends belief" or "suspends doubt," to what extent does he "take the role of the other," in the words of George Herbert Mead? Must he necessarily have a "reference group" that legitimizes any of his beliefs that go against those prescribed by his age role?

One path toward understanding the conditions leading to legitimation and delegitimation is based on the social exchange theory of Peter Blau and Richard Emerson.[9] Emerson lists four exchange factors that affect the balance of power between individuals or groups:

1. The individual or group can supply others with a service that they want badly, thus placing themselves in an excellent bargaining position for demanding services in return.
2. The individual or group can avoid dependence on others by obtaining in some other way services that these others would normally provide.
3. The individual or group can obtain a service from others without thereby entering into a state of dependence to them through coercing them to furnish their service.

[5] George Herbert Mead, *Mind, Self, and Society* (Chicago: U. of Chicago, 1962).
[6] Herbert Marcuse, *Eros and Civilization: A Philosophical Inquiry into Freud* (New York: Random House, Inc., Vintage Books, 1955).
[7] Edmund Husserl, *Phenomenology and the Crisis of Philosophy,* trans. by Quentin Lauer (New York: Harper, Torchbooks, 1965).
[8] Alfred Schütz, *The Problem of Social Reality,* Collected Papers, Vol. 1 (The Hague: Martinus Nijhoff, 1967).
[9] Richard M. Emerson, "Power-Dependence Relations," *American Sociological Review,* **27** (February 1962), pp. 31–41. For an elaboration of these ideas, see Peter M. Blau, *Exchange and Power in Social Life* (New York: Wiley, 1964), especially pp. 115–42.

4. The individual or group may avoid dependence on others by learning to resign themselves to do without the services that these others would normally provide.

Suppose that instead of thinking of power relations between individuals or groups, we think of power relations between an individual and his role, for example, his age role. The individual's "power" to delegitimize his age role would, on the basis of this analogy, depend on Emerson's four factors. With regard to (1), for example, an individual who is able to identify himself as middle-aged may be able to offer others—as a result of his better adjustment—satisfactions that cannot be offered by an individual identifying himself as old. Because of his higher degree of adjustment, such an individual may not need the approval of those others who expect him to conform to the role of the aged, and thus—relative to (2), (3), and (4)—he moves into a powerful position. Of course, once again this discussion adopts the formist framework of either-or thinking, whereas a more sophisticated approach to legitimation would take into account matters of degree, complex relationships, and changes among these relationships.

Carrying this mode of thinking one step further, we might ask what forces would limit the continuing accumulation of power on the part of the individual who identifies himself as middle-aged? Also, we might ask the converse of this question: what forces would limit an increasing dependence on the part of an individual who identifies himself as old? Here, the concepts of negative loop and positive loop help to illuminate the situation. We might see the situation of both kinds of individuals as a combination of positive and negative loops, with the negative loop predominating, as illustrated in Figure 4-1. I make an assumption that for some reasons—as indicated by the arrows showing pressures to conform—*both* individuals who identify themselves as middle-aged *and* individuals who identify themselves as old shift from a positive to a negative loop. Thus, both increasing power and increasing dependence are self-limiting propositions. But, then, what are those reasons? Is it possible, for example, for the individual to continually increase his power? Is power a fixed, or zero-sum, pie, where one individual's gain is another's loss? Is it, on the contrary, an expanding pie? Or is it some complex combination of these two alternatives?

These theoretical considerations were not developed at the time the aging and adjustment study was undertaken, but only just now, many years after its completion. In Chapter 5, Section 5.2, I will present a picture of the way in which the research problem was theoretically defined at the time. Here, however, I wanted to illustrate a more effective approach to defining a problem, one that builds on the major theoretical traditions available. These theoretical considerations remain, of course, only speculations until they become translated into specific tools of measurement and enter a re-

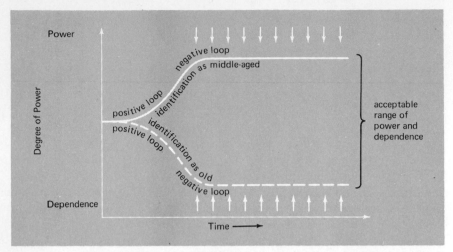

Figure 4-1.
Social Exchange Theory and Age Identification.

search process where they can be tested. Some of these considerations are carried forward in the aging study described in Section 4.4. There, the contrast between the formist paradigm behind the aging and adjustment study and the pragmatist paradigm behind the aging process study will be discussed.

4.2 Occupational Choice

I shall begin by relating the medical student study described in Section 2.2 to the types of sociological theory discussed in Section 4.1, continue with a discussion of the mechanistic paradigm behind much of this theory, and conclude with an analysis of some methodological implications of the theory.

Occupational Choice and Sociological Theory

Suppose that we examine another role in addition to that of age: the occupational role. Let us transfer the theoretical insights of Section 4.1 to the present study. Starting with the Marxist concept of alienation, a key question suggested by the preceding discussion is whether or not the individual can choose to escape from the alienating aspects of his occupational role. Is there some choice he can make analogous to the older individual's self-identification as middle-aged? The concept of "role distance" is relevant here: to what extent is a given surgeon, for example, a prisoner of his role, and to what extent does he feel free to develop an occupational role based largely on his own personality and style? Can he learn to see his role from a distance, and thereby retain some personal leverage with respect to it? As for the medical student, must he assume fixed possibilities for fulfilling or not fulfilling his various goals within the different medical fields? Or should he count on being able to alter those possibilities so as to shape his role in accordance with his own needs?

From a structural-functional perspective, we might wonder how functional it is—both for the individual and for society—for the medical student to learn to conform neatly to existing expectations within the various fields of medicine? For example, to what extent does the existing division of labor among the fields of medicine make good medical sense? Does illness tend to cut across fields sufficiently to reduce the effectiveness of the highly specialized physician? And what about the existing hierarchy between physician and patient: to what extent does it produce the kind of dependence in the patient that stifles his own possible development toward better health? To what extent does it tend to dampen the potential for widespread and effective health education? Would it be more functional for both the individual and society if medical students considered other kinds of role relationships than bureaucratic ones?

For the medical student to explore other possibilities—especially possibilities that challenge deeply existing role relationships—he would have to learn to delegitimate what exists and legitimate what does not yet exist. But how would he learn to do this, to express his "I" in the face of his "me" or of societal repressive pressures? How might he learn to transcend the partial nature of an external horizon in which medical roles are defined in traditional ways? How might he learn to suspend belief in those roles? And what about his own set of goals: to what extent are they changeable, and to what extent is he a prisoner of them? Is it possible for the individual to learn to delegitimate those goals in favor of goals with, say, increasing levels of aspiration?

Turning to exchange theory, let us examine the medical student's power to delegitimize both existing medical roles and his own given goals. Is it possible for him to find a way of doing so and, at the same time, to offer to society and self more effective medical care and greater satisfactions, respectively, than he would be able to do otherwise? If so, then he is in an excellent bargaining position—vis-à-vis existing medical roles—with respect to being able to reconstruct those roles as opposed to being shaped by them. That bargaining position would be improved further to the degree that his "internal horizon" and "role distance" developed to the point where he was less dependent on the approval of others.

And once again we can apply the cybernetic concepts of negative and positive loops. Assuming that the individual's accumulation of power to reconstruct his medical roles—as well as his increasing dependence on existing role definitions—are self-limiting, what forces produce this negative loop? What is the nature of the social and personality forces that make it very difficult for the individual to go beyond certain boundaries, limiting the degree to which he can reconstruct his medical roles, and the degree to which he allows his personality to be shaped by these same roles? Why do the positive loops give way to the negative loops, producing the familiar S-shaped curves?

The Mechanistic Paradigm

If the sociologist assumes that his research is directed only by his sociological theory, he is paying too little attention to other forces shaping his investigations. In particular, the paradigms, or world views, discussed in Chapter 2—formism, mechanism, organicism, and pragmatism—illustrate such forces. They are products of history, society, and culture, and they work their way into the fabric of institutions and personalities. For example, the various theoretical discussions in this chapter—dealing with conflict theory, structural-functionalism, exchange theory, phenomenology, and symbolic interactionism—have all had a formist cast to them because of the formist cast implicit in verbal communication and in human phenomena.

Embedded deep within these sociological theories is a mechanistic paradigm[10] as well, a world view, or folk model, that has developed largely within the period of the industrial revolution. In mechanism—related to the metaphors of the machine and the continuum—we move toward a more active conception of human phenomena, analogous to the physical science notion of force: society is seen as pushing or pulling the individual in various directions and in powerful ways. We also move toward a more integrated, or synthetic, view, going beyond very partial and disparate pieces of knowledge. And there is a definite direction along which gradations occur, which is the idea of the continuum.

In structural-functionalism, for example, we have the idea of a social system as a whole. When we ask whether something is functional for society, we are attempting to put together a great many pieces of knowledge. There is also directionality to the question. A system is seen as more than the simple sum of its parts: it is an integration of those parts. Also, the social system tends to be viewed by sociologists as extremely powerful, shaping personalities and human phenomena generally.

As for conflict theory, the individual is seen as becoming alienated as a result of his placement within a given situation in society, such as a given medical role. In social exchange theory the individual's success in his medical role is seen as being dependent on his bargaining situation: to what extent can he offer valued services and to what extent does he require

---

[10] For further discussion of mechanism, see Donald A. Schon, "Theories of the Mind: Mechanism and Dynamism; Atomism," in *Invention and the Evolution of Ideas* (London: Social Science Paperbacks, 1967), pp. 140–70.

the services offered by others? When we move from structural-functional-ism, conflict theory, and social exchange theory to phenomenology and symbolic interactionism, we move from a kind of social determinism to a kind of individual determinism. The phenomenologist might see the medi-cal student as reconstructing or failing to reconstruct his medical role on the basis of whether he is able to suspend belief in that role. The symbolic interactionist might see this choice as based on the student's self-image.

Methodological Implications

Just as sociological theory is permeated by various paradigms, so is it also permeated by methodological perspectives. It is not enough, in an attempt to understand a theory, to look to its abstract ideas or its underly-ing assumptions: we must also look to the ways in which it is practiced. The researcher may not practice what he preaches, but then we are in a position to distinguish two kinds of sermons: that which is communicated by words, and that which is communicated by deeds. One aspect of the methodology of the medical student study that reflects and reveals the theo-retical perspective is the indexing approach that was used. In place of sep-arate tables, each of which incorporates a piece of the study's data—as in the case of the age and adjustment study—one table (Table 2-4) is able to reveal, with the aid of an integrative index, the implications of a wide range of data. Resultant Goal Commitment encompasses a number of specific goals as well as the individual's corresponding expectations for fulfilling them. It also takes into account the degree of commitment to each goal as well as the degree to which the individual expects to fulfill that goal within a given medical field.

We might designate this as an integrative, or synthetic, approach to in-dexing or measurement, contrasting it with the analytic measurement orien-tation illustrated by the aging study. Rather than setting one approach against the other, we might see them as complementary, as in Figure 4-2. We might begin with either analysis or synthesis and proceed to create a positive loop—moving in the direction of measurements yielding ever more accurate predictions—by moving back and forth between analysis

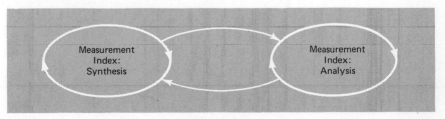

Figure 4-2.
A Positive Loop for Measurement: Synthesis and Analysis.

and synthesis. For example, one could start with a comprehensive index such as that represented by Resultant Goal Commitment. On the basis of working with that index and testing its effectiveness in predicting preference for the medical fields, the investigator would learn something of the index's strengths and weaknesses. That knowledge could be the basis for splitting the index, analytically, into component parts, each constituting a more clearly defined aspect of behavior than the more global index represented. Once again, this might yield additional insights, and the investigator might try to capitalize on them so as to produce even more accurate predictions by constructing an improved synthetic index.

A second methodological aspect of the medical student study is its emphasis on correlation and prediction. Beyond the establishment of the *existence* of a relationship between two factors—such as revealed within the aging and adjustment study—is the uncovering of a high *degree* of relationship between factors. This is important because it moves the investigator in the direction of being able to predict one factor from the other. Here once again we need not choose between the two approaches, as illustrated in Figure 4-3. We might begin by establishing the existence of a relationship, then proceed—via improved measurement and theory—to develop a closer relationship between the factors, and continue to improve our understanding of the type of relationship to the point where we can achieve accurate prediction. To do so, we would probably have to take into account the positive loop for measurement discussed in the preceding paragraph.

This approach may sound perfectly reasonable and perfectly obvious, yet there is a tendency within modern quantitative sociology to apply only the analytic measurement approach of Figure 4-2, thus failing to achieve the positive loop. For example, attention is paid to the very careful analytic efforts of the physicist, to the clarity of his definitions, to his ability to develop specific tools (like thermometers) for getting at unambiguous concepts (like temperature), and to a view of scientific development as the piling of one analytic study on top of another. This understanding fails to take into account the basis of physical science in general theory—with mathematics as a vital tool in achieving that generality—and the synthetic nature of seemingly simple measurements (like thermometer readings) be-

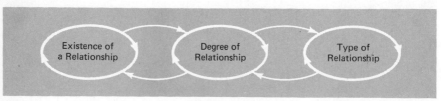

Figure 4-3.
From Existence to Degree to Type of Relationship: Positive Loops.

cause of their link with theory. One must have a general vision of a house if one is to build any small piece of it; this is a more productive view than the emphasis on analysis, where the house of science is built by piling brick on brick until the house as a whole somehow emerges.[11]

If the paradigm of the investigator—whether it be formist, mechanistic, or whatever—plays so vital a part in the research process, how is it possible to achieve scientific "objectivity"? If our conclusions are based largely on what we ourselves bring to the research scene, how is science to differ from an endless discussion where each person argues for his particular point of view and there is no movement toward an enlargement of understanding? As discussed in Section 1.4, we need not abandon objectivity in order to focus on the importance of investigator effect. We begin by assuming that there is no way of separating the scientist from the phenomena under investigation so that he can passively observe what is occurring. The problem becomes, then, one of assessing what his impact is on the course of his research, and his paradigm is a force helping to produce that impact. By addressing this problem, we are able to achieve a higher level of objectivity—in the sense of taking into account the relevant factors operating within the research situation—than by sweeping it under the rug.

By adopting the mechanistic world view, we commit ourselves to a fundamentally Newtonian view of human behavior, and we also help to create that mode of behavior. Within the context of the medical student study, this becomes a view of the individual as a rational man who makes choices in an attempt to maximize the fulfillment of his goals. Just like a billiard ball, he is impelled along by forces over which he has no control. Some of these are external: the available medical roles from among which he chooses. Others are internal: his goals and his expectations for achieving them in the various medical fields. All of these forces are fixed, and together they determine human behavior.

Of course, it is easy for the sociologist to find fault with such a model of human behavior, yet it has its uses, just as does the formist model. By applying it, we are able to pull together a good deal of human experience, more than we can within the separate tables dictated by the formist approach. The result is the possibility of establishing closer relationships between variables and moving further on the road to accurate prediction. Also, we are able to learn just how far the model is able to take us and how much it cannot do for us. It leaves open questions like the following: Why do a proportion of individuals make choices in seemingly irrational ways? How do the individual's goals and expectations change? How do

---

[11] For a less distorted view of modern physics, one that pays attention to history and provides a balanced view of analysis and synthesis, see Gerald Holton, *Thematic Origins of Scientific Thought: Kepler to Einstein* (Cambridge, Mass.: Harvard U.P. 1973). See also Thomas S. Kuhn, *The Structure of Scientific Revolutions* (Chicago: U. of Chicago, 1962).

the medical roles themselves change? How can the individual learn to re-construct his roles, his goals, and his expectations?

4.3   Community Development

In this section as in the preceding one we shall deal with the study's relationship to sociological theory, to a paradigm—the organicist one in this case—and to methodology. Once again, the view I put forward is that, although a study may appear to have a life separate from these larger issues, actually it is enmeshed in them completely. Therefore, to avoid facing them is to bury one's head in the sand, for one necessarily does a study within a given world view, theoretical perspective, and methodological framework. The question is not *whether* these orientations are involved but rather *which* stances are taken.

Community Development and Sociological Theory

Sociological theory has been closely associated with the industrial revolution, and we can thus bring a variety of theoretical perspectives to a study bearing on industrialization. Let us focus in particular on the study's search for positive loops linking the scientific-industrial revolution with the quality of life. To what extent is this positive loop idea, as well as the more particular idea of an association between these two phenomena, central to sociological theory?

One problem in seeking such relationships is that current styles of writing and thinking tend to hide the value commitments of the investigator. Since a positive loop has a given direction, we must seek to uncover the implicit directions within sociological theory. Some of the earlier sociologists—such as Comte (from mathematics to mechanics, physics, chemistry, biology, and sociology), Maine (from status to contract), Durkheim (from mechanical solidarity to organic solidarity), Marx (from a dialectic between the forces and relations of society to the end of such conflict within a classless society), Spencer (from homogeneity to heterogeneity), and Weber (from charismatic to rational-legal authority)—were far more explicit in the directions they saw society taking than modern sociologists tend to be.

However, if we understand modern sociology as built on the basis of this earlier work, and if we look for these same directions, then it is possible to find them despite the fact that they tend to be hidden. For example, within the work of Talcott Parsons (structural functionalism) there is a view of society as becoming increasingly universalistic versus particularistic, specific versus diffuse, and affectively neutral versus affective,[12] cor-

---

[12] Talcott Parsons, *Societies: Evolutionary and Comparative Perspectives* (Englewood Cliffs, N.J.: Prentice-Hall, 1966).

responding to the conceptions of Weber, Durkheim, Spencer, and others. Modern conflict theory tends to revise the work of Marx but not to reject his fundamental ideas. The exchange theory of George Homans follows much of the tradition of learning theory in psychology, with the individual learning to develop goals (thus moving away from a purely mechanistic model of fixed goals) on the basis of rewards and punishments.[13] As for phenomenology and symbolic interaction, they seem to be pointing in a direction that does not conflict with the earlier one but adds a new dimension to it: We are alerted to the directions that the individual can take, and we learn to perceive ways in which he can affect, as well as be affected by, the directions of society.[14]

The central problem of the community development study may be restated in this way: How can we penetrate sufficiently deeply the complexity and dynamism of a modern urban community, with its multitudes of economic, political, religious, scientific, educational, and psychological problems, so as to reveal a direction for incrementally solving its problems? How can we make use of a sociological heritage that teaches us to see societal directions—many of which appear to be quite worthwhile—in the context of modern problems? Perhaps that heritage is no longer useful. Perhaps it was a child of an age of reason that no longer exists, an Enlightenment era that has been drowned by increasing illustrations of man's inhumanity to man. It is one thing to talk of progress in the middle of the nineteenth century, but it is quite another to do so in the last quarter of the twentieth century.

Yet sociological theory is not so time-bound as to offer no major insights into modern problems generally or this study in particular. For example, Durkheim distinguishes between an "abnormal" division of labor, where there is little effective coordination among specialists, and a normal division of labor.[15] Perhaps, then, the problem of community development hinges largely on finding ways for specialists to communicate with one another and integrate their knowledge so that we can move from an abnormal to a normal division of labor. As another illustration, Weber provides a portrait of bureaucracy—seen as an ideal type—in which rationality and efficiency prevail, yet this is not the bureaucracy of human experience. The coordination of roles that is supposed to take place never does take place effectively, and we have a situation comparable to Durkheim's abnormal division of labor. With respect to Marx, there is the vision of a society in which the relations of production no longer contradict the forces of pro-

[13] George C. Homans, *Social Behavior: Its Elementary Forms* (New York: Harcourt, 1961).

[14] For a work that illustrates fundamental developments in phenomenology as well as in the sociology of knowledge, see Peter L. Berger and Thomas Luckmann, *The Social Construction of Reality* (Garden City, N.Y.: Doubleday, Anchor, 1967).

[15] Émile Durkheim, *The Division of Labor in Society*, trans. by George Simpson (New York: Free Press, 1947).

duction, and where the individual is no longer alienated. In such a society, the individual would no longer function as a mere specialized tool of the productive process but would somehow be able to be much more his own master.

These theoretical perspectives all point toward the kind of specialization developed in modern society—that which blocks communication—as a key source of its problems. They point toward the importance of improved communication. For example, there is the communication between industry, the Hispanic community, and the East European community, or communication between those making scientific assessments, community planners, and social science technologists. But communication cannot be improved greatly unless the structural basis for such improved communication is laid. Where there is little chance for upward economic mobility on the part of the lower class, where the educational gaps and the gaps in social services between the rich and poor are great, we might expect little interest in opening up channels of communication. For under those circumstances of scarcity, the haves are interested in maintaining their position against the have-nots, and the have-nots are interested in obtaining a larger piece of the pie. It is also possible, however, that the pie itself can continue to expand, with an upward positive loop developing between the scientific-industrial revolution and the quality of life. Under such circumstances communication can open up and a normal division of labor can be created, along with rationality and efficiency in organizations and less and less alienation.

The Organicist Paradigm

If we now move beyond the ideas of academics and intellectuals to ideas current in industrialized society as a whole, we shall note that the organicist idea of societal progress—while it has received very serious blows—is not yet dead. Three major processes occurring in modern society are industrialization, bureaucratization, and urbanization. Relating to each of these, the idea of somehow finding ways of solving existing problems is very much alive. We still see society as continuing to move in these directions whether or not we succeed in solving the problems associated with these trends.

To begin with the industrialization process, it is widely accented—an idea not generally contradicted within academia[16]—that economic forces are central to whatever happens in society, and that other institutions must adapt themselves to economic ones. We can see this in the plans of school systems to emphasize the kind of education that will gear into the needs of the economic system, in the widespread recognition that styles of life vary on the basis of economic factors, and in the efforts of governments

---

[16] For a view of sociology that focuses on the ways in which the industrial revolution has continued to alter all social institutions, see Bernard S. Phillips, *Sociology: Social Structure and Change* (New York: Macmillan, 1969).

to foster the economic development of the society. The progress of the individual as well as of the society tends to be seen as linked to economic forces, granting that there is increasing recognition of the power of these forces for evil as well as good.

Along with the industrialization process has come a process of increasing bureaucratization, that is, an ever greater degree of specialization, or finer division, of labor and an ever higher hierarchy, analogous to the development of a giant beehive with a great many columns (representing the division of labor) and a great many rows (representing the hierarchy). All of this tends to be associated with progress in the popular mind. A World War II, a Vietnam, a Watergate, and an energy crisis—all jar us out of our complacent view of the continuation of progress, but somehow we still return to that view. With regard to the community development study, I was able to unearth a wide range of extremely serious problems characteristic of urban, industrial, bureaucratic society. None of the major problems involved has yet yielded to a solution. And yet my optimism is retained throughout it all, my faith that it is possible to develop a better and better society.

A second fundamental idea stemming from the organicist paradigm that influenced the community development study is the idea of the power of the social system. The industrialization, bureaucratization, and urbanization processes have alerted us to the importance for our lives of the way human beings are organized, or interact, that is, the structure of human relationships. If we wish to solve some larger problem, we almost automatically turn to techniques for changing large social systems, whether by developing new laws, voting new people into power, or altering the consciousness of the masses. And if we are facing a set of interrelated and highly complex problems, as in the community development study, then we must seek to reconstruct the network of social systems that create those problems. Solutions to existing problems are seen as available to us provided that we can tap the power of social systems.

Methodological Implications

For all of the sophistication of the theory involved in the community development study, the actual techniques of research fall appallingly short of that level of sophistication. If social systems were seen as in continuing flux and moving along various dimensions, where were the methodological tools for measuring such movement? If the various social systems were seen as interrelated in complex ways, how were such interrelationships to be assessed? This is an illustration of the wide gap prevailing between theory and research. On the one hand, our theory poses a high level of aspiration; on the other hand, the methods are very far from producing the kind of data appropriate for that level. In particular, there is only minimal application of powerful mathematical tools for integrating data. A major reason for this gap is the deterministic flavor associated with most uses of mathematics. Within an organicist perspective, there is an emphasis on change and growth. The mechanistic world view, by contrast, centers on the workings of and existing set of forces. Another reason—perhaps a more important one—is simply a lack of awareness of the existence of the gap.

Given this situation, one alternative is to accept what appears to be a widening gap between theory and methods, granting that theoretical developments recently have been outstripping methodological developments. The key problem here is ineffectiveness, for it is the interaction between theory and research that is the basis for the continuing development of scientific knowledge. With this large gap, such interaction is minimized. Indeed, we might go so far as to say that when large gaps exist, the scientific method is no longer at work.

A second alternative is to lower our level of aspiration so that the theory put forward is in line with the methodology used. For example, we might limit ourselves to studies like that of the medical students, where we do not attempt, theoretically, to deal with changes in societal roles or in individual goals or beliefs. Or we might confine our investigations to those like the aging and adjustment study, where we attempt to discover whether or not relationships between pairs of variables exist. A major problem here is that such studies—whether based on the formist or the mechanistic paradigm—provide little basis for moving into an organicist framework. Such a framework has been dominant in sociological theory since the origins of sociology, and it holds forth a yet unfulfilled aspiration. Perhaps more important, the alternative of maintaining a low level of aspiration holds out little hope for dealing with pressing societal problems.

A third alternative is to fulfill that level of aspiration by developing methodology to the point where it can provide the data essential for testing and developing an organicist model. Such data would have to deal with changes in both the environment and the individual. If it were to incorporate the organicist idea of progress and point in both upward and downward directions, then it might deal with these changes along continua, or dimensions, just as an organicist theory has generally done. This would not only fulfill the promise of sociological theory but would also incorporate the insights from the formist and mechanistic paradigms. The distinction between upward and downward, as well as most of the language and thought that goes into such studies, would be formist, while the concept of the continuum and efforts to integrate the various pieces of the study would be mechanistic.

We might gain insight into this choice among three alternatives by applying Davies' theory of revolution, as illustrated in Figure 4-4.[17] This theory

---

[17] James C. Davies, "Toward a Theory of Revolution," *American Sociological Review,* **27** (February 1962), p. 6, Fig. 1.

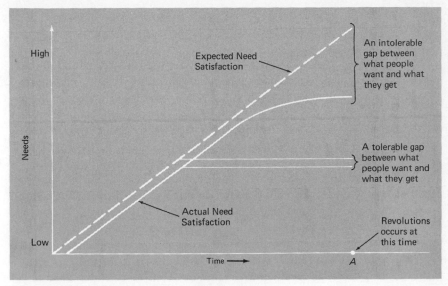

Figure 4-4.
Davies' Theory of Revolution.

has only been applied to the kinds of societal revolutions involving violence, but it can also be applied to intellectual revolutions. The theory
contends that revolutions are likely to occur in situations where expected
need satisfactions have been rising (the same as Adlai Stevenson's concept
of the "revolution of rising expectations") and actual need satisfactions
along with them. Revolutions occur when the latter falls relative to the
former and the gap between the two becomes intolerable.

Time A—the time when the gap becomes intolerable—corresponds
roughly to the current relationship between sociological theory (expected
need satisfaction) and research methods (actual need satisfaction). If
Davies' theory applies, then our first alternative cannot remain open for
long: we cannot choose to continue with a widening gap between theory
and method, for something will have to give. In our second alternative,
it is theory that gives: we lower our theoretical aspirations so that they
come closer and closer to the current methodological situation. This would
be analogous to attempting to teach individuals in a revolutionary situation
that they should give up their aspirations for a better way of life. Our third
alternative is to raise our methodological performance so that it comes to
be in step with our theoretical aspirations. I believe that the latter is not
only desirable but is also a very probable solution, provided that we apply
our increasing theoretical knowledge to the task of improving our research
tools.

4.4   The Aging Process

In this section my procedure will be to combine theory, paradigm, and methodology in one discussion. Just as pragmatism builds on formism, mechanism, and organicism, so does this study build on the ideas and techniques of the preceding ones. In addition, it goes beyond them in certain ways, although it also has its limitations relative to the other studies.

I want to begin with the study's dependent, or effect, variable, contrasting the aging study's focus on adjustment (Section 4.1) with this study's emphasis on mental health. I conceive of mental health, in this study, as a variable that is also a continuum extending in both directions, with no limit at the positive mental health end of the scale. Adjustment, by contrast, was conceived of in an either-or fashion: respondents were divided into those who were adjusted and those who were maladjusted. The same contrast between a dichotomy and a continuum also divides the two studies with regard to the independent, or causal, factors: self-identification as old or middle-aged (for example), on the one hand, and a continuum of degree of role breadth on the other.

Let us turn to Figure 4-5 to explore some of the implications of this difference between a dichotomy and a continuum, which is also a key difference between a formist world view and the others presented. On the left-hand side we see a diagram very similar to that of Figure 4-1, where my emphasis was on the relationship between social exchange theory and

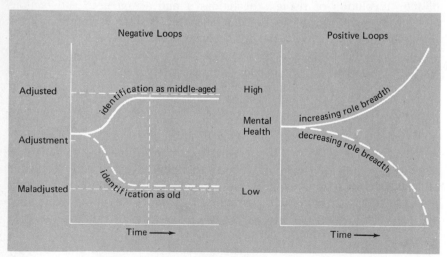

Figure 4-5.

Formism and Pragmatism: Negative and Positive Loops.

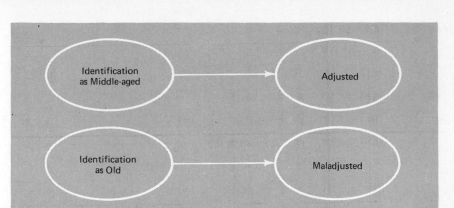

Figure 4-6.
Age Identification and Adjustment: A Formist Perspective.

that study of the aged. Each of the two negative loops—the one corresponding to a self-identification as middle-aged as well as the one corresponding to a self-identification as old—is associated with a different level of adjusment. Because both the independent and the dependent variable are conceived of dichotomously, there is little or no focus on factors that push the individual further down or further up the adjustment scale. Indeed, there is very little interest in the time axis at all: the focus is not on the *process* of age identification, over a period of time, with its implications for adjustment at various stages of the process (the period prior to "A"), but on the result, or *product,* namely, self-identification as middle-aged or old. Perhaps a more accurate way of depicting such an approach is contained in Figure 4-6, which does not have a time axis and is as a result closer to a formist perspective. In addition to the dichotomies for both independent and dependent variables, there is no feedback relationship.

Now let us examine a relationship that is characteristic of a pragmatist perspective: that between role breadth and mental health, as depicted in Figure 4-7 (the same as that presented in Figure 3-4, except that system dynamics notation is omitted here). Time is exceedingly important for such a structure of mutual and self causation, for the value of each variable is dependent on the stage of the process that we are examining. For example, an individual might begin to question his conformity to a role for aged individuals that restricts his social and sexual activities, thus moving toward greater role breadth. Such questioning in turn might produce better mental health on his part. That, in turn, might encourage him still further to free himself from role restrictions. This snowballing process, or positive loop, might also take place *within* the role breadth variable and *within* the health variable. For example, an opening up with respect to role restric-

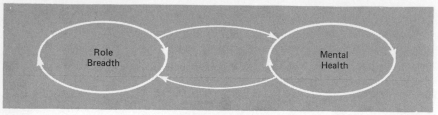

Figure 4-7.
Role Breadth and Mental Health: A Pragmatist Perspective.

tions in one area of life can encourage the individual to open up with regard to role restrictions in other areas, or an improvement in one aspect of mental health can lead to an improvement in other aspects.

The right-hand side of Figure 4-5 depicts the results of both upward and downward snowballing. Here we have the phenomenon of the positive loop, that is, a situation of acceleration or deceleration, where deviations from an initial point continue to be amplified in the same direction. Because the focus here is on a continuum, dichotomous points along the continuum—such as those on the left-hand side of Figure 4-5—are incorporated within the continuum. This is what is meant by the idea that a pragmatist approach incorporates a formist approach yet goes beyond it.

But what are the processes that produce an upward versus a downward positive loop? This question suggests the possibility that individuals can learn to continue to improve their health. By contrast, the left-hand side of Figure 4-5 appears to be quite pessimistic. The best that the individual can hope for is to become adjusted as distinct from maladjusted. The researcher tends to accept this level of aspiration for the individual and then proceeds to inquire into the forces that produce adjustment versus those that produce maladjustment. The pragmatist approacsh, then, not only focuses on change but also on "development," or the snowballing of change in a given direction, as distinct from the relatively static formist approach. Of course, all of the curves in Figure 4-5 are vastly oversimplified; they are only meant to be suggestive of different possibilities.

Having outlined these contrasting approaches to the study of the aging process, we can now ask how the pragmatist orientation relates to sociological theory, taking into account the discussion of the relation between the formist approach and theory in Section 4.1. To illustrate, we might begin with structural functionalism. One of its central concerns is an understanding of the conditions that make for the survival or extinction of a given social system. One problem here is a lack of focus on process: the concern is with a dichotomous view of phenomena, that is, with survival or lack of survival. The approach, which is similar to the formist orientation pictured in Figure 4-6, contrasts a set of conditions associated with survival of the social system with a set associated with the extinction of the system. Thus, the temporal dimension is not a core consideration here. Spatially, structural functionalism tends to focus on large-scale social systems or entire societies, as distinct from small groups or personality systems. This is a very severe limitation in the context of the study under discussion, for I am concerned with the individual's health in relation to his set of roles.

Social exchange theory is closer to the small group and the personality system, but then it has less to say about large-scale structures. I am assuming that the problem at hand has to do with personality systems *and* small groups *and* large-scale systems. For example, the societal definition of the role of the aged affects how open or constricting that role is for the individual and, hence, his mental health. That societal definition may depend on many factors, such as the level of industrialization of the society and the needs of various segments of society for the services of the aged. Even in the context of the individual and the small group, there are limitations to social exchange theory. Much of its heritage comes from psychological learning theory, but that theory has tended to see the individual as a passive organism, responding to stimuli from his environment, as distinct from an active participant in the kind of two-way interaction that is pictured in Figure 4-7. Finally, social exchange theory suffers from the same ahistorical and atemporal bias that is associated with structural-functionalism: the central question for Blau and Emerson, for example, is the exercise of power rather than the long-term development or loss of power.

Conflict theory tends to be much more historically, or temporally, oriented, although we might distinguish here between a short-term and a long-term perspective. Whereas conflict theory does more justice to long-term changes, the situational approach of exchange theory does more justice to detailed changes over a short period. Yet I might argue that we cannot afford to choose between these two orientations if we are to understand the dynamics of Figure 4-7: long-term changes are built up on the basis of short-term ones, and long-term changes in turn influence the short-term picture. In addition to this, there is another temporal problem that tends to be associated with conflict theory: a more or less deterministic perspective, perhaps related to the Marxist emphasis on science. History is seen as moving inexorably from one class conflict to another, all based on the dialectical conflict between the forces and relations of production, with the classless society waiting at the end of the rainbow. Yet conflict theory is not alone in its deterministic perspective, and indeed, it is easy to take into account because it is above the surface. Covert species of determinism tend to be associated with structural functionalism and exchange theory, whether it be the inevitable shaping of the individual by his social environment or the implicit assumption of a movement "from homogeneity to heterogeneity," from *gemeinschaft* to *gesellschaft,* toward ever higher hierarchies and an ever more detailed division of labor. In addition to all these limitations of conflict theory along the temporal dimension, there are its spatial limitations: its focus is on the large-scale institutions of society, and the problem at hand is small-scale as well as large-scale. The significance of a deterministic perspective can be understood by examining Figure 4-7 once again: to the degree that any determinism exists, the complex set of interacting arrows becomes superfluous. If things will necessarily happen in a certain way, then all forces within the situation except one are superfluous.

Both symbolic interactionism and phenomenology give more attention to the possibility of autonomous action by the individual, although this is less true of symbolic interactionism than of phenomenology. For Mead, the individual is socialized by society, with no consideration given to the process by which the individual "socializes" society. However, Mead does allow for an autonomous "I" that is distinct from the socially oriented "me." Phenomenologists along with symbolic interactionists tend to stick to the small group context, avoiding analysis of large-scale social structures. Unfortunately, this narrowing of context tends to be associated with an atemporal orientation. Linguistic and mental processes tend to be seen outside of any particular historical context. Yet for all these limitations, these two theoretical perspectives help to redress the dominant sociological focus on the large social systems and the dominant view of the almost deterministic power of the group over the individual. However, it is no solution to recommend—as in the case of much of phenomenology—a reverse kind of determinism, whether explicitly or implicitly.

Having explored both paradigmatic and theoretical aspects of the study of the aging process, let us turn now to methodological implications. To begin with, these perspectives call for the kind of study that traces changes over time. To move from a dichotomous to a gradational view, we must trace a sequence of occurrences. The study in fact does center on obtaining time-series information by restudying the same group of individuals. This is known as a "panel study." In addition, many of the questionnaire items called for retrospective as well as prospective information. Granting the limitations of this procedure relative to a genuine time series, it nevertheless does point in the appropriate direction.

Moving from the temporal to the spatial dimension, one characteristic of the methodological approach is the construction of scales of measurement on the basis of multiple items covering diverse kinds of behavior, as suggested in Figure 2-4. Such measurements deal not only with phenomena at the role level of analysis (role breadth) but also at the personality level (mental health). This measurement approach appears to be suited to a pragmatist paradigm, which supposedly incorporates the formist, mechanistic, and organicist paradigms. Also, it seems appropriate for a study that has been defined as being relevant to such macrolevel theory as structural functionalism and conflict theory as well as such microlevel theory as exchange theory, symbolic interactionism, and sociological phenomenology,

One additional methodological approach is the development of a computer-based model that takes into account the various feedback loops depicted in Figure 4-7. The beginnings of this approach were developed in Section 3.2, where the beaker metaphor was discussed and system dynamics notation was introduced. Further details will be presented in Chapter 5, where each of the four studies will once again be presented, this time within the context of a series of case studies that attempt to recapture the flavor of what occurred in each project.

4.5 Summary

Between the high level of abstraction of the paradigm and the low level of abstraction of the research procedure lies the level of abstraction represented by theory. We might see all three as constituting a continuum along which the researcher continues to move up and down as he proceeds to shift from the context of discovery to the context of verification. Using as illustrative contexts the previously discussed studies of aging and adjustment, occupational choice, community development, and the aging process, five theoretical schools of thought from sociology were presented: structural functionalism, conflict theory, social exchange theory, symbolic interactionism, and phenomenological sociology. Table 4-1 lists ideas from these schools relating to each of the four studies. By exploring the theoretical and paradigmatic implications of particular research procedures being employed, the social scientist can become aware of—and move to correct—conflicts between methods and theory or methods and paradigm or theory and paradigm.

If the social researcher is to achieve genuine advances in knowledge, he must build on what has already been done. The physical scientist has an easier time of it here because his theory is already well codified. Also, physical phenomena are far less interactive than human phenomena, so that narrow specialization can still yield important findings. The social scientist, however, faces a much different situation. There is no one accepted theoretical framework, and the interactive nature of the phenomena he deals with tends to make narrow specialization a path to triviality. Given this situation, one direction for him to take (if he is a sociologist) is to explore within any given study its relationships to the five dominant theoretical schools of thought. By limiting oneself to one school or to a few important ideas within a given school, one increases the danger of becoming a "new Columbus."

Table 4-1

Theoretical Ideas Relating to the Four Illustrative Research Projects

	Aging & Adjustment	Occupational Choice	Community Development	Model of Aging
Conflict Theory (e.g.: Marx, Coser)	Alienation from meaningless age roles	Alienation from meaningless occupational roles	Avoiding conflict between forces and relations of production	Emphasis on long term historical factors
Structural Functionalism (e.g.: Durkheim, Weber)	Conformity to legitimized role expectations	How functional for society is individual conformity to occupational roles?	Movement to a "normal" division of labor and rational role coordination	Survival of the social system as a prelude to understanding processes for strengthening it
Symbolic Interactionism (e.g.: Mead, Goffman)	Assertion of "I" to delegitimate role expectations	Expression of "I" in the face of repressive role expectations	Development of data on changes in the individual as well as society, e.g., the gap between expected need satisfactions and actual need satisfactions. In this way, transcending the organicist paradigm	Possibility of autonomous actions by the individual to create higher levels of mental health
Phenomenology (e.g.: Schutz)	"Suspension of belief" in immediate role situation	Trenscending the "profile" of the occupational role		
Exchange Theory (e.g.: Homans, Blau)	Development of the individual's power to delegitimate his role	Individual's bargaining position for reconstructing his occupational role		Emphasis on situational and small group factors involved in mental health

Exercises

1. Select any current research article from a sociology journal and relate it to the five schools of sociological theory discussed in the chapter: structural functionalism, conflict theory, social exchange theory, phenomenology, and symbolic interactionism.

2. Following up exercise #1, make use of your theoretical work to define a new problem for investigation, based on both the earlier study and the theoretical work you have done.

3. Discuss some of the concrete research implications of the positive loop between synthesis and analysis in relation to measurement, as described in the last part of Section 4.2.

4. What is the relationship between Davies' theory of revolution, as presented in Figure 4-4, and our discussions of negative loops and positive loops?

Annotated References

MILLS, C. WRIGHT (ed.). *Images of Man.* New York: George Braziller, Inc., 1960. Mills' presentation of the classical tradition in sociological thinking includes selections from the work of Marx and Engels, Weber, Veblen, Mosca, Michels, Pareto, Spencer, Schumpeter, Thomas and Znaniecki, Simmel, Durkheim, and Mannheim.

RITZER, GEORGE. *Sociology: A Multiple Paradigm Science.* Boston: Allyn and Bacon, Inc., 1975. Ritzer presents three paradigms to be found within sociology: the social facts paradigm, which includes much of conflict theory and structural-functionalism, the social definition paradigm, incorporating much of symbolic interactionism and phenomenology, and the social behavior paradigm, which includes exchange theory.

WEBER, MAX. *The Protestant Ethic and the Spirit of Capitalism.* New York: Charles Scribner's Sons, 1958. Weber puts to work his sense of history and his breadth of knowledge about human societies to develop and give evidence for a sociological theory of the dynamics involved in one important phase of history. Weber provides the student with an illustration of the best that sociological theory has produced.

ZEITLIN, IRVING M. *Rethinking Sociology: A Critique of Contemporary Theory.* New York: Appleton-Century-Crofts, 1973. Zeitlin presents five schools of sociological theory: structural functionalism, social exchange theory, conflict theory, phenomenology, and symbolic interactionism. In his final chapter, "Toward a Synthesis of Marx, Mead, and Freud," he integrates many of the critical ideas developed throughout the book.

chapter 5

Case Studies
in Defining and
Redefining the
Problem

The time has come to pull together the ideas from Chapters 2, 3, and 4 to give coherence to the focus of Part Two: the definition of a research problem.

My approach will be to present once again the four studies discussed in preceding chapters, only this time viewing the studies through a contextual and personal lens. These case studies are not meant to give the reader illustrations of the best possible ways of defining research problems. Indeed, if a given study is evaluated from the perspective of the ideas in the preceding chapters, it will be found to be seriously limited. I present these studies in order to illustrate the process I experienced insofar as I understand that process and can present it. I am attempting to get as close as I can to the logic-in-use of a given study, but the reader should be aware that what emerges is a reconstructed logic.

5.1 The Process of Defining a Research Problem:
An Overview

Before plunging into the aging and adjustment study, it is useful to pull together from the preceding chapters what we have learned about the general process of defining a research problem. I begin with the analogy from Chapter 1 between the scientific method and human interaction, as portrayed in Figure 1-1 (The Scientific Method as a Feedback Process) and Figure 1-2 (Human Interaction as a Feedback Process). The everyday process of covert rehearsal, where the individual considers and traces out the consequences of a range of possible actions, corresponds to the scientific definition of a problem. Just as covert rehearsal takes place almost continually, whether implicitly or explicitly, so does the process of defining a research problem: the initial definition is followed by a continuing series of redefinitions. Usually, however, such redefinitions remain at the unconscious level: the researcher consciously commits himself at the beginning of his investigation to a certain course of action, and he tends to be relatively unaware of the various ways in which he departs from that course throughout the research process. To the extent that he can legitimize such departures and learn to make them explicit, he stands a much better chance of taking whatever steps are necessary within the research process to collect the data essential for his problem. Also he comes to be in a much better position to communicate effectively the results of his studies, for otherwise a widening gap develops between his reconstructed logic and his logic-in-use.

Pursuing this analogy between scientific and everyday behavior, the definition of the problem motivates the scientist to take action, just as covert rehearsal motivates the individual. Without going through a covert rehearsal process we do not weigh the relative advantages and disadvantages of various courses of action. In the medical student study, for example, such a process of weighing was part of the process by which students chose their field of medicine. For the scientist, defining a problem also gives him a sense of direction and motivation, even a sense of urgency. This sense of problem is essential if he is to organize his efforts effectively throughout the project. And it is not something that can be done initially and then let lie: the scientist's project moves from one phase to another, with new things occurring all the time. The context of the investigation changes as initial findings begin to be collected. Thus, a sense of problem as well as specific directions for research must be recaptured throughout the investigation.

If it is true, then, that the scientist is continually redefining his problem, and that this is the basis of his retaining a sense of direction throughout the investigation, what can be said about the nature of this direction? Is this something about which we can say nothing, since the scientist himself must decide the most appropriate direction? Or is he in need of any methodological guidance? I think he is, because he is nowhere near as free as he tends to think he is: he tends to follow the dominant paradigm, which has generally become the basis for his thought processes. To become freer to make intelligent choices, then, he must uncover the paradigm, or world view, that guides his behavior. In this direction, according to Thomas Kuhn,[1] lies the construction of scientific revolutions. Failing this, our work tends to be less scientific because of its basis in unquestioned assumptions.

In Chapter 2, four paradigms are explored: formism, mechanism, organicism, and pragmatism. From formism we have, in incipient form, the

---

[1] Thomas S. Kuhn, *The Structure of Scientific Revolutions* (Chicago: U. of Chicago, 1962).

idea of progress, an idea that lies at the heart of the process of problem definition. Why bother to define a scientific problem if we can expect to achieve nothing by so doing? However, once we assume that it is possible to move beyond the known into the unknown—the idea of scientific progress—then this effort is worthwhile. The idea of progress helps to create progress in scientific endeavor, although it does not guarantee such progress. Of course, all of this is only incipient in formism: we have the simple dichotomy between one thing and another, such as between man and God. Yet once the dichotomy is established, and once one end of the dichotomy is valued over the other, it becomes the basis for motion in that direction, just as two points can determine a vector.

As for mechanism, its root metaphor is the machine, connoting man's active shaping of his environment. In applying this idea, the researcher attempts to achieve conscious control over the research environment with the aid of his definition of the problem. If this sounds immoral, it should be understood that the researcher's choice is not between shaping and not shaping, but between shaping consciously and shaping unconsciously. By choosing, for example, to construct the kind of research environment within which both researcher and respondent reveal themselves as much as possible, the researcher works to reveal the forces operating there.

Organicism suggests the researcher's adaptation to his research environment, an adaptation that sensitizes him to external phenomena and helps him to understand such phenomena. To achieve such sensitivity we must first distinguish ourselves from our environment (formism), and we must become convinced that adaptation to our environment gives us some power to shape that environment (mechanism). We must learn to be objective in the sense that we do not allow our own wishes about the environment to prevent us from seeing that environment as it might be seen by others. We should strive, then, for the kind of problem definition that is not limited to our own narrow experience but includes, insofar as possible, the experiences of others. Organicists among the early sociologists, such as Marx and Weber, illustrate this breadth of perspective in their problem definitions.

If the researcher is to move from an incipient idea of progress (formism) to a conviction that he can shape his environment (mechanism) to a sensitivity to his environment (organicism), then how is he to learn to do so? He can of course conform to what other scientists are doing, but that may not suit his own purposes, and he may do poorly as a result. Somehow, he must learn not only to be sensitive to his external environment but to be sensitive to himself as well, that is, he must become reflexive. After all, it is he who is responsible for the research process, and a great deal of what occurs within that process is a product of whatever he is. Such inner sensitivity—coupled with an outer orientation—is the basis for a pragmatist perspective. With it, the investigator can move back and forth from an external to an internal sensitivity, continuing to redefine his problem as he sees the repercussions of his actions on his environment and himself.

In Chapter 3, two vital tools involved in defining research problems are discussed: language and cybernetics. Language is obviously involved in problem definition, but how can the analysis of language of Chapter 3 help us to do a better job? The key idea here is that each paradigm is associated with a particular approach to language. Thus, we can become alert to our underlying paradigm by looking carefully at the language we use to define our research problem. Also, we are in a position to alter our language as an aid to moving toward a different paradigm if we so desire. Thus, for example, we can move from the formist distinction between adjustment and maladjustment to the pragmatist distinctions among degrees of mental health, as in Figure 4-5.

The second tool discussed in Chapter 3 is cybernetics, with a linguistic emphasis on gradational concepts providing its basis. Thinking in terms of the first cybernetics, we can learn to be wary of erecting any methodological or theoretical tools—as we proceed to define a problem—into ends in themselves, and thus creating a negative loop within the research process. That is the story of the failure to achieve scientific revolutions: scientists unwittingly adopt the dominant paradigm when they define problems, failing to realize its limitations. As for the positive loop idea of the second cybernetics, this serves to emphasize the importance of a sequence of problem definitions, with each one building on the preceding ones. The idea of the positive loop is most encouraging: it holds out to us possibilities for going far beyond where we are now, and doing so at an accelerating pace. The third cybernetics—with its focus on cybernetic thinking—helps us to retain a sense of proportion and a humanistic thrust. Cybernetics is seen as being no more than a tool for enlarging human understanding: we must define and redefine our problems bearing in mind that the enlargement of our understanding is far more vital than the use of specialized tools of any type.

If problems are to be defined in such a way that the results of research can be communicated to a given audience, then we must take into account the theoretical literature that audience is familiar with. In Chapter 4 I illustrate this for a sociological audience, discussing five categories of sociological theory: structural functionalism, social exchange theory, conflict theory, phenomenology, and symbolic interactionism. We can make use of such theories—as well as a widening range of research literature—by defining our problems so as to take into account more and more of the phenomena called for by all of them. For example, one of the major thrusts of structural functionalism, social exchange theory, and conflict theory is to sensitize us to the power of the social system to shape the individual.

A vital thrust of phenomenology and—to a lesser extent—of symbolic interactionism is a sensitivity to the power of the individual to shape and construct his social environment. What would an approach taking both thrusts seriously imply? For one thing, the investigator would come to realize that he himself plays an important role in the construction and/or interpretation of whatever social systems he investigates, and he would have to define his problem so as to be in a position to measure investigator effects.

5.2   A Case Study of Aging and Adjustment

In the preceding chapters, I have referred to the study of aging and adjustment as an illustration of a formist perspective, but I now submit that such a designation was no more than a convenient stereotype. Any study is far too complex to be understood by a mere category. In this section I shall try to relive some of what I experienced while undertaking that study, with the purpose of achieving greater insight into the process of effective problem definition. I shall divide the discussion into three segments, corresponding to three different stages of my work.

The earliest stage revolves around my doctoral dissertation at Cornell University, completed in 1956. Some of the flavor of this study, "A Role Theory Approach to Predicting Adjustment of the Aged in Two Communities," may be obtained from this selection, taken from my dissertation abstract:

Data are based on interviews with 500 respondents in the Kips Bay–Yorkville Health District of New York City and 468 respondents in Elmira, N.Y. Interviews were held with probability samples of the non-institutionalized aged populations sixty years old or older in the two areas. . . .

Adjustment is conceived of as a state in which needs are satisfied by rewards. The measure of adjustment is a Guttman scale of three items. . . .

In each of the four role-areas considered, the relationship between role change and adjustment is statistically significant. . . .

Additional results show that age-identification may operate in part as an intervening variable in its effect on adjustment. Role changes in the employment and marital roles, i.e., retirement and death of spouse, respectively, are related to felt age, which in turn is related to adjustment.

Our general conclusion is that we have contributed to demonstrating the utility of a role theory approach to predicting the adjustment of the aged.[2]

[2] Bernard S. Phillips, "A Role Theory Approach to Predicting Adjustment of the Aged in Two Communities," (Ph.D. dissertation, Cornell University, 1956), abstract.

Formism is definitely in evidence here, as illustrated by the emphasis on statistical significance and the yes-no demonstration of the utility of a role theory approach. There is also formism in the somewhat pretentious use of technical terms such as "probability samples," "Guttman scale," "role areas," and "statistically significant." Mechanism is in evidence as well. First, there is the emphasis on prediction. Also, a Guttman scale sets up a continuum. In addition, there is an air of impersonality conveyed by "our" versus "I" and the use of the passive voice, all of which I felt at the time conveyed the kind of objective scientific attitude to be found in the physical sciences. Behind all the formism and mechanism is a certain arrogance: here I was finally proving the truth of ideas that might have been discussed for hundreds or thousands of years with no definitive results. And what I conveyed, in properly humble language, was truth: a role theory approach has been demonstrated to be useful in predicting the adjustment of the aged.

Before even coming to Cornell, I had been imbued with a kind of missionary spirit, a spirit that I now feel departed very much from a scientific attitude. I had just emerged from a year at Washington State University, where I had fallen under the influence of Wesley Salmon, a philosopher who had studied with Hans Reichenbach, perhaps the most eminent of the American positivists (those who emphasize the context of verification far more than the context of discovery). I felt deeply that what sociology needed, and the whole world as well, was the rigorous statistical testing of hypotheses against data. I was, in the words of Sorokin, a "new Columbus": I felt that what I was doing was brand new, that the past was littered with unclear ideas and inadequate data and could be safely rejected, and that the world was waiting breathlessly for what I might have to say.

The second stage of my research on aging and adjustment centered on an article based on my dissertation that was submitted to the *American Sociological Review* and was accepted. I quote from my concluding paragraphs:

> This paper has outlined a theoretical framework that may be utilized in predicting the degree of adjustment of the aged. . . .
>
> The role changes considered are significantly related to maladjustment, although there is little tendency for multiple role changes to cumulate and result in a closer relation to the adjustment variable. . . .
>
> Age identification can reverse the expected relation between any one of the role changes considered and adjustment. Where two role changes are combined, however, this reversal does not generally take place.
>
> It is hoped that future studies of adjustment will further specify the relatively crude variable of role change. In addition, the significance of the age-identification variable for adjustment indicates a need for further investigation of this and other aspects of the self-image.[3]

[3] Bernard S. Phillips, "A Role Theory Approach to Adjustment in Old Age," *American Sociological Review,* **22** (April 1957), p. 217.

There is less audacity here. For example, there is no claim that "we have contributed to demonstrating the utility of a role theory approach." Instead, there are such qualified statements as, "This paper has outlined a theoretical framework that may be utilized in predicting. . . ." There is also some disappointment hidden within these words. For example, I knew that "The role changes considered are significantly related to maladjustment," but that statement is qualified with the realization that "there is little tendency for multiple role changes to cumulate and result in a closer relation to the adjustment variable." I had hoped to move from establishing the *existence* of a relationship to understanding how to achieve a closer *degree* of relationship. Also, I was rooting for the power of age-identification to alter the situation produced by role changes, and I was only able to achieve a qualified success. Although age identification can reverse the impact for any one role change, it cannot do so for more than one.

The over-all change from my dissertation abstract to this article—which involved some additional research—was a movement from an upward positive loop (with reference to my assessment of the importance of what I was doing) to a negative loop. My earlier zeal about changing the world through science had run up against the complexities of the world and deficiencies in my tools. I had learned to accept a lower level of aspiration, but not without disappointment. I hoped that "future studies of adjustment will further specify the relatively crude variable of role change." This S curve of upward acceleration (the positive loop part) followed by a leveling off (the negative loop part) was characteristic of my earlier academic experiences as well. For example, I remember studying for my oral qualifying examination for the doctorate at Cornell. While reading a great many argumentative book reviews in the *American Sociological Review,* in which some reviewers completely demolished the work of others, it gradually dawned on me that much of what was being done in the discipline was quite worthless. I had suspected this earlier—in my undergraduate days at Columbia when I had been deeply influenced by the iconoclasm of C. Wright Mills—but the feeling had become more powerful: I felt that *I* could demolish the work of others. I began thinking in these terms about major theorists and pieces of research, and I did not find myself wanting. In my imagination, I kept accelerating in this vein, developing an approach of my own that superseded all the others. My earlier exposure to positivism, with its dismissal of vast areas of human knowledge, had fortified me for this task. I felt that there was no limit that I could not surpass in sociology. And then I experienced my examination. I did quite well throughout most of it, but was suddenly floored by a very simple question: What is a statistical test of significance? I mentally blocked on the question, for all my background in mathematics and statistics. Robin Williams and Philip McCarthy—my examiners—desperately tried to help me, giving me all kinds of hints, but I was too far gone. I was conscious of being a tremendous hypocrite, parading my knowledge and interest in a mathematical approach to sociology and performing at what I considered to be a despicable level of achievement. In retrospect, I believe that I was a victim of my own lack of self-confidence and maturity. Unfortunately, it took me many years to recover my short-lived feeling that there is no limit to what I can do in sociology.

A third stage of research associated with aging and adjustment relates to an article I wrote some five years later, "Role Change, Subjective Age, and Adjustment: A Correlational Analysis." It was based on additional data relating to the earlier study: 257 of the sample of 500 from New York City had a member of their family or a friend who was interviewed as well, and my investigation centered on these two sets of 257 individuals, the older people and their associates. I felt at the time that if statistical tests of significance were limited in what they could tell us, then perhaps a correlational approach, with its emphasis on degree of relationship, might do more. I had not given up on what I believed to be the most important finding of my earlier study: that age-identification—and, more generally, self-image—was the key to understanding the whole process. My summary of results reads in part as follows:

> While the zero order correlational analysis produces a predominance of situations where role change is related both to adjustment and subjective age, with subjective age being related to adjustment, the partial correlational analysis results in a predominance of situations where role change and subjective age are each related to adjustment without being related to one another. *The relatively low magnitude of the correlations indicates that a good deal is left unexplained in the processes affecting the adjustment of the aged.*[4]

Here once again was my sequence from positive loop to negative loop, my S curve. I had had great aspirations for my correlational tools, feeling that whatever limitations were inherent in my original study would be remedied by these more powerful techniques, especially since I had access to excellent data. It was—and is—a rare study where one attains information from both a sizable sample and from their close associates. Yet I was to discover that you can't make a silk purse out of a sow's ear: using correlation coefficients and a fancy partial correlational analysis does not by itself produce high correlations. My foray into sophisticated quantitative analysis enabled me to conquer a new methodology, but that methodology was not sufficient in itself to produce what I wanted. Once again I had moved outside of my shell of previous knowledge only to experience a larger shell.

[4] Bernard S. Phillips, "Role Change, Subjective Age, and Adjustment: A Correlational Analysis," *Journal of Gerontology,* **16** (October 1961), pp. 351–52.

5.3   A Case Study of Occupational Choice

It seems that the lessons of history—including personal history—are learned only slowly and painfully, yet at least it is possible to learn from them. If correlational techniques are not sufficient in themselves to yield accurate predictions, then perhaps mathematical models—aided by wide-ranging theory—can solve the problem. Yet I was working in an era—the late fifties and very early sixties—when data processing technology had not developed very far. Of course, there were some specialized techniques—such as factor analysis—that had been developed. But when it came to putting together one's own mathematical model of phenomena, I had few precedents to go by, either in the sociological literature or with respect to the use of data processing equipment. So I once again moved outside my shell.

As discussed in Section 2.2, the mechanistic paradigm was deeply involved in my theoretical and methodological approaches as I proceeded with studying the choice of fields of medicine by medical students. Fresh out of graduate school, I was determined to put what little knowledge of mathematics I had to work, and I was convinced that a formist emphasis on tests of significance was quite limited in the insights it could yield. Perhaps my own view of the human being as fundamentally rational contributed to my interest in developing a mathematical model. I remember that my typical expectations of self and others were substantially ahead of people's performances—my own included—as evidenced by my recurrent surprise and disappointment with the behavior of others. If a lack of living up to these high standards was a surprise to me, then my normal expectation was that people generally behaved the way they should. From here, it was an easy step to construct a rational model of human choices, where individuals choose so as to maximize expected goal fulfillment and minimize expected goal deprivation. Of course, my frame of reference should not be surprising in relation to my academic background, for I had been deeply influenced by the effectiveness of mathematics and the physical sciences.

My sense of problem, then, was based on convictions as to the limitations of existing research techniques and the importance of mathematical models. Those twin feelings resulted, after a number of years of research, in the close relationship between resultant goal commitments and actual preferences for fields of medicine (Table 2-4). Delays and obstacles resulted in a June 1964 publication of the basic results of a study undertaken in 1956, and even that publication was so hedged with cautious statements that it would have been difficult for a reader to understand its significance. Sometime in 1960, after complex manipulations of the data, I was able to construct Table 2-4, and I was overjoyed at the result. At last, my vision of a mathematical approach to sociology was proving fruitful. As I proceeded to write up the results and to obtain criticism from others, my confidence in the achievement started to ebb. First of all, I had difficulty in communicating effectively what I had done. It was one thing to write up the aging study in article form, because I had seen that same approach in so many other articles. But here was a quite different situation: complex data manipulations and a mathematical model to be explained to a predominantly nonmathematical audience. In addition, others suggested that my results were trivial: wasn't it already obvious that people made choices on the basis of goals or values? And even if I was able to demonstrate this with high correlation coefficients and a wide range of percentages, was I really predicting which medical field the students actually entered, or was I merely predicting their relatively changeable preferences? Why didn't I follow up the students over a number of years to see which fields they actually entered?

The crowning blow—which very nearly resulted in the study never being published in article form or becoming an important illustrative basis for the first and second editions of this book—came through my correspondence with the editors of *Sociometry*. My paper was initially rejected because a reader felt that my approach to measurement, where I subtracted and summated scores for a number of questionnaire items in order to obtain my over-all index of resultant goal commitment, was not appropriate. My measurement technique was ruled out not because it was not fruitful—indeed, it was able to yield excellent correlations—but because I had no definite evidence that I had a right to add, subtract, and divide on the basis of my measurement procedures. After a short period when I was convinced that my years of work had indeed been wasted, I recovered my confidence sufficiently to reply in detail to the editor, explaining that the scientist evaluates methodology pragmatically—on the basis of its results—and does not rule a technique out because it isn't supposed to be an appropriate one. At that point, the editor agreed to send my paper out for another review, this time to someone he described as very well known in the discipline. And for the second time I received a rejection, but this time there was room for revising the paper with a few minor changes. And once again I was crushed, although briefly, but then I recovered and made the necessary revisions, the most important of which was the following footnote:

> It is recognized that the operations of subtraction and summation, both of which are required for the calculation of EVD [Expected Goal Commitment, previously designated as "expected value deprivation"], are undefined for ordinal scales. These operations are justified pragmatically on the basis that there is no alternative procedure which can utilize the basic idea of value deprivation and can be defined for ordinal scales, the level of measurement which is presently attainable. As a consequence

of the undefined procedures utilized, results obtained should be treated with caution. It should be noted, however, that the measurement of expected value deprivation attains construct validity to the extent that EVD subsequently is shown to enter into a series of relationships which are of theoretical consequence.[5]

The paper was accepted. I won the skirmish, but in the process I lost the battle. Somehow, I was never quite convinced of the importance of the study for the development of methodological techniques such as synthetic indexes (depicted in Figure 2-4 and described in Section 4.2). I sat back and waited for reactions to the article, but no reaction of consequence came. Then an unusual opportunity presented itself. A student of mine[6] approached me about the analysis of questionnaire data from a study of 10,000 U.S. naval officers, a study focusing on their decision to remain in the service or retire. I suggested an approach analogous to the one I took in the medical student study, and subsequently I was most surprised to be presented with the following data.

Table 5-1
Synthetic Measurement: Goal Commitment and Retirement

| | Goal Commitment | | | | | | | | |
| | High | | | | | | | | Low |
	1	2	3	4	5	6	7	8	9
Remain in the service	93%	88%	78%	67%	52%	35%	28%	16%	23%

The results were just as striking as the medical student data: almost all officers with the highest goal commitment intend to remain in the service, whereas only a small proportion among those with the lowest goal commitment intend to do so.

One problem with these data was that the study was classified at the time, and somehow my own knowledge of the data was not enough for me: I needed the reactions of others. I knew that these results, when combined with those of the medical student study, gave great weight to the importance of a synthetic approach to measurement. But my intellectual "knowing" did not add up to an emotional "feeling." I had sufficient confidence in the medical student study to use it as a major example in the

---

[5] Bernard S. Phillips, "Expected Value Deprivation and Occupational Preference," *Sociometry*, **27** (June 1964), p. 155.
[6] Mr. Jack Kinney.

first two editions of this book, but not enough to think about and develop the methodological implications of the study.

My treatment of the study in this book constitutes a third stage in this case study. Over these last five years my intellectual convictions have grown into emotional feelings, so much so that I have been both seeing that study as illustrating general synthetic procedures for measurement and also attempting to go beyond this mechanistic world view with organicist and pragmatist procedures without abandoning either formism or mechanism. Many things have contributed to this change in me. There are, for example, changes in society—the counterculture, Vietnam, Watergate, the women's liberation movement, the energy crisis, inflation, unemployment—pointing up the poverty of existing modes of societal organization. There are also changes within academia, and sociology in particular, pointing up the ineffectiveness of existing approaches for dealing with societal problems. And there are the many things that have happened to me personally, not the least of which has been my attempting to communicate the relevance of existing knowledge to students who wish to solve important problems in the world. All of this adds up to a sense of urgency that was communicated to me and affected my own approach to defining research problems.

In looking back over the various stages of my inquiries into the occupational choices of medical students, I find once again that I can summarize a great deal by using the concepts of positive loop and negative loop. I seem to have undergone a series of S curves, such as are presented in Figure 5-1, with each positive loop followed by a negative loop. The crucial

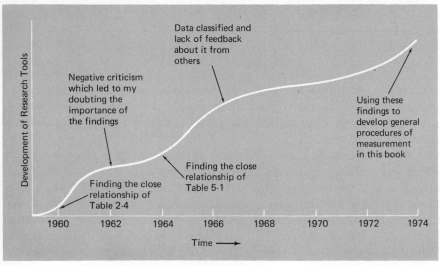

Figure 5-1.
Positive and Negative Loops in the Development of Research Tools.

factor in the emergence of the negative loop seems to have been a lack of direction for going beyond that point and a lack of confidence to move in that direction. Thus, the given development—say a specific technique for synthetic measurement—is seen at a given time as an end in itself. This factor seems also to have, in large part, produced the negative loops that developed during the aging and adjustment study (see Section 5.2). For example, at the time that the partial correlational analysis proved to be so disappointing, I had no vision of the possibility of moving to a mathematical model—as I did with the occupational choice study—and I had no conviction as to the importance of doing so. In summary, I might say that I was largely in the grip of formist and mechanistic world views, respectively, for these two studies, and I lacked a pragmatist ability to take a deep reflexive look at the limitations of the tools I had committed myself to.

5.4   A Case Study of Community Development

One vital problem posed in the foregoing case studies is how to reduce the length of time during which the researcher enters and remains in a research plateau, or negative loop. Is it possible to make such periods shorter and shorter? This case study, which was described in Section 2.3, had to do with the construction of a community social profile and a sociocultural impact statement. That impact statement analyzed the social and cultural impacts projected for three alternative decisions relative to an oil refinery in an ethnically divided urban community: conversion to a storage facility, modernization with no increase in production, and modernization with an increase in production. The latter alternative was seen to provide a basis for an upward (favorable) positive loop between quality of life and the continuing scientific-industrial revolution.

This positive loop is portrayed in Figure 5-2. On the left-hand side is the structure of the relationship between (1) a host of factors involved in a continuation of the scientific-industrial revolution and (2) the quality of life. That host of factors was detailed in a series of recommendations contained in a first draft of the sociocultural impact statement. On the right-hand side of Figure 5-2 is the hypothesized dynamic behavior of the quality of life. The key problem involved in Figure 5-2 is that it is based primarily on speculation: it is an educated guess as to what set of forces can revive a divided community with economic and social problems that has lost confidence in itself.

The writing of that first draft of the sociocultural impact statement constitutes an upward positive loop section of the curve of this case study of community development, at least in its addressing the magnitude and comprehensiveness of the problems involved. What followed, however, was

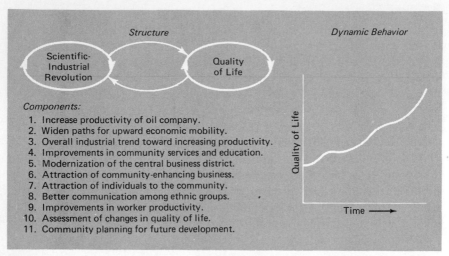

Figure 5-2.
Scientific-Industrial Revolution and Quality of Life.

the almost complete elimination of that statement by the organization responsible for the impact statement, an organization dominated by engineers who respected mathematics and tables but not what they considered to be vague discussions of possible occurrences. Here, then, was the beginning of a negative loop, but for how long was it to continue? If my experience here was to parallel that in the medical student study, it would take a number of years to learn how to go beyond the tools and perspectives I was using. But as a matter of fact, it was only a matter of months before I had conceived of an alternative methodology designed to deal with the difficulties.

As I perceived the situation, the fundamental mistake I made was characteristic of the organicist approach generally: I had not incorporated sufficiently the power of the mechanistic world view and provided the hard scientific facts, stated in the form of mathematics and tables, that the engineers could not have ignored. Of course, what was required in order to do this was the kind of research on the community that would provide those facts, and the kind of theory that was sufficiently systematic so as to organize those facts well enough to deal with the fantastic complexity involved in a study of community development. The community profile that had been done was not focused on this kind of need, although it might well have been.

Yet I did not reach this conclusion immediately. I must confess that for a brief period of time—perhaps two weeks—I was in some doubt as to the value of the impact statement. Was it really possible, I thought, for a sociologist to deal with as many complex and changing factors as are involved in a community? Was it not a vast oversimplification to seize on the potential positive loop between quality of life and the continuing industrial revolution, virtually ignoring the multitudes of other loops operating in the community? At the same time, however, I was convinced that no one else was in a better position to do this than myself. The systems engineers had far more knowledge of, and experience with, the cybernetic tools I was using, but their experience was with physical and not human phenomena. And those few systems engineers who were working with predicting complex urban phenomena—such as the systems dynamicists (see Section 8.4 for an illustration)—had little knowledge of the social science literature.

I soon had an opportunity to become more specific about my ideas, this time in the context of a highway planning study. Its aim was to provide information that would help engineers plan the exact route of the projected widening of a highway by taking into account—within certain cost limitations—the desires of the residents. This was a much simpler situation than an effort to deal with the multiple problems involved in community development, but perhaps that was for the best, since the conceptual and measurement problems were difficult enough if I was to incorporate a mathematical approach. I decided to adopt an approach similar to the one I used in the medical student study, only adapted to an organicist emphasis on change and development.

To start with my orientation to change, I focused on three separate groups: individuals who had recently experienced the highway widening (based on the location of their homes), individuals who were now experiencing it, and individuals living in the area where the widening was to take place. Ideally, to understand dynamics one should follow the same group or individual over a number of points in time. Failing this, one can learn about dynamics by examining different groups or individuals at various stages of a process, as in this study, if one assumes that the groups or individuals are very much the same relative to the factors under investigation. Here, then, is a way of going beyond the medical student study, which did not focus on changes in values or expectations: study individuals or groups at different stages of a process in which values and expectations are altered in order to investigate the forces that produce the changes.

My measurement approach—discussed in the last part of Section 4.2—was the same as that used in the medical student study. I was interested in pulling together a great deal of information in order to demonstrate quite clearly that an individual's plans to move—just like his plans to choose a medical field or to retire—can be predicted by taking into account his goals and his set of expectations for achieving those goals under different conditions. I centered on four goals relating to reactions to the highway: (1) avoiding traffic noise, (2) avoiding air pollution, (3) not seeing the traffic, and (4) avoiding walls around the highway. The strength of each goal was measured by a question like this:

Are you affected by air pollution in any of the following ways?
(CHOOSE AS MANY ANSWERS AS FIT THE QUESTION)
1   when looking out from inside your home
1   when working around the house or taking a walk
1   when playing games or in recreational activity
1   when sleeping, relaxing, or taking life easy
1   when driving on the highway

I took the number of situations in which an individual said he was affected by air pollution to constitute a rough measure of the strength of his goal of avoiding air pollution. Thus, where no situation was mentioned, the individual received a score of 1, while five situations mentioned produced a score of 6. I could have used 0 and 5 instead, but I wanted to avoid zero, since this score was to be multiplied by another, and a zero would cancel the other score out.

That other score was derived from questions as to the chances that changes in air pollution, for example, would affect the individual adversely, e.g., a weight of 6 was assigned to "a certainty," and a weight of 1 to "no chance." These scores became multipliers of the goal strength measures, so that an individual with a strong goal of avoiding air pollution (score of 6) who *also* thought that a change in air pollution would affect him (score of 6) received a score of 6 times 6, or 36, for this one pair of questions, as contrasted with a score of 1 times 1, or 1, for an individual who had no goal of avoiding air pollution and who believed air pollution wouldn't affect him. If these two individuals also felt the same way about the other three goals, and also had corresponding beliefs about those conditions affecting or not affecting them, then the first individual would receive four scores of 36, or a total of 144, while the latter would receive four scores of 1, or a total of 4. Thus, individuals in the sample might range from a minimum score of 4 to a maximum of 144 when their answers to this group of forty-eight questions are combined into one score. Let us designate this score "expected deprivation."

Expected deprivation scores were then to be related to a measure of the individual's desire to move, derived from this question:

What are the chances that you would move if any or all four of these things happened: walls around the Turnpike, increase in air pollution, seeing traffic, and an increase in traffic noise levels as a result of a widening of the Turnpike?
(1) no chance   (2) 25% chance   (3) 50% chance
          (4) 75% chance   (5) a certainty

For example, the expected deprivation scores might first be combined into nine groups and given a ranking of 1 to 9 as follows:

Expected Deprivation Score	Expected Deprivation Rank	Expected Deprivation Score	Expected Deprivation Rank
1–16	1	81–96	6
17–32	2	97–112	7
33–48	3	113–128	8
49–64	4	129–144	9
65–80			

These ranks might then be related to the measure of the individual's desire to move in a simple table, if we dichotomize that measure into these two parts: those who think there is no chance or little chance of their moving (scores of 1 or 2), as contrasted with those who think there is an even chance or higher of moving (3, 4, or 5). The table emerging from this cross tabulation of expected deprivation rank and intention to move might, *hypothetically,* look like this, analogous to Tables 2-4 and 5-1 for the medical student study and the officer retirement study, respectively:

				Expected Deprivation Rank					
	Low								High
	1	2	3	4	5	6	7	8	9
Little or no chance of moving	12%	21%	26%	33%	44%	52%	65%	66%	81%

My reason for this kind of projected analysis was to provide irrefutable data to the highway engineers on the importance of taking into account such intangible factors as people's goals and beliefs. I felt that such a close relationship between expected deprivation and chances of moving would clearly demonstrate that social science can achieve mathematical relationships similar to those achieved in the physical sciences. Further, I felt that a detailed analysis of the three contrasting groups of homeowners—those who had just undergone a widening of the highway, those who were presently experiencing it, and those in the target area—would yield a more dynamic picture of the processes involved. However, I failed to take into account sufficiently the situation at hand: construction had already been delayed for some time. Costs were soaring, and answers were needed extremely rapidly. Even though this sophisticated analysis would not have taken more than about a month, there was no time for it, and a rougher analysis—focusing on the percentages of homeowners who had various goals and beliefs—was all that could be utilized.

Here was another failure, another negative loop. But that loop can once again be converted to an upward positive loop. After all, a good deal had been accomplished: a method of analysis and data based on that method. What is required at this point, more than anything, is faith in the importance of what has been done so as to provide the motivation and time necessary to complete the analysis. We might, then, apply Figure 5-1 to the various phases of this case study of community development. The three positive loop components correspond to the writing of the impact statement, the collection of the highway data on the basis of a new approach to measurement, and the potential analysis of these data. The two negative loops correspond to the rejection of the impact statement and the decision to proceed with highway construction without the mathematical analysis.

5.5 A Case Study of the Aging Process

This case study may be seen as a continuation of my previous work with aging and adjustment (see Sections 2.1 and 5.2), with a gap of ten years between the last phase of that study and the beginning of this one. I described some aspects of this recent study in Section 2.4, but not in the manner of this chapter: an exploration of the context of the research, of what was going on in my head, of what I was feeling at the time. As a result of discussing these kinds of factors, I hope to attain additional insight into the forces that produce positive loops and inhibit negative loops in the development of research tools.

For several years prior to this study, I had become fascinated with the possibilities of computer-based modeling, or computer simulation, as a way of moving beyond the limitations of deterministic mathematical models, which have difficulty in dealing with complex data involving a number of feedback loops. I felt that very little sociological data offered opportunities for testing computer-based models, since data at several points in time are required. I was thus attracted to the panel, or time series, data being collected by the Normative Aging Study in the Veteran's Administration Outpatient Clinic in Boston. I had become aware of the study because its assistant director was a graduate student of mine at Boston University.[7] Also, he knew of my earlier work with aging and adjustment and attempted to interest me in returning to a subject to which I had once been committed.

When I started to work with the Normative Aging Study, I was anxious

[7] Charles L. Rose.

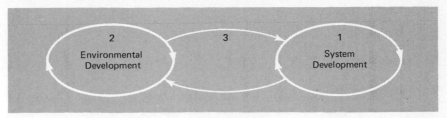

Figure 5-3.
Model 1 of Human Development: Flow Diagram.

to make use of what I called "Model 1 of Human Development,"[8] a general-purpose model that centered on a system of three positive loops, as pictured in Figure 5-3: system development, environmental development, and the interaction between the two. In the first, an increase in the system's level of development leads to information about that increase being fed back to the system, encouraging it to attain a further increase, and so on. In the second, the same kind of thing can occur for the environment. In the third, the system and the environment stimulate one another—on the basis of information feedbacks—to develop. By "development," I mean the continuing amplification of deviation in a direction that enables system and environment to widen their cognitive horizons, express more of their fundamental goals, and become more effective in solving problems. Of course, this model does not assume that development is inevitable: deviations may be amplified in any direction whatsoever, and any or all of these positive loops may go downward as well as upward.

It is important as an initial step to see how the model works metaphorically. In Section 3.2 I presented the beaker metaphor as it applies to mental health, but actually I first used that metaphor in the present general context of system and environmental development before applying it to a medical context. The reader can also trace in Section 3.2 the relationship between the beaker metaphor and system dynamics notation.

In Figure 5-4 I present Model 1 with the aid of the notation of system dynamics. The model is the same as that of Figure 3-4, except that the latter deals with more specific factors. The notation of valves and rectangles is best understood with the aid of the beaker metaphor, as presented in Figure 3-3: each valve is analogous to a faucet and each rectangle is analogous to a beaker. To follow the analogy, however, we must assume that the faucet can pull water out of the beaker as well as put it in, that is, that there is a process that can drain each beaker.

[8] This model was developed in association with Mr. Bruce Morgenstern, who was at the time a senior in the Boston University College of Engineering. Mr. Morgenstern constructed the model as his term project on the basis of the theory I presented during the semester.

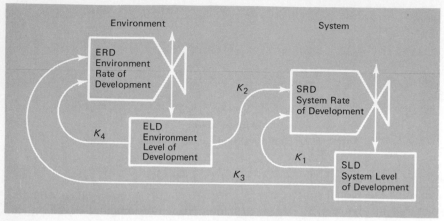

Figure 5-4.
Model 1 of Human Development: System Dynamics Notation.

The different K's refer to the various loops in Model 1, loops that are the same as those in Figure 5-3. K_1 has to do with the internal system development loop (loop 1 of Figure 5-3), K_4 with the external environmental development loop (loop 2 of Figure 5-3), and K_2 and K_3 deal with the interactive loop from environment to system and back from system to environment (loop 3 of Figure 5-3). We can use the beaker metaphor to gain insight into the workings of the model. For example, in the case of an upward positive loop for the system, we might imagine that the rising of the water in the beaker causes the faucet to open wider, that the wider faucet causes the water to rise still faster in the beaker, that this in turn produces a beaker that expands vertically, and so on. The same analogy could be used in the case of an upward positive loop for the environment. As for the interactive loop, we might imagine two sets of faucets and beakers connected in such a way that an increase in the rate of flow in any one stimulates a corresponding increasing rate of flow in the other, and vice versa.

An essential ingredient of any computer-based model is the mathematics involved. There are three kinds of factors to be dealt with in Model 1: (1) the "state variables" (*SLD* and *ELD*), (2) the "parameters" (K_1, K_2, K_3, K_4, and two additional parameters that get at factors outside of the immediate situation, A and B), and (3) the rates (*SRD* and *ERD*). The state variables are time-dependent variables, that is, they can easily change (although they do not necessarily change) from one time unit to the next. The parameters, by contrast, are factors, or variables, that generally may be treated as constants within a given problem, or may be seen as changing slowly. All of this information may be put together-within the context of the rates: this model may be defined largely by a set of two equations, one for each rate, that specify the relationships between the state variables and parameters, on the one hand, and the rates of development (*SRD* and *ERD*), on the other. These are

$$SRD = e^{At}(K_1SLD + K_2ELD). \qquad (51)$$

$$ERD = e^{Bt}(K_3SLD + K_4ELD). \qquad (52)$$

where $e = 2.714$ (the base of the natural logarithms), and where t is the amount of time over which the process continues.

The parameters A and B outside of the parentheses are exponentials and thus can alter *SRD* and *ERD* dramatically. We can begin to gain insight into the way this works by contrasting two situations: when A and B are negative numbers, and when A and B are positive numbers. In the first case, both e^{At} and e^{Bt} become fractions, since $e^{-At} = 1/e^{At}$ by definition. But these fractions get smaller and smaller as the process continues over time, since t is increasing, and they thus approach zero. And as they get close to zero, they work to cancel out the terms inside of the parentheses. Thus, *SRD* as a whole—and *ERD* as well—tends to approach zero, that is, the rates of development tend to zero. Metaphorically, the faucets tend to stop flowing and the water levels tend to reach an equilibrium. Or, if the faucets were draining the water, they tend to stop draining.

In the second case, when A and B are positive, e^{At} and e^{Bt} grow very rapidly because t is growing, and t is also multiplied by the positive A or B. The growth of e^{At} and e^{Bt} is extremely rapid because of the increasing value of their exponents. What happens to *SRD* and *ERD* depends on the total value of what is inside the parentheses. Thus, *SRD* could be zero, positive, or negative, depending on that total value. There would be a rapid acceleration or deceleration of *SRD* and *ERD* if the total value inside the parenthesis is positive or negative, respectively.

We can gain insight into the ways in which different combinations of values for A and B, as well as for the K's, are manifested in the various kinds of positive and negative loops shown in Figure 5-5. Let us note that, although Figure 5-5 deals with the parameters relating only to *SRD* (System Rate of Development), *ERD* (Environment Rate of Development) works analogously. For cell 1, *SRD* is an upward positive loop, since an exponentially increasing factor (e^{At}) is multiplied by the positive factor within the parenthesis. For cell 2, *SRD* is a downward positive loop, since the negative factor in the parenthesis converts the exponentially increasing e^{At} to an exponentially decreasing factor. In cell 3 we have an upward negative loop for *SRD*, since e^{At} is approaching zero

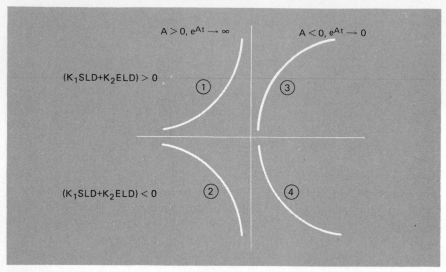

Figure 5-5.
System Rate of Development for Different Parameter Values in Model 1.

and thus continues to dampen the positive factor in the parenthesis. In cell 4 it is the negative factor in the parenthesis which is dampened by e^{At}.

Thus far, Model 1 has been outlined mathematically and metaphorically, but I have said little about it paradigmatically, theoretically, or from a measurement perspective. In brief, Model 1 fits into a pragmatist paradigm with a structure where a given system can alter its environment as well as be altered by its environment. And in line with a pragmatist perspective, Model 1 (in common with other system dynamics models) can deal with extremely rapid change as well as accumulation or development (or the reverse) because it incorporates the mathematics of the differential equations. If we conceive, for the moment, of the system as an individual and of the environment as society, then we can gain some insight into the relevance of sociological theory. Roughly, the structural functional and conflict theory traditions emphasize the importance of K_4 and K_2: changes in society and how these affect the individual. The symbolic interactionist and phenomenological traditions have more to say about the importance of K_1 and K_3: how the individual undergoes change and how he affects his society. Exchange theory may be applied to both of these phenomena.

From a measurement perspective, then, the K's can be seen (in this illustration) as factors that weight the relative importance of the individual and the society or group in producing changes in individual and social systems. More specifically, we might define the two levels of development (the state variables SLD and ELD) as positive so that the various K's can shift the expressions inside the parentheses in either a positive or negative direction, depending on whether they take on positive or negative values. We might think of all these K's as centering on any given situation. In that situation, an individual can be oriented to develop himself or the reverse (K_1 can be positive or negative); he can also be affected positively or negatively by his social system (K_2 can be positive or negative); he can also be developing or hindering his social system (K_3 can be positive or negative); and his social system can be oriented positively or negatively (K_4 can be positive or negative). Note that "positive" and "negative" in this context are used synonymously with "developmental" and "antidevelopmental," and not with reference to positive and negative loops. Whether a system moves into a positive loop or negative loop depends on the functioning of the entire model and not on only a portion of it.

Given this interpretation for the K's, what meaning can be given to A and B, and why should these be conceived of as such powerful forces? If the K's are situationally based, then we may conceive of A and B as the long-term structure of the personality and the social system, a structure that has been built up over the entire history of the organism or the group. A and B, then, encompass multitudes of situations and thus might well be expected to be more powerful than the various K's. For example, an individual with a very developmental personality (let us say that his A flashes into the positive range quite frequently) may initially do poorly in a given situation that he is ill prepared for (let us say that the various K's are extremely small positive numbers). However, over a period of time his exponential (A) will take over and produce rapid development as he learns to apply himself to the situation.

Getting back to my early situation in working with the Normative Aging Study, I came there armed with this general model, and I expected that it could solve all problems in short order. After all, I had been able to pull together a great many theoretical insights within the framework of the model, and that process had in turn yielded further insights. I might say, then, that Model 1 represented for me an important positive loop in my attempt to go beyond the limitations of the earlier aging and adjustment study as well as the more recent medical student study and the still more recent community development study. But once again I was due for a surprise that resulted in a plateau, or negative loop: I had not taken into account the effort that would be required to measure the state variables and the parameters. A model is theoretical, and in order to apply it to any given situation we must develop the kinds of measurements for that situation that provide indices for the model's parameters. In addition to this measurement requirement, I had yet to apply the model more specifically to the context of the aging process. As a result of these two lacks—measurement and specific theory—I spent several months wondering why things weren't working beautifully before realizing what was happening and redefining my research problem accordingly.

The result of this redefinition was the adaptation of Model 1 to the aging process that is illustrated in Figure 3-4 and reproduced with the K's added as Figure 5-6. The upper part of Figure 5-6 presents a flow diagram of the four loops involved, whereas the lower part presents the same relationships in system dynamics notation.

To illustrate the dynamic behavior of Model 1 as applied to the mental health area, let us contrast the situations of two individuals in their late sixties, O and M, where O identifies himself as old and M identifies himself as middle-aged. On the basis of the aging study described in Section 2.1—where M would tend to be better adjusted than O—we might see these differences in age identification also as differences in the basic mental health of the two, differences intimately associated with their personality structures. The result would be (1) differences in Level of Mental Health, and (2) differences in the parameter A between the two, with individual M tending to have a higher Level of Mental Health and a more positive A than individual O. Now suppose each individual finds himself in a roughly equivalent situation, say, an environment where others expect him to "act his age" and accept limited opportunities and a lowered status.

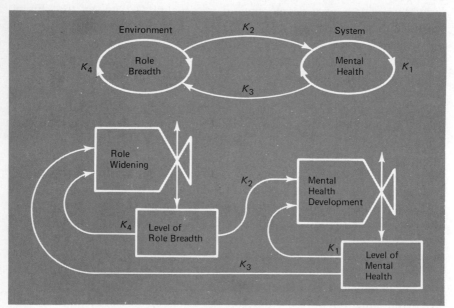

Figure 5-6.
Model 1 Applied to Role Breadth and Mental Health.

In such a situation, the Level of Role Breadth for each individual is low, and let us say that K_2 is a negative number.

In the same kind of situation, the dynamic behavior of these two individuals will be quite different. Individual O would tend to have the same limiting orientation to himself possessed by those who expect him to act his age, that is, his K_1 would also tend to be negative. The result for O would tend to be a downward negative loop with reference to his development in the situation: he would level off asymptotically at the point where he is conforming to the low expectations he and others have for his behavior. Not so for individual M: his positive K_1 would battle the negative K_2 within the parenthesis, and if his K_1 is sufficiently high relative to the negative K_2, the parenthesis would be positive. Now, if his A is only very slightly negative, then he would exhibit an upward negative loop at a high level of development. If his A is positive, then he would exhibit an upward positive loop for as long as A remained positive (assuming that the expression within the parenthesis remained positive).

One function of a model is to open up more complex and dynamic ways of thinking, and this is what I attempted to do in the context of the Normative Aging Study. In addition to this modeling activity, I proceeded to develop a questionnaire, which was partially illustrated in the last part of Section 2.4 and will be illustrated further in Chapter 9, "Interviews, Questionnaires, and Surveys." The questionnaire centers on the measurement of all the parameters called for by this model of mental health development, including A and B. As a result of this specific modeling of health development and of my questionnaire construction work, I was once again able to move from a negative loop to an upward positive loop in that study. I had redefined my research problem to focus on these new activities, just as I will have to redefine it over and over again so long as this research continues.

5.6 Summary

This completes my four case studies, illustrating the process of defining a research problem and, hopefully, providing insight into ways of continuing to redefine research problems so as to avoid negative loop plateaus and achieve upward positive loops in the direction of ever greater research effectiveness. This process is summarized in Table 5-2. Yet all of this constitutes only a beginning in an attempt to provide such insight, for the achievement of increasingly effective research is a process that is largely unknown. Researchers tend to focus on one project at a time, failing to learn about the research process itself based on sequences of research projects. We might put Model 1 to work here to gain additional insight.

Table 5-2
Stages in the Definition of Research Problems

	Aging & Adjustment	Occupational Choice	Community Development	Model of Aging
Stage 1	Yes-no demonstration of the existence of relationships between role changes and adjustment	Attempt to predict medical preferences using mechanistic theory	Verbal explanation of the complex forces producing community development	Attempt to use "Model 1" to deal with the aging process
Stage 2	Exploration of the degree of relationship between age identification and adjustment	Attempt to predict retirement of naval officers with mechanistic theory	Using mathematical tools to choose highway path which minimizes expected goal deprivation	Development of specific theory and measurements to adapt "Model 1" to the aging process
Stage 3	Same goal as stage 2 with additional data and the use of sophisticated correlational tools	Present interest in predicting changes in occupational goals, expectations, choices	A future problem: using these mathematical tools to deal with the stage 1 problem of community development	Changes in theory and measurement on basis of analysis of questionnaire results

Suppose that the researcher's *A*—and society's *B*—is negative; then no matter what the researcher did, assuming that no change occurred in *A* or *B,* he could not achieve an upward positive loop.

I believe that it is possible to establish an upward positive loop for social science provided that we include this concern in our definition of research problems. Once we understand the existence of a problem, we have taken the most important step toward dealing with it, and such a reflexive approach can be incorporated within any research endeavor. It is our ability to define a problem, and to continue to redefine it, that lies at the heart of the research process and moves it forward. But a heart requires other organs and limbs in order to function effectively, as we shall see in the remaining chapters. The scientific method is a feedback loop that includes the context of verification as well as the context of discovery.

Exercises

1. Write up your own case study of your efforts to solve some problem—not necessarily a research problem—paying special attention to your successive redefinitions of the problem. Can you gain any insight into the process of staying on an upward positive loop of increasing effectiveness in problem solving from your case study?

2. Develop a chart of your case study corresponding to Figure 5-1, identifying various positive and negative loops that might be involved. Use the chart to sensitize yourself to crucial phases of your case study, attempting to increase your insight by adding to the case study.

3. The case studies of occupational choice and community development both illustrate a synthetic approach to measurement and both employ mathematics to integrate a number of measures so as to predict people's choices. Apply this approach to a problem of your own selection, constructing the various measurements and the technique for combining them.

4. Apply Model 1 to some research study you are familiar with: (1) locate the system and the environment, (2) define *SLD* and *ELD* so that each represents a continuum, and (3) define all the parameters in relation to aspects of the situation being studied. Do some analysis of the dynamic behavior that would result if the model is correct. Does this give you any further insight into the situation investigated?

Annotated References

HAMMOND, PHILLIP E. (ed.) *Sociologists at Work.* New York: Basic Books, Inc., Publishers, 1964. This book presents detailed discussions of the context of twelve research projects, including why the research was undertaken, what happened when plans didn't work, how researchers capitalized on lucky accidents, how theory was adapted to fit a given situation, and how procedures were improvised.

MEADOWS, DONELLA H., et al. *The Limits to Growth.* New York: Universe Books, 1972. This is the first popular book-length illustration of the system dynamics approach to problem definition and theory construction. It is a report on the Project on the Predicament of Mankind, which attempts to take into account such world-wide problems as poverty, degradation of the environment, uncontrolled urban spread, insecurity of employment, alienation of youth, and inflation.

THOMPSON, WILLIAM IRWIN. *At the Edge of History: Speculations on the Transformation of Culture.* New York: Harper and Row, Publishers, Colophon Books, 1972. If a researcher's definition of a problem is linked to his world view, and if that in turn is linked to the world view prevailing in his society, then we must examine the latter in order to understand what goes into the way research problems are defined. Thompson gives us a personal account of his attempts to understand where we are going and where we might go, involving his travels from L.A. to Big Sur to M.I.T. to Toronto.

part III
Measurement and Data Construction

The scientific method is a feedback process where ideas within the context of discovery are subjected to testing within the context of verification. It is tempting for all of us to assume that we already have the answers for existing questions or problems, yet by so doing we fail to take into consideration the limitations of our own experience. Freud and Marx, among many others, have contributed to the idea that our conscious views of the way things are themselves products of internal and external forces that we barely understand. If this be so, then it becomes important to find ways of dealing with these distortions, ways that subject ideas to testing against a widening range of experience. As we move from Part Two to Part Three, we carry the idea of problem definition into this arena of human experience.

From this perspective, the researcher is not a passive observer, an individual who simply collects data from his environment: whether he is aware of it or not, he actively constructs the data he observes. He comes to the research process with assumptions and theoretical perspectives, with a complex system of goals and beliefs, and there is no way in which he can eliminate the powerful forces that he himself brings to the research process. This active role is as old as the scientific process itself; what is new is a rapid growth in our awareness of the nature of this role. As a result, we are now in a position to greatly improve the effectiveness of scientific research. We can focus the spotlight of investigation on both *the forces introduced by the investigator and the external forces he is attempting to understand.*

In Part Three we center on a variety of processes of data construction, conceiving them in this interactive way. In this light, experimental and simulation procedures are not the only techniques for collecting data in which the researcher introduces changes into the research situation. This also occurs in the case of observation, surveys, and the analysis of available data. No procedure for data collection can escape the impact of the investigator. It follows, then, that the various investigative techniques have a great deal in common. In Part Three a dominant theme is the unity of the various procedures, which do vary in the emphasis they give to the research process. Each one can add to our understanding of the fantastic complexities involved in human behavior.

chapter 6

Strategies for Measurement and Scaling

In Figure 3-1 I presented a formist image of scientific theory, centering on an attempt to attain correspondences between points in the "plane of truth," hovering overhead, with points in the "plane of observation," representing our research experiences. This is also the familiar Platonic distinction between the Idea and our shadow experiences and, indeed, results from a very long tradition within Western civilization that separates mind from body, or the inner world from the external one. Such a perspective has proved to be extremely valuable within the history of social research. It has helped to motivate generations of social scientists to challenge taken-for-granted assumptions about the nature of reality, and to put forward alternative views. The concept of a scientific truth that could challenge religious or political or common sense dogmas has helped to create a powerful force for the expansion of human knowledge.

But this concept is also a two-edged sword: it can motivate the development of new knowledge, but it can also stultify continuing development in this direction to the degree that we believe we have arrived at truth. For example, suppose that we take the formist view of scientific theory—as presented in Figure 3-1—as truth. Then a number of implications follow: (1) There is a static view of phenomena, that is, concepts just lie there in their plane of truth, corresponding to the formist view that A is A. (2) Associated with this static view is a lack of direction beyond truth, with truth becoming a self-justifying end in itself rather than an orientation providing a direction for ever greater understanding. (3) There is a spatial narrowness implied: we are encouraged to exclude from consideration all other phenomena outside the plane of observation. (4) The over-all assumption is that the scientist is merely a passive observer of reality and not a changer of reality by his own actions.

In Figure 6-1 below I present a pragmatist image of scientific theory. This is a combination of the beaker metaphor presented in Figure 3-3 with

135

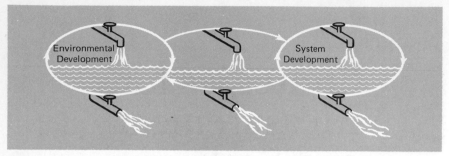

Figure 6-1.
Pragmatist Image of Scientific Theory.

the flow diagram of Model 1 of Human Development from Figure 5-3. The result is that we have in the same figure not only the cybernetic, or interactive, structure of phenomena but also the dynamic behavior, or resultants, that derive from that structure in the form of the flows and accumulations or losses of water. What happens to these flows over time may be described by such concepts as negative loop and positive loop, as illustrated in Figure 3-5, 3-6, 3-7, and 3-8. Let us view the level of the water within the various loops as "the state of nature," or "reality," or "truth."

Now that we have an alternative to the formist view of scientific theory and measurement, we are able to examine its implications, which contrast with those stemming from the formist view: (1) There is a dynamic view of phenomena, with expansion and/or contraction occurring everywhere, and with a potential for exponential growth or decay. (2) As for direction, since truth (the level of water in the various loops and the rates of flow) is ever-changing, then more knowledge about the nature of phenomena is always required, and interest turns to the context of discovery as well as to the context of verification. (3) Spatial breadth is attained because all phenomena are seen as intimately interrelated: the rate of flow and level of water in any one part of the system-environment affect rates and levels in other parts. (4) Since all phenomena—including the investigator himself—are seen as located within the system or the environment, the investigator can no longer see himself as a *deus ex machina* but will have to see himself as actively involved in the research context. In this chapter we shall discuss some of the implications of this pragmatist image for measurement, scaling, and data construction. We shall discover that we cannot afford to narrow our view as we become involved in the details of our subject. Indeed, our best tools for penetrating deeply into those details are our most comprehensive orientations, such as those discussed in this brief introduction to the chapter.

6.1 Measurement

All of us are continually engaged in the measurement process all the time, in line with the image of human interaction as a feedback process that was presented in Figure 1-2. We covertly review the results of our communication with others or, more generally, of our interaction with the environment. Within that review we apply informal measurement processes to assess various aspects of what has taken place, such as the level of effectiveness of our own behavior, the attitudes of others, and changes in the situation. These informal and largely covert procedures are analogous to the more explicit procedures of the scientist, as portrayed in Figure 1-1. In both cases, measurement is an essential component of the feedback process in that it enables the individual or the scientist to steer the course he has charted, or to chart a more sensible course than the one he initially chose. Measurement is a process by which the individual obtains information, and as such it is fundamental not only to the cybernetic process in science and everyday life but also to life itself. By acquiring information, the organism moves beyond the narrowness of its previous experience and learns to adapt more effectively to its environment as well as to change that environment to suit its own needs.

Measurement Validity

We are here concerned not with whether hypotheses or propositions are valid or true but rather with the validity of the measurement of a given concept. Although validity is a synonym for truth, let us use it in the context of the pragmatist image (Figure 6-1) as distinct from the formist image (Figure 3-1). By so doing, however, we need not abandon the insights stemming from the latter. Let us introduce them via a dichotomy between the actual level of water within a given loop (or beaker) and the perceived or measured level of water, corresponding to the distinction between the plane of truth and the plane of observation, as illustrated in Figure 6-2. Let us see this beaker as a detailed view of the system development beaker of Figure 6-1, with the scientist seen as the system. Suppose, for example, that the scientist is not aware of his formist perspective or the ways in which it limits his research effectiveness. Thus, his actual level of understanding of the research situation is far less than his perceived level, as in Figure 6-2. Then he will not question in any fundamental way his ability to define a research problem—that is, his force for development will be limited—resulting in a feeble rate of development and perhaps even an over-all decay. However, if the information feedback he obtains leads him to perceive his actual level correctly, then the gap between

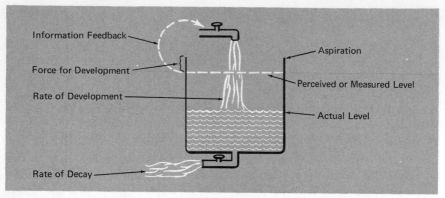

Figure 6-2.
Actual Versus Perceived Levels in the Beaker Metaphor.

aspiration and achievement will be great, and so will the rate of development. This rate of development can continue, or even increase, in an upward positive loop provided that the researcher learns to continually raise his aspiration relative to his perceived achievements (the height of his beaker relative to the height of his water).

Using this metaphor, the problem of measurement validity becomes that of obtaining correct information about a given level. But this problem becomes quite difficult as we look to see how the scientist proceeds in assessing the rates of flow and level of water within the environment. Just as there is a gap between the scientist's perception and the actuality of his own performance, so also is there the same kind of gap for the scientist's measurement of the environment. Spatially, the three beakers of Figure 6-1 are interconnected, and anything that we observe is the combined product of all of them. Temporally, the level generally is changing from moment to moment, and a measurement that is valid for one moment may not be valid for the next. As for the impact of the investigator, his own ability to assess accurately the limitations of his research tools—as well as other factors in the situation under investigation—will profoundly affect his ability to define a research problem effectively as well as the effectiveness of the research *in toto*.

We are now in a position to discuss three validation procedures: face validation, criterion validation, and construct validation. In each case we are concerned with obtaining valid measurement, that is, with achieving a correspondence between our perception or measurement and the actual phenomenon, as in Figure 6-2. *Face validation* procedures involve, simply enough, a brief evaluation of how well, "on the face of it," such a correspondence appears to have been achieved. Thus, for example, measurement based on projective techniques or indirect procedures (see the last part of Section 9.2) have less face validity than more direct techniques.

This approach frequently is taken as a substitute for criterion validation and construct validation, and it appears—in general—to have little to recommend it other than that the time saved here may be put to good use in other aspects of the research process. One problem is that appearances are often deceptive, especially when the researcher may be unaware of the possibility of a large gap between his perceptions and the actual situation. In a situation where an individual may not be able to admit to himself or another his true situation, projective or indirect tests may be more accurate than measures with high face validity, provided that the investigator himself is sensitive to what is going on. Another problem with face validation is similar to that with criterion validation: there is a narrow spatial focus on the achievement of a one-to-one correspondence between a measurement and one's idea as to a valid measurement, as distinct from a broader perspective that takes into account a host of relationships such as those portrayed in Figure 6-1. In addition, there is no sense of the development of an upward positive loop from measurement—as portrayed in Figure 4-2—where there is continuing development of both a measurement's integrative capabilities and its analytic incisiveness.

Criterion validation procedures stem quite directly from the formist perspective: We begin by selecting as our criterion—against which we shall test the new measure or index we are concerned with—an old or previously established measurement, with this criterion being seen as residing in the plane of truth. We then find the degree of association (see Chapter 13 for a discussion of measures of association) between the criterion and the new measurement, and this constitutes our assessment of criterion validity. For example, in studying the aging process we may select an old established measure of adjustment as our criterion. Then, if individuals receive very much the same kinds of scores on the criterion as they do on a new measure of adjustment that we are attempting to assess—e.g., if the r (a measure of association) between the two is as high as .80—we conclude that the new measure has a high degree of criterion validity.

The problems here are similar to those for face validation, although criterion validation procedures are widely used and well accepted. With respect to spatial narrowness, there is the same formist assumption that a measurement can be isolated from its context within the plane of observation, and that a concept can be isolated from this theoretical context within the plane of truth. Yet it is even more presumptuous to take a measurement developed in one context and designate it as a criterion for a measurement in another context. As for the temporal limitations of criterion validation procedures, there is a conservative bias in the direction of seeing the criterion as excellent, as distinct from pushing to go far beyond the limitations of the criterion.

Construct validation procedures[1] stem from the pragmatist perspective. Spatially, the focus is no longer on a one-to-one correspondence between a criterion and a new measurement but rather is on the complex theoretical relationships within which the concept being measured is enmeshed, and also on the complex situation within which the measurement is being obtained. A measurement of a given concept has construct validity to the degree that—when it is employed in research—it is able to yield an entire set of relationships that makes good theoretical sense to the researcher. A measurement that yielded only a few of the theoretical relationships that other research indicated the investigator had a right to expect would have less construct validity than a measurement that yielded a great many such relationships.

To illustrate, suppose that once again we are attempting to measure the adjustment of older individuals. Theoretically, we might expect adjustment to be related to a host of factors such as how old a person feels, employment status, and marital status (Section 2.1). At a higher level of abstraction, we might see the degree of role breadth of a great many kinds of roles as related to various aspects of mental and physical health, including adjustment (Section 5.5). Then we can test for the construct validity of any given measure of adjustment by assessing the number of expected theoretical relationships that measure yields when it is applied to a set of individuals. Such an assessment generally is presented by means of a discussion of how well or poorly the new measure works theoretically, and not by putting forward any quantitative index.

Construct validation procedures are sufficiently broad to be able to incorporate elements of both criterion validation and face validation. In the former case, we might view the relationship between the criterion and the new measurement as one among the many relationships forming a network with this new measurement. Whether or not a relationship between the new measurement and the criterion is established will constitute only partial evidence with respect to the validity of the new measurement. Furthermore, in this way we might be able to learn a great deal more about the nature of the criterion: we will see it within a theoretical context. Perhaps we will learn, on the basis of such procedures, directions for improving the criterion—now seen as only one among many factors—as well as paths for improving our ability to measure the other factors.

As for face validation, our focus here is on the degree of correspondence between the researcher's idea of a valid measurement and the measurement in question. This correspondence or lack of it cannot be isolated from the

[1] For a detailed rationale for construct validation procedures that links them to philosophical considerations, see Lee J. Cronbach and Paul E. Meehl, "Construct Validity in Psychological Tests," *Psychological Bulletin,* **52** (1955), pp. 281–302.

milieu in which it occurs, according to the pragmatist perspective; many factors within the personality of the researcher and within the measurement situation are involved. Construct validation procedures can incorporate these sets of factors along with the others under consideration. Furthermore, these additional considerations can help the validation process by opening up new questions and providing new answers. In addition, the researcher can learn from such procedures to do a more intelligent job the next time he attempts to assess face validity.

Reliability and Precision

If the validity of a measurement, in relation to Figure 6-2, is an assessment of the gap between the perceived or measured level of water in the beaker and the actual level, then the reliability of a measurement is an assessment of changes in the perceived or measured level of water. The two fundamental approaches to measuring reliability have to do with the stability of the measurement of the water level at successive points in time and the equivalence of measurements taken by different observers or the same observer using slight variations of the measurement at roughly the same time.[2] A measurement is reliable, then, to the degree that it does not vary over time (stability) and to the degree that the same basic measurement procedure employed in different contexts at the same time yields the same result (equivalence).

The key problem associated with reliability comes from forgetting its relation to validity. Researchers are interested in learning where the water level is, and anything that helps them in this endeavor is valuable. If the investigator becomes fascinated by the achievement of a high degree of reliability, then all that he may be accomplishing is the acquisition of greater confidence in his ability to come up with a grossly invalid measurement every single time without fail. A broken spring scale may be perfectly reliable and invalid. Reliability is not only useless without validity: it is downright misleading. To correct this kind of narrowness, we might think of a feedback loop between validity and reliability, as indicated in Figure 6-3. Here, we cannot omit thinking of reliability without also thinking of validity. And once we think of validity, we must think of the entire theoretical matrix within which the concept being measured is located.

Using this image of the measurement process, which stems from the pragmatist view, let us now contrast its implications for reliability with those stemming from the formist image of a plane of truth and a plane of observation. Temporally, the formist view pushes us toward seeing a high reliability coefficient, as measured by some measure of degree of asso-

---

[2] This distinction between stability and equivalence is developed by L. J. Cronbach in "Coefficient Alpha and the Internal Structure of Tests," *Psychometrika,* **16** (1951), pp. 297–339.

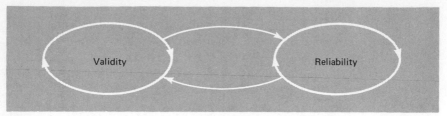

Figure 6-3.
The Validity and Reliability Feedback Loop.

ciation, as a kind of end point to the measurement process: one is able to pinpoint one's measurement within the plane of observation. For the pragmatist, however, one may actually have focused on a point very far from the one that actually does reflect the concept under investigation. In order to go further, one must explore the meaning of attaining that reliable measurement. As a result of such explorations, the investigator might achieve a clearer understanding of his concept and of the validity of the measurement he is using. That in turn could give him the ability to produce a measurement that has more validity. Now he can focus once again on the reliability of that measurement, and this process can continue in an upward positive loop ad infinitum.

Spatially, the formist perspective is exceedingly narrow, with a focus on only one spot on the plane of observation. But when reliability comes to be seen as linked to validity in an upward positive loop, then the investigator must take into account the entire plane of observation as well as the entire plane of truth; or, in the metaphor of the pragmatist view, he must take into account the perceived and actual levels of water in the loops of Figure 6-1. This is so because validity deals with the relationship between these two planes (or between the perceived and actual water levels), and also because construct validity—which is the most comprehensive way of dealing with the various approaches to validation—comes to be involved. It will be recalled that construct validity takes into account not merely a single isolated proposition but the entire theoretical matrix within which a given concept is enmeshed.

In the scale of relative importance, precision is to reliability as reliability is to validity. The precision of a measurement device refers to the smallest interval that it is able to detect. It is very easy for precision to become an end in itself, thereby losing sight of both reliability and validity. What good is an assessment of water level to the centimeter if that assessment varies greatly from one instant to the next and from one observer to the next, and if that assessment is completely invalid? Yet when we take into account both reliability and validity, as in Figure 6-4, then precision becomes an exceedingly important tool within the research process. We have

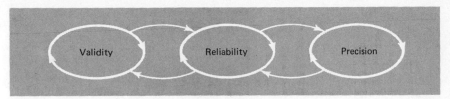

Figure 6-4.
The Validity, Reliability, and Precision Feedback Loop.

only to look to the role of precision in the development of the physical sciences to gain evidence of its potential.

6.2   Scales of Measurement

Scaling procedures are techniques designed to achieve precise measurement. As such, they have the potential for helping the investigator to continue to improve his research effectiveness by linking improvements in precision with improvements in reliability and validity, as portrayed in Figure 6-4. What is commonly meant by more precision is that scales or measurements take on more and more of the mathematical properties of numbers. The progression from nominal scales to ordinal, interval, and ratio scales—as illustrated in Figure 3-2.—takes measurement from the formist properties of ordinary language (identity, excluded middle, noncontradiction) to such mathematical, or mechanistic, properties as meaningful multiplication and division. In Section 6.2 we shall begin with a discussion of the functions of scaling procedures and conclude with examining the properties of nominal, ordinal, interval, and ratio scales. Only so much can be meaningfully said about scaling outside of the context of specific approaches to data collection. Consequently, detailed discussions of particular scaling techniques as well as treatment of other issues relating to scaling are reserved for the various chapters on data collection within Part Three. In particular, Chapter 9—"Interviews, Questionnaires, and Surveys—will present several scaling techniques, since most such procedures have been developed within a survey context.

Functions of Scaling Procedures

Before getting deeply into the nature of various kinds of scales, we must understand something of the scientific motivation behind being concerned with them at all. The sociologist walks a tightrope between the humanities and the physical sciences. To one side he is pulled by a humanistic tradition as well as sociological theory, both of which alert him to the importance of verbal descriptions of human behavior. To the other side there is a physical science tradition that has leaned heavily on the language of mathematics. How can he utilize this latter language, which has proved to be so successful in enabling man to shape his physical environment, in his efforts to probe the complexities of human behavior?

One direction that sociologists and other social scientists have taken is to state social science theory in the language of mathematics. I have illustrated this with the study of the occupational choices of medical students in Section 2.2. Such a mathematical approach goes beyond the use of statistical tests (to be described in Chapter 12). Those tests primarily function in a formist way, as illustrated by the aging and adjustment study of Section 2.1. But how, then, does the social scientist proceed in this mathematical way? In order to apply mathematical procedures, one must work with elements to which the rules of mathematics can be applied. The mathematician works with numbers, and the physicist works with variables like force and distance to which numbers can readily be applied. But how are we to multiply or divide occupation, religion, ethnic group, or voting preference? How are we to take advantage of the power of mathematics if the entities with which we deal are simply verbal categories and do not appear to have numerical properties?

One approach the social scientist can take is to make use of procedures that impart to phenomena the properties of numbers. This is an active role for him, departing from a view of the social scientist as a passive observer of the phenomena around him. By so doing, however, does he not sacrifice an objective approach? Does he not thereby shape the data so as to achieve the results he desires? If we adopt a pragmatist perspective, then we will understand that the social scientist can no more choose to avoid affecting the research process than an observer can choose to see a given phenomenon without hitting it with photons of light. The choice, then, is not between influencing and not influencing the phenomena under investigation, but among the various ways of influencing those phenomena. For example, we can ask individuals—as was done in the formist study of aging and adjustment—whether they identified themselves as middle-aged or old, resulting in a nominal scale. Or we can ask them how old they feel in years, pushing them to think in ratio terms. Either way we ask the question, we are influencing the respondent.

By choosing to obtain measurements with, say, ratio as distinct from nominal scale properties, we lay the basis for bringing to bear on the research process the powerful mathematical tools developed over hundreds of years. The researcher himself learns to see phenomena with mechanistic as distinct from formist eyes. One of the achievements that can result is an ability to achieve much closer relationships than are generally attained with nominal scales, as illustrated by the occupational choice study. This is no mean achievement. It moves the researcher from being able to demonstrate relatively minute relationships among variables to demonstrating a high degree of relationship between a given pair of variables. The problems associated with the former state of affairs are discussed by Gouldner as follows:

> There is a fairly widespread tendency among sociologists to rest content with a demonstration that some sociological variable "makes a difference." If a variable can be shown to control even the smallest proportion of the variance in a problematic pattern, it is all too readily regarded as a memorable contribution to sociology and all too ceremoniously ushered into its theoretical hall of fame. . . . Unless sustained interest is manifested in the *degree* of variance which a variable controls, and, unless, further, we can identify sociological variables that certifiably control substantial proportions of the variance of the specified patterns of human behavior, sociology will remain scientifically immature and practically ineffectual.[3]

Yet despite the achievements of mechanism beyond formism, this world view also has its limitations, as we have seen in our previous discussions. In the occupational choice study (Section 2.2), for example, although it was possible to develop a very close relationship between resultant goal commitment and preference for a field of medicine, no attempt was made to explore the conditions that produce changes in goals and changes in expectations about the various medical fields. The mechanistic world view projects an image of a closed universe, a clock-world where fundamental change does not take place. In addition, there is a degree of spatial narrowness associated with this type of study: it tends to ignore the rich complexity that verbal sociological theory within the organicist tradition alerts us to. Also, it tends to ignore the role of the investigator in this whole process, which distinguishes it from the pragmatist perspective.

Nominal, Ordinal, Interval, and Ratio Scales

In our discussion of formism in Section 2.1 and later in Section 3.1, formist assumptions involved in language—and also in nominal scales—were presented. These are (1) the principle of identity, which asserts that if a proposition is true, it is true (or A is A); (2) the principle of contradiction, asserting that no proposition can be both true and false (a thing cannot be both A and not-A); and (3) the principle of the excluded middle, stating that any proposition must be either true or false (a thing must be either A or not-A). *Nominal scales,* by incorporating these assumptions, have both the strengths and weaknesses of ordinary language. *Gemeinschaft* and *gesellschaft,* mechanical solidarity and organic solidarity, male and female, Italian, Japanese, and Irish, are some examples of nominal scales.

[3] Alvin W. Gouldner, "Reciprocity and Autonomy in Functional Theory," in Llewellyn Gross (ed.), *Symposium on Sociological Theory* (New York: Harper, 1959), pp. 247–48.

Ordinal scales are based on the same principles of identity, contradiction, and excluded middle that are the foundation for nominal scales. These principles are carried forward to encompass the idea of linear, or simple, order, which involves a rank-ordering phenomena. An ordinal scale with respect to the height of individuals, for example, would involve their lining up in such a way that their height increases from the front to the back of the line. Each individual would either have a greater height or a lesser height than every other individual (in the case of ties, we refer to the scale as being "partially ordered" rather than "simply ordered" or "linearly ordered"). The axioms on which a simply ordered scale is based, given that C is any collection whose elements are called points (denoted by small letters), and given that "precedes" (denoted by $<$) is a relation existing between all points, are

1. If x and y are distinct points of C, then $x < y$ or $y < x$.
2. If $x < y$, then x and y are distinct.
3. If $x < y$ and $y < z$, then $x < z$.[4]

I might illustrate these axioms for simple order by defining the points as basketball teams and C as a basketball league, with precedes ($<$) defined as "invariably loses to." From axiom 1, for any two teams, one must invariably lose to the other. From axiom 2, if a team invariably loses to another team, then the two are separate (and not the same) teams. From axiom 3, if team x invariably loses to team y, and if team y invariably loses to team z, then team x invariably loses to team z. In attempting to apply these axioms to any actual basketball league, we would find it extremely difficult to satisfy axioms 1 and 3, with axiom 2 being trivial and easily satisfied. All is not lost, however, if we change our definition of precedes from "invariably loses to" to "loses more than half of the time to." In this way, it becomes much easier to find a simply ordered collection of basketball teams. Under what conditions should we alter such definitions, and what is accomplished by all this? We should not lose sight of our over-all purpose of gaining deeper understanding of phenomena. The import of producing, or failing to produce, a simply ordered scale must be measured against its contribution to this.

For an *interval scale* we have a simply ordered scale and, in addition, the distance from one element to the next is the same as the distance from that next element to the following one. For example, individuals ordered in terms of height would constitute an interval scale if the tops of their heads would form a straight line, indicating a uniform change in height

[4] Raymond L. Wilder, *Introduction to the Foundations of Mathematics* (New York: Wiley, 1952), pp. 45–46.

of attaining social status. The dominant theme of the conflict subculture is the acquisition of "reputation" through the successful use of violence and coercion. Individuals and gangs gain honor and respect by showing that they are tough and fearless. The final subculture, the "retreatist" pattern, is composed of adolescents who have limited access not only to criminal opportunities but to the conflict pattern. Retreatism is the subculture of drug-using "cats," for example, who withdraw from and repudiate conventional success-goals and the means for attaining them. The retreatist withdraws from conventional society and pursues a "kick" (drugs, music, sexual experiences). The kick is usually maintained through a lucrative "hustle," but the hustle is secondary to the kick. One hustles to maintain one's kick and a "cool" life style (nice clothes, chicks), not to attain economic success per se. Unlike the conflict pattern, the cat avoids violence and prides himself in his ability to survive by outwitting or conning others (Cloward and Ohlin, 1960:20–27).

Given the diversity of these works, it is difficult to summarize and evaluate subcultural theories of delinquency (for a critique and review of these theories see Bordua, 1961). Two features shared by subcultural theories is that delinquency is a group or subcultural phenomenon rather than an individual phenomenon, and is more common in the lower class. Such theories are therefore inadequate for explaining middle-class delinquency or delinquency that does not occur within a group context. Of the theories Cloward and Ohlin's "delinquent opportunities" is probably the most complete, recognizing internal differences among lower-class delinquent subcultures. There is certainly a great difference between the delinquent who is apprenticing in the world of professional crime, the tough who derives "rep" from the use of violence, and the "cool cat" who grooves on drugs. All three engage in delinquent activities but for vastly different reasons and with different consequences. Cohen's theory of delinquent subcultures and Miller's focal concerns are inadequate for understanding this complexity. Cloward and Ohlin also consider nondelinquent patterns. They present a typology that distinguishes between delinquents and lower-class youth who seek membership in the middle class. The lower-class youth who aspires to be upwardly mobile desires to change his membership group and his entire life style; the delinquent strives for economic success while retaining his basic identification with the lower-class value system. Finally, Cloward and Ohlin attempt to synthesize anomie theory and differential association by expanding and devising Merton's typology so that it incorporates the cultural transmission that occurs within delinquent subcultures.

A major weakness of subcultural theories is that they explain only a fraction of delinquent activities. It has been estimated that Cloward and Ohlin's delinquent subcultures may account for less than 10 percent of the cases appearing before the juvenile court (Toby, 1961:284). If one adds unreported delinquency, the figure is probably lower. Critics argue that subcultural theorists have overestimated the extent to which delinquent gangs are well-integrated subcultures or cohesive groups. Yablonsky (1959) maintains that delinquent gangs are near-groups with a loose and amorphous organization that is intermediate in structure between a well-organized collective and an anonymous mob. Other sociologists question the assumption that the values of the delinquent subculture somehow reject or are in conflict with those of the larger society. David Matza and Gresham Sykes (1961) argue that many so-called deviant or delinquent values, such as Miller's focal concerns, are expressions of subterranean, or unspoken, values in the larger society. Subterranean values are in conflict with other dominant values, but they are recognized and accepted by many in the society. The values of the delinquent subculture are consistent with the values of the "leisure class" idealized by society. The delinquent's disdain for work, pursuit of kicks or thrills, desire for the "big score" by outwitting or conning others, and the quest to demonstrate masculinity through toughness are deeply rooted in the American value system. Although delinquents have internalized the norms and values of the society, they are able to engage in delinquent acts by employing a series of mechanisms that neutralize the effectiveness of these controls (Sykes and Matza, 1957). These techniques of neutralization justify the delinquent's actions, enabling him, in a sense, "to have his cake and eat it too." The delinquent can violate the law without feeling deviant or rejecting larger societal values by employing one or more of the following techniques of neutralization:

1. *The denial of responsibility.* The delinquent is a victim of forces beyond his control.
2. *The denial of injury.* No one is really hurt by delinquent acts.
3. *The denial of the victim.* The victim deserves what he gets.
4. *The condemnation of the condemners.* Those who condemn delinquents are crooked and hypocritical.
5. *The appeal to higher loyalties.* Under certain circumstances larger societal norms may be violated in favor of others that are more pressing.

The new labeling perspective challenges conventional conceptions of delinquency. According to this perspective, "delinquency" is a label that is successfully applied by the dominant society to certain adolescents (for a more general discussion of labeling see the Introduction to Part Two). Labeling theory focuses on the labeling process rather than on the behavior of delinquents. Previously, sociological theories had asked: Why do certain adolescents violate the law while others remain law abiding? Labeling theory asks: If all adolescents engage in actions for which they could be adjudicated as delinquent, why are some labeled "delinquent" while others are not?

While the labeling perspective has been applied to a variety of deviant acts, it seems especially relevant for the study of delinquency. Traditionally, the police and courts were viewed as "passive responders to the active behavior or misbehavior of juveniles" (Wheeler and Cottrell, 1966:22).

Today it is clear that official agencies play a major role in defining delinquency. The criteria for defining delinquency are so broad that much discretion must be employed in the disposition of cases (Wheeler and Cottrell,
1966:22–27). The concept of secondary deviation is especially applicable
to delinquency. There is a great difference between committing a delinquent *act*, primary deviation, and identifying with a delinquent *career*,
secondary deviation (Wheeler and Cottrell, 1966:22–27). Most juveniles
who engage in delinquent acts do not see themselves as delinquent. The
delinquent role is adopted through an interactional process involving the
society and the adolescent. After being defined as deviant or delinquent
by the schools, police, and the courts, the adolescent applies the label to
himself. Labeling theory has some interesting implications for the treatment
of juvenile offenders. One of these is that in cases in which delinquent acts
do not present a clear threat to society, more harm than good may come
from official reaction (Wheeler and Cottrell, 1966:22–27). No action at
all may be better than official intervention and the ensuing labeling of
misbehavior as "delinquency."

Labeling is potentially a very promising perspective, but it leaves some
important questions unanswered. Is it a "theory," or explanation, of deviant
behavior or simply a conceptual framework? If it is intended as an explanation, it does not answer three basic questions: "(1) Why does the incidence
of a particular act vary from one population to the next? (2) Why do some
persons commit the act while others do not? (3) Why is the act in question
considered deviant and/or criminal in some societies but not in others?"
(Gibbs, 1966:12.) These are important questions that labeling theory has
yet to answer adequately. It should be noted, however, that some of the
criticisms of labeling are based on misconceptions of the theory. The
labeling perspective does *not* attempt to explain why "some individuals
engage in deviant acts while others do not" because such a question is
inconsistent with its most basic assumptions. The question implies a static
conception of social norms and deviant behavior: Certain acts are automatically deviant because they violate a norm or a law. Labeling rejects
this traditional view and suggests instead that the essence of deviance is
not in an act or acts but in the conditions under which the act occurs and,
most importantly, the meaning attributed to the act by participants. If a
policeman shoots an innocent black militant, he is "upholding the law"
and his actions are applauded by the larger society, but if a black militant
kills a policeman, whom he perceives as a representative of an oppressive
system, he is a murderer. Both have engaged in essentially the same act of
killing another human being, but the consequences of their actions will be
very different. Since deviance is a social definition, the labeling perspective
assumes that the behavior of the deviant is of secondary importance to the
reaction of the society. One could even be labeled "socially deviant" without violating social norms (e.g., an innocent man convicted of murder).

Despite the shortcomings of labeling theory, though, it has sensitized us to the role played by agents of social control in the process of defining persons as deviant or delinquent. It is the antithesis of biological theories that treated deviance as something emanating from within the person.

REFERENCES

Bordua, David J.
1961 "A Critique of Sociological Interpretations of Gang Delinquency." 338 (November):120–136.

Cloward, Richard A., and Lloyd E. Ohlin
1960 Delinquency and Opportunity: A Theory of Delinquent Gangs. New York: Free Press.

Cohen, Albert K.
1955 Delinquent Boys. New York: Free Press.
1966 Deviance and Control. Englewood Cliffs, N.J.: Prentice-Hall.

Cohen, Bruce J.
1970 Crime in America. Itasca, Ill.: Peacock.

Cortés, Juan B., and Florence M. Gatti
1972 Delinquency and Crime: A Biopsychosocial Approach. New York: Seminar Press.

Empey, Lamar T.
1967 "Delinquency Theory and Recent Research." Journal of Research in Crime and Delinquency. 4 (January):28–42.

Gibbs, Jack P.
1966 "Conceptions of Deviant Behavior: The Old and the New." Pacific Sociological Review 9 (Spring):9–14.

Glueck, Sheldon, and Eleanor Glueck
1950 Unraveling Juvenile Delinquency. New York: Commonwealth Fund.
1956 Physique and Delinquency. New York: Harper & Row.
1962 Family, Environment and Delinquency. Boston: Houghton Mifflin.

Gordon, Robert A.
1967 "Issues in the Ecological Study of Delinquency." American Sociological Review 32 (December):927–944.

Kitsuse, John I., and David C. Dietrick
1959 "Delinquent Boys: A Critique." American Sociological Review 24 (April):208–215.

Matza, David, and Gresham M. Sykes
1961 "Juvenile Delinquency and Subterranean Values." American Sociological Review 26 (October):712–719.

Miller, Walter B.
1958 "Lower Class Culture as a Generating Milieu of Gang Delinquency." Journal of Social Issues 14 (No. 3):5–19.

Munn, Norman L.
1956 Psychology. Third ed. Boston: Houghton Mifflin.

Nye, F. Ivan, James F. Short, Jr., and Virgil J. Olson
1958 "Socioeconomic Status and Delinquent Behavior." American Journal of Sociology 63 (January):381–389.

Piliavin, Irving, and Scott Briar
1964 "Police Encounters with Juveniles." American Journal of Sociology 70 (September):206–214.

President's Commission on Law Enforcement and Administration of Justice
1967a The Challenge of Crime in a Free Society. Washington, D.C.: GPO.
1967b "The Administration of Juvenile Justice—The Juvenile Court and Related Methods of Delinquency Control." Pp. 1–40 in Juvenile Delinquency and Youth Crime. Washington, D.C.: GPO.

Reckless, Walter C., Simon Dinitz, and Barbara Kay
1957 "The Self-Component in Potential Delinquency and Potential Non-Delinquency." American Sociological Review 22 (October): 566–570.
1958 "A Self-Gradient Among Potential Delinquents." Journal of Criminal Law, Criminology, and Police Science 49 (September-October):230–233.

Reckless, Walter C., Simon Dinitz, and Ellen Murray
1956 "Self-Concept as an Insulator Against Delinquency." American Sociological Review 21 (December):744–746.
1957a "Teacher Nominations and Evaluations of 'Good' Boys in High Delinquency Areas." Elementary School Journal 57 (January):221–223.
1957b "The 'Good' Boy in a High Delinquency Area." Journal of Criminal Law, Criminology, and Police Science 48 (June):18–25.

Reiss, Albert J., Jr., and A. Lewis Rhodes
1964 "An Empirical Test of Differential Association Theory." Journal of Research in Crime and Delinquency 1 (January):5–18.

Roebuck, Julian B., and Ronald C. Johnson
1962 "The Jack-of-All-Trades Offender." Crime and Delinquency 8 (April): 172–181.
1964 "The 'Short Con' Man." Crime and Delinquency 10 (July):235–248.

Schur, Edwin M.
1969 Our Criminal Society. Englewood Cliffs, N.J.: Prentice-Hall.

Shaw, Clifford R., et al.
1929 Delinquency Areas. Chicago: University of Chicago Press.

Shaw, Clifford, and Henry McKay
1969 Juvenile Delinquency and Urban Areas. Chicago: University of Chicago Press.

Sheldon, William H.
1949 Varieties of Delinquent Youth. New York: Harper & Row.

Short, James F., Jr.
1957 "Differential Association and Delinquency." Social Problems 4 (January):233–239.
1958 "Differential Association with Delinquent Friends and Delinquent Behavior." Pacific Sociological Review 1 (Spring):20–25.
1960 "Differential Association as a Hypothesis: Problems of Empirical Testing." Social Problems 8 (Summer):14–25.

Short, James F., Jr., and F. Ivan Nye
1958 "Extent of Unrecorded Juvenile Delinquency: Tentative Conclusions." Journal of Criminal Law, Criminology, and Police Science 49 (November-December):296–302.

1957–58 "Reported Behavior as a Criterion of Deviant Behavior." Social Problems 5 (Winter):207–213.

Sutherland, Edwin H., and Donald R. Cressey

1970 Criminology. Eighth ed. Philadelphia: Lippincott.

Sykes, Gresham M., and David Matza

1957 "Techniques of Neutralization: A Theory of Delinquency." American Sociological Review 22 (December):664–670.

Toby, Jackson

1961 "Delinquency and Opportunity." The British Journal of Sociology 12 (September):282–289.

Valentine, Charles A.

1968 Culture and Poverty: Critique and Counter-Proposals. Chicago: University of Chicago Press.

Vold, George B.

1958 Theoretical Criminology. New York: Oxford University Press.

Voss, Harwin L.

1964 "Differential Association and Reported Delinquent Behavior: A Replication." Social Problems 12 (Summer):78–85.

1966 "Socio-Economic Status and Delinquent Behavior." Social Problems 13 (Winter):314–324.

1969 "Differential Association and Containment Theory: A Theoretical Convergence." Social Forces 47 (June):381–391.

1970 Society, Delinquency, and Delinquent Behavior. Boston, Mass.: Little, Brown.

Washburn, S. L.

1951 "Review of W. H. Sheldon, Varieties of Delinquent Youth." American Anthropologist 53 (December):561–563.

Wheeler, Stanton, and Leonard S. Cotrell, Jr.

1966 Juvenile Delinquency: Its Prevention and Control. New York: Russell Sage.

Yablonsky, Lewis

1959 "The Delinquent Gang as a Near-Group.". Social Problems 7 (Fall): 108–117.

INTRODUCTION TO THE READINGS

In the first article Michael Lewis presents an excellent review and critique of subcultural theories of delinquency. He isolates two dominant views of lower-class delinquency. One assumes that lower-class culture contains certain themes that are deviant with larger societal norms and that lower-class adolescents become delinquent simply by adhering to these norms (e.g., Miller). The second holds that lower-class adolescents subscribe to the same success-goals as the rest of society but their access to these goals is blocked (e.g., Merton). Delinquency therefore represents a deviant means of attaining desired goals. Despite differences between the views, both are criminogenic; delinquent behavior is "intrinsically deviant." Conventional theories of delinquency fail to distinguish between activities that are structurally deviant and those that are normatively deviant. While "the hustle" and "the gang" involve illegal behavior, they are expressions of commitment to norms and values that pervade our society.

The second selection can be used to illustrate the labeling view of delinquency. For a long time the police and the courts were seen as passive agencies that detect and deter crime and delinquency. Labeling theory shifted the focus from the criminal or delinquent and his attributes (e.g., body build, personality) to the audience. From this perspective the police and the courts, far from being passive agencies, play an important part in creating delinquency. Piliavin and Briar show how an adolescent's demeanor, appearance, and race are more important than the offenses he commits in determining the disposition of juvenile cases.

Structural deviance and normative conformity: the "hustle" and the gang

MICHAEL LEWIS

INTRODUCTION

There are two basic sociological interpretations of slum crime and delinquency. The first posits the presence of cultural emphases or themes in the slum (or among lower-class groups) which, because they deviate from mainstream American (or middle-class) cultural expectations, lead those who behave in terms of them into conflict with the law and with law enforcers. The second interpretation holds that slum crime and delinquency are largely the products of blocked access to desired conventional (or mainstream) careers and rewards. . . .

In spite of the substantive differences between these two positions they do have one very important quality in common. They are both *criminogenic* interpretations. Whatever their differences, both positions take for granted that the evoked behavior is *intrinsically deviant*; that given the conventional standards of "right and wrong" in contemporary society these behaviors are "wrong" because they *violate* the institutionalized expectations for the "right." Implicit in both interpretations is the view that behavioral norms and conceptions of legality are inextricably wed; that behavior which is criminal (or delinquent) must, of necessity, be behavior which violates common conceptions of what is generally accepted and valued in our society. In other words, to say that certain behavior violates the law is also to say that it violates our broader normative sense of the kinds of things people ought to do.

It is the intention of this paper to present an interpretation of two major forms of slum crime and delinquency —"the hustle" and "gang behavior"— which is unequivocally dissimilar from either of the positions sketched above in that it does not view such behaviors as *intrinsically deviant*. In the argument presented below I eschew the necessary connection between illegality (or criminality) and normative deviance. I shall posit that while much of the behavior I am discussing is illegal it is also within the range of that which is normatively valued in the cultural mainstream of contemporary society.

THE HUSTLER

The common conception of the hustler holds him to be a small-time, petty criminal who "lives by his wits." He is the "fence," the "pimp," the "numbers runner," the "crap shooter," or perhaps even the small-scale purveyor of "grass" (marijuana) or "horse" (heroin). Superficially the hustler seems to fit very well into Robert Merton's characterization of *innovative anomie*. The *innovator*, says Merton, is the individual who, having internalized a common conception of success and finding legitimate means to its realization blocked, undertakes deviant practices as substitute means to his desired goal.[1] The hustler seems to be doing just that. In the first place he usually comes from the "bottom of the heap." He is characteristically a member of a socially stigmatized and disinherited group—a familiar figure, for example, in the black ghettos of American cities.[2] Typically, his formal education is limited while he pursues material rewards which are usually inaccessible to the majority of those who are similarly stigmatized but who do not hustle. The pursuit of such rewards which are symbolic of conventional success seems to integrate the hustler into the mainstream—at least as far as ends or goals are concerned. At the same time, however, the nature of his "hustle," numbers running, procuring, etc., seems to be a deviant means to conventional success which the conditions of his identity force him to adopt in lieu of conventional access modes such as legitimate business, entrepreneurial, or otherwise. If, because of who [he] is, he cannot sell stocks and bonds, he *can* "make it" by taking bets on the numbers.

Some of the facts which lead to such an interpretation are obviously incontrovertible. It is beyond question, for example, that Negroes as members of a stigmatized group have characteristically been denied conventional access to material rewards. It is also true, subcultural arguments notwithstanding, that there is no appreciable difference between white and black when it comes to material aspirations. More-

over, it may even be granted without fear of serious challenge that the hustle represents an adaptation to exclusion from what we commonly perceive as standard modes of access to material rewards. However, there is some question as to the "deviant" nature of the innovation or the "hustle."

If we follow Merton's argument we are forced to characterize the behavior of the hustler as essentially deviant, because it is illegal and often evokes a moralistic repugnance from us. Such an approach equates the nature of the behavior with the way it is commonly *labeled* in society at large. In a very real sense such an approach leaves the behavior in question unanalyzed. Its use tells us little about the essence of the "deviant" behavior or its *social meaning* for the behaver. The position taken here is (1) that from the hustler's perspective his means behavior is in conformity with much of the means behavior employed in "legitimate or conventional" access modes to material reward (the integrating goal), and (2) that the sociologist who looks carefully at the hustler's behavior must concur that while it is often prohibited by law it is only infrequently deviant in terms of social meaning for the actors involved—the "hustler" and, indeed, the "hustled." . . .

Whatever the hustle, it invariably involves a high degree of *rational planning* and the exercise of mental agility. Not only does the hustler have to "outwit the law," but he must also be several jumps ahead of his clientele. For example, there are some who hustle "their bread" by selling goods they purchase from junkies who no doubt have stolen them. Trafficking in contraband, the hustler has to escape public attention in order to stay in business. Beyond this he must also engage in a market analysis of considerable sophistication. He has to take on goods

---

[1] Robert Merton, "Social Structure and Anomie," in *Social Theory and Social Structure*, rev. ed., (Glencoe, Ill.: The Free Press, 1957), pp. 131–160.

[2] See, for example, the depiction of the "hustler" in *The Autobiography of Malcolm X* (New York: Grove Press, 1964).

which are likely to have a fast turn-over on the market to which he has access. This means that the hustler has to assess accurately local taste and consumer demand. Like the legitimate buyer for a retail outlet, if he makes an incorrect assessment he will be stuck with the goods, which besides representing an economic loss also represents an increased possibility of detection (on the assumption that these are contraband). Beyond maintaining a market or consumer analysis, the hustler who is "fencing" must also work out acceptable profit margins in his "retailing" operation. He knows that in order to make a sale he must offer his goods at prices below those asked on the legitimate market. He offers no guarantees and provides no service; thus, if he did not undersell his legit competitors he would soon lose his clientele. If he must undersell or underprice his goods while at the same time be far enough ahead to make his efforts worthwhile, he must pass on, as it were, the disparity between his retail price and that of his legitimate competition to his suppliers. Thus, he must find suppliers who not only can provide him with goods for fast turnover but who also are in desperate need of quick cash so that they are willing to sell to a middle man even though this means accepting a very tangible economic loss. It would indeed be difficult to find in a legitimate economic enterprise endeavors which exceed this hustle in the exercise of sophistication and rationality.

Other examples of hustlers commonly found in black ghettos also illustrate this emphasis on rational planning and market analysis. Numbers running and policy, common forms of gambling in these areas, are small bettor games which enable low income players to continue playing even when they lose consistently. The numbers

and policy both promise the possibility of a very big payoff for a small investment—although the odds are overwhelmingly against it—and in areas where money is short and releases from the desultory routines of daily life are few, each of these games fits a need. If the player is lucky he can "win big." At the very least, each time he plays he can partake of the *excitement* which inheres in the *possibility* that he might win. Those who run such games know their clientele. The numbers runner, for example, is a master psychologist in his environment, knowing very well the meaning of his game in the lives of those who play. It would be an overstatement to say that this awareness consciously led to the emergence of the numbers (or policy) as a characteristic hustle in the ghetto; yet it is clear that hustlers who "turn their bread" in this game know their market and sell to the needs which abound therein, the needs for money and for the possibility of the unexpected. They are full of stories about big winners and, like any good legitimate salesman, they keep their clientele interested by keeping alive those myths of possibility which draw them in. There is little difference between them and the "legitimate" myth makers, the advertising copy writers, or the used car salesmen.

Besides the planning rationality or the market awareness typically a part of the hustle, there are two other themes which run through this behavior and define its social meaning. They are (1) an emphasis upon achievement and the demonstration of personal skill, and (2) an emphasis upon dependability and integrity—or, in other words, honesty.

There is probably no social milieu which is more achievement oriented and in which demonstrations of personal skill are more admired than the hustler's world. The hustler is always "scuffling" or working at his "hustle." In part this is so because only infrequently does he get far enough ahead financially to ease off for a while. Also, many hustlers such as runners, pimps, pushers, and bootleggers (those who sell liquor without a liquor license) have a regular clientele who require that the hustler and his product be available on a regular basis. Whatever his hustle, the individual who "brings it off with style" excites the admiration of his fellows. The pimp who can keep a long string of prostitutes "sweet for him" is usually perceived as an expert in the psychology of women and in the context of his operations he probably is just that. Certainly he is adept at manipulating his women to the point that they are willing to go along, although each knows that she is just one of a number of his women. The bootlegger whose after-hours place is always well stocked and available for drinking and gambling and is free of "The Man's" (police) interference will attract a permanent following who will extoll his shrewd business head even while he is taking their change.

. . .

At first surmise it would seem that any concept of honesty as applied to the hustler involves a self-contradiction. The hustler operates outside the law and would appear to be, by definition, lacking in honesty. In fact this is a simplistic notion which really obfuscates a more complex and truly fascinating reality. While it is undeniably true that some hustlers involve themselves in activities such as theft or one of the variety of con-games which clearly involve the victimization of the "sucker" by the hustler, most hustles involve the maintenance of a relationship between the hustler and the client which presupposes reliability

and integrity. Curious as it may at first seem, the hustler seems to have a *professional* relationship with the "suckers" (if, indeed, the term is appropriate) characterized by an implicit code of ethics. The clientele link themselves with the hustler on a voluntary basis, coming to him for a service or for goods which they know he can provide. If the hustler fails to provide or otherwise measure up to expectations he will lose his clientele, his reputation in the hustle will be damaged, and he will be unable to attract new customers. Moreover, because the service provided or the goods purchased often involve a violation of the law and/or in some cases—as in a visit to a prostitute—a violation of conventional mores on the part of the customer, the hustler, if he is to maintain his reputation, must keep his relationship with his clients confidential. If he should expose a client for any reason, or even threaten to do so, he would soon lose his clientele. . . .

There are always those who violate the ethics of the hustle, but it would be a mistake not to recognize that these ethics do exist and that they are central to the hustler's style. Without the tacit understandings between hustler and client which govern the behavior of the former there would be no *trust*. Paradoxically, it is trust or faith in the hustler's honesty which is absolutely necessary to the client who is about to violate the law or the conventional standards of his community. Its subrosa nature makes every transaction with a hustler something of a risk for the client. It is only the hustler's reputation which allays the anxiety and at least to some extent routinizes the transaction. A dishonest hustler gives the *profession* a bad name and drives the customers away.

If you accept as accurate the above depiction of the hustler's world, it must follow that the behaviors involved are not simply deviant means to an institutionalized or legitimate goal. The three themes which permeate the hustler's behavior—*rationality, the emphasis upon achievement by individual skill*, and *honesty*—are norms which we ascribe to economic activity in the "square world" of the American middle class. Thus, the hustler, even when he is in violation of the law, typically goes about his business in a manner which attests to his substantial integration into the normative mainstream of contemporary society. We can accept Merton's notion that such behavior is deviant in that it violates legal specifications about what *is* and what *is not* a legitimate way of pursuing success goals. Structurally, the hustler *is* an innovator, a deviant; but it would be an error to equate this *structural deviance* (violation of the law) with the presence of deviant social meanings in the behavior. In terms of its social meaning for those who participate, hustling is more *imitative* than *innovative*.

Merton writes of the imperfect socialization of the innovator. He accounts for the abandonment of institutionalized means while aspirations for conventional success are maintained by suggesting that the innovator is, by virtue of his position in society, someone whose connection with legitimate means behavior is tenuous. Thus, when the will to success is overpowering and the conventional access ways are blocked, the individual easily casts off the restrictions imposed by the institutionalized prescriptions and proscriptions regarding means behavior.[3] As far as the hustler is concerned, however, our depiction of the meanings in his behavior allows for an opposite formulation in explanation of his *illegal or structurally deviant endeavors.*

If the social meanings in the hustler's behavior indicate that he is normatively integrated with the mainstream even while his behavior is illegal then it would seem, paradoxically, that such behavior is a function of normative integration at the means level in situations which only permit of its behavioral expression in ways which are more likely than not to be outside the law. If an individual is socialized to appreciate the importance of rational planning and control in economic endeavors, if he is socialized to the importance of building a personal reputation based upon skill, recognizable achievement, and integrity in his economic dealings with others, then depending upon his social location he will be on his way to becoming either a legitimate businessman, a professional, or a hustler. If he happens to have been born into the white upper middle class we can expect one of the former; if he happens to have been born into the black lower class (or some similar group) we can expect the latter.

It is indisputable that a lower-class Negro who is socialized to the norms of rational planning and reputation based upon achievement, demonstrable skill, and integrity is confronted with a legitimate opportunity structure which is less than encouraging. Imbued with a desire for material reward earned by these normative means, the lower-class Negro simply does not find positions open to him in the legitimate structure which permit such achievement. Given the technological sophistication of the legitimate economy, jobs which pay well and allow their incumbents to engage in rational planning, which allow them to develop a reputation based upon demonstrable competence and personal integrity, require a high degree of formal training

[3] Merton, *op. cit.*, p. 149.

and certification usually necessitating prolonged periods of preparation in the educational system. For a host of reasons—some economic, some having to do with social conditions in his immediate environment, and some having to do with the quality of education available in the schools he has access to—the lower-class Negro finds it difficult, and in some cases impossible, to obtain the training and certification necessary to qualify for positions in the legitimate economy where he could realize his conventional normative needs with reference to both *ends* and *means*. The greater his commitment to the conventional norms of rationality, achievement, and demonstrable responsibility and reliability in dealing with a public together with a desire for greater than average material reward, the more his situation—his social location—stymies his desire to enter the legitimate economy. For those whose commitment to these norms (both of means and ends) is less intense—whose aspirations are not as high—there are increasingly opportunities opening in the legitimate economy. But for those whose conventional normative commitment is high and who consequently would have to enter the economy nearer the top of the occupational pyramid, there are few opportunities for which their situation allows them to qualify. . . .

THE JUVENILE GANG

. . . In the public mind juvenile gangs have been identified as a major menace to person and property in the city. Consequently, there are few if any cities which have not committed at least some public resources (although often not enough) to efforts aimed at their pacification. Special police units, youth board street work-ers, and social workers can all be found in the high delinquency areas of any city while sociologists and psychologists have been busy in attempts to unravel the "why's" and "how's" of the juvenile gang and its opposition to conventional society. Out of this melange of activity there have emerged a number of explanations of the gang phenomenon. I shall here try to deal critically with two of the more important sociological formulations.

Walter Miller's view of the genesis of gang delinquency represents an extreme form of the subcultural argument.[4] For Miller, gang delinquency is not a reaction to *anything* like blocked access to status or material rewards; it is rather the natural outgrowth of a behavioral realization of the normative content of lower-class culture. Delinquent gangs in this view run afoul of the law because they are collectivities oriented toward the realization of norms in behavior which, because they are lower class, violate dominant middle-class expectations. . . .

The lower-class culture generating gang delinquency in the aforementioned manner is, according to Miller, constituted of a rank order of focal concerns inclusive of (1) Trouble, (2) Toughness, (3) Smartness, (4) Excitement, (5) Fate, and (6) Autonomy. These are themes which generate commitment in some instances and avoidance in others. The gang is the collectivity in which lower-class adolescents are perceived as working out their behavioral relationships to these themes or concerns.[5]

[4] Walter Miller, "Lower Class Culture as a Generating Milieu of Gang Delinquency," *The Journal of Social Issues,* Vol. XIV, No. 3 (1958), 5–19.

[5] *Ibid.,* p. 17.

Our criticism of this formulation is two-fold. First, on the basis of my research I would reject the notion that there is a "lower-class" culture so distinct from a dominant "middle-class" culture that behavior calculated to realize the normative content of the former automatically violates law which is based on the latter. My second criticism is based in part on the first. I find that certain normative qualities typical of middle-class existence and certain idealizations of "Americanisms" are the underlying themes of gang organization and activity. Thus, contrary to Miller and in conjunction with the argument developed with regard to the hustler, I perceive the gang as a mechanism for the realization of mainstream norms in situations which impede most "legitimate" expressions of them. The gang in this view is not delinquent in response to deviant norms; but it is delinquent to the extent that its members are socialized to mainstream norms while at the same time they find themselves impeded from expressing their commitments in the manner of the middle class. . . .

In a manner similar to Merton's formulation, Albert Cohen argues that in an open-class society such as that characteristic of present-day America, all individuals irrespective of their class identities are exposed to, and to some degree internalize, the dominant normative qualities of that society.[6] Thus, says Cohen, in American society "it is difficult to find a 'working class' milieu in which 'middle class' standards are not important."[7] As this is the case,

working-class (lower-class for our purposes) youth are confronted with a mighty dilemma. On the one hand they cannot escape measuring themselves against middle-class standards. The mass media, the schools, and even their peers who seem to be "getting ahead" all attest to the importance of middle-class life styles in this society. On the other hand, because of their working-class status, their socialization has rendered them deficient in attributes which would allow them to compete successfully for opportunities and rewards generally accessible to the middle class.

. . . The delinquent subculture in Cohen's view consists of a grand repudiation of everything middle class. It is in every sense a *contra-culture* in which middle-class values and standards are inverted. Because the middle-class standards are perceived as unattainable, their value or importance is denied, indeed even ridiculed, by an orientation to their opposites. In the acts of denial the delinquent establishes for himself a status which he can regard as superior to that which those who accept middle-class standards aspire. Thus, the delinquent gang is a collectivity which in effect gives legitimacy to the individual's *reaction-formation* (Cohen himself regards this term as applicable) against the middle-class normative universe. For as long as the lower- or working-class adolescent accepts that universe as important he must live with the realization of his own status inadequacy. . . .

Although Cohen's formulation is superior to Miller's from the perspective of this essay, there are some important questions which should be raised about its overall adequacy as an analytic treatment of gang delinquency. On the basis of my research I agree with Cohen's assertions that working- or lower-

[6] Albert Cohen, *Delinquent Boys: The Culture of the Gang* (Glencoe, Ill.: The Free Press, 1955), p. 122.

[7] *Ibid.*, p. 124.

class youth are exposed to mainstream norms, and that the delinquent gang represents an attempt to deal with situationally based impediments to their realization in the manner of the middle class. However, I find it difficult to accept the notion that the delinquent gang represents a collective reaction-formation in denial of middle-class morality.

In the first place it is difficult to conceive of a collectivity whose only basis for existence is a psychological defense mechanism "writ large."[8] In order for any collectivity to persist it must be possessed of positive functional attractions from the perspective of its membership. Even recognizing, as Cohen does, that motivation for membership in the gang may vary from one member to the next does not clearly depict the attractions of the collectivity *as a collectivity* for the lower-class adolescent. What can he derive from membership in the gang which meets his needs for the behavioral realization of the norms to which he subscribes? What does the collectivity "do" for its members which they themselves would be unable to accomplish as solitary individuals? Again it is not enough to argue as Cohen does that the gang is the reference group sustaining the individual's reaction formation against middle-class morality. . . .

Second, in his description of gang characteristics Cohen highlights only those which seem to fit his contra-cultural thesis. It may indeed be true that juvenile gangs engage in property destruction and it may be true that gang members can be found who are ma-

licious and "short-run hedonists,"[9] but it is certainly nothing short of arbitrary to assert that these characteristics (along with *group autonomy*, etc.) to the exclusion of others, define the behavioral universe of the gang. As we shall see below there are other qualities of the delinquent gang which do not fit the contra-cultural thesis quite so well. In this vein it is important to note that Cohen virtually ignores the social organization of the gang. Little attention is paid to differential roles or status within the gang and the rules governing behavior within the gang. A focus upon these extremely important sociological characteristics, I submit, would lead to conclusions less supportive of the contra-cultural thesis. Indeed, by placing the contra-cultural characteristics in the context of the social organization of the gang we reach the conclusion that the gang is more mainstream than deviant. . . .

More interesting sociologically and more to the point of the argument I am pursuing are those *organized gangs* which are also very much a part of the slum-ghetto scene. The organization of the *organized gang* is taken seriously by its members and so ought to be viewed similarly by sociologists. Such gangs display the kind of formal organization we usually associate with large-scale collectivities characteristic of the nondelinquent or "straight" world of middle-class adults. The organized gang invariably has a president, at least one vice president and sometimes a treasurer, and a war minister. In some instances where the gang is really a federation of a number of smaller gangs (as is the case of some of the large gangs in New York City and is apparently true of some of the

---

[8] In positing his sub-cultural thesis W. Miller makes essentially the same criticism. See Miller, *op. cit.*, p. 19.

[9] See Cohen, *op. cit.*, pp. 24–32.

larger Chicago gangs), there is a hierarchical structure of control and authority with a governing council of representatives from the constituent subunits.[10] . . .

A major concern of the organized juvenile gang is its sovereignty over a "turf" or territory. In this the gang acts as a kind of local shadow government monitoring the comings and goings of individuals in its age category and often exerting social control over members and nonmembers as well. There are, for example, reported incidents in which gang members, with considerable effect, have both "encouraged" or "discouraged" school attendance among adolescents living on their turf. This collective concern for sovereignty can hardly be designated as normatively deviant in terms of the American mainstream, except in the sense that the gang has no legal right to exercise it. The attempt to exercise sovereignty is legally deviant because the gang has no recognized mandate from the state to do so, but the aspiration to organized authority over a constituency is as American as apple pie. Thus, the concern for territorial sovereignty is itself imitative of a common-place theme in middle-class-dominated American life.

As a general matter, the concept of sovereignty has two major implications. It implies first that rules, norms, and protections against harm are applicable to all who fall under or owe allegiance to the sovereign authority,

and second that none of these is extended to those who are beyond its pale. The notion of sovereignty, in effect, distinguishes between an in-group for whom a series of moral imperatives exists and out-groups whose treatment by members of the in-group is not necessarily governed by such imperatives. . . .

Juvenile gangs usually attempt to establish their sovereignty according to the following dimensions. They first try to establish unchallenged authority over a "turf" or physical territory which has fairly specific boundaries. Those who live within these boundaries are considered by gang members to be subject to their "authority." Second, they establish age limits on their sovereignty, usually only an upper limit. This limit may not be explicitly recognized and it may even be revised upward or downward depending upon the power of the gang, but it does, nevertheless, exist. Thus, the gang concerns itself with its sovereignty over individuals up to a certain age living within a specified physical area.

I would venture that a considerable amount of the illegal or structurally deviant gang activities (except for hustling) victimizes only those who in one way or another are beyond the boundaries of the gang's sovereignty and are thus not protected by the usual in-group moral codes. Much of the violence, for example, which seems characteristic of the gang occurs when the gang is either seeking to extend its sovereignty or, conversely, is seeking to protect it from incursions by other gangs or outsiders. And what seems to be wanton property damage and non-utilitarian theft is not an indication of a generalized repudiation of the middle-class valuation of property. Much of this destructive activity is aimed at one or another of the out-groups—

[10] Note: I am indebted to Mr. Howard Altstein for information on the formal structures of large scale gangs. As a social worker in New York City's Youth House for Boys, Mr. Alstein had the opportunity to collect information on gang organization in New York. He has kindly shared this information with me.

adults or other adolescents outside the turf—and is a purposive act of aggression against those whose interests are defined as inimical to those of the gang. In-group property is respected while out-group property can be destroyed with impunity and without eschewing its value. . . .

In order to understand what has just been described, one has to have some sense of what the organized gang does for its constituents and why it seems to be a collectivity associated with lower-class slum-ghetto areas in American cities. It would seem abundantly clear that the organized gang is a setting in which conventional normative content is realized, although in a manner which quite often violates law, just as was shown for the hustle. Where in the conventional opportunity structure can these ghetto adolescents so readily gain recognition for their leadership ability and their interpersonal competence? Where in the conventional opportunity structure can these ghetto adolescents experience organizational participation in which they have as visible a chance of rising to the top by their own merits? Where can they exercise highly valued rationality? And in which conventional contexts can they participate in controlling their own destinies by determining what is right and what is wrong and who their enemies are? All of these are conventional aspirations which, given the stigmatization and functional incapacity for mainstream achievement, can only be realized by many slum-ghetto youth in a context at once imitative of but divorced from the mainstream. The organized gang provides just such a context. Its rules and regulations are real enough; it rewards achievement, control, rationality, and courage; it makes social control accessible to those who are otherwise powerless by scaling things down to a

point where sovereignty is a realistic concern. The gang, it may be said, is the "imitation of life." Not a reaction-formation writ large but an imitation of American reality writ small. The gang's violence, its aggressiveness, is legally or structurally deviant because the gang is a sovereignty without a charter. But it is not normatively deviant.

CONCLUSION

In this paper I have argued against explanations of structurally deviant behaviors which imply their normative deviance. Quite to the contrary, in the cases which I have analyzed, the hustle and the organized juvenile gang, I have concluded that the existence of illegal behavior or behavior which is structurally deviant is paradoxically the function of intense commitment to normative qualities which are well within the conventional range in American society in situations (the slum ghettos) which make their behavioral realization in the legitimate opportunity structure all but impossible. If this is indeed so, then there are several implications which those who are interested in reform and in the reduction of crime must confront.

As long as situational impediments remain, approaches which attempt to change the offender's behavior are likely to fail. It does no good to tell a highly successful hustler about the gratifications of being a lathe operator; he is deriving conventional rewards from his hustle which he could never derive at the lathe. Moreover he would probably cling to the hustle even if he earned as much money at the lathe, for the hustle offers him an opportunity to achieve some of the gratifications many middle-class people value in their work. Likewise, it does no good to tell a gang leader to give up his role. Only if he were willing to give up some of the conventional satisfactions which so many middle-class people take for granted would he be willing to do so.

If the impeding situation does not change, as long as there is normative conventionality in the slum ghetto there will be structural deviance. (How much easier it would be if their commitments were deviant; we would argue that ours are better and that they should change, but *their* commitments are *our* commitments; *their* values are *our* values.) Since we cannot deprive these individuals of their commitments, we must either give legal sanction to at least some of their presently regarded deviant behaviors or we must change some of the requirements for entrance at relatively high levels into the "legitimate opportunity structure." Maybe a successful numbers banker would make an equally good stockbroker. He certainly has the same normative commitments as the stockbroker and in spite of limited formal education his success attests to his cerebral acuity. Perhaps this hustler would become a stockbroker; he certainly would refuse to become a lathe operator. Maybe gang leaders ought indeed be placed in situations of trust; maybe the gang's concern with sovereignty could be put to good use in developing the reconstruction of the slum ghetto. Since the gangs already have a constituency and since they function to serve conventional aspirations, why not build conventional organizations for them from the ground up in such areas?

It should be clear that if it is not deviant norms which must be changed, the existing criminality and delinquency is ultimately a function of a situation. If this is so, then all the "therapy" of probation officers, social workers, psychologists, vocational rehabilitators, etc., will be too little or no avail. If this is so, it is not the criminal who must change, but the situation which turns his conventionality toward illegal expression. If this is so, social reform is needed in place of the various and sundry individual "therapies" which are imposed upon the violator of law.

Police encounters with juveniles[1]

IRVING PILIAVIN and
SCOTT BRIAR

As the first of a series of decisions made in the channeling of youthful offenders through the agencies concerned with juvenile justice and corrections, the disposition decisions made by police officers have potentially profound consequences for apprehended juveniles. Thus arrest, the most severe of the dispositions available to police, may not only lead to confinement of the suspected offender but also bring him loss of social status, restriction of educational and employment opportunities, and future harassment by law-enforcement personnel.[2] According to some criminologists, the stigmatization resulting from police apprehension, arrest, and detention actually reinforces

deviant behavior.[3] Other authorities have suggested, in fact, that this stigmatization serves as the catalytic agent initiating delinquent careers.[4] Despite their presumed significance, however, little empirical analysis has been reported regarding the factors influencing, or consequences resulting from, police actions with juvenile offenders. Furthermore, while some studies of police encounters with adult offenders have been reported, the extent to which the findings of these investigations pertain to law-enforcement practices with youthful offenders is not known.[5]

The above considerations have led the writers to undertake a longitudinal study of the conditions influencing, and consequences flowing from, police actions with juveniles. In the present paper findings will be presented indicating the influence of certain factors

[1] This study was supported by Grant MH-0632802, National Institute of Mental Health, United States Public Health Service.

[2] Richard D. Schwartz and Jerome H. Skolnick, "Two Studies of Legal Stigma," *Social Problems*, X (April, 1962), 133–42; Sol Rubin, *Crime and Juvenile Delinquency* (New York: Oceana Publications, 1958); B. F. McSally, "Finding Jobs for Released Offenders," *Federal Probation*, XXIV (June, 1960), 12–17; Harold D. Lasswell and Richard C. Donnelly, "The Continuing Debate over Responsibility: An Introduction to Isolating the Condemnation Sanction," *Yale Law Journal*, LXVIII (April, 1959), 869–99.

[3] Richard A. Cloward and Lloyd E. Ohlin, *Delinquency and Opportunity* (Glencoe, Ill.: Free Press, 1960), pp. 124–30.

[4] Frank Tannenbaum, *Crime and the Community* (New York: Columbia University Press, 1936), pp. 17–20; Howard S. Becker, *Outsiders: Studies in the Sociology of Deviance* (New York: Free Press of Glencoe, 1963), chaps. i and ii.

[5] For a detailed accounting of police discretionary practices, see Joseph Goldstein, "Police Discretion Not To Invoke the Criminal Process: Low Visibility Decisions in the Administration of Justice," *Yale Law Journal*, LXIX (1960), 543–94; Wayne R. LaFave, "The Police and Non-enforcement of the Law—Part I," *Wisconsin Law Review*, January, 1962, pp. 104–37; S. H. Kadish, "Legal Norms and Discretion in the Police and Sentencing Processes," *Harvard Law Review*, LXXV (March, 1962), 904–31.

on police actions. Research data consist primarily of notes and records based on nine months' observation of all juvenile officers in one police department.[6] The officers were observed in the course of their regular tours of duty.[7] While these data do not lend themselves to quantitative assessments of reliability and validity, the candor shown by the officers in their interviews with the investigators and their use of officially frowned-upon practices while under observation provide some assurance that the materials presented below accurately reflect the typical operations and attitudes of the law-enforcement personnel studied.

The setting for the research, a metropolitan police department serving an industrial city with approximately 450,000 inhabitants, was noted within the community it served and among law-enforcement officials elsewhere for the honesty and superior quality of its personnel. Incidents involving criminal activity or brutality by members of the department had been extremely rare during the ten years preceding this study; personnel standards were comparatively high; and an extensive training program was provided to both new and experienced personnel. Juvenile Bureau members, the primary subjects

[6] Approximately thirty officers were assigned to the Juvenile Bureau in the department studied. While we had an opportunity to observe all officers in the Bureau during the study, our observations were concentrated on those who had been working in the Bureau for one or two years at least. Although two of the officers in the Juvenile Bureau were Negro, we observed these officers on only a few occasions.

[7] Although observations were not confined to specific days or work shifts, more observations were made during evenings and weekends because police activity was greatest during these periods.

of this investigation, differed somewhat from other members of the department in that they were responsible for delinquency prevention as well as law enforcement, that is, juvenile officers were expected to be knowledgeable about conditions leading to crime and delinquency and to be able to work with community agencies serving known or potential juvenile offenders. Accordingly, in the assignment of personnel to the Juvenile Bureau, consideration was given not only to an officer's devotion to and reliability in law enforcement but also to his commitment to delinquency prevention. Assignment to the Bureau was of advantage to policemen seeking promotions. Consequently, many officers requested transfer to this unit, and its personnel comprised a highly select group of officers.

In the field, juvenile officers operated essentially as patrol officers. They cruised assigned beats and, although concerned primarily with juvenile offenders, frequently had occasion to apprehend and arrest adults. Confrontations between the officers and juveniles occurred in one of the following three ways, in order of increasing frequency: (1) encounters resulting from officers' spotting officially "wanted" youths; (2) encounters taking place at or near the scene of offenses reported to police headquarters; and (3) encounters occurring as the result of officers' directly observing youths either committing offenses or in "suspicious circumstances." However, the probability that a confrontation would take place between officer and juvenile, or that a particular disposition of an identified offender would be made, was only in part determined by the knowledge that an offense had occurred or that a particular juvenile had committed an offense. The bases for and utilization of non-offenses related criteria by police in accosting and disposing of juveniles are the focuses of the following discussion.

SANCTIONS FOR DISCRETION

In each encounter with juveniles, with the minor exception of officially "wanted" youths,[8] a central task confronting the officer was to decide what official action to take against the boys involved. In making these disposition decisions, officers could select any one of five discreet alternatives:

1. Outright release
2. Release and submission of a "field interrogation report" briefly describing the circumstances initiating the police-juvenile confrontation
3. "Official reprimand" and release to parents or guardian
4. Citation to juvenile court
5. Arrest and confinement in juvenile hall.

Dispositions 3, 4, and 5 differed from the others in two basic respects. First, with rare exceptions, when an officer chose to reprimand, cite, or arrest a boy, he took the youth to the police station. Second, the reprimanded, cited, or arrested boy acquired an official police "record," that is, his name was officially recorded in Bureau files as a juvenile violator.

Analysis of the distribution of police disposition decisions about juveniles revealed that in virtually every category of offense the full range of official disposition alternatives available to officers was employed. This wide range of discretion resulted primarily

8 "Wanted" juveniles usually were placed under arrest or in protective custody, a practice which in effect relieved officers of the responsibility for deciding what to do with these youths.

from two conditions. First, it reflected the reluctance of officers to expose certain youths to the stigmatization presumed to be associated with official police action. Few juvenile officers believed that correctional agencies serving the community could effectively help delinquents. For some officers this attitude reflected a lack of confidence in rehabilitation techniques; for others, a belief that high case loads and lack of professional training among correctional workers vitiated their efforts at treatment. All officers were agreed, however, that juvenile justice and correctional processes were essentially concerned with apprehension and punishment rather than treatment. Furthermore, all officers believed that some aspects of these processes (e.g., judicial definition of youths as delinquents and removal of delinquents from the community), as well as some of the possible consequences of these processes (e.g., intimate institutional contact with "hard-core" delinquents, as well as parental, school, and conventional peer disapproval or rejection), could reinforce what previously might have been only a tentative proclivity toward delinquent values and behavior. Consequently, when officers found reason to doubt that a youth being confronted was highly committed toward deviance, they were inclined to treat him with leniency.

Second, and more important, the practice of discretion was sanctioned by police-department policy. Training manuals and departmental bulletins stressed that the disposition of each juvenile offender was not to be based solely on the type of infraction he committed. Thus, while it was departmental policy to "arrest and confine all juveniles who have committed a felony or misdemeanor involving theft, sex offense, battery, possession of dangerous weapons, prowling, peeping, intoxication, incorrigibility, and disturbance of the peace," it was acknowledged that "such considerations as age, attitude and prior criminal record might indicate that a different disposition would be more appropriate."[9] The official justification for discretion in processing juvenile offenders, based on the preventive aims of the Juvenile Bureau, was that each juvenile violator should be dealt with solely on the basis of what was best for him.[10] Unofficially, administrative legitimation of discretion was further justified on the grounds that strict enforcement practices would overcrowd court calendars and detention facilities, as well as dramatically increase juvenile crime rates—consequences to be avoided because they would expose the police department to community criticism.[11]

In practice, the official policy justifying use of discretion served as a demand that discretion be exercised. As such, it posed three problems for juvenile officers. First, it represented a departure from the traditional police practice with which the juvenile officers themselves were identified, in the sense that they were expected to justify their juvenile disposition decisions not simply by evidence proving a youth had committed a crime—grounds on which police were officially expected to base their dispositions of non-juve-

nile offenders[12]—but in the *character* of the youth. Second, in disposing of juvenile offenders, officers were expected, in effect, to make judicial rather than ministerial decisions.[13] Third, the shift from the offense to the offender as the basis for determining the appropriate disposition substantially increased the uncertainty and ambiguity for officers in the situation of apprehension because no explicit rules existed for determining which disposition different types of youths should receive. Despite these problems, officers were constrained to base disposition decisions on the character of the apprehended youth, not only because they wanted to be fair, but because persistent failure to do so could result in judicial criticism, departmental censure, and, they believed, loss of authority with juveniles.[14]

DISPOSITION CRITERIA

Assessing the character of apprehended offenders posed relatively few difficulties for officers in the case of youths who had committed serious crimes such as robbery, homicide, aggravated assault, grand theft, auto theft, rape, and arson. Officials generally regarded these juveniles as confirmed delin-

---

[9] Quoted from a training manual issued by the police department studied in this research.

[10] Presumably this also implied that police action with juveniles was to be determined partly by the offenders' need for correctional services.

[11] This was reported by beat officers as well as supervisory and administrative personnel of the juvenile bureau.

[12] In actual practice, of course, disposition decisions regarding adult offenders also were influenced by many factors extraneous to the offense per se.

[13] For example, in dealing with adult violators, officers had no disposition alternative comparable to the reprimand-and-release category, a disposition which contained elements of punishment but did not involve mediation by the court.

[14] The concern of officers over possible loss of authority stemmed from their belief that court failure to support arrests by appropriate action would cause policemen to "lose face" in the eyes of juveniles.

quents simply by virtue of their involvement in offenses of this magnitude.[15] However, the infraction committed did not always suffice to determine the appropriate disposition for some serious offenders;[16] and, in the case of minor offenders, who comprised over 90 percent of the youths against whom police took action, the violation per se generally played an insignificant role in the choice of disposition. While a number of minor offenders were seen as serious delinquents deserving arrest, many others were perceived either as "good" boys whose offenses were atypical of their customary behavior, as pawns of undesirable associates or, in any case, as boys for whom arrest was regarded as an unwarranted and possibly harmful punishment. Thus, for nearly all minor violators and for some serious delinquents, the assessment of character—the distinction between serious delinquents, "good" boys, misguided youths, and so on—and the dispositions which followed from these assessments were based on youths' personal characteristics and not their offenses.

Despite this dependence of disposition decisions on the personal characteristics of these youths, however, police officers actually had access only to very limited information about boys at the time they had to decide what to do with them. In the field, officers typically had no data concerning the

past offense records, school performance, family situation, or personal adjustment of apprehended youths.[17] Furthermore, files at police headquarters provided data only about each boy's prior offense record. Thus both the decision made in the field—whether or not to bring the boy in—and the decision made at the station —which disposition to invoke—were based largely on cues which emerged from the interaction between the officer and the youth, cues from which the officer inferred the youth's character. These cues included the youth's group affiliations, age, race, grooming, dress, and demeanor. Older juveniles, members of known delinquent gangs,

TABLE 1
Severity of police disposition by youth's demeanor

Severity of police disposition	Youth's demeanor		
	Co-op- erative	Unco-op- erative	Total
Arrest (most severe)	2	14	16
Citation or official reprimand	4	5	9
Informal reprimand	15	1	16
Admonish and release (least severe)	24	1	25
Total	45	21	66

[15] It is also likely that the possibility of negative publicity resulting from the failure to arrest such violators—particularly if they became involved in further serious crime—brought about strong administrative pressure for their arrest.

[16] For example, in the year preceding this research, over 30 percent of the juveniles involved in burglaries and 12 percent of the juveniles committing auto theft received dispositions other than arrest.

[17] On occasion, officers apprehended youths whom they personally knew to be prior offenders. This did not occur frequently, however, for several reasons. First, approximately 75 percent of apprehended youths had no prior official records; second, officers periodically exchanged patrol areas, thus limiting their exposure to, and knowledge about, these areas; and third, patrolmen seldom spent more than three or four years in the juvenile division.

Negroes, youths with well-oiled hair, black jackets, and soiled denims or jeans (the presumed uniform of "tough" boys), and boys who in their interactions with officers did not manifest what were considered to be appropriate signs of respect tended to receive the more severe dispositions.

Other than prior record, the most important of the above clues was a youth's *demeanor*. In the opinion of juvenile patrolmen themselves the demeanor of apprehended juveniles was a major determinant of their decisions for 50–60 percent of the juvenile cases they processed.[18] A less subjective indication of the association between a youth's demeanor and police disposition is provided by Table 1, which presents the police dispositions for sixty-six youths whose encounters with police were observed in the course of this study.[19] For purposes of this analysis, each youth's demeanor in the encounter was classified as either co-operative or unco-operative.[20] The

[18] While reliable subgroup estimates were impossible to obtain through observation because of the relatively small number of incidents observed, the importance of demeanor in disposition decisions appeared to be much less significant with known prior offenders.

[19] Systematic data were collected on police encounters with seventy-six juveniles. In ten of these encounters the police concluded that their suspicions were groundless, and consequently the juveniles involved were exonerated; these ten cases were eliminated from this analysis of demeanor. (The total number of encounters observed was considerably more than seventy-six, but systematic data-collection procedures were not instituted until several months after observations began.)

[20] The data used for the classification of demeanor were the written records of observations made by the authors. The classifications were made by an independent judge not associated with this study.

results clearly reveal a marked association between youth demeanor and the severity of police dispositions.

The cues used by police to assess demeanor were fairly simple. Juveniles who were contrite about their infractions, respectful to officers, and fearful of the sanctions that might be employed against them tended to be viewed by patrolmen as basically law-abiding or at least "salvageable." For these youths it was usually assumed that informal or formal reprimand would suffice to guarantee their future conformity. In contrast, youthful offenders who were fractious, obdurate, or who appeared nonchalant in their encounters with patrolmen were likely to be viewed as "would-be tough guys" or "punks" who fully deserved the most severe sanction: arrest. The following excerpts from observation notes illustrate the importance attached to demeanor by police in making disposition decisions.

1. The interrogation of "A" (an 18-year-old upper-lower-class white male accused of statutory rape) was assigned to a police sergeant with long experience on the force. As I sat in his office while we waited for the youth to arrive for questioning, the sergeant expressed his uncertainty as to what he should do with this young man. On the one hand, he could not ignore the fact that an offense had been committed; he had been informed, in fact, that the youth was prepared to confess to the offense. Nor could he overlook the continued pressure from the girl's father (an important political figure) for

In classifying a youth's demeanor as co-operative or unco-operative, particular attention was paid to: (1) the youth's responses to police officers' questions and requests; (2) the respect and deference—or lack of these qualities—shown by the youth toward police officers; and (3) police officers' assessments of the youth's demeanor.

the police to take severe action against the youth. On the other hand, the sergeant had formed a low opinion of the girl's moral character, and he considered it unfair to charge "A" with statutory rape when the girl was a willing partner to the offense and might even have been the instigator of it. However, his sense of injustice concerning "A" was tempered by his image of the youth as a "punk," based, he explained, on information he had received that the youth belonged to a certain gang, the members of which were well known to, and disliked by, the police. Nevertheless, as we prepared to leave his office to interview "A," the sergeant was still in doubt as to what he should do with him.

As we walked down the corridor to the interrogation room, the sergeant was stopped by a reporter from the local newspaper. In an excited tone of voice, the reporter explained that his editor was pressing him to get further information about this case. The newspaper had printed some of the facts about the girl's disappearance, and as a consequence the girl's father was threatening suit against the paper for defamation of the girl's character. It would strengthen the newspaper's position, the reporter explained, if the police had information indicating that the girl's associates, particularly the youth the sergeant was about to interrogate, were persons of disreputable character. This stimulus seemed to resolve the sergeant's uncertainty. He told the reporter, "unofficially," that the youth was known to be an undesirable person, citing as evidence his membership in the delinquent gang. Furthermore, the sergeant added that he had evidence that this youth had been intimate with the girl over a period of many months. When the reporter asked if the police were planning to do anything to the youth, the sergeant answered that he intended to charge the youth with statutory rape.

In the interrogation, however, three points quickly emerged which profoundly affected the sergeant's judgment of the youth. First, the youth was polite and cooperative; he consistently addressed the officer as "sir," answered all questions quietly, and signed a statement implicating himself in numerous counts of statutory rape. Second, the youth's intentions toward the girl appeared to have been honorable; for example, he said that he wanted to marry her eventually. Third, the youth was not in fact a member of the gang in question. The sergeant's attitude became increasingly sympathetic, and after we left the interrogation room he announced his intention to "get 'A' off the hook," meaning that he wanted to have the charges against "A" reduced or, if possible, dropped.

2. Officers "X" and "Y" brought into the police station a seventeen-year-old white boy who, along with two older companions, had been found in a home having sex relations with a fifteen-year-old girl. The boy responded to police officers' queries slowly and with obvious disregard. It was apparent that his lack of deference toward the officers and his failure to evidence concern about his situation were irritating his questioners. Finally, one of the officers turned to me and, obviously angry, commented that in his view the boy was simply a "stud" interested only in sex, eating, and sleeping. The policemen conjectured that the boy "probably already had knocked up half a dozen girls." The boy ignored these remarks, except for an occasional impassive stare at the patrolmen. Turning to the boy, the officer remarked, "What the hell am I going to do with you?" And again the boy simply returned the officer's gaze. The latter then said, "Well, I guess we'll just have to put you away for a while." An arrest report was then made out and the boy was taken to Juvenile Hall.

Although anger and disgust frequently characterized officers' attitudes toward recalcitrant and impassive juvenile offenders, their manner while processing these youths was typically routine, restrained, and without rancor. While the officers' restraint may have been due in part to their desire to avoid accusation and censure, it also seemed to reflect their inurement to a frequent experience. By and large, only their occasional "needling" or insulting of a boy gave any hint of the underlying resentment and dislike they felt toward many of these youths.[21]

PREJUDICE IN APPREHENSION AND DISPOSITION DECISIONS

Compared to other youths, Negroes and boys whose appearance matched the delinquent stereotype were more frequently stopped and interrogated by patrolmen—often even in the absence of evidence that an offense had been committed[22]—and usually were given more severe dispositions for the same violations. Our data suggest, however, that these selective apprehension and

[21] Officers' animosity toward recalcitrant or aloof offenders appeared to stem from two sources: moral indignation that these juveniles were self-righteous and indifferent about their transgressions, and resentment that these youths failed to accord police the respect they believed they deserved. Since the patrolmen perceived themselves as honestly and impartially performing a vital community function warranting respect and deference from the community at large, they attributed the lack of respect shown them by these juveniles to the latters' immorality.

[22] The clearest evidence for this assertion is provided by the overrepresentation of Negroes among "innocent" juveniles accosted by the police. As noted, of the seventy-six juveniles on whom systematic data were collected, ten were exonerated and released without suspicion. Seven, or two-thirds of these ten "innocent" juveniles were Negro, in contrast to the allegedly "guilty" youths, less than one-third of whom were Negro. The following incident illustrates the operation of this bias: One officer, observing a youth walking along the street, commented that the youth "looks suspicious" and promptly stopped and questioned him. Asked later to explain what aroused his suspicion, the officer explained, "He was a Negro wearing dark glasses at midnight."

disposition practices resulted not only from the intrusion of long-held prejudices of individual police officers but also from certain job-related experiences of law-enforcement personnel. First, the tendency for police to give more severe dispositions to Negroes and to youths whose appearance corresponded to that which police associated with delinquents partly reflected the fact, observed in this study, that these youths also were much more likely than were other types of boys to exhibit the sort of recalcitrant demeanor which police construed as a sign of the confirmed delinquent. Further, officers assumed, partly on the basis of departmental statistics, that Negroes and juveniles who "look tough" (e.g., who wear chinos, leather jackets, boots, etc.) commit crimes more frequently than do other types of youths.[23] In this sense, the police justified their selective treatment of these youths along epidemiological lines: that is, they were concentrating their attention on those youths whom they believed were most likely to commit delinquent acts. In the words of one highly placed official in the department:

If you know that the bulk of your delinquent problem comes from kids who, say, are from 12 to 14 years of age, when you're out on patrol you are much more likely to be sensitive to the activities of juveniles in this age bracket than older or

[23] While police statistics did not permit an analysis of crime rates by appearance, they strongly supported officers' contentions concerning the delinquency rate among Negroes. Of all male juveniles processed by the police department in 1961, for example, 40.2 percent were Negro and 33.9 percent were white. These two groups comprised at that time, respectively, about 22.7 percent and 73.6 percent of the population in the community studied.

younger groups. This would be good law enforcement practice. The logic in our case is the same except that our delinquency problem is largely found in the Negro community and it is these youths toward whom we are sensitized.

As regards prejudice per se, eighteen of twenty-seven officers interviewed openly admitted a dislike for Negroes. However, they attributed their dislike to experiences they had, as policemen, with youths from this minority group. The officers reported that Negro boys were much more likely than non-Negroes to "give us a hard time," be un-co-operative, and show no remorse for their transgressions. Recurrent exposure to such attitudes among Negro youth, the officers claimed, generated their antipathy toward Negroes. The following excerpt is typical of the views expressed by these officers:

They (Negroes) have no regard for the law or for the police. They just don't seem to give a damn. Few of them are interested in school or getting ahead. The girls start having illegitimate kids before they are 16 years old and the boys are always "out for kicks." Furthermore, many of these kids try to run you down. They say the damnedest things to you and they seem to have absolutely no respect for you as an adult. I admit I am prejudiced now, but frankly I don't think I was when I began police work.

IMPLICATIONS

It is apparent from the findings presented above that the police officers studied in this research were permitted and even encouraged to exercise immense latitude in disposing of the juveniles they encountered. That is, it was within the officers' discretionary authority, except in extreme limiting cases, to decide which juveniles were to come to the attention of the courts and correctional agencies

and thereby be identified officially as delinquents. In exercising this discretion policemen were strongly guided by the demeanor of those who were apprehended, a practice which ultimately led, as seen above, to certain youths, (particularly Negroes[24] and boys dressed in the style of "toughs") being treated more severely than other juveniles for comparable offenses.

But the relevance of demeanor was not limited only to police disposition practices. Thus, for example, in conjunction with police crime statistics the criterion of demeanor led police to concentrate their surveillance activities in areas frequented or inhabited by Negroes. Furthermore, these youths were accosted more often than others by officers on patrol simply because their skin color identified them as potential troublemakers. These discriminatory practices—and it is important to note that they are discriminatory, even if based on accurate statistical information—may well have self-fulfilling consequences. Thus it is not unlikely that frequent encounters with police, particularly those involving youths innocent of wrongdoing, will increase the hostility of these juveniles toward law-enforcement personnel. It is also not unlikely that the frequency of such encounters will in time reduce their significance in the eyes of apprehended juveniles, thereby leading these youths to regard them as "routine." Such responses to police encounters, however, are those which law-enforcement personnel perceive as indicators of the serious delinquent. They thus serve to vindicate and reinforce officers' prejudices, leading to closer sur-

[24] An unco-operative demeanor was presented by more than one-third of the Negro youths but by only one-sixth of the white youths encountered by the police in the course of our observations.

veillance of Negro districts, more frequent encounters with Negro youths, and so on in a vicious circle. Moreover, the consequences of this chain of events are reflected in police statistics showing a disproportionately high percentage of Negroes among juvenile offenders, thereby providing "objective" justification for concentrating police attention on Negro youths.

To a substantial extent, as we have implied earlier, the discretion practiced by juvenile officers is simply an extension of the juvenile-court philosophy, which holds that in making legal decisions regarding juveniles, more weight should be given to the juvenile's character and life-situation than to his actual offending behavior. The juvenile officer's disposition decisions— and the information he uses as a basis for them—are more akin to the discriminations made by probation officers and other correctional workers than they are to decisions of police officers dealing with non-juvenile offenders. The problem is that such clinical-type decisions are not restrained by mechanisms comparable to the principles of due process and the rules of procedure governing police decisions regarding adult offenders. Consequently, prejudicial practices by police officers can escape notice more easily in their dealings with juveniles than with adults.

The observations made in this study serve to underscore the fact that the official delinquent, as distinguished from the juvenile who simply commits a delinquent act, is the product of a social judgment, in this case a judgment made by the police. He is a delinquent because someone in authority has defined him as one, often on the basis of the public face he has presented to officials rather than of the kind of offense he has committed.

Crime

6

SOCIAL NORMS AND CRIME

Every society faces the perennial problem of social control, of devising ways of inducing conformity to its cherished values and norms. In simpler societies, such as Durkheim's "mechanical" society and Tönnies' Gemeinschaft (see Chapter 4), social control was accomplished through informal mechanisms as time-honored traditions were passed on from generation to generation. Deviant behavior was handled through community pressure, ridicule, or ostracism. As societies became larger and more complex, a need for more formal controls developed. The state stepped in, not only to settle disputes among individuals but to discourage transgressions against the collective.

In order to understand the relationship between social norms and crime it is necessary to distinguish among three different types of norms: folkways, mores, and law. Folkways, as noted in the Introduction to the book, are procedural rules that facilitate social interaction, and they may be violated without incurring strong societal reaction. Mores,

on the other hand, are considered essential for the survival of the group. Folkways and mores are typically enforced through a variety of informal controls employed by the society and its social institutions, but some, especially those considered important, are also enforced by formal agencies of social control. "The law, as a type of formal social control, consists of (1) explicit rules of conduct, (2) planned use of sanctions to support the rules, and (3) designated officials to interpret and enforce the rules" (Quinney, 1970a:9). The authority to legislate and enforce the law through the use of coercive sanctions is given to the state. Thus law differs from folkways and mores in that offenses and the mechanisms for its enforcement are explicitly and formally defined.

The law is split into two primary classes: civil and criminal. Civil law is concerned with wrongs committed against the individual, criminal law with crimes against the state or the society as a whole (Sykes, 1967:17). The civil law attempts to bring about restitution of wrongs against persons (e.g., property rights, inheritance) rather than to punish violators as such. While many crimes also involve injury to the victim (assault), they are considered as transgressions against society as a whole. The distinction between civil and criminal offenses is not always clear, since "many illegal acts may be treated as either crimes *or* civil wrongs, depending on the circumstances of the case" (Sykes, 1967:17). Adultery, as a case in point, is sometimes treated as a crime; at other times it becomes the basis for a civil suit as in divorce (Sykes, 1967:17–18).

Some criminologists have attempted to expand the definition of crime to include not only violations of the law but other behavior that is injurious to society (Sykes, 1967:10). They argue that if criminology is to have universal applicability, it must deal with behavior that is harmful to society, not merely with violations of the legal code. Sellin (1938:19–32) suggested abandoning the study of variable legal definitions and concentrating instead on violations of conduct norms that are found universally. Unfortunately, Sellin and other critics of the legal definition of crime do not identify the universal standards that are socially injurious (Tappan, 1947). Such a perspective assumes that criminal law and social norms necessarily correspond. It fails to distinguish between deviant behavior and crime (Quinney, 1965). Although many laws such as those concerning incest and rape are broadly supported, others either lack normative support or conflict with dominant values. The various logical combinations of law and norms are presented in the following table[1]:

	Deviant	Normative
Illegal	Deviant criminal	Normal criminal
Legal	Deviant noncriminal	Conforming noncriminal

[1] It should be noted that these types refer to acts or situations, not to persons.

The deviant criminal pattern is one in which behavior is both illegal and deviant (e.g., rape). Normal crime, on the other hand, involves behavior that violates the law but is not deviant according to larger societal norms. Laws pertaining to restraint of trade, false advertising, and gambling, for example, do not seem to have much support in the normative structure. In the area of sexual behavior, masturbation, premarital coitus, and hetero-sexual mouth-genital contact have been termed "normal deviance" because a large proportion of the population take part in these acts and they do not conflict with societal norms (Gagnon and Simon, 1967:8). The third type, behavior that is deviant but not criminal, has been grossly neglected by sociologists. Many persons who are subjected to social "stigma" (Goffman, 1963) fall into this category. It is not criminal to have a physical disability or deformity or to be an ex-mental patient, but such persons are considered deviant and suffer from what Erving Goffman calls "spoiled identity." The last category consists of behavior that is neither deviant nor criminal.

One of the most important implications to be drawn from this typology concerns the effect of the normal criminal pattern on society. When the legal statutes are not supported by social norms, an anomic situation results in which the law is applied selectively and enforcement is viewed as arbitrary by societal members. Enforcement is very difficult under such conditions, adherence to the law being motivated by fear of punishment rather than by moral commitment.

The typology assumes a uniform set of laws and norms across the society. In reality there is wide internal variation not only in legal statutes but also in social norms. Some acts are illegal in one state or locality and not in another, and penalties for various offenses are not imposed uniformly throughout the United States. Perhaps the subcultural variations in norms and values are more important. An act may be deviant when viewed from one set of norms but not from another. Smoking marijuana deviates from traditional middle-class norms and conforms to the norms of the youth culture. Differential norms become especially important in a complex, heterogeneous society having many diverse and conflicting groups. A single, simple theory of crime cannot explain the wide diversity of criminal activities in a complex society. Theories of crime must take into account not only the correspondence between law and norms but also the variety of normative systems.

CONCEPTIONS OF CRIME

The legal definition of crime and the "socially injurious" view discussed in the preceding section are but two of many diverse conceptions of crime. Here let us focus on two dominant perspectives of the study of crime—order-pluralistic and conflict (for a detailed discussion of these terms see Chapters 2 and 3).

The order and conflict perspectives, it will be recalled, have antithetical conceptions of society. Those who adhere to an order perspective adopt a pluralistic model of society, according to which diverse segments of the society are integrated into a cohesive whole with a common value system. The conflict perspective, on the other hand, sees society as a composite of conflicting interest groups with different values and norms. Two distinctive conceptions of crime, corresponding to the order and conflict models, are found in criminology today. The order, or pluralistic, conception is the oldest and the most widely held. Much of the legal theory that has accumulated appears to be based on an order model of society. "The ideas of the early sociologists directly influenced the school of legal philosophy that became a major force in American legal thought—sociological jurisprudence—in which Roscoe Pound was the principal figure" (Quinney, 1970b:30).

Pound's theory of interests was based on an order, consensus model of society.[2] He felt that the law is a barometer that measures the moral consciousness of society at any given time. The primary function of the law is to adjust and resolve conflicting interests. In a pluralistic society the interests of the society as a whole are reflected in the law:

Looked at functionally, the law is an attempt to satisfy, to reconcile, to harmonize, to adjust these overlapping and often conflicting claims and demands, either through securing them directly and immediately, or through securing certain individual interests, or through delimitations or compromises of individual interests, so as to give effect to the greatest total of interests or to the interests that weigh most in our civilization, with the least sacrifice of the scheme of interests as a whole (Pound, 1943:39).

The pluralistic, order model has been challenged in recent years by a number of criminologists who subscribe to a conflict perspective. The conflict perspective sees law not as a compromise of interests, but rather as the imposition of some interests over others (Quinney, 1970b:39). Groups with power are able to gain control of governmental processes and to pass laws that help them maintain their position. According to the conflict view:

Society is characterized by diversity, conflict, coercion, and change, rather than by consensus and stability. . . . law incorporates the interests of specific persons and groups; it is seldom the product of the whole society. Law is made by men, representing special interests, who have the power to translate their interests into public policy. Unlike the pluralistic conception of politics, law does not represent a compromise of diverse interests in society, but supports some interests at the expense of others (Quinney, 1970b:35).

Power groups control not only the creation of law but also its administration; the police and the courts are representatives of the dominant interest structure in society. Power groups also shape public conceptions of crime.

[2] Much of this discussion of Pound is taken from Quinney (1970b:29–35).

They control task force reports, the mass media, the police, and other agencies that help to formulate public conceptions of crime. Conflict theory maintains that the pluralistic, order model is itself an ideological tool employed by representatives of the power structure (e.g., the police, legal scholars, and sociologists) to legitimize the exploitation of the weak by the powerful. The broad acceptance of the pluralistic view throughout the society indicates that social control has been so effective that people do not see themselves as controlled. They are duped into believing that the legal system represents the interests of all of us, not just some of us.

The pluralistic, order model of political society is usually linked to Durkheim, who maintained that crime is normal behavior (1964:65–73). Crime is a universal phenomenon found in all societies and at all time. It is not pathological, but rather a normal expression of the collective conscience. ". . . the only common characteristic of all crimes is that they consist . . . in acts universally disapproved of by members of each society" (Durkheim, 1933:73). Although Durkheim believed that crime is the collective embodiment of society, he, unlike other order theorists, rejected the view that crime is necessarily injurious to society:

. . . there are many acts which have been and still are regarded as criminal without in themselves being harmful to society. What social danger is there in touching a tabooed object, an impure animal or man, in letting the sacred fire die down. . . . Moreover . . . an act can be disastrous to society without incurring the least repression (Durkheim, 1933:72).

Durkheim's conception of crime is basically consistent with contemporary labeling theory (see the Introduction, Part Two). Crime is ultimately an arbitrary definition created and applied by society. Acts are not inherently criminal or deviant, but rather derive their meaning from social definitions: ". . . we must not say that an action shocks the common conscience because it is criminal, but rather that it is criminal because it shocks the common conscience. We do not reprove it because it is a crime, but it is a crime because we reprove it" (Durkheim, 1933:81). Durkheim was also concerned with the nature of punishment. The primary social function of punishment is not to, deter future offenders but to reinforce societal norms. "Its true function is to maintain social cohesion intact, while maintaining all its vitality in the common conscience" (Durkheim, 1933:108).

According to Durkheim, changes in societal complexity brought about changes in the nature of punishment. Primitive societies, in which solidarity is mechanical, are characterized by repressive sanctions (for a discussion of mechanical and organic solidarity see Chapter 4). The purpose of law is to punish an outrage to the collective morality. As society moves from mechanical to organic solidarity, repressive law tends to be replaced by restitutive law.[3] In a complex society law "is not expiatory, but consists

[3] Some believe that this claim is highly questionable (Timasheff, 1963:109).

of a simple *return in state*" (Durkheim, 1933:111). The purpose of law is to restore damages to injured parties, not to punish. Civil law and contracts assume an increasingly important role in societies with organic solidarity.

CRIME IN AMERICA

Volume and trends

There is much concern with crime in American society today. "Crime in the streets" is a recurrent political issue on both the national and local levels. Many Americans, but especially those who reside in metropolitan areas, are afraid to walk the streets at night. The President's Commission on Law Enforcement and Administration of Justice (1967a:V), in a study of high-crime areas in two large cities, found that because of their fear of crime 43 percent of the respondents stay off the streets at night, 35 percent do not speak to strangers, 21 percent use cars and cabs at night, and 20 percent would like to move to another neighborhood.

The public's fear of crime is supported by crime statistics, which indicate that the volume of crime has risen at an alarming rate.[4] Crimes of violence and property offenses increased between 1933 and 1965 both in total numbers and in the rate per 100,000 population (President's Commission, 1967a:23).[5] However, those offenses that the public fears most, violent crimes, increased less rapidly than other offenses. In the 1933–1965 period the rate tripled for forcible rape and doubled for aggravated assault, but the willful homicide rate decreased to 70 percent of its high rate in 1933 (President's Commission, 1967a:23). Property crimes have risen at a much faster rate than crimes of violence. The greatest increase is found for larceny of $50 or more, a 550-percent increase from 1933 to 1965. Table 1 presents a picture of trends in serious crimes in the past decade. According to the FBI Uniform Crime Reports (UCR), between 1960 and 1972 the rate for crimes of violence increased 149 percent, while the rate for property offenses was up 152 percent. The table shows clearly that those crimes that receive the most publicity (crimes of violence) increased less rapidly than other crimes. The rate for murder was up only 70 percent; the rate for larceny of $50 and over was up 212 percent.

[4] Official statistics, of course, underestimate the total volume of crime, since many crimes are not reported. A survey by the Law Enforcement Assistance Administration in five major cities found that only about one-third to one-half of all crimes are reported (Associated Press, 1974).

[5] These figures should be interpreted cautiously, since their reliability is questionable. The United States, unlike several European nations, did not start keeping national crime statistics until 1930. Moreover, because of changes in reporting, earlier figures are not fully comparable to nor as reliable as figures obtained since 1958 (President's Commission, 1967a:23).

TABLE 1
National crime, rate, and percent change

Crime index offenses	Estimated crime 1972		Percent change over 1971		Percent change over 1967		Percent change over 1960	
	Number	Rate per 100,000 inhabitants	Number	Rate	Number	Rate	Number	Rate
Total	5,891,900	2,829.5	−1.7	−2.7	+54.6	+46.9	+191.7	+151.2
Violent	828,150	397.7	+2.2	+1.3	+67.1	+58.8	+189.6	+149.3
Property	5,063,800	2,431.8	−2.3	−3.3	+52.7	+45.1	+192.1	+151.6
Murder	18,520	8.9	+5.0	+4.7	+52.6	+45.9	+105.0	+78.0
Forcible rape	46,430	22.3	+10.8	+9.9	+69.6	+61.6	+172.6	+134.7
Robbery	374,560	179.9	−2.9	−3.8	+85.5	+76.2	+248.9	+200.3
Aggravated assault	388,650	186.6	+6.6	+5.5	+52.9	+45.2	+154.7	+119.3
Burglary	2,345,000	1,126.1	−1.0	−1.9	+45.6	+38.3	+160.4	+124.3
Larceny $50 and over	1,837,800	882.6	−2.0	−2.9	+75.1	+66.4	+262.3	+212.0
Auto theft	881,000	423.1	−6.4	−7.3	+34.5	+27.8	+170.3	+132.9

SOURCE: FBI *Uniform Crime Reports* (1973:2).

The table also shows that violent crimes account for a very small proportion of all crimes. The FBI Uniform Crime Report Index includes the seven most "serious" offenses. Four of these, murder, rape, aggravated assault, and robbery, are violent crimes; the others, burglary, larceny of $50 and over, and auto theft, are property offenses. In 1972 only 14 percent of the reported UCR offenses were crimes of violence (FBI, 1973:1). Violent crimes account for an even smaller proportion of all crimes, since many property crimes are excluded from the Crime Index (e.g., embezzlement, fraud, loan sharking, tax evasion, bribery, and graft). The UCR Index also excludes "drunkenness," for which more persons are arrested than any other offense (FBI, 1973:122). Criminal homicide, probably the most feared of all crimes, is a very low-volume offense, constituting about 2 percent of the crimes of violence and less than one-half of 1 percent of all Crime Index offenses (FBI, 1973:6). There were only 8.9 murders per 100,000 persons in 1972 (FBI, 1973:6).

Characteristics of offenders

Crime is not peculiar to any group, but rather is ubiquitous to American society. Whereas earlier biological and psychological theories treated "criminals" as a distinctive category, today it is clear that crime cuts across all social and economic groups. Each of us, at one time or another, violates the law. A study of 1700 adults, most from the state of New York, found that 91 percent admitted committing offenses for which they could have received jail or prison sentences (President's Commission, 1967a:43). Most persons who violate the law, however, are not officially labeled "criminals." The criminal label is a social definition applied selectively by the police and the courts to certain segments of the population.

Age is a persistent correlate of crime. Adolescents and youthful offenders comprise a large proportion of the criminal population. The President's Commission on Law Enforcement and Administration of Justice concluded that:

America's best hope for reducing crime is to reduce juvenile delinquency and youth crime. In 1965 a majority of all arrests for major crimes against property were of people under 21, as were a substantial minority of arrests for major crimes against the person. The recidivism rates for young offenders are higher than those for any other age group (1967a:55).

Although adolescents and young adults appear to be the most criminally prone age groups, the relationship between age and crime varies considerably according to the type of offense. Persons under twenty-five years of age have high rates of arrest for all of the serious crimes in the URC Index. Table 2 shows that this age group accounts for 75 percent of the arrests for serious crimes in the United States. Approximately 59 percent of the arrests for crimes of violence and 80 percent of property offenses were of persons under twenty-five. But when all crimes are considered, about half

TABLE 2
Total arrests of persons under 15, under 18, under 21, and under 25 years of age, 1972
[6,195 agencies; 1972 estimated population 160,416,000]

Offense charged	Grand total all ages	Number of persons arrested				Percentage			
		Under 15	Under 18	Under 21	Under 25	Under 15	Under 18	Under 21	Under 25
Total	7,013,194	665,887	1,793,984	2,753,814	3,751,878	9.5	25.6	39.3	53.5
Criminal homicide:									
(a) Murder and nonnegligent manslaughter	15,049	221	1,634	3,709	6,578	1.5	10.9	24.6	43.7
(b) Manslaughter by negligence	2,986	33	282	778	1,398	1.1	9.4	26.1	46.8
Forcible rape	19,374	818	3,842	7,752	12,135	4.2	19.8	40.0	62.6
Robbery	109,217	11,387	34,823	59,005	82,900	10.4	31.9	54.0	75.9
Aggravated assault	155,581	9,094	27,256	47,095	73,569	5.8	17.5	30.3	47.3
Burglary—breaking or entering	314,393	68,087	160,376	219,377	261,980	21.7	51.0	69.8	83.3
Larceny—theft	678,673	165,360	336,983	442,828	523,809	24.4	49.7	65.2	77.2
Auto theft	121,842	16,711	65,255	87,155	102,107	13.7	53.6	71.5	83.8
Violent crime [a]	299,221	21,520	67,555	117,561	175,182	7.2	22.6	39.3	58.5
Property crime [b]	1,114,908	250,158	562,614	749,360	887,896	22.4	50.5	67.2	79.6
Subtotal for above offenses	1,417,115	271,711	630,451	867,699	1,064,476	19.2	44.5	61.2	75.1

Offense								
Other assaults	307,638	25,237	60,322	98,068	149,790	8.2	19.6	31.9	48.7
Arson	10,645	4,251	6,203	7,248	8,132	39.9	58.3	68.1	76.4
Forgery and counterfeiting	44,313	690	4,311	12,320	23,418	1.6	9.7	27.8	52.8
Fraud	96,713	1,069	3,705	13,227	33,481	1.1	3.8	13.7	34.6
Embezzlement	6,744	112	379	1,054	2,525	1.7	5.6	15.6	37.4
Stolen property; buying, receiving, possessing	71,754	6,932	21,988	36,736	49,901	9.7	30.6	51.2	69.5
Vandalism	129,724	57,490	91,586	103,697	112,371	44.3	70.6	79.9	86.6
Weapons; carrying, possessing, etc.	119,671	4,928	18,656	35,612	57,374	4.1	15.6	29.8	47.9
Prostitution and commercialized vice	44,744	127	1,399	10,132	26,968	.3	3.1	22.6	60.3
Sex offenses (except forcible rape and prostitution)	51,124	4,037	10,977	17,471	25,753	7.9	21.5	34.2	50.4
Narcotic drug laws	431,608	12,865	98,308	227,048	338,327	3.0	22.8	52.6	78.4
Gambling	70,064	267	1,728	4,668	10,679	.4	2.5	6.7	15.2
Offenses against family and children	52,935	270	1,034	7,855	17,983	.5	2.0	14.8	34.0
Driving under the influence	604,291	168	7,568	50,749	131,432	°	1.3	8.4	21.7
Liquor laws	207,675	7,609	76,894	150,948	166,302	3.7	37.0	72.7	80.1
Drunkenness	1,384,735	4,964	40,625	127,898	264,323	.4	2.9	9.2	19.1
Disorderly conduct	582,513	46,446	127,756	218,297	311,251	8.0	21.9	37.5	53.4
Vagrancy	55,680	1,060	5,547	14,337	31,728	1.9	10.0	25.7	57.0
All other offenses (except traffic)	966,722	96,954	256,815	412,258	580,204	10.0	26.6	42.6	60.0
Suspicion	41,475	3,784	12,421	21,181	30,149	9.1	29.9	51.1	72.7
Curfew and loitering law violations	116,126	33,610	116,126	116,126	116,126	28.9	100.0	100.0	100.0
Runaways	199,185	81,306	199,185	199,185	199,185	4.8	100.0	100.0	100.0

SOURCE: FBI *Uniform Crime Reports* (1973:128).

[a] Violent crime is offenses of murder, forcible rape, robbery and aggravated assault.
[b] Property crime is offenses of burglary, larceny and auto theft.
[c] Less than one-tenth of 1 percent.

241

of offenders are over twenty-four. "Offenders over 24 make up the great majority of persons arrested for fraud, embezzlement, gambling, drunkenness, offenses against the family, and vagrancy" (President's Commission, 1967a:44).

Another factor that is related to crime is sex. Most persons arrested for crimes are men. The ratio of arrests is about six males for every female (FBI, 1973:34). UCR figures show that 10 percent of the arrests for violent crimes and 20 percent of those for property offenses involved women (FBI, 1973:34). Women's primary involvement was in larceny, which accounted for 19 percent of all female arrests (FBI, 1973:34). Although women account for a small proportion of all crime, their criminal involvement appears to be increasing. Between 1960 and 1970 arrests for females under 18 increased 204 percent; in comparison arrests for males in this age group increased only 98 percent. During the same period UCR Index crimes rose 73 percent for males and 202 percent for females (FBI, 1971:36).

Crime rates are much higher in large cities than in rural areas. According to the President's Commission:

Twenty-six core cities of more than 500,000 people, with less than 18 percent of the total population, account for more than half of all reported Index crimes against the person and more than 30 percent of all reported Index property crimes. One of every three robberies and nearly one of every five rapes occurs in cities of more than 1 million (1967a:28).

In 1972 the total UCR rate of crime per 100,000 inhabitants was 4947.9 for cities over 250,000 and 2363.6 for suburban areas and only 1084.4 for rural areas (FBI, 1973:2). The level of crime is highest in the inner-city slums of large metropolitan areas. Numerous studies have shown that robbery, burglary, and violent crimes typically "occur in areas characterized by low income, physical deterioration, dependency, racial and ethnic concentrations, broken homes . . . and high population density" (President's Commission, 1967a:35). Crime rates tend to decrease as one moves outward from the inner city.

Crime in the United States varies by region. When all UCR offenses are considered, the crime rate is highest in the Western states (4030.3) and lowest in the South (2462.7). The Northeastern (2840.6) and the North Central (2480.7) states have intermediate rates. There are, however, internal variations according to the offense. The rates for murder and aggravated assault, for example, are highest in the South (FBI, 1973:2).

The victims of crime

The typical conception of the criminal is one of a stranger lurking in the shadows, waiting to prey on innocent and helpless victims. Such a conception is not supported by the data on victimization. The victim and the offender in violent crimes are rarely complete strangers, and in many cases they are relatives or intimate acquaintances. In a famous study of homicide in Philadelphia, Wolfgang (1957) found that in only 12.2 percent of the cases was the assailant a stranger. About one-fourth of all murders occur within a family unit (FBI, 1973:8). Most murders are unplanned and explosive, resulting from family arguments, altercations among friends and acquaintances, or lovers' quarrels and romantic triangles. Felony murders, "defined as those killings resulting from robbery, sex motive, gangland slaying, and other felonious activities" (FBI, 1973:8), account for only 22.1 percent of the total (another 5.3 percent are suspected felony murders). It is also interesting to note that males outnumber females as victims of murder by about 4 to 1 (FBI, 1973:6).

Although national data on the victim-offender relationship are only available for homicide, studies in a number of cities suggest that the pattern is very similar for rape and aggravated assault. Amir (1967:56) found in a study of rape that 48 percent of the victim-offender relationships could be classified as "primary" relationships. He also rejected a number of popular misconceptions about rape:

1. *Negroes are more likely to attack white women than Negro women.* (Most rapes were intraracial.)
2. *Rape usually occurs between total strangers.* (In only a minority of cases were the victim and offender strangers.)
3. *Rape victims are innocent persons.* (Twenty percent of the victims had a police record, especially for sexual offenses. Another 20 percent had "bad" reputations.)
4. *Rape is predominantly an explosive act.* (In about 71 percent of the cases the rape was planned.)
5. *Rape is mainly a dead-end street or dark-alley event.* (Rapes usually occurred in the place where the victim and offender first met.)
6. *Rape is a violent crime in which brutality is inflicted upon the victim.* (In 87 percent of the cases only temptation and verbal coercion were used to subdue the victim.)
7. *Victims generally resist their attackers.* (Over half did not resist their attackers in any way.)

Findings obtained by the District of Columbia Crime Commission are consistent with Amir's data. The commission found that:

Almost two-thirds of the 151 [rape] victims surveyed were attacked by persons with whom they were at least casually acquainted. Only 36 percent of the 224 assailants about whom some identifying information was obtained were complete strangers to their victims: 16 (7 percent) of the attackers were known to the victim by sight, although there had been no previous contact. Thirty-one (14 percent) of the 224 assailants were relatives, family friends or boy friends of the victims, and 88 (39 percent) were either acquaintances or neighbors (President's Commission, 1967a:40).

As in homicide and rape, victims and offenders in assault cases are seldom strangers. "Most aggravated assaults occur within the family unit, and among neighbors or acquaintances" (FBI, 1973:10). In the District of Columbia study only 19 percent of the victims did not know their assailants (President's Commission, 1967a:40). Eleven percent of the attacks involved a spouse, 10 percent other relatives, and in 60 percent of the cases the victim and offender were at least casually acquainted (President's Commission, 1967a:40).

As was noted in the discussion of Amir's study of rape, a common misconception is that crimes of violence are interracial. The vast majority of murders, rapes, and assaults involve persons of the same race. A study in Chicago found "that Negroes are most likely to assault Negroes, whites most likely to assault whites. Thus, while Negro males account for two-thirds of all assaults, the offender who victimizes a white person is most likely also to be white" (President's Commission, 1967a:40). Although middle-class whites fear "crime in the streets" and call for "law and order," they are relatively immune from victimization. The President's Commission (1967a:42) reported that "the burglary victimization rates were highest in the districts where the overall crime rates were highest." Most persons who commit serious crimes victimize others with similar social characteristics. Victims of crime, like offenders, are typically male, nonwhite, and in lower-income groups (President's Commission, 1967b:80–84). Lower-income groups are more likely to be victims of rape, robbery, and burglary. The only UCR offense in which the chances of victimization clearly increase with income is larceny of $50 and over (President's Commission, 1967b:80–84). Similarly, blacks are more likely than whites to be victimized for all Index offenses except larceny (President's Commission, 1967b:80–84). The chance of victimization for crimes of violence is greatest for men between the ages of twenty and twenty-nine (except for rape of course).

THE CREATION OF PUBLIC CONCEPTIONS OF CRIME

Much of the public's perception of crime is based on images presented by the mass media and police agencies (for an excellent discussion of criminal conceptions see, Quinney, 1970b:277–302). Evidence suggests that public attitudes toward crime are shaped more by mass media presentations than by the actual incidence of crime. Since most crimes are not experienced directly, the coverage of crime plays an important role in creating conceptions of crime. One study reported that there was no relationship between the volume of crime news presented in four Colorado newspapers and crime statistics for the state (Davis, 1952). What is critical is that public opinion with respect to crime corresponded more closely to variations in news coverage than to the actual volume of crime in these localities. Perception of crime is then, at least partly, dependent on media exposure.

Even within the same city the mass media may present very different portrayals of crime. A content analysis of two New York City newspapers over a three-month period showed that *The Daily News* included almost two items on juvenile delinquency for every item on the same subject included by *The New York Times*. *The Daily News* was four times as likely as the *Times* to carry front-page coverage of delinquency, and its stories were typically more emotional and sensational (Bachmuth, Miller, and Rosen, 1960).

A second important source of conceptions of crime is crime statistics. While local crime statistics shape attitudes toward crime, the most complete and influential statistics are those presented by the FBI's Uniform Crime Reports. The UCR, published yearly, is based on voluntary reports from local law-enforcement agencies. The FBI furnishes local police officials with a *Uniform Crime Reporting Handbook* as a guide for preparing the reports. Crimes are divided into two categories. Part I includes the seven most "serious" offenses that make up the Crime Index. Part II includes other, less serious offenses. There is a difference in the way offenses are tabulated; Part I offenses are recorded as "crimes known to the police," Part II offenses as the number of persons "charged by the police." Part I "crimes were selected for use in the Crime Index because, as a group, they represent the most common local crime problem. They are all serious crimes, either by their very nature or due to the volume in which they occur" (FBI, 1972:5).

The FBI Index can be criticized on several levels. First, an index is assumed to be a representative sampling of a larger universe. In the case of crime in the United States, however, the larger universe—all crimes committed—is unknown. The Crime Index then is a measure of crimes that come to the attention of the police, but we do not know if there is a constant ratio between crimes known to the police and all crimes committed (Wolfgang, 1963). The process through which crimes become known to the police is selective rather than random. Since the police are representatives of the power structure, they are more sensitive to the crimes committed by people who lack power, namely, the poor and members of social minorities. This bias is evident even in the construction of the Crime Index, which excludes white-collar crimes on the grounds that they are "not important." ". . . the underlying defect of police reporting as a measure of the volume of crime is that the police have only a very limited function in crime control, and the crimes reported by the police are only a fraction of those that occur" (Shulman, 1966:483). Since crimes generally come to the attention of the police as a result of citizen complaints, "crimes without victims" (e.g., prostitution, gambling, and homosexuality) and those involving sex and family relationships are likely to go unreported (Shulman, 1966). Other crimes that do not come to the attention of the police are tax evasion, embezzlement, shoplifting by middle-class persons, forged and fraudulent checks for small amounts, gambling offenses, and bribes of public officials (Shulman, 1966). In addition, many crimes such as restraint of trade and price fixing are not considered violations of the criminal law and are dealt with under administrative and civil law. Finally, the UCR does not include violations of federal law.

Although the Crime Index reputedly contains the seven most "serious" crimes, the rationale for including these offenses and excluding others has never been clear. Arson, kidnapping, and assault and battery may inflict as much physical harm as Index crimes (Wolfgang, 1963). There is no apparent explanation for why crimes such as embezzlement, which results in great property losses, are omitted while larceny over $50 is included (Wolfgang, 1963). Moreover, items are not weighed according to the seriousness of the offense. A larceny of $50 contributes as much to the total Index as a homicide. Since burglary makes up about 40 percent of all Index offenses (FBI, 1971:18), a slight change in the burglary rate will have a substantial impact on the total Index, whereas a large change in homicide will have a negligible effect on the Index.

Another difficulty with the Index is that much crime is hidden by the method of classifying multiple offenses. The *Uniform Crime Reporting Handbook* instructs law-enforcement officials to tabulate only the most serious crime when more than one offense is committed in a criminal event. The Manual gives the following illustration:

Problem: A holdup man forces a husband and his wife to get out of their automobile. He shoots the husband and leaves in the automobile after taking money from the husband. The husband dies as a result of the shooting.

Solution: In the problem we can recognize robbery and murder as well as auto theft. . . . only one offense of murder is scored (FBI, 1966:41).

Perhaps the most serious criticism that can be made of UCR figures is that the police are able to manipulate public conceptions of crime by either under- or overreporting. If a police department wants to create the impression that crime is being "reduced," it can accomplish this reduction statistically. Ironically, more efficient law enforcement and improved reporting will result in an increased crime rate. Conversely, poor law enforcement and underreporting of crime will result in a reduction in crime.

The inadequacies of the UCR Index are an issue of concern because of the impact of these statistics on public opinion. The FBI figures are widely disseminated and publicized by the mass media. They are read not only by the average citizen but also by legislators and other public officials who make decisions about the funding of law-enforcement agencies. The manner in which crime statistics are presented seems designed to shock the public and to create a crime scare (for a discussion of "the crime control establishment," see Silver, 1974). The FBI has "time clocks" that inform us that so many crimes occur each minute or fraction of a minute. The figure that follows, for example, shows that one rape occurs every eleven minutes and one burglary every thirteen seconds. Although these statistics might

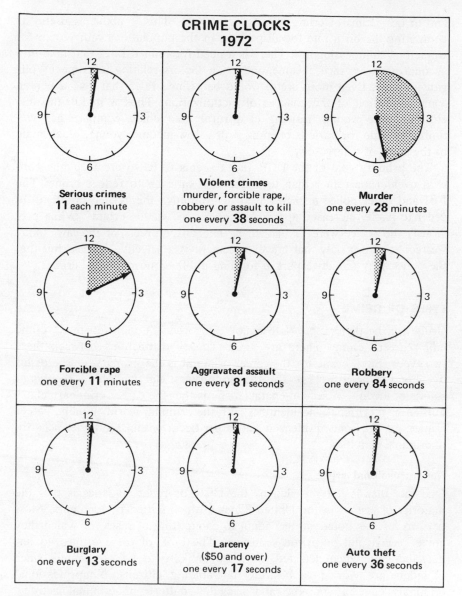

CRIME CLOCKS
1972

Serious crimes
11 each minute

Violent crimes
murder, forcible rape,
robbery or assault to kill
one every **38** seconds

Murder
one every **28** minutes

Forcible rape
one every **11** minutes

Aggravated assault
one every **81** seconds

Robbery
one every **84** seconds

Burglary
one every **13** seconds

Larceny
($50 and over)
one every **17** seconds

Auto theft
one every **36** seconds

Source: FBI *Uniform Crime Reports* (1973:30).

make for interesting reading, they tell us nothing about changes in the incidence of crime nor about the chances of victimization. The clocks create the impression that crime has reached epidemic proportions without taking into account changes in the population. The UCR Index does present crude rates per 100,000 persons, but there is an implicit assumption that all persons in the population are equally likely to commit crimes and to be victims of crime (Wolfgang, 1963). This is about as useful as computing the birth rate for all persons in the populations rather than for women of childbearing age. There is a need for refined rates that take into account age, sex, race, income, and other factors relating to crime (Wolfgang, 1963). Even more useful would be refined rates that give a person some indication of the chances of victimization. Thus a middle-income, elderly, white woman residing in a rural area could compare her victimization rate for various offenses with a low-income, young, black male in the slum of a large city.

The primary goal of the UCR Index seems to be to create public concern over crime rather than to understand or even to reduce crime. The FBI and other police agencies need to dramatize the "crime problem" in order to justify increased appropriations for a "war on crime." While previously the police were thought to be neutral enforcers of the law, today we recognize not only that law enforcement is a selective process but that the police play an active part in forming public conceptions of crime.

TYPES OF CRIME

Crime can be divided into two major categories: "nonprofessional" crime and "career" crime. There are three primary distinctions between these two types. First, crime for the career criminal is the primary source of his livelihood, whereas crime for the nonprofessional is only a secondary source of income. A second characteristic is that the career criminal defines himself as a criminal and identifies with the criminal world. Finally, career crimes are not isolated offenses, but rather occur within a broader network of criminal activities.

Nonprofessional crime

One fact that is not revealed by the UCR or other statistics is that the majority of crimes in the United States are committed by amateurs. Most persons, as was noted earlier, admit to committing offenses for which they could receive jail or prison sentences. The bulk of these crimes go undetected, and when detected, they are unlikely to be prosecuted, since offenders are viewed as basically law-abiding citizens. Nonprofessional criminals have a sporadic and irregular pattern of criminal activity. ". . . most people do not persist in committing offenses" (President's Commission, 1967a:44). The crimes of the amateur are likely to be relatively minor offenses such as shoplifting of items under $10 in value. "However, it is the total volume, rather than individual acts, that makes shoplifting a serious problem for most commercial enterprises. Nationally most large retail businesses estimate their overall inventory shrinkage due to shoplifting, employee theft, and accounting errors at between 1 and 2 percent of total inventory" (President's Commission, 1967a:42).

Business establishments need to contend not only with crimes committed against them by the public but also with crimes of their own employees. The President's Commission observed:

. . . theft by employees accounts for a considerably larger volume of theft than shoplifting. . . . Employee theft is also a problem in many industrial concerns. A recent survey by the National Industrial Conference Board of 473 companies indicated that 20 percent of all companies and nearly 30 percent of those with more than 1,000 employees had a serious problem with employee theft. . . . More than half of the companies with a problem of employee theft indicated trouble with both white and blue collar workers (1967a:43).

Although employee theft occurs among both blue- and white-collar workers, sociologists have been particularly interested in white-collar crime. The term white-collar crime, introduced by Edwin H. Sutherland, refers to "crime committed by a person of respectability and high social status in the course of his occupation" (Sutherland, 1949:9).

Sutherland's research has become the classic statement on white-collar crime. Dissatisfied with traditional sociological theories that relied heavily on poverty and social class to explain crime, he suggested "that persons of the upper socio-economic class engage in much criminal behavior; that this criminal behavior differs from the criminal behavior of the lower socioeconomic class principally in the administrative procedures which are used in dealing with the offenders . . ." (Sutherland, 1949:9). Sutherland felt that conventional theories were based on biased statistics. The upper-status person has the power and influence to avoid prosecution. When charged, he can employ skilled attorneys and more effectively escape conviction. Even more serious is the class bias involved in the administration of the law. We have two sets of laws—one applies only to business and the professions, the other to the rest of the society. "Persons who violate laws regarding restraint of trade, advertising, pure food and drugs are not arrested by uniformed policemen, are not often tried in criminal courts, and are not committed to prisons . . ." (Sutherland, 1949:8). Their cases come before administrative commissions or civil courts. Sutherland undertook an ambitious study of 70 of the 200 largest corporations in the United States. Although many suits against corporations are not made public, he was able to document 980 decisions against these corporations in their lifetimes (Sutherland, 1949:20). The range of decisions against individual corporations was from 1 to 50 with an average of 14. The decisions involved restraint of trade, "infringement," unfair labor practices, rebates, misrepresentation in advertising, and various miscellaneous offenses.

Sutherland's research has been subjected to a number of criticisms. According to Vold (1958:243), it is "ambiguous, uncertain, and controversial." Some feel that the theory is too broad and imprecise. Sutherland sometimes appears to "personify" corporations and to treat them as individuals (Geis, 1962). He failed to distinguish adequately between the crimes of corporations per se and those of executives, arguing that the crimes of corporations are the crimes of executives and managers. He maintained that executives are aware of corporate crimes and should be held responsible for them (Sutherland, 1949:54). Geis' (1962) study of General Electric and violations of the Sherman Antitrust Act found that a number of executives were not aware of price-fixing activities. This study also questions the assumption that white-collar offenders do not think of themselves as criminals. A number of antitrust violators regarded themselves as criminals and felt "stigmatized" as a result of their conviction. Probably the most serious criticism of white-collar crime is that most of the activities that are subsumed under this rubric are not criminal offenses but violations of civil law, administrative rules, or simply immoral or unethical practices. Robert G. Caldwell (1958) argues that most so-called white-collar crimes are not crimes at all. Although we may question many business activities as immoral or unethical, they are not criminal unless someone is convicted of violating a criminal statute (Caldwell, 1958).

While Sutherland's theoretical formulations have many weaknesses, there is no doubt that he made a valuable contribution by shifting the focus of criminology from class theories to more inclusive explanations. Even if many white-collar offenses are not technically crimes, they can be shown to be socially injurious. One certainly cannot dismiss these as minor, or inconsequential, offenses, for literally billions of dollars are lost annually to white-collar crime. "The financial cost of white collar crime is probably several times as great as the financial cost of all the crimes which are customarily regarded as 'the crime problem'" (Sutherland, 1949:12). Perhaps more important than the financial cost of crime is the effect that crime committed by respectable citizens has on societal morale and on respect for law and order. "There is an obvious and basic incongruity involved in the proposition that a community's leaders and more responsible elements are also its criminals" (Vold, 1958:253).

Career crime

Career crime can be divided into two basic subtypes—professional crime and organized crime. Professional criminals frequently have a symbiotic relationship with organized criminals, but they are not part of organized crime. "Often they may be hired to do special jobs by the established figures in the world of organized crime, but they are not regarded as permanently a part of that world" (President's Commission, 1967a:46). This distinction is not intended to suggest that members of organized crime are somehow less "professional" than other criminals, but rather that there are enough differences between them to warrant two separate, though overlapping, categories.

Professional crime

The pioneer study of professional crime was Edwin H. Sutherland's, *The Professional Thief* (1937). The book, written in collaboration with a professional thief (Chic Conwell), provides an inside look at professional crime. The picture of the professional thief which emerged from this description was in sharp conflict with the stereotyped conception of a ruthless psychopathic killer. He showed that professional thieves typically abhor the use of violence and rely instead on intelligence and cunning. There is "honor among thieves" in the sense that relations are regulated by a complex system of norms and values, and by a strict code of ethics. These norms and values, as well as the techniques for committing offenses, are learned through differential association (see Chapter 5 for a detailed discussion of this concept). Sutherland (1937:197–215) outlined five basic characteristics of professional crime:

1. *The profession of theft as a complex of techniques.* Like other professionals, the professional thief develops a complex of abilities and skills that facilitate the execution of crime. "Manual dexterity and physical force are a minor element in these techniques. The principal elements in these techniques are wits, 'front,' and talking ability."
2. *The profession of theft as status.* There are a number of status gradations among professional thieves. One's status is determined not only by financial success but also by connections, power, technical skills, and overall knowledge.
3. *The profession of theft as consensus.* There is general consensus among thieves with respect to attitudes and beliefs concerning clients (victims), the police, and many other issues. Since professional thieves are considered outcasts from legitimate society, they develop their own subcultural norms and values. A code of ethics emerges to regulate social relations and guard against activities that are harmful to the group (e.g., "squealing" and breaking commitments).
4. *The profession of theft as differential association.* Most professional thieves regard nonprofessionals, including white-collar criminals, with contempt. Professional theft is defined by differential association. "The group defines its own membership. A person who is received in the group and recognized as a professional thief is a professional thief"
5. *The profession of theft as organization.* Professional crime is "organized" in the sense that it occurs within a system of unity and reciprocity. Professional crime is a collective enterprise. Admission into the group is based on selection and tutelage by other professional criminals. Among the characteristics used in selection are wits, nerve, talking ability, and, most importantly, "honesty" in dealing with other criminals.

Between the professional thief and the amateur criminal there are numerous criminals who are habitual offenders or at best semiprofessionals. "The small-time professional spends virtually all of his time directly engaged in crime. . . . The more successful professional criminals spend a greater proportion of their time on planning and other preparation" (President's Commission, 1967a:46). While the more successful professional can spend weeks planning a promising "caper," the "small-time" operator is constantly "hustling" in many diverse activities. At one end of the continuum are "big-con" men (e.g., jewel thieves) who engage in transactions involving hundreds of thousands of dollars. At the other extreme we find "short-con" men, shoplifters, and pickpockets (President's Commission, 1967a: 46). Roebuck and Johnson's (1962) study of "The Jack-of-All-Trades Offender" provides an interesting contrast with the professional criminal. These are habitual, nonspecialized offenders who make their living at crime but who never develop special skills and have very low status among criminals. The most striking characteristic was their naïveté in committing crimes. They took unusual chances; their burglaries were not specialized (they "took everything that wasn't nailed down"); they seldom made connections with a "fence" before committing a crime, and they went through with a job even when something went awry. As a result of their ineptness and frequent arrests, these men were not accepted by professional criminals.

Our knowledge of professional crime is extremely limited, based on scattered anecdotal material. *The Professional Thief* (1937) remains a primary source of information even though it is not clear if this description of professional crime is still applicable today (for a more recent statement on professional crime, see Letkemann, 1973). A pilot study sponsored by the President's Commission (1967b:96–101) in which law-enforcement agents and professional criminals were interviewed in four cities—Atlanta, Chicago, New York, and San Francisco—has called into question some of Sutherland's basic assumptions. Contrary to Sutherland's assertion, most professional criminals in this study were generalists not specialists; nor were they especially loyal to their colleagues. There was an absence of strong ethical codes and the "honesty" that Sutherland emphasized.

It is difficult to interpret the findings of the President's Commission, since we do not know whether the incongruity between them and Sutherland's work is due to changes in the world of professional crime or to differences in the definition of crime employed by the two studies. The commission's definition of crime bears little resemblance to Sutherland's. Professional crime was defined as crime committed for personal economic gain, whereas Sutherland was emphatic in asserting that all persons who make their living at crime are not necessarily professionals. Such a conception views professional crime as an individual phenomenon and neglects the role played by differential association in the selection and tutelage of criminals. Finally, about two-thirds of the 50 criminals studied by the commission were in jail or prison. Sutherland maintained that the truly professional criminal has "connections" that enable him to engage in illegal activities without fear of prosecution. When all these factors are considered, they suggest that the commission studied habitual criminals known to the police rather than an elite group of professional criminals.

There is reason to believe that the world of professional crime is undergoing change; Irwin and Yablonsky (1965) maintain that the "professional" is gradually being replaced by a criminal pattern that resembles "The Jack-of-All-Trades Offender." The "old," skilled professional who relies on wits, talking ability, and the capacity to outfox others (Roebuck and Johnson, 1964:235) is apparently on the demise. His place is being taken by a "new" criminal who is typically unskilled, works alone, and is not bound by subcultural norms or a code of ethics.

Organized crime

Few topics have aroused more interest or created greater controversy than organized crime. The world of organized crime is part of American folklore, depicted graphically in the mass media and simultaneously feared and envied by the public. While most Americans take the existence of organized crime for granted, there has been considerable controversy among criminologists, journalists, and public officials over its existence. Few would deny that there are organized criminal activities in the large cities of the United States, but there is some question as to the extent to which such activities are "organized." Some argue that there is a national syndicate or cartel that organizes criminal activities in the United States on a national level. Skeptics, on the other hand, maintain that these crimes are carried out on a local or, at best, regional level and that the evidence of a national crime syndicate has not been produced. Most of the evidence supporting the idea of a national crime syndicate has come from agencies of the federal government, Senate investigating committees, and law-enforcement officials. Typical of these is the position taken by the President's Commission on Law Enforcement and Administration of Justice (1967a: 192).

Today the core of organized crime in the United States consists of 24 groups operating as criminal cartels in large cities across the Nation. Their membership is exclusively Italian, they are in frequent communication with each other, and their smooth functioning is insured by a national body of overseers. To date, only the Federal Bureau of Investigation has been able to document fully the national scope of these groups, and FBI intelligence indicates that the organization as a whole has changed its name from the Mafia to La Cosa Nostra.

The late J. Edgar Hoover informed a House of Representatives Appropriations Subcommittee that La Cosa Nostra "operates on a nationwide basis, with international implications, and until recent years it carried on its activities with almost complete secrecy" (President's Commission, 1967a: 192).

Although the President's Commission (1967a:196) acknowledges that information on organized crime is sketchy and incomplete, it does present a fairly detailed description of the internal structure of organized crime. According to the commission (1967a:192–193), organized crime is controlled by 24 "families" with membership in a family ranging from 20 to 700. The figure that follows presents the structure of an organized crime family. The hierarchy bears some resemblance to a feudal, military kingdom, although more direct precedent for the American Mafia is found in

An organized crime family

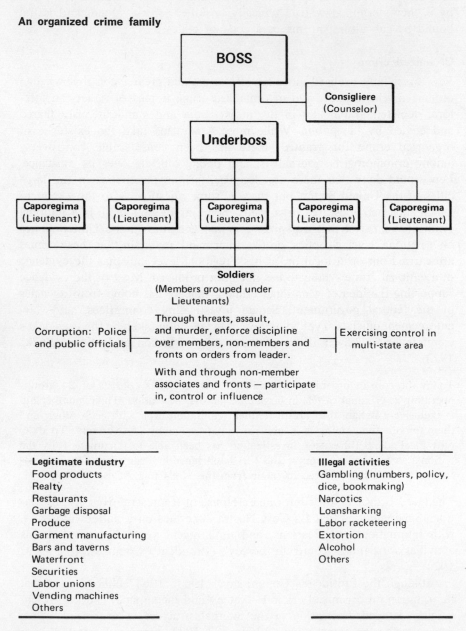

Source: President's Commission on Law Enforcement and Administration of Justice (1967a:194).

the Sicilian Mafia (President's Commission, 1967a:193). "Each family is headed by one man, the 'boss,' whose primary functions are maintaining order and maximizing profits" (President's Commission, 1967a:193).

The "underboss" is next in command and acts for the boss in his absence. He coordinates relations and messages between the boss and subordinates. The "counselor," or *consigliere*, occupies an important position roughly at the same level as the underboss, but he operates outside of the hierarchy in a staff capacity. This position is usually assumed by an older, experienced member of the family. The "lieutenants" (*caporegime*) are below the underboss and may serve as "buffers" between the higher echelons and lower-level members. Lieutenants usually head operating units and act in a supervisory capacity. The lowest-ranking members of the family are soldiers (*soldati*). "A soldier may operate a particular illicit enterprise (e.g., a loan-sharking operation, a dice game, a lottery . . .) on a commission basis, or he may 'own' the enterprise and pay a portion of its profit to the organization . . ." (President's Commission, 1967a:193). While the boss is the head of the family, the ultimate authority rests in the "commission," which acts as the ruling body over the 24 families. The commission is composed of from 9 to 12 bosses from the most influential families. It has authority to set policy and arbitrate disputes.

Discipline among members of organized crime is maintained through secrecy and a strict code of conduct. The code, patterned after the Sicilian Mafia's code of *omerta* or "manliness" (Cressey, 1967:41), elicits "loyalty, honor, respect, absolute obedience . . . through material rewards, and through violence" (President's Commission, 1967a:195). It works to maintain the position of power of high-ranking members, who typically avoid contact or communication with lower-level members. There is general agreement that the major source of income for organized crime is gambling (President's Commission, 1967a:188). It includes the "numbers" game, offtrack betting, dice games, and wagers on sporting events. Gambling operations are carefully organized into elaborate hierarchies, with profits eventually accruing to leaders of organized crime. Loan sharking, "the lending of money at higher rates than the legally prescribed limit, is the second largest source of revenue for organized crime" (President's Commission, 1967a:189). Among those who borrow illicitly are gamblers, narcotics users, and small businessmen. Interest rates may be as high as 150 percent a week (President's Commission, 1967a:189). The third major source of income is the sale of narcotics. The distribution of narcotics is organized along the lines of a sophisticated import-export business. The sale of heroin, for example, passes through four or five levels from the importer to the pusher on the street. The involvement of organized crime is primarily on the level of importing and wholesale distribution rather than direct sale to addicts (President's Commission, 1967a:189).

While this description of organized crime has been disseminated by the mass media and is widely accepted by the public, a number of writers have challenged the idea of a national crime syndicate. They maintain that the existence of organized crime, or the Mafia, has not been demonstrated beyond the assertion that it exists. Daniel Bell believes that although very little evidence has been produced concerning the existence of the Mafia, Americans continue to believe in the myth of the Mafia. "There is . . . in the American temper, a feeling that 'somewhere,' 'somebody' is pulling all the complicated strings to which this jumbled world dances" (Bell, 1960:127). Gus Tyler (1962a:324) has also noted that the existence of the Mafia is, as yet, unproved. One of the most comprehensive reviews and critiques of the evidence regarding the existence of the Mafia, Gordon Hawkins' article "God and the Mafia," is reprinted at the end of the chapter.

OUR CRIMINAL SOCIETY

Americans are engaged in an endless struggle against crime. Millions of dollars are spent yearly combating crime, and issues such as crime in the streets and law and order command much attention. Crime is viewed as an external evil or as a foreign element rather than as an integral part of society. Gus Tyler has observed that the criminal is usually:

. . . an outsider, an outcast, a foreign element to the society. The criminal has a different-shaped head, a faulty intellect, a demon inside him. . . . The criminal can resemble anything except our normal selves. The search for the criminal is a manhunt *outside* our own skins, the yearning for a scapegoat (Tyler, 1962b:327–328).

We are obsessed with crime flooded with crime statistics, continually shocked by the discovery of crime scandals. Our response is to set up commissions, committees, and task forces to investigate the problem and provide solutions. But the recommendations of the experts are typically ignored, and we continue to be shocked by crime.

This tendency is neither new nor peculiar to American society, for Durkheim noted many years ago that crime is a normal phenomenon, an expression of the collective conscience. Crime reinforces societal norms and defines the group's boundaries. The criminal, "as a trespasser against the group norms, . . . represents those forces which lie outside the group's boundaries: he informs us, as it were, what evil looks like, what shapes the devil can assume. And in doing so, he shows us the difference between the inside of the group and the outside" (Erikson, 1964:15). Our interest in crime seems to reflect a greater concern with our own morality than with crime per se. It is designed to expiate our sins rather than to reduce crime. In earlier times criminals were paraded in the town square, and public executions drew thousands of law-abiding citizens. Today, mass media coverage of crime fulfills the same functions previously carried out by public hangings and the use of stocks (Erikson, 1964:14).

Our search for a scapegoat is frustrating, since criminal statistics and commission studies typically do not support our misconceptions about crime. We find that counter to our expectations the violent criminal is not an evil stranger who attacks innocent victims, but rather someone with whom we have a primary relationship. The chances of being raped, assaulted, or murdered by a complete stranger are much lower than by an intimate acquaintance or relative. Most property offenses are also committed by nonprofessionals. It is estimated that more money is lost yearly to amateur and white-collar offenders than to career criminals. Even the career criminal does not typically exploit innocent victims. The professional thief, for example, could not carry out a successful con game without the help of a dishonest accomplice who, in attempting to con a third party, unwittingly becomes the victim: "True confidence games always make use of the avarice and dishonesty of the victim. Their common element is showing the victim how to make money, or gain some other advantage, in a dishonest manner and then taking advantage of his dishonesty. A true confidence game leaves no innocent victim" (Gasser, 1963:47). It is not surprising that the professional thief develops a cynical attitude toward conventional society, since the belief that all people are criminals at heart is repeatedly reinforced. The confidence man believes that while he is more successful as a thief, "he . . . is no more guilty" than his victim (Gasser, 1963:48). The implication of the victim in the confidence game provides the con man with considerable protection from prosecution.

Although organized crime is depicted as a menace to society by law-enforcement agencies, it could not exist without the help and cooperation of legitimate society, including public officials and law-enforcement officers who directly or indirectly support its illicit activities (see Conklin, 1973). Organized crime is successful to the extent that it is able to provide goods and services that are in great demand. Its major income-producing activities—gambling, loan sharking, and drugs—are in a sense "victimless crimes." Victims willingly and voluntarily seek out goods or services. And in regard to crime in general the term "crimes without victims" refers to activities involving "a willing and private exchange of strongly demanded yet officially proscribed goods and services; this element of consent precludes the existence of a victim—in the usual sense of the word" (Schur, 1965:v). Abortion, drugs (particularly the nonaddictive), gambling, vagrancy, and sexual offenses among consenting adults (e.g., homosexuality) fall into this category. The consensual nature of crimes without victims makes them virtually unenforceable.

Since our society views crime as an external force, in combating crime it turns to external forms of control. Characteristically, we pass more laws or call for stronger law enforcement. Our efforts are based on the assumption that crime is something that others do, not something we do. Crime will be reduced substantially not by stronger legislation or more effective enforcement but by basic changes in American society and its value system so that there is greater respect for the law and the conditions that breed violence are altered. Crime is a complex and pervasive phenomenon that cuts across all segments of society and cannot be explained by a single and simple class theory.

The manifest rationale behind the criminal law is to protect the society from acts that are injurious, either to the collective or to individuals, but throughout most of our history the law has been used to legislate morality. Guided by the Puritan Ethic and heritage (Erikson, 1966), we have attempted to control behavior that is viewed as offensive or indecent. By attempting to legislate morality we have engaged in "what might be termed *the criminalization of deviance* . . ." (Schur, 1965:5). Our contemporary crime crisis appears to be more one of "overcriminalization" than of "undercriminalization" (Kadish, 1967). But to advocate the repeal of laws regarding crimes without victims is not to necessarily condone such activities but to realize that they are beyond the scope of the criminal law.

In short, we need no longer search for scapegoats in trying to deal with the problem of crime. Solutions to the crime problem lie within ourselves, not outside. Crime, like literature, music, and philosophy, is both a part and a product of the society (Tyler, 1962b:327). The distinction between the criminal and the noncriminal, morality and immorality, is a false dichotomy; they are necessarily linked. In a sense "morality and immorality meet at the public scaffold, and it is during this meeting that the community declares where the line between them should be drawn" (Erikson, 1964:14).

REFERENCES

Amir, Menachem
  1967 "Forcible Rape." Federal Probation 31 (March):51–58.
Associated Press
  1974 "Only One Half of Crimes Reported." Grand Forks Herald, Grand Forks, N.D. (April 15):8.
Bachmuth, Rita, S. M. Miller, and Linda Rosen
  1960 "Juvenile Delinquency in the Daily Press." Alpha Kappa Delta 30 (Spring):47–51.
Bell, Daniel
  1960 The End of Ideology. New York: Free Press.
Caldwell, Robert G.
  1958 "A Re-examination of the Concept of White-Collar Crime." Federal Probation 22 (March):30–36.
Conklin, John E.
  1973 The Crime Establishment. Englewood Cliffs, N.J.: Prentice-Hall.
Cressey, Donald R.
  1967 "The Functions and Structure of Criminal Syndicates." Pp. 25–60 in the President's Commission on Law Enforcement and Administration

of Justice, Task Force Report: Organized Crime. Washington, D.C.: GPO. Appendix A.

Davis, F. James
1952 "Crime News in Colorado Newspapers." American Journal of Sociology 57 (January):325–330.

Durkheim, Emile
1933 The Division of Labor in Society. (Translated by George Simpson). New York: Free Press.
1964 The Rules of Sociological Method. (Translated by Sarah A. Solovay and John H. Mueller, ed. by George E. G. Catlin). New York: Free Press.

Erikson, Kai T.
1964 "Notes on the Sociology of Deviance." Pp. 9–21 in Howard S. Becker (ed.), The Other Side. New York: Free Press.
1966 Wayward Puritans: A Study in the Sociology of Deviance. New York: Wiley.

Federal Bureau of Investigation
1966 Uniform Crime Reporting Handbook. U.S. Department of Justice. Washington, D.C.: GPO.
1971 Uniform Crime Reports—1970. U.S. Department of Justice. Washington, D.C.: GPO.
1972 Uniform Crime Reports—1971. U.S. Department of Justice. Washington, D.C.: GPO.
1973 Uniform Crime Reports—1972. U.S. Department of Justice. Washington, D.C.: GPO.

Gagnon, John H., and William Simon (eds.)
1967 Sexual Deviance. New York: Harper & Row.

Gasser, Robert Louis
1963 "The Confidence Game." Federal Probation 27 (December):47–54.

Geis, Gilbert
1962 "Toward a Delineation of White-Collar Offenses." Sociological Inquiry 32 (Spring):160–171.

Goffman, Erving
1963 Stigma. Englewood Cliffs, N.J.: Prentice-Hall.

Irwin, John, and Lewis Yablonsky
1965 "The New Criminal: A View of the Contemporary Offender." The British Journal of Criminology. 5 (April):183–190.

Kadish, Sanford H.
1967 "The Crisis of Overcriminalization." The Annals of the American Academy of Political and Social Science 374 (November):157–170.

Letkemann, Peter
1973 Crime as Work. Englewood Cliffs, N.J.: Prentice-Hall.

Pound, Roscoe
1943 "A Survey of Social Interests." Harvard Law Review 57 (October): 1–39.

President's Commission on Law Enforcement and Administration of Justice
1967a The Challenge of Crime in a Free Society. Washington, D.C.: GPO.
1967b Task Force Report: Crime and Its Impact—An Assessment. Washington, D.C.: GPO.

Quinney, Richard
1965 "Is Criminal Behaviour Deviant Behaviour?" The British Journal of Criminology 5 (April): 132–142.
1970a The Problem of Crime. New York: Dodd, Mead.
1970b The Social Reality of Crime. Boston: Little, Brown.
Roebuck, Julian B., and Ronald C. Johnson
1962 "The Jack-of-All-Trades Offender." Crime and Delinquency 8 (April): 172–181.
1964 "The 'Short Con' Man." Crime and Delinquency 10 (July):235–248.
Schur, Edwin M.
1965 Crimes Without Victims. Englewood Cliffs, N.J.: Prentice-Hall.
Sellin, Thorsten
1938 Culture Conflict and Crime. New York: Social Science Research Council. Bulletin 41.
Silver, Isidore
1974 The Crime-Control Establishment. Englewood Cliffs, N.J.: Prentice-Hall.
Shulman, Harry Manuel
1966 "The Measurement of Crime in the United States." The Journal of Criminal Law, Criminology, and Police Science 57 (November):483–492.
Sutherland, Edwin H.
1937 The Professional Thief. Chicago: University of Chicago Press.
1949 White Collar Crime. New York: Holt, Rinehart & Winston.
Sykes, Gresham M.
1967 Crime and Society. Second ed. New York: Random House.
Tappan, Paul W.
1947 "Who Is the Criminal"? American Sociological Review 12 (February): 96–102.
Timasheff, Nicholas S.
1963 Sociological Theory: It's Nature and Growth. Revised ed. New York: Random House.
Tyler, Gus
1962a Organized Crime in America. Ann Arbor, Mich.: University of Michigan Press.
1962b "The Roots of Organized Crime." Crime and Delinquency 8 (October):325–338.
Vold, George B.
1958 Theoretical Criminology. New York: Oxford University Press.
Wolfgang, Marvin E.
1957 "Victim-Precipitated Criminal Homicide." Journal of Criminal Law, Criminology, and Police Science 48 (May-June):1–11.
1963 "Uniform Crime Reports: A Critical Appraisal." University of Pennsylvania Law Review 111 (April):708–738.

INTRODUCTION TO THE READINGS

The selections in this chapter are designed to illustrate the two major types of career crime—professional crime and organized crime. The first selection, based on the confessions of a successful con man, provides an inside view of the confidence game. The game discussed by "Yellow Kid" Weil, the faro bank payoff, is an example of the "big con" or "long con." It includes many props and accomplices, is carried out by skilled professionals, and requires careful and complicated planning. Although the short-con game requires fewer props and players, less planning and skill, it includes the same basic elements. Con games of all varieties rely typically on cunning and deceit and avoid violence. They are successful only to the extent that the victim is willing to engage in illegal or dishonest behavior. The implication of the victim in illicit activities makes it easier to "cool off the mark" so that he accepts the situation, regains his self-respect, and does not complain to the police (Roebuck and Johnson, 1964).

The second article carefully examines evidence concerning the existence of the Mafia. Hawkins shows how the belief in the Mafia is part of our cultural folklore and mythology. Attempts to prove the existence of the Mafia parallel arguments for the existence of God. The Mafia has divine attributes: invisibility, omnipresence, omnipotence, immateriality, and eternity.

From "Yellow Kid" Weil—Con Man

JOSEPH R. WEIL

One of the oldest gambling games is faro bank. I don't know just when it first became popular. But I do know that it dates back to the Pharaohs of ancient Egypt, from whom the name was derived. It has long been popular in France.

In the early days faro was dealt from an open deck, without the box. Louis XIV was one of the first to try to legislate it out of existence. The French nobles gambled so recklessly and lost so consistently at faro bank that many became penniless. Louis issued a decree banning the game, but still it flourished. For centuries, it has been a favorite of Parisian and other French gaming resorts. It became a major attraction at Monte Carlo. In the early days of the United States, faro bank was popular in the frontier towns.

My own experience with the game began soon after my return from Baltimore. I was in Tommy Defoe's tailor shop in the Railway Exchange building. Tommy's place was a regular hangout for con men. If we wanted to pass the word along to a fellow worker, Tommy always obliged.

John Strosnider, who could be as smooth as silk, was sitting at a table shuffling cards. He was a wizard at cards. He could deal from the bottom and the average person would never know it. He also had a gadget for pulling a card up his sleeve which consisted of a wire extending from the foot, up through the trousers, under the shirt, through the sleeve at the shoulder, and out the coat sleeve. On the end of the wire at the sleeve was a clip-like finger. With this, John could palm the card he wanted and make any other card disappear faster than you could see it.

Now he was shuffling the cards, doing tricks and playing with his faro box. He had two new gadgets he was demonstrating. Both were bits of wire he manipulated with his left hand. He called one "the thief" and the other "the knife." With "the thief" he could remove any card he wanted from the deck, with "the knife" he could cut the deck and put the bottom card on top. He was practicing various other manipulations.

After a while I tired of watching him and picked up a newspaper. I turned to the classified column. I soon came across a want ad that interested me.

A Mrs. Kingston was going to California for six months and wanted to lease her nine-room apartment on the Gold Coast. I lost no time in calling on Mrs. Kingston. She showed me the apartment.

It was furnished luxuriously, and in excellent taste. The floors were covered with fine Oriental rugs. The large drawing-room was hung with priceless oil paintings. The other rooms were elegantly appointed, and there were two bathrooms.

The kitchen was completely equipped. Next to the pantry, there was a wine room.

It was an ideal setup. I succeeded in convincing Mrs. Kingston that I would take good care of her furnishings—and this was a prime consideration. I agreed to the $200 a month she asked,

From Joseph R. Weil (as told to W. T. Brannon), "Yellow Kid" Weil—Con Man (New York: Pyramid Publications, 1957), pp. 123–133. Reprinted with permission of Pyramid Publications.

and paid her six months rent in advance.

Returning to Tommy Defoe's tailor shop I found Strosnider still practicing with his cards. I told him of the apartment and of my plans for it.

"We need a couple more good men to complete our organization," I added.

"How about the Deacon and Jimmy Head?" he proposed.

I had known Fred "The Deacon" Buckminster, one of Chicago's top confidence men, casually for a number of years but had never worked with him. Buck had been doing errands for Barney Bertsch, Chicago's big fixer. But things were hot for Barney, and Fred was ready to pull out.

He was a big, portly fellow, with the most innocent face you ever saw. Looking at him you would have sworn that he could not be anything but honest. His eyes were as innocent as a baby's and his features were positively cherubic. His demeanor was so decorous he actually radiated an air of piety. This had earned him the sobriquet "The Deacon" by which he is still known, although he is now an old man.

"He is a good detail man," Strosnider told me.

Fred seldom slipped up on the small things which are very important in any good con game.

Jimmy Head was from Texas. I have heard that he was from a good family and that his real name was not Head. He was a medium-sized man, nearing middle age, with a mild and pleasing manner and a slight Southern accent. In any crowd he would be inconspicuous, for he was a good example of the average citizen.

Head was also smooth. He was polite and his soft-spoken pleasantries made a favorable impression on the victims. He was the sort of fellow you would have expected to find in a teller's cage at your bank. We engaged a private room and I told Strosnider, Head and Buck of my plan. We would set up an establishment more lavish than any gambling club in Chicago. The story to our victims would be that it was a club maintained by the Jettison estate—one of a chain of such clubs scattered throughout the country.

They were enthusiastic about my scheme and agreed to play the roles I assigned to them.

As soon as Mrs. Kingston had vacated the apartment, we moved in. Of course there had to be some rearrangement. Buckminster arranged for a roulette wheel and I had a number of tables brought in. In addition to the roulette table, we set up tables for poker and dice and, of course, a table for faro bank.

In a corner near the entrance we set up a cashier's cage and installed Jimmy Head as cashier. He also kept the register and the membership book. This roster contained most of the biggest names in Chicago. Jimmy was supplied with large stacks of boodle, which were always in plain view. A victim always believes he has a chance of winning if there is a lot of cash in sight.

Strosnider was to be the manager of the club and also was to deal the faro bank game. Buckminster was the "overseer," an official whose headquarters were supposedly in New York. The story was that he went from club to club, checking to see that each was being operated properly.

The apartment was ideal. Only a very wealthy person, such as the millionaire Jettison, could have assembled such rich furnishings. It was not difficult for an outsider to believe that the club was frequented only by the socially elite. Indeed it would have been hard to convince the average person that anybody other than a millionaire was behind the club.

Strosnider became "John Steele," manager of the club. Buckminster became "Mr. McFetridge," the director from New York. My own place in the scheme was to pose as an outsider with inside connections.

As first victim I selected a man named Orville Hotchkiss. I had met him a year before when for a short time I operated a paint factory. Hotchkiss owned a retail paint store and had bought products of the factory. I knew he had no money to speak of, but I also knew that he was a fast friend of a man named McHenry, a sports promoter in Aurora. Though I brought in Hotchkiss, my ultimate victim was to be McHenry.

"Orville," I told him when I called, "I want you to help me out."

"Sure, Jim. What can I do?" Hotchkiss knew me as James R. Warrington.

"I have an uncle," I said, "who is the manager of one of the gambling clubs operated by the Jettison estate. You've heard of these clubs, haven't you?"

"Of course."

I knew he hadn't, but I also knew he had heard of the Jettison estate and the fabulous man who had founded it.

"My uncle has been with Jettison for twenty years," I continued. "He's served faithfully. He expected to get a raise last week, but what happened? They gave him a cut. He's plenty mad about it and wants to quit. But before he does he wants to make a killing.

"He knows that the New York overseer, a man named McFetridge, is back of it. McFetridge doesn't like my uncle and that's the reason for the cut. At the first opportunity he'll fire my uncle. But my uncle isn't going to give him a chance. He's going to clean up and retire."

"I don't blame him," said Hotchkiss. "What do you want me to do?"

"I want you to go in and make a big wager at the faro bank table. My uncle will be dealing. He'll let you make a killing—providing you split with him."

"Why don't you do it, Jim?"

"I would," I replied, "but they know me at the club. They know that Mr. Steele is my uncle. I couldn't get away with it."

"It's all right with me," returned Hotchkiss, amiably, "but what am I going to use for money?"

"Don't worry about that. My uncle will tell you how to do it."

I arranged a meeting with "Mr. Steele." He brought the faro box along.

"It's a case of rank ingratitude, Mr. Hotchkiss!" Strosnider said heatedly. "I've given Jettison the best years of my life. I certainly was entitled to a raise, if anything. But no, I get a cut." Strosnider was a good actor and there was bitterness in his voice.

"That's too bad," Hotchkiss commiserated with him.

"It's a rotten shame," Strosnider said with feeling. "But I don't intend to let them rub my nose in the dirt. I'm going to get even. Do you blame me?"

"Of course not," Hotchkiss replied.

"Ordinarily I wouldn't consider doing anything dishonest," John went on, "but this is different. I feel it's what I've got coming to me." He shuffled the cards. "Do you know anything about faro bank, Mr. Hotchkiss?"

"No, I don't."

"Well, you will when I get through."

For two hours Strosnider rehearsed Hotchkiss in how to play. He showed him how, by shielding the cards with his big hands, he could always see what was coming out before it was dealt. He arranged a series of signals so Hotchkiss would know how to bet. They went over it time after time, until

Hotchkiss was letter perfect in receiving the signals.

"Now, I'll let you win all through the deck," Strosnider said, "but wait until the last turn to bet all your chips. I'll give you the signal just before the deal. Now is that clear?"

"Yes," Hotchkiss replied, "but there's one thing that isn't. What am I going to use for money?"

"You can write a check, can't you?"

"Sure, but it wouldn't be any good."

"Don't let that worry you," said John. "You can cover it the next day. It'll be plenty good with all the money you'll win."

"Suppose they won't take a check?"

"Oh, they'll take it. All the big men who come to the club write checks. You just hand me a check for $50,000 and I'll give you the chips."

Strosnider produced two elaborately engraved guest cards. He wrote "James R. Warrington" on one and "Orville Hotchkiss" on the other and handed them to us.

"Come in about ten," he said, shook hands and left.

Promptly at ten that evening we were at the Gold Coast building that housed the Kingston apartment. Hotchkiss knew he was in an aristocratic section. He knew also that only wealthy people inhabited this building.

We were admitted by a man in an impressive butler's outfit. He took our hats and escorted us to where the manager sat. Strosnider got up, shook hands, and greeted us profusely.

"We're happy to have you gentlemen as our guests," he declared.

He led us across the room towards the kitchen. The activities of the club were in full swing. My friend's eyes popped when he saw the lavish appointments. About two dozen men in evening dress were at the various gaming tables and with them a number of women in formal gowns.

Hotchkiss thought he had indeed landed in the very midst of Gold Coast society. He had no way of knowing that the men were all stooges, minor con men hired for the occasion. Each was paid $25. Each man furnished his own clothes and his own woman companion. I've no doubt that many of the girls thought the place a swank gambling club, just as Hotchkiss did.

Each man was plentifully supplied with chips. They strolled about the room, trying their luck at all the games. It didn't matter whether they won or lost. The chips weren't worth anything. But Hotchkiss didn't know that. He gaped at the piles of crisp greenbacks in Jimmy Head's cage.

We made our way across the room in leisurely fashion so that our guest could absorb all the atmosphere. Then, we went through the kitchen and into the wine room where we found a bottle of champagne in a bucket of ice. The chef—a genuine chef, incidentally —was preparing sandwiches to serve the "club members."

Strosnider poured the champagne. "Here's to the Jettison Club!" he cried. We drank the toast.

"You gentlemen make yourselves at home," said Strosnider. "I have to see if there is anything I can do for the guests. When you feel like it come over to the faro bank table and we'll have a little game."

For perhaps a half hour we wandered about the big room, watching the various games. The butler came in with a big tray of sandwiches and passed them among the "club members." Later he returned with the beverages. Hotchkiss was thoroughly sold on the idea that it was a high-class club.

"I see my uncle is not occupied

now," I told him. "Suppose we go over and play."

Hotchkiss agreed, and we walked over to the faro bank table.

"I'd like to buy some chips," he said. "I don't have much cash with me. Will a check do?"

"Of course," said Mr. Steele (Strosnider). "How much did you wish to play?"

"Fifty thousand dollars."

"Just make the check payable to cash." He began to count out chips with an expression that implied this club thought nothing of a mere fifty-thousand-dollar bet.

Hotchkiss wrote the check and Strosnider handed him the chips.

"Step up, gentlemen, and place your bets," he said briskly.

Two or three stooges at the table put chips down on the board. Hotchkiss won small bets consistently, aided by Strosnider's signals, and had $75,000 in chips when the last turn came.

"The last turn, gentlemen," Strosnider called. "There are three cards left. You must call the first two to win. The winner gets four to one."

But the other players apparently had had enough. They left the last turn entirely to Hotchkiss. Strosnider signaled, and he put his chips down on low-high. The last turn was dealt and the first two cards to appear were Four-Queen.

"I congratulate you, sir," said Strosnider, pushing $300,000 in chips to Hotchkiss. "You have been—"

He didn't finish the sentence. He looked up and there, standing behind Hotchkiss, was a big, imposing figure. He was immaculately groomed and he watched with great interest as Hotchkiss picked up the chips and walked to the cashier's cage.

"Hello, Mr. McFetridge," Strosnider greeted him with a sickly grin. "This is an—ah—unexpected pleasure."

"Mr. McFetridge" nodded curtly and followed Hotchkiss to the cashier's window.

Hotchkiss unloaded his chips and Jimmy Head counted them. "Three hundred thousand," he said. "Is that correct, sir?"

"Yes," Hotchkiss replied, obviously with a lump in his throat. You could tell that the mere thought of $300,000 all in one bundle frightened him.

Jimmy Head reached for the pile of boodle and started counting out crisp hundred-dollar bills.

"Just a moment!" It was the commanding voice of Mr. McFetridge.

"Mr. McFetridge!" Head exclaimed. "When did you get in?"

"I just came in as this gentleman called the last turn," the big fellow replied. "Are you a new member, sir?" he asked Hotchkiss. "I don't seem to recall you."

"Why, no," Hotchkiss replied. "I'm a guest."

"I see," said McFetridge. "I was over at the faro bank table and I noticed that you bought your chips with a check."

"Yes. Isn't that all right?"

"Of course," Mr. McFetridge replied. "Our members do it regularly. But we know them and we know their checks are good. But the rules of the house require that a guest pay cash for his chips."

"I can do that," Hotchkiss retorted crimsoning. "If you'll just wait until I collect my winnings, I'll be glad to redeem the check in cash."

"I'm sorry," said Mr. McFetridge, gently but firmly. "That's against the rules of the house too. I am sure that you can see our position. Suppose you had lost. Would the check have been good?"

"Certainly it would!" I cut in.

"I have no doubt that it is good. But

we must be sure before we can pay your winnings."

"What do you want me to do?" asked Hotchkiss.

"Just let us put your check through the bank," the overseer said amicably. "It will take only a couple of days. Then we'll be very glad to pay you your $300,000."

"In other words," I said, "if Mr. Hotchkiss can prove he had $50,000 in cash, you will pay him?"

"Certainly," said the overseer. "The money is his. He won it. All we ask is that he demonstrate his ability to pay if he had lost."

"Then why not give him back his check? He can cash it and return tomorrow with the money."

"That is agreeable to me," said Mr. McFetridge. "If he brings in $50,000 in cash tomorrow, we'll gladly pay him what he won." He turned toward the faro bank table. "Oh, Steele!"

Strosnider came over, a hang-dog look in his eyes.

"You know the rules of the house," McFetridge said sternly. "You know that only members are allowed to use checks to buy chips."

"Yes, sir," the other murmured abjectly. "But Mr. Hotchkiss has a guest card—"

"I have no doubt that Mr. Hotchkiss is as good as gold," McFetridge cut him off. "But the rules of the house must be obeyed. I'm afraid I'll have to report this infraction of the rules to the New York office."

"I'm sorry," the faro bank dealer apologized.

"Now give Mr. Hotchkiss his check back," the overseer ordered.

Strosnider handed the check to Hotchkiss.

"We'll be in tomorrow with the cash," I said. "Please have the money ready."

"It will be ready," returned the big fellow, with a sweep of his hand toward the pile of boodle in the cashier's cage.

Once we were outside I muttered, "It would be just our luck to run into that overseer."

"What are we going to do now?" Hotchkiss asked.

"What can we do?" I shrugged. "I haven't got $50,000 and I don't know anybody who has."

"Well, I do," he said. "And I don't intend to pass up my share of that $300,000."

"You do know somebody with that much money?"

"Yes. You remember McHenry?"

"McHenry?" I hesitated. "McHenry. Oh, you mean the man who helped you in the paint deal?"

"Yes. He's got $50,000. If I give him half of my share, he'll come in with me. Or I think he will."

"So what are you going to do?"

"I'm going to Aurora first thing in the morning."

"Good! We'll put one over on that McFetridge yet."

I parted from Hotchkiss after arranging to meet the one o'clock train from Aurora on which he expected to return. As I have said, we had slated McHenry as the real victim and Hotchkiss was doing exactly what I expected him to do.

When the train came in I was there. Hotchkiss got off and so did McHenry. We shook hands and went into the station restaurant for lunch.

We discussed the deal and McHenry took the bait. "Suppose we go up there now," he proposed. "Will anybody be in?"

"Yes," I replied. "My uncle is always there in the afternoon."

"All right," said McHenry. "Let's go."

We took a cab to the Gold Coast apartment. Strosnider admitted us.

I introduced him to McHenry and said: "We've come to collect. Mr. McHenry has the $50,000."

"McFetridge isn't here, the dirty rat!" Strosnider said bitterly. "He's got all the funds locked in the vault. You'll just have to wait until he comes. He's threatened to fire me."

"Well," I declared softly, "after this deal you won't have to work for him, Uncle John."

"I have a better idea," offered Strosnider. "You gentlemen come with me."

He led the way to a sun room which was comfortably furnished with tables and chairs. "Have a seat and I'll be right back."

When he returned he had his faro box.

"Do you know anything about faro bank?" he asked, addressing McHenry.

"Not much," McHenry admitted.

"Well, we've got plenty of time. I'm going to teach you."

"What for?"

"I'm going to give that McFetridge a real double-crossing," Strosnider replied. "You've got $50,000 in cash. You can buy chips with that and I'll let you win. You can win $300,000 and give Mr. Hotchkiss $50,000 and let him collect his bet, too."

All afternoon Strosnider rehearsed McHenry in how to play faro bank, how to bet, and the signals. Finally McHenry said he had practiced enough.

"Are you sure you understand it?" John asked.

"Positive," McHenry insisted.

"All right but I don't want any slips. Are you sure you don't want to go over it again?"

"No. There won't be any slips. I understand it perfectly."

He didn't, of course, but we didn't want him to. Strosnider wrote out a guest card for McHenry and we departed. I took them to dinner and at nine that night we went back. Our purpose in going early was to allow McHenry to make his play before McFetridge showed up.

The same group was on hand, going through the same motions. McHenry, like Hotchkiss, was very much impressed. But there was a difference between the two men. Hotchkiss frankly admitted he didn't know his way around gaming circles. But McHenry was the type that would today be called a "wise guy." He looked upon everything with a knowing eye.

When he approached the faro bank table he was set for the kill. He put down $50,000 in cash and received the equivalent in chips.

The game started, with a few stooges playing alongside McHenry. They all dropped out before the last turn. He won regularly with the help of Strosnider's signals. He had more than $75,000 in chips when the last turn came.

"Step up, gentlemen," Strosnider called. "It's the last turn. You can bet any of six ways. There are three cards remaining in the deck—a King, Ten, and Ace. You can call it high or you can call it low. If you call the cards, you get four to one."

This was the signal for McHenry to bet. The cards were in the box exactly as Strosnider had called them. But McHenry got his signals mixed when John said, "You can call it high or you can call it low." That was in reality the signal that high card would be first.

McHenry put all the chips he had on Ace-King to show in that order. Strosnider started to deal, then looked up. Behind McHenry was the formidable bulk, of Buckminster (Mr. McFetridge). Strosnider signalled frantically to McHenry to withdraw. This was to make it seem realistic to McHenry.

Buckminster spoke up. "The bet stands," he said icily.

Strosnider hesitated, looking from McHenry to McFetridge, with a harried expression.

"Deal the last turn!" McFetridge commanded.

"Sure, go ahead and deal," McHenry said confidently.

Strosnider dealt the cards. The first was a King, the second a Ten, the last an Ace.

Sorrowfully, Strosnider raked in the chips. McHenry turned pale, as if he could not believe his eyes.

"I've been cheated!" McHenry muttered.

"Come on," I said, grabbing his arm. "Let's get out of here."

"You can go with them," said McFetridge. "Steele, you're fired!"

The three of us went out and stopped in the nearest buffet.

"Whatever possessed you to bet on Ace-King?" Strosnider demanded as soon as we had been seated.

"You signalled to bet on the high card," McHenry defended himself.

"Certainly I did," Strosnider replied. "Why didn't you?"

"But I did. I bet on the Ace—"

"The Ace? Why, you stupid idiot, everybody knows that the Ace is low card in faro bank."

"I didn't."

"Well, why didn't you ask?" Strosnider demanded bitterly. "I thought you said you knew everything about this game."

"I'm sorry that I muffed it."

"A lot of good that does now. Not only did you muff our chance to make a killing but you caused me to lose my job. I hope that I never run into anybody like you again!"

On this note we parted company. I later saw Hotchkiss many times. He laughed about the whole thing when he learned my real identity. . . .

God and the mafia

GORDON HAWKINS

A perplexing and elusive problem confronts the student seeking information about organized crime. It concerns the concept "organized crime" itself. For a curious feature characterizes almost all the literature on the subject, up to and including the Task Force Report on this topic published in 1967 by the President's Commission on Law Enforcement and Administration of Justice. This is that a large proportion of what has been written seems not to be dealing with an empirical matter at all. It is almost as though what is referred to as organized crime belonged to the realm of metaphysics or theology.

. . .

Take first the question of the existence of organized crime, a matter about which, like the existence of God, doubts have been expressed. On this subject Estes Kefauver, in his *Crime in America*, which is based on testimony taken at the hearings before, and upon reports of, the Senate Crime Committee between 1950 and 1951, writes as follows:

A nationwide crime syndicate does exist in the United States of America, despite the protestations of a strangely assorted company of criminals, self-serving politicians, plain blind fools, and others who may be honestly misguided, that there is no such combine. . . . The national crime syndicate as it exists today is an elusive and furtive but nonetheless tangible thing. Its organization and machinations are not always easy to pinpoint. . . . However, by patient digging and by putting together little pieces of a huge and widely scattered puzzle, the picture emerges. . . . Behind the local mobs which make up the national crime syndicate is a shadowy, international criminal organization known as the Mafia, so fantastic that most Americans find it hard to believe it really exists.

Now, apart from the bizarre nature of its content, one of the most remarkable facts about this quite categorical statement, which occurs in the first chapter of Kefauver's book, is that the evidence necessary to substantiate it is never produced. Indeed Daniel Bell in his *The End of Ideology* comments as follows:

Unfortunately for a good story—and the existence of the Mafia would be a whale of a story—neither the Senate Crime Committee in its testimony, nor Kefauver in his book, presented any real evidence that the Mafia exists as a functioning organization. One finds public officials asserting before the Kefauver committee their *belief* in the Mafia; the Narcotic Bureau *thinks* that a world-wide dope ring allegedly run by Luciano is part of the Mafia: but the only other "evidence" presented—aside from the incredulous responses both of Senator Kefauver and Rudolph Halley when nearly all the Italian gangsters asserted that they didn't know about the Mafia—is that certain crimes bear "the earmarks of the Mafia." (Author's italics.)

Others have been equally skeptical. Thus, Burton B. Turkus, in *Murder Incorporated*, writing at the time when the Senate Crime Investigating Committee was publishing its findings, said:

If one such unit had all crime in this country under its power, is it not reasonable to assume that somewhere along the line, some law agency—federal, state, county or municipal—would have tripped it up long before this? No single man or

---

group ever was so clever, so completely genius, as to foil all of them forever. . . . In fact, as a factor of power in national crime, Mafia has been virtually extinct for two decades.

Gus Tyler, editor of *Organized Crime in America*, prefaces the section devoted to the Mafia with an essay in which he says that the Mafia "whose existence is assumed by some government agencies" is "a still unproven fact." He adds, however, that "while the existence of the Mafia is still legally conjectural, theories of its existence cannot be ignored."

But the "theories of its existence" prove on examination to consist of little more than a series of dogmatic assertions. Thus, the Final Report of the California Special Crime Study Commission on Organized Crime (1953) speaks of The Mafia, which it says is "now known as L'Unione Siciliana," as "the most sinister and powerful criminal organization in the world (with) headquarters on at least two continents." But after giving a somewhat desultory account of a variety of "illegal enterprises," and making further reference to "a criminal organization extending all over the world," the report falls back on the argument that "The study of these crimes over the years shows a definite pattern, the repetition of which in case after case cannot be laid to coincidence." This incidentally bears an extraordinary resemblance to one of the best known arguments for the existence of God: that is "the argument from design" in the form in which it was used by the eighteenth- and nineteenth-century rationalist theologians. But it is neither probative nor particularly persuasive.

DIVINE ATTRIBUTES

Another respect in which assertions about the existence of organized crime

in general, and a Mafia in particular, resemble statements about the existence of God is that in neither case is it clear what would be regarded as constituting significant counterevidence. Thus, in the Third Interim Report of the Special Committee to Investigate Organized Crime in Interstate Commerce (i.e., the Senate Crime Committee, or the Kefauver Committee), it is said that "Almost all the witnesses who appeared before the committee and who were suspected of Mafia membership, either denied that they had ever heard of the Mafia, which is patently absurd, or denied membership in the Mafia."

The only exception to this which stood up under cross examination was a witness who said "that the Mafia was freely discussed in his home when he was a child." It is not at all clear what the significance of this childhood reminiscence is supposed to be. What is perfectly clear however is that *whatever* witnesses had said would have been construed as evidence *for* the existence of Mafia. Acknowledgment of membership in, or awareness of the existence of a Mafia would have been accepted at face value. Denials, on the other hand, merely demonstrate that the Mafia "is a rare 'secret' society whose existence is truly secret"; secrecy being enforced by "Mafia killings" that themselves "are surrounded with the secrecy that has proved to be most difficult to penetrate."

But even when organized crime is not identified with a Mafia it is still referred to in terms that imply divine attributes, such as invisibility, immateriality, eternity, omnipresence, and omnipotence. Thus, in the President's Commission Task Force Report on Organized Crime, it is said that "organized crime affects the lives of millions of Americans, but . . . preserves its *invisibility*." Again, organized crime is said to have its own discipline, but "the laws and regulations they obey, the procedures they use, are private and secret ones that they devise themselves, change when they see fit, and administer summarily and *invisibly*." Moreover, "Agents and employees . . . cannot implicate the highest level figures, since frequently they have neither spoken to *nor even seen them*." Another Task Force Report, "Assessment of Crime," states that "Organized crime thrives on *invisibility*. . . . No one knows whether it is getting bigger or smaller. . . ." And F. J. Cook, in *The Secret Rulers*, speaks of "a secret organization, an *invisible* government of crime." (Hawkins' italics.)

As for immateriality, we are also told by the President's Commission:

But to discuss the impact of organized crime in terms of whatever direct, personal, everyday effect it has on individuals is to miss most of the point. Most individuals are not affected in this sense, very much. . . . Sometimes organized crime's activities do not directly affect individuals at all.

And one writer, "the former attorney for an illicit New York organization," is quoted as speaking in mystical terms of "a mysterious, all pervasive reality."

The Task Force Report also emphasizes the perpetually enduring nature of organized crime. "[O]rganized crime maintains a coherent, efficient organization with a *permanency of form that survives changes* in working and leadership personnel." And Gus Tyler, in an article on "The Roots of Organized Crime," speaks of ". . . its *eternal life* . . . an institutional longevity extending far beyond the natural life span of its more mortal leadership." (Hawkins' italics in both cases.)

With regard to omnipresence and omnipotence, Robert F. Kennedy said that "The insidious influence of organized crime can reach into almost every facet of our life, corrupting and undermining our society." The Task Force Report goes further and states that "Organized criminal groups are known to operate in all sections of the Nation." Professor D. R. Cressey writing of "the American confederation of criminals," in his paper on "The Functions and Structure of Criminal Syndicates," which is printed as an appendix to the Task Force Report, says that "while organized criminals do not yet have control of all the legitimate economic and political activities in any metropolitan or other geographic area of America," they have started "to undermine basic economic and political traditions."

As with the Deity, moreover, direct knowledge of this phenomenon is apparently not vouchsafed to us. "While law-enforcement officials now have detailed information about the criminal activities of individual men," Professor Cressey writes, "knowledge of the structure of their confederation remains fragmentary and impressionistic." He goes on to say that "Our knowledge of the structure that makes 'organized crime' organized is somewhat comparable to the knowledge of Standard Oil that could be gleaned from interviews with gasoline station attendants." But there is nothing tentative about his explicit statement that "in the United States, criminals have managed to organize a nationwide illicit cartel and confederation." And in a lengthy chapter beginning, "The structure of the nationwide cartel and confederation which today operates the principal illicit businesses in America, and which is now striking at the foundations of legitimate business and government as well came into being in 1931," sufficient baroque detail is provided to suggest that interviews with gasoline station attendants may not be totally uninformative for those with ears to hear.

THE CODE OF THE UNDERWORLD

Yet, as Professor Cressey acknowledges, "some officials, and some plain citizens, remain unconvinced." And, although he regards skepticism as "misplaced," he does not, like Senator Kefauver, define unbelievers as criminals, self-servers, blind fools, and so on. This is, in the circumstances, prudent. For when only "fragmentary and impressionistic" data about an "elusive and furtive" phenomenon are available for judgment, it is unwise to assume that doubt must be disingenuous or perverse.

Thus, as an instance of the sort of thing that might occasion doubt on the part of a plain citizen, consider the tenets of the code that Professor Cressey says "form the foundation of the legal order of the confederation." He states frankly that he was "unable to locate even a summary statement of the code" and that his statement of it is based only on "the snippets of information we have been able to obtain." Yet, on this presumably exiguous basis, he constructs a code that, in regard to form and content, compares favorably with more easily accessible examples of such systems of general rules regarding conduct.

The sinister underworld code that "gives the leaders exploitative authoritarian power over everyone in the organization," reads like the product of collaboration between Rudyard Kipling and Emily Post. Most of it would not appear incongruous if embroidered on a sampler. Organized criminals are enjoined to "be loyal members of the organization," to "be a member of the team," to "be independent," and yet not to "rock the boat." At the same time, they are told to "be a man of honor" and to "respect womanhood and your elders."

The organized criminal "is to be cool and calm at all times"; "is not to use narcotics . . . not to be drunk on duty . . . not to get into fights. . . ." "He does not whine or complain in the face of adversity." "The world seen by organized criminals is a world of graft, fraud, and corruption, and they are concerned with their own honesty and manliness as compared with the hypocrisy of corrupt policemen and corrupt political figures."

In a world of corrupt police and politicians, it must be difficult to preserve these standards. But Professor Cressey explains that, by a "process of recruitment and indoctrination," the leaders of organized crime "have some degree of success" in inculcating "a sense of decency and morality—a sense of honor—so deep that there will be absolute obedience." It is no surprise when we are told that Mr. Vito Genovese, who is said to have been, in 1957, leader of the "All-American 'Commission'" which is "the highest ruling body in the confederation," was "invested with charismatic qualities by his followers. He was almost revered, while at the same time being feared, like an Old Testament divine. Even his name had a somewhat sacred quality. . . ."

The truth is that this sounds very much like what Gus Tyler calls "the fantasy of the Mafia," and Daniel Bell refers to as the "myth of an omnipotent Mafia" all over again. . . . For others, however, the same sparsity of data supports an equally grandiose inferential superstructure. "Since we know so little," Professor Cressey says, "it is easy to make the assumption that there is nothing to know anything about." But the scarcity of "hard facts" does not appear to constrict him unduly. And although some of what he says sounds plausible in a non-derogatory sense, when it comes to the question of the *existence* of "the American confederation of criminals" he uses a form of argument that comes close to what one might call logical legerdemain.

The argument is worth examining briefly. Under the heading, "The Structural Skeleton," Professor Cressey provides an outline of the "authority structure" or " 'organizational chart' of the American confederation." Twenty-four criminal "families," each with its "boss," are said to operate under the "commission" that "serves as a combination board of business directors, legislature, supreme court and arbitration board." After giving some details of "the formal structure of the organization," Professor Cressey deals briefly with street-level operations and more informal functions. He then concludes briskly:

[T]he skeleton has more bones than those we have described, as our discussion of informal positions and roles indicates. *The structure outlined is sufficient to demonstrate, however, that a confederation of "families" exists.* (Hawkins' italics.)

It scarcely seems necessary to point out that if "to demonstrate" here means "to prove by reasoning" or "to establish as true," the existence of the confederation cannot be said to have been demonstrated.

. . .

But we come now to what must in this context and in the present state of knowledge be crucial questions. The first of these concerns what may be called the mythopeic factors that operate in this field. For it is important to recognize that, quite apart from the evidence available, the notion that behind the diverse phenomena of crime there exists a single mysterious om-nipotent organization that is responsible for much of it, is one that has long exerted a powerful influence on the minds not only of journalists, but also of law enforcement agents and serious students of crime. The second question which we have to ask is, leaving aside nonevidential and irrational considerations, what kinds of evidence may be regarded as providing a means of ascertaining the truth in this matter. . . .

FOLKLORE AND MYTH

With regard to the first question, it is evident that there is a considerable *folklore* relating to organized crime. Much of the literature on the subject consists of myths and folktales. The point is made in Earl Johnson's article, "Organized Crime: Challenge to the American Legal System" that:

America has a new folklore. This folklore has grown up around—organized crime. Next to Westerns, war and sex, it is probably the chief source of material for TV plots, books—both fiction and non-fiction—and newspaper exposés. . . .

The significance of this development has nowhere been fully analyzed, but in the light of the functionalist interpretation of myth made by anthropologists, it would be unwise to dismiss it as of little account. Bronislaw Malinowski, for example, holds that "Myth fulfills in primitive culture an indispensable function: it expresses, enhances and codifies belief; it safeguards and enforces morality; . . ." Nor, is this something confined to primitive cultures, although the character of the myths will obviously be different in different cultures. In regard to our own society, Ruth Benedict has pointed out that "the fundamental opposition of good and evil is a trait of occidental folklore that is expressed equally in Grimms' fairy tales and in the *Arabian Nights*." . . .

Another function of mythology, however, is that it provides an *explanation*, in that it helps to introduce some intelligible order into the bewildering diversity of phenomena surrounding us. . . .

Yet, something more than a demand for simplicity and order is involved. In this connection, the way in which anger and distress lead to a demand for the identification of a responsible individual or group, which is brought out by Professor Allport in his discussion of the psychological process of "scapegoating," is directly relevant to our discussion. "The common use of the orphaned pronoun 'they,'" says Allport, "teaches us that people often want and need to designate out-groups —usually for the purpose of venting hostility. . . ." And Daniel Bell attributes part of the attractiveness of the

theory of a Mafia and national crime syndicate to the fact that there is in the American temper, a feeling that "somewhere," "somebody" is pulling all the complicated strings to which this jumbled world dances. In politics the labor image is "Wall Street" or "Big Business"; while the business stereotype was the "New Dealers."

In the field of crime, the national crime syndicate provides a specific focus or target for fear and discontent.

. . .

WHAT IS "ORGANIZED CRIME"?

. . . At this point, it is necessary to define the question at issue a little more precisely than has been done so far. In the first place, there is no doubt that small groups of criminals organized for carrying out particular kinds of crime have existed for centuries. . . .

The question we are considering, however, is whether . . . there is a national syndicate that dominates organized crime throughout the country —one large nationwide criminal organization that controls the majority, if not all, of the local undertakings. For the concept of organized crime that was presented in the evidence given by Attorney General Robert F. Kennedy before the Permanent Subcommittee on Investigations of the Committee on Government Operations (McClellan Committee) in 1963 involves

a private government of organized crime, a government with an annual income of billions—run by a commission (which) makes major policy decisions for the organization, settles disputes among the families and allocates territories of criminal operation within the organizations.

ENTER VALACHI

Clearly a crucial question in this context concerns the evidence on which the Attorney General based his contention that such a government and such an organization existed. The nature of that evidence became clear as the McClellan Committee Hearings proceeded. For, at those Hearings, as Senator McClellan himself put it: "For the first time a member of the secret underworld government, Cosa Nostra, testified under oath describing the operations of that criminal organization, and the misguided and dedicated loyalty of its members." The witness referred to was Joseph Valachi, a sixty-year-old man with a long criminal record, at that time serving a life sentence for murder and a twenty-year sentence for a narcotics offense.

Of the significance attached to Valachi's evidence there seems to be no doubt. The Attorney General described his disclosures as "the biggest intelligence breakthrough yet in combating organized crime and racketeering in the United States." William George Hundley, head of the Justice Department's Organized Crime Section, was even more revealing. He said:

Before Valachi came along *we had no tangible evidence that anything like this actually existed.* He's the first to talk openly and specifically about the organization. In the past we've heard that so-and-so was a "syndicate man" and that was all. Frankly I always thought it was a lot of hogwash. But Valachi named names. He showed us what the structure is and how it operates. . . . (Hawkins' italics.)

It becomes necessary therefore to examine Valachi's testimony critically. In this connection, it has to be remembered that, prior to his giving evidence, Valachi, who had the year before (June 1962) murdered a fellow prisoner, was, according to his own statements, in fear of his life. He claimed that his former criminal associates intended to kill him. His feelings for them were no less inimical. When asked why he had decided to cooperate with the Department of Justice, he replied: "The main answer to that is very simple. Number one: It is to destroy them." With such an objective in view, the witness could not be regarded as totally disinterested. Moreover, on his own evidence, he clearly did not regard veracity as always obligatory when speaking to law enforcement agencies.

In the circumstances, it is understandable that Senator McClellan attached importance to securing some corroboration for Valachi's testimony. Thus, in opening the Hearings, he said: "We believe a substantial part of his testimony can and will be corroborated." And, in closing them, he said: "The corroboration furnished by law enforcement officers makes Valachi's

testimony more credible and important."

We may ask therefore how far that verdict is borne out. For in such a case as this, the corroborative process assumes unusual significance.

COSA NOSTRA OR MAFIA?

Let us take first a point of detail that has already attracted some comment. What was the name of the organization about which Valachi testified? According to Valachi, it was "Cosa Nostra." He was asked if the organization was "anything like the Mafia, or is it part of the Mafia, or is it the Mafia?" He replied:

Senator, as long as I belong to this Cosa Nostra, all I can tell you is that they never express it as a Mafia. When I was speaking, I just spoke what I knew. . . . I know this thing existed a long time, but in my time I have been with this Cosa Nostra and that is the way it was called. . . .

On this, F. J. Cook, in his *The Secret Rulers*, comments that:

there is a consensus among the nation's best investigators, men with the most intimate knowledge of the underworld and its rackets that they had never heard the name before Valachi used it. . . . This has cast some doubt upon the validity of Valachi's story.

It is not a doubt that troubles Mr. Cook however. "Regardless of name," he says, "the vital fact remains: the criminal organization exists. . . . The name itself is secondary. What matters is the reality of a secret organization, an invisible government of crime. . . . " Yet for those more skeptical than Mr. Cook, and concerned about the *corroboration* of Valachi's testimony, it is not a matter that can be passed over so lightly. For the fact is that on this point Valachi's evidence was *never* corroborated, although a large number of expert witnesses were examined on this subject. . . . It seems a little surprising that out of all those who appeared before the commission not one person was found to confirm Valachi's evidence on this matter.

INITIATION RITES

But if the question of nomenclature is regarded as of no great significance, there are what may be seen as more substantial matters about which the state of the evidence is equally unsatisfactory. Take, for example, the question of initiation rites, about which a great deal has been written in the literature. The Attorney General told the McClellan Commission: "They literally take an oath and they have the bloodletting. I think it will be described to you before the committee, but those who are members of this organization, take the oath."

When he testified on this, Valachi described a ceremony at which thirty-five or forty persons were present in the course of which he took an oath ("I repeated some words they told me, but I couldn't explain what he meant."); burnt a piece of paper ("Well then he gave me a piece of paper, and I was to burn it."); had his finger pricked ("With a needle and he makes a little blood come out."); and repeated some more words ("I never asked what it meant.").

Now the purpose of this meeting, according to Valachi, was "to make new members and *to meet all of them*." Yet later, when questioned, Valachi, although he claimed to have proposed others for membership, twice stated that he couldn't remember being "invited to participate at any other initiation ceremony." No member of the committee thought to ask him how

it was that subsequently—from 1930 onward—no new member was ever to meet *him* at an initiation ceremony. . . .

THE GENOVESE "FAMILY"

We come now, however, to what is unquestionably a matter of substance, to that part of Valachi's testimony that dealt with the membership and organizational structure of the Vito Genovese "family" in New York to which he belonged. It was in this connection that his evidence was said to be most valuable and reliable. John F. Shanley, Deputy Chief Inspector in the Central Investigations Bureau, which is the intelligence unit concerned with organized crime in the New York City Police Department, stated, "His strength is in the Genovese chart, his greatest strength. . . ."; the chart referred to being one prepared by the Central Investigations Bureau showing details of the Vito Genovese "family." It is important, therefore, to see how far Valachi's evidence was corroborated by the police. In this connection, the evidence given by Deputy Chief Shanley reveals that the information given by Valachi coincided with that put forward by the police in a number of respects. Yet an examination of the record reveals other facts which also make it clear that:

1. It would have been very surprising indeed if the police evidence had not agreed with that of Valachi, and,
2. To talk of the police evidence as *corroborating* Valachi's testimony is to totally misrepresent the situation.

In order to demonstrate this point, it is only necessary to reproduce two brief passages from Deputy Chief Inspector Shanley's testimony. The first passage is taken from the beginning of that testimony:

The Chairman: Have you gone over the information that the committee has obtained and conferred with the staff regarding it, and also with this witness, Joe Valachi?
Mr. Shanley: I haven't conferred with the witness.
The Chairman: You never conferred with the witness?
Mr. Shanley: No, sir.
The Chairman: So, what you are going to testify here is not a result of any conference you have had with Valachi?
Mr. Shanley: No, sir.
The Chairman: Very well, you may proceed.

The second passage occurs toward the end of Deputy Chief Inspector Shanley's evidence, after he had produced the chart referred to above and testified about the Genovese "family." It runs as follows:

The Chairman: Senator Muskie, you have a question?
Senator Muskie: You testified earlier, Inspector Shanley, that you had not personally talked to Mr. Valachi.
Mr. Shanley: That is right.
Senator Muskie: Yet these charts are based heavily on his information, am I correct?
Mr. Shanley: That is correct.
Senator Muskie: What was the source of your access to his information?
Mr. Shanley: The Committee.
Senator Muskie: These hearings?
Mr. Shanley: Yes, sir. We received the information prior to the hearings.
Senator Muskie: Would it have been possible for you to reconstruct these charts without his testimony?
Mr. Shanley: No, sir.
Senator Mundt: Mr. Chairman.
The Chairman: Senator Mundt.
Senator Mundt: While we are talking about the value of the charts, you have been in the hearing room, I think, Inspector, since the very beginning of the

Valachi testimony. Is that right?
Mr. Shanley: Yes, sir.

It is only necessary to add that sedulous reproduction is not the same thing as substantiation. Nor is it sufficient merely to assert, as Mr. Shanley did, that Valachi's information possessed "an apparent authenticity that is hard to doubt." . . .

ORGANIZATIONAL DISCIPLINE

We turn now from "the corroboration furnished by law enforcement officers [that] makes Valachi's testimony more credible and important," to what, in the circumstances, is the only other criterion of validity available, that is, the internal consistency of the evidence. Here there are a variety of matters that might be considered. In view, however, of the great emphasis that is always placed, in the literature, on the strictness of organizational discipline, and the obvious necessity for this if such an organization is to cohere and continue to exist, it is interesting to examine first the evidence on this topic.

In this connection, Senator McClellan spoke in his opening address of "the strict discipline imposed upon the members." He said: "This tightly knit association of professional criminals demands and gets *complete dedication and unquestioned obedience* by its members to orders, instructions and commands from the ruling authority or boss or bosses thereof." Subsequently, many witnesses were to refer to this. Thus, William H. Schneider, commissioner of police of Buffalo, spoke of the syndicate as "a multibillion dollar syndicate which depends on brutal assault and murder as its means of *cold, dispassionate discipline.*" (Hawkins' italics.) Valachi was

asked about this by Senator McClellan.
The Chairman: [T]hat (i.e., Cosa Nostra) is an organization, is it that requires *absolute obedience and conformity* to its policy as handed down by those in authority? (Hawkins' italics again.)
Mr. Valachi: Yes, sir.

. . .

The Chairman: Is that correct?
Mr. Valachi: Yes, sir.

It is interesting to compare these statements with some passages in Valachi's later testimony. It appears that, because of "the heat of the narcotics prosecutions, and the investigations and the publicity" in 1957, "those in authority" decreed that there was to be no more dealing in narcotics among members of Cosa Nostra. As Valachi put it: "No narcotics. You are in serious trouble if you were arrested for narcotics. You had to prove to them —you have another trial after having a trial with the government." His examination on this topic ran as follows:

Mr. Valachi: After Anastasia died in 1957, all families were notified—no narcotics.
Mr. Adlerman: Who laid down that rule?
Mr. Valachi: That was a rule that was discussed by the bosses themselves.
Mr. Adlerman: Was that the consigliere and the bosses themselves made that rule?
Mr. Valachi: That is right; that covered all families.

It is instructive to read what came next:

Mr. Adlerman: Was the narcotics trade one of the principal moneymakers for the members of the Cosa Nostra?
Mr. Valachi: Yes, it was.
Mr. Adlerman: And was this rule disregarded to a large extent?
Mr. Valachi: You mean there were lots of people in business?
Mr. Adlerman: That is right.
Mr. Valachi: Yes, sir.

Valachi went on to say that even some of "the bosses" violated the rule and he was then asked:

Mr. Adlerman: What was the reason why the members, the soldiers and so forth, and even some of the bosses disregarded the rule?
Mr. Valachi: Because of the moneymaking, the profit in it.
Mr. Adlerman: There was big money?
Mr. Valachi: They would chance their own lives.
Mr. Adlerman: And there was a conflict between the desire to make money and the desire to obey the rules; is that right?
Mr. Valachi: Well, they just defied the rules.
Mr. Adlerman: They defied the rules?
Mr. Valachi: That is the way I can explain it that way.

In the light of what had been said earlier about "complete dedication and unquestioned obedience," it was not an entirely satisfactory explanation. But then no explanation, however ingenious, could encompass the logically impossible task of reconciling the development described with the concept of a ruthless, unquestionable authority imposing "cold, dispassionate discipline" and securing "absolute obedience and conformity." . . .

MUTUAL AID?

It is, in fact, extremely difficult to understand what membership of the organization was supposed to entail either in the way of rights or duties. When Valachi was describing his initiation, he was asked:

Senator Mundt: In executive session you said when you had your hands all clasped together and repeated some words in Italian or Sicilian, that what it meant was "One for all and all for one."

Mr. Valachi: Yes; that is the way I explained it.

Senator Mundt: One for all and all for one.

Mr. Valachi: That is right. But I didn't know the words, Senator. You remember, I didn't know the words.

Senator Mundt: That is right, but you said that is the reaction you got.

Mr. Valachi: That is correct.

Senator Mundt: All right, then you became there a full-fledged member.

Mr. Valachi: Yes, sir.

It would seem reasonable to assume that the slogan, assuming that Valachi understood it correctly, implied some kind of mutual aid and protection. Certainly Senator McClellan had told the committee that "The benefits of membership . . . are a share in its illicit gains from criminal activities and protection from prosecution and the penalties of the law. . . ." Later Valachi was asked:

Senator Mundt: I want to ask you a couple of questions dealing with the first part of your testimony. You belonged to Cosa Nostra for about 30 years?

Mr. Valachi: Since 1930.

Senator Mundt: What was your average income from your criminal contacts during those 30 years, your average annual income?

Mr. Valachi: Senator, I wouldn't be able to tell you. Sometimes I was doing bad, sometimes I was going good.

Senator Mundt: What I am trying to establish is that you were working as a soldier in this family, I am trying to determine what your income was as a soldier working for Genovese.

Mr. Valachi: You don't get any salary, Senator.

Senator Mundt: Well, you get a cut then.

Mr. Valachi: You get nothing, only what you earn yourself. Do you understand? . . .

Senator Mundt: You say the only thing you got out of your membership and for carrying out your assignments that

Genovese gave you was protection?

Mr. Valachi: Yes. . . .

So much then for Senator McClellan's "share in its illicit gains." What about "protection from prosecution and the penalties of the law"? Deputy Chief Inspector Shanley had told the Committee that "[T]he family will help with lawyers, bail bondsmen, *et cetera*, if anything goes wrong."

The following passages are relevant here:

Senator Javits: Were you represented, for example, by lawyers in that time when you were picked up?

Mr. Valachi: When you are picked up, sometimes yes; sometimes no. Sometimes you don't even require a lawyer.

Senator Javits: How did you seek the help of your family when you were picked up?

Mr. Valachi: I used to get my own help. What family do you mean?

Senator Javits: The family to which you belonged, the Genovese family.

Mr. Valachi: I never bothered them. If I got picked up, I got myself out, I got my own lawyers.

Senator Javits: Did they give you any protection in the 35 years?

Mr. Valachi: No.

Senator Javits: They did not furnish lawyers?

Mr. Valachi: Never.

Senator Javits: Or bondsmen?

Mr. Valachi: Never, I got my own bondsmen, my own lawyers.

. . .

Senator Javits: Do you attribute the fact that you were not convicted of a crime for 35 years to your membership in this family? Do you connect the two at all?

Mr. Valachi: No.

Senator Javits: You were just lucky?

Mr. Valachi: That is right.

Senator Javits: And you changed the nature of activities?

Mr. Valachi: Put it that way.

Senator Javits: So your membership in the

family had nothing to do, in your opinion . . .

Mr. Valachi: I was never in a position, if I was I would tell you, Senator, I was never in a position where the family helped me.

In his evidence before the McClellan Committee, the Attorney General spoke of the commission ("We know that Cosa Nostra is run by a commission. . . .") as a body that "makes major policy decisions for the organization, settles disputes among families and allocates territories of criminal operation within the organizations." It sounds a very businesslike and efficient operation on the part of men about whom the committee were later told "frequently they don't make out in the legitimate business" because they are "not very smart businessmen." But it is hardly consistent with Valachi's testimony. He was asked:

Senator Curtis: In that connection, did they divide up the territory? Even though you operated on your own, you knew where you could operate?

Mr. Valachi: No, you see, Senator, you take Harlem, for instance. We have about four families all mixed up there. *There isn't any territory.* You find Brooklyn gangs in New York and New York into Brooklyn. They get along very well. If anything, you have in Brooklyn, in fact they help protect it for you. *I would not say it is territories.* You take for instance in Harlem, we have about three families bumping onto one another. You have the Gambino family, the Lucchese family, and you have the Genovese family right in Harlem. . . . You have three families right there. You have members there from all different groups. (Hawkins' italics.)

PRECEPTS AND RULES

We may deal briefly with one other matter and then leave the McClellan Committee. Senator McClellan told members that "The penalty for disloyalty or any serious deviation from the precepts, rules and dictates of the order is usually death." But what were the precepts and rules of the order? We have already noted Professor Cressey's remarkable "code of good thieves everywhere." What did Joseph Valachi have to say on the subject? He stated that at the time of his initiation he was told that he must never divulge the secrets of the initiation ceremony or of the organization. On this point, he said:

As to what I am telling you now, I need go no further to say nothing else but this here, what I am telling you, what I am exposing to you and the press and everybody. This is my doom. This is the promise I am breaking. Even if I talked, I should never talk about this, and I am doing so. That is my best way to explain it.

His examination continued as follows:

The Chairman: . . . Were any of the rules explained to you there, or were they explained to you later?
Mr. Valachi: Just two rules at this time.
The Chairman: Just two at that time?
Mr. Valachi: At this time.
The Chairman: What were they?
Mr. Valachi: One was the secret which I was just telling you about, and the other rule was, for instance, a wife, if you violate the law of another member's wife, or sister, or daughter, these two rules were told; in other words, you had no defense.
The Chairman: You have no defense?
Mr. Valachi: These two main rules. If you give away the secret or you violate—at this time that is all of the rules I was told.
The Chairman: Those two.
Mr. Valachi: At this time.
The Chairman: If you violated the family relationship of a husband and his wife, and if they were members of Cosa Nostra; is that all?

Mr. Valachi: If they were members. If they were members of Cosa Nostra.

The Chairman: You were prohibited from violating the rules of family relationship.

Mr. Valachi: That is right.

The Chairman: Those two at that time.

Mr. Valachi: That is right.

But, although Valachi testified that later on he "learned the rules," the only other example he gave was, "For instance you can't hit another member with your fist." He admitted having broken this rule himself when he found his partner "was stealing most of the profit." Senator McClellan seems to have scented another rule at this point, for he asked: "Was that against your code, to steal from each other?" But Valachi's reply was somewhat equivocal. "Well yes," he said, "against my code it was." And that was all the committee learnt about "the code" which, according to the President's Commission Task Force Report on Organized Crime "gives the leaders exploitative authoritarian power over everyone in the organization."

Of the three rules he mentioned, Valachi had avowedly broken two. Was he unusual in this? He was certainly not unique in becoming an informer. According to the Attorney General, the *main* thing that distinguished him was that he was willing to "come and testify in public." . . . But, apart from this sort of disloyalty, did the chivalric code of "One for all and all for one" otherwise prevail? Almost everything in Valachi's testimony suggests the opposite. He spoke of vicious power struggles and murderous internecine conflicts like the Masseria-Maranzano war and the Gallo-Profaci feud. He spoke of "the bosses" as being "very bad to the soldiers and they have been thinking for themselves, all through the years." He portrayed Professor Cressey's "almost revered" Vito Genovese as mean, murderous, and megalomaniacal. If there existed anywhere amongst organized criminals that "sense of decency and morality— a sense of honor," which Professor Cressey remarks as characteristic of them, it seems to have escaped Joseph Valachi's notice.

In sum then, what can be said about the Valachi evidence? . . . Despite what Senator McClellan said about his evidence being corroborated, it was not corroborated on any points essential to the hypothesis we are considering. It was neither consistent with itself nor with other evidence that was presented to the Committee. Valachi both contradicted himself and was contradicted by others. Moreover, what the Attorney General called "the biggest intelligence breakthrough yet" appears to have produced nothing in the way of tangible results.

. . .

APALACHIN

There is one other piece of "evidence" which should be mentioned here before we conclude. This relates to what J. Edgar Hoover called the "meeting of hoodlums at Apalachin, N.Y.," which has been referred to somewhat more grandly by others as the "Crime Convention at Apalachin" and the "historic rally of the Mafia at Apalachin." . . .

There seems to be general agreement that on November 14, 1957 a number of individuals, most of whom "had criminal records relating to the kind of offense customarily called 'organized crime,' " gathered at the home of Joseph Barbara in Apalachin, N.Y., and that the gathering was interrupted by the police. But, beyond that point, the evidence becomes extraordinarily confused. Indeed, even such basic information as how many persons were present at the gathering is lacking. . . .

Where such discrepancies exist about a matter that is, at least in principle, subject to quantitative measurement, it is not surprising that there is disagreement about less objective features. . . .

Consider, for instance, the question of the nature of the gathering at Apalachin. John T. Cusack, District Supervisor for the Federal Bureau of Narcotics, testified before the New York State Legislative Committee that "the meeting at Apalachin, New York, should be considered a meeting of the Grand Council" of "the Mafia Society." Attorney General Robert Kennedy, in his evidence to the McClellan Committee, cited "the meeting at Apalachin" as an example of a meeting of the commission that runs Cosa Nostra and "makes major policy decisions for the organization." But he also testified that "membership in the commission varies between 9 and 12 active members." He made no attempt to reconcile this evidence with his earlier statement that "more than a hundred top racketeers" were present at Apalachin. Senator McClellan allowed himself a rhetorical flourish. "The meeting of the delegates to the Apalachin convention," he said, "suggests a lawless and clandestine army . . . at war with the government and the people of the United States." He failed to mention, however, that not one of these lawless warriors was armed, and that only one (a parole violator from New Jersey who should not have left the state) was wanted anywhere by the police.

. . . When, subsequently, twenty of those present at Apalachin were charged with "conspiring to obstruct justice and commit perjury," the government frankly admitted at the outset of the trial "that it would not be able to show what was going on at the meeting." Regarding this trial, the *Task Force Report: Organized Crime* says: "In 1957, twenty of organized crime's top leaders were convicted (later reversed on appeal) of a criminal charge arising from a meeting at Apalachin, N.Y." It is characteristic of the inconsequential way in which the whole subject is treated in both official and unofficial reports that the defendants are said to have been convicted in 1957 of charges on which they were not even indicted until May 1959. But the report is accurate in stating that all the convictions were reversed on appeal.

. . . One thing is certain: the information available about Apalachin provides no serious evidence that "a single national crime syndicate" dominates organized crime in America; nor does it make this seem probable.

AN ARTICLE OF FAITH

Yet if the evidence for the existence of an All-American crime confederation or syndicate is both suspect and tenuous to the point of nullity, it is clear that for the believer there is nothing that could count decisively against the assertion that it exists. Indeed, precisely those features that in ordinary discourse about human affairs might be regarded as evidence in rebuttal are instantly assimilated as further strengthening the case *for* the hypothesis. The absence of direct evidence, apart from Valachi's uninhibited garrulity (and other unspecified informants), merely demonstrates "the fear instilled in them by the code of nondisclosure." Thus, denials of membership in, or knowledge of, the syndicate can not only be dismissed as self-evidently false, but also adduced as evidence of what they deny. If there is gang warfare, this indicates that "an internal struggle for dominance over the entire organization" is going on; and also provides "a somber illustration of how cruel and calculating the underworld continues to be." If peace prevails this may be taken either as evidence of the power of the syndicate leadership and the fear in which it is held; or alternatively as reflecting the development of "the sophisticated and polished control of rackets that now characterize that organization."

It is said that "practically all" the members of the organization "are of Sicilian birth or ancestry." Professor Cressey, for example, speaks of "the Italian-Sicilian apparatus [that] continues to dominate organized crime in America." But counterevidence relating to the activities of those from other ethnic backgrounds (e.g., Meyer Lansky, said by J. Edgar Hoover to be "generally recognized as one of the most powerful racketeers in this country"), can easily be accommodated as illustrating the "characteristic Mafia method of utilizing non-Sicilian associates where it serves its criminal objectives." In the end, it is difficult to resist the conclusion that one is not dealing with an empirical phenomenon at all, but with an article of faith, transcending the contingent particularity of everyday experience and logically unassailable. . . .

Drugs

7

DRUGS IN HISTORICAL PERSPECTIVE

There is much controversy today over the so-called drug problem. Parents and other concerned citizens are alarmed by the emergence of a drug subculture among American youth. Concern with the drug menace tends to obscure the fact that drugs are not a new or even recent phenomenon. "Drug use, in one form or another, has been a common feature of most cultures throughout history" (National Commission on Marihuana and Drug Abuse, 1973:37).

One of the most widely used drugs in various societies is opium. Its use can be traced to as early as 4000 B.C. in Sumeria and 3500 B.C. in Egypt (Kramer, 1972:32). It was also found in ancient Assyria, Babylonia, Persia, and Greece (Kramer, 1972:32; Blum, 1967b: 41). "The euphoriant effects of the opium poppy are implied in Sumarian [sic] records of 4000 B.C. Greek and Roman records are replete with historical references" (Gay and Way, 1972:47). In Homer's *Odyssey*, for instance, we are told that

". . . Helen, the daughter of Zeus, turned her thoughts elsewhere. Straightway she cast into the wine of which they drunk, a drug which quenches pain and strife and brings forgetfulness of every ill." While opium was recognized for its therapeutic and medicinal value, particularly as a painkiller, widespread private, recreational consumption was uncommon in this early period. "By 1000 A.D. opium was already being widely used in China and the Far East as an indulgence . . ." (Lindesmith, 1965:194). The problem was so intense that in 1729 the Chinese emperor decreed the first prohibitory laws. Punishment was specified for anyone involved in the opium trade, except the user, and the punishment for those who kept opium shops was death by strangulation (Lindesmith, 1965:194). Penalties were eventually extended to include the user. Government attempts to control opium use by forbidding its importation led to the Opium War (1839–1842) with Great Britain (McGrath and Scarpitti, 1970:1). The prohibition system remained in effect until 1858 when the sale of opium was legalized (Lindesmith, 1965:194). The drug problem in China continued, however, and repressive measures were periodically reinstituted during the twentieth century.

Opium use spread to other Far Eastern nations and eventually to the West Coast of the United States, particularly San Francisco's Barbary Coast (Gay and Way, 1972:49). Before the Civil War the use and distribution of opium and morphine was largely unregulated (National Commission on Marihuana and Drug Abuse, 1973:14). "Cure-all" medicines such as "Dover's Powder" and "Dr. Barton's Brown Mixture," containing opium extracts, were widely used during the nineteenth century (Gay and Way, 1972:49). The use of narcotic drugs, however, remained a relatively minor problem until after the Civil War. Morphine "was used indiscriminately during the Civil War for the wholesale relief of pain and, most significantly, to treat common gastrointestinal ailments. After the War, morphine was widely used in medical practice and was easily available outside the medical system in proprietary medicines" (National Commission on Marihuana and Drug Abuse, 1973:15). In 1898 heroin was introduced by the German pharmaceutical firm, Bayer, and hailed as a new cough suppressant and a cure for morphine dependence (Gay and Way, 1972:45).

Although the use of opium and its derivatives was mostly uncontrolled during the nineteenth century, there were sporadic attempts to regulate its sale and use. As early as 1842 a tariff was assessed on imported opium, and in 1888 the possibility of banning the importation and smoking of opium was considered (Kramer, 1972:37). The first prescription law was passed by Pennsylvania in 1860, and "in 1875, San Francisco enacted an ordinance prohibiting the smoking or possession of opium, the possession of opium pipes and the maintenance of 'opium dens.' As the practice spread, it generated a succession of similar state laws and local ordinances" (National Commission on Marihuana and Drug Abuse, 1973:15). Concern with the problem of addiction grew, leading in 1914 to passage of what was to become the dominant drug-control law—the Harrison Act. The act was designed as a revenue measure—drug transactions were to be recorded and taxed by the Treasury Department, but the law came to be interpreted as a legislative measure that denied addicts access to legal drugs (Lindesmith, 1965:4). The addict was placed in an ambiguous position. "The Act did not make addiction illegal and it neither authorized nor forbade doctors to prescribe drugs regularly for addicts" (Lindesmith, 1965:5). Drugs were to be dispensed "for legitimate medical purposes" and "prescribed in good faith," but it did not specify what was meant by these phrases.

A series of Supreme Court decisions between 1915 and 1925 had the effect of denying addicts access to drugs (for a discussion of these cases see Lindesmith, 1965:5–11). These decisions were reexamined in the 1925 *Linder* case in which the Court ruled that addicts could receive bonafide medical treatment if the physician was acting in good faith. This interpretation was affirmed by the Court in 1962 in *Robinson* v. *California*. Despite the importance of the *Linder* decision, it was ignored both by the Federal Bureau of Narcotics and by prosecutors. It is estimated that in the twelve years following passage of the Harrison Act 25,000 doctors were arraigned on charges of selling narcotics and 3,000 were sentenced to prison terms (Goode, 1972:191). Physicians, fearing prosecution, censure by the medical profession, and the revocation of their licenses, have since been reluctant to treat addicts. It is ironic that while the government has opposed the use of drugs by physicians to ease the distress of withdrawal, informers of drug activities are frequently given drugs in exchange for cooperation with the police and prosecutors (Lindesmith, 1965:17). Our attitudes toward narcotics users have been punitive and inflexible. Addiction is viewed as deviant behavior, and a drug-fiend mythology has emerged to support this view. The addict is viewed as a wild and dangerous animal who presents a threat to society; addiction is willful and immoral behavior, not an illness or disease. The dominant attitude toward addicts is typified by a 1957 Indiana law making it illegal for an addict to appear in public unless he can demonstrate that he is undergoing treatment by a physician. The law simultaneously forbids physicians to provide drugs for habitual addicts (Lindesmith, 1965:34). The addict is placed in an impossible situation in which he must either undergo painful solitary withdrawal or seek illicit drugs.

Our punitive attitude toward drug users is a social phenomenon that is as worthy of study as addiction itself. This punitive attitude will be discussed later in the chapter; now it is important to note that our reaction to drug addiction far exceeds the damage it has done to society. Certainly alcohol abuse is far more widespread and has more important consequences; yet our reaction to alcoholics and drunken offenders is much less severe. Even if one believes that narcotic drugs are harmful, the addict is generally a willing victim. Our punitive legislation is designed to "protect" the addict from himself.

DEFINITION OF TERMS

Terms such as "addiction," "dependence," and "drug abuse" have been used in a confusing and careless manner. If such terms are to be used in systematic analyses, it is necessary that they be defined more carefully and with greater precision (President's Commission, 1967b:1). Physiologically, the term "addiction" refers to physical dependence on a drug, but it is sometimes confused with psychological dependence and with social integration into a drug-using subculture (President's Commission, 1967b:1). The World Health Organization has recommended substituting the term "drug dependence" for "drug addiction," but we continue to use "addiction" as a medically recognized term (President's Commission, 1967b:2). Addiction has a more negative connotation, consistent with the drug-fiend mythology. The term "psychological dependence," or "emotional dependence," has been used loosely and adds little to our understanding of drug use. It refers to nothing more than habit-forming behavior. Thus some persons are psychologically dependent on marijuana in the same sense that others are dependent on ice cream. In this discussion the term "addiction" will refer to physiological dependence on a drug so that immediate withdrawal produces severe illness. Persons may become physically dependent on substances that are not normally thought of as drugs (e.g., alcohol and coffee). A term that is frequently associated with dependence is "tolerance." When tolerance to a drug occurs, increased dosages are required to attain the same effect.

"Narcotics" is a much abused term. It is a legal rather than a medical or sociological term. The substances defined as narcotics by the law share few pharmacological properties. A variety of substances, including the opiates, cocaine, and marijuana, are narcotics according to federal laws and many state statutes. ". . . the word 'narcotics' had been purged of its scientific meaning and became, instead, a symbol of socially disapproved drugs" (National Commission on Marihuana and Drug Abuse, 1973:17). The term "drug" is equally ambiguous. Although we commonly refer to certain substances as "drugs," the label seems to be based more on social than on chemical criteria. Technically, a drug is any substance that is used as a medicine. However, it is typically applied to substances that are socially disapproved. Alcohol and coffee, for example, are not considered drugs in the United States today, but they were considered drugs at an earlier period because they were socially disapproved (Clausen, 1971:189). Here the term "narcotics" will be discarded, and "drugs" will refer to substances that are socially and legally proscribed when used in a nonmedicinal setting.

DRUGS AND THEIR EFFECTS

The opiates

Opium and its various derivatives are powerful depressants that are widely prescribed in medical treatment as painkillers, or analgesics. They include morphine, codeine, dilaudid, laudanum, and paregoric (Goode, 1972:161). Morphine, for example, is used to relieve pain and codeine to reduce cough. The opiates have substantial medicinal value, but prolonged use leads to tolerance and physical dependence.

Heroin, a morphine derivative, "is the chief drug of addiction in the United States" according to the President's Commission (1967b:2). Unlike other opiates, heroin cannot be used in medical practice; its manufacture or importation, for any purpose, is illegal. Although it is commonly asserted "that heroin is outlawed because of its special attractiveness to addicts and because it serves no known medical purpose not served as well or better by other drugs" (President's Commission, 1967b:3), heroin and morphine are very similar pharmacologically and biochemically.

An experienced drug addict would probably not be able to discern the difference between comparable doses of heroin and morphine, and a pharmacologist would have to look very, very closely to distinguish the laboratory effects. . . . Nonetheless, heroin is declared to have no medical uses whatsoever. . . . Morphine, on the other hand, is regarded as a boon to mankind (Goode, 1972:6).

The difference in our reaction to these two drugs, in short, is not explained by their pharmacological properties, but rather by differential meanings that are assigned to them by society (Goode, 1967:6). Heroin "relieves anxiety and tension and diminishes the sex, hunger, and other primary drives" (President's Commission, 1967b:2). Its effects are extremely variable, however, not only according to the potency and purity of the drug but, more importantly, according to the context and meaning of use. "Heroin use . . . is almost exclusively a group phenomenon" (Goode, 1972:167). One's initial experience may be unpleasant, but through subcultural definitions it can be defined as an extremely pleasurable and euphoric experience. The decreased sex drive that frequently accompanies heroin use is not surprising, since for many its effects parallel and exceed those of sexual orgasm (Goode, 1972:171).

While heroin is generally labeled as a "dangerous" drug, it is, except for the danger of overdosing,[1] relatively nontoxic (Gay and Gay, 1972:27). Physicians and other respectable members of society have used heroin in a controlled medical setting for many years with little damage to the body. Diseases such as hepatitis and tetanus, which are commonly associated with addiction, result from unsterilized needles and unsanitary conditions

---

[1] There is not much difference between an effective and a lethal dose of heroin.

(Gay and Way, 1972:51). Many other negative effects can also be traced to impurities that are found in the heroin purchased by street addicts. In short, the negative effects of heroin "are a product of the present legal and social system surrounding addiction, and almost not at all a function of the drug itself" (Goode, 1972:164). The drug-fiend mythology supports the view that heroin consumption, even in minute quantities, leads to instant addiction. While repeated heroin use produces tolerance and dependence, most persons who try heroin do not become dependent (National Commission on Marihuana and Drug Abuse, 1973:144). It is also possible to stabilize doses so that tolerance is kept under control (Weil, 1973:57–58). Those who become dependent do so generally after repeated use within a context that defines the experience and its effects as pleasurable.

Cocaine
"Cocaine is obtained from the leaves of Erythroxylon shrubs which grow in the Andes" (National Commission on Marihuana and Drug Abuse, 1973:163). Although cocaine is classified as a narcotic by law, it is a potent stimulant with effects similar to those of the amphetamines. Its effects are, however, of shorter duration than those of amphetamines. Cocaine produces neither tolerance nor dependence.

Amphetamines
Although a variety of substances, including cocaine, serve as stimulants to the central nervous system, amphetamines are the most widely prescribed in medical practice. They are used in weight-control programs, to relieve depression, to treat behavior disorders in children, and by persons seeking high levels of alertness and vigor (Blum, 1967a:29). Amphetamines have become part of the drug problem as many persons seeking a high or a kick have turned to them for recreational use. "Uppers" (or "speed") produce a feeling of well-being and euphoria. Large doses may produce violent behavior, paranoia, delusions, and psychotic episodes. When a person uses them over a prolonged period of time, he builds up tolerance and requires increasing doses to attain the same high. Experts differ on whether amphetamines produce physical dependence (Goode, 1972:136). For a long time it was believed that one did not become dependent, but recent evidence suggests that "the cessation of repeated use of high doses of amphetimines [sic] generally causes the user to feel irritable, fatigued and depressed; and a type of withdrawal occurs, although it is qualitatively different from and not as uniquely characteristic as the withdrawal syndrome associated with cessation of heroin use" (National Commission on Marihuana and Drug Abuse, 1973:160).

Barbiturates
With the exception of alcohol, barbiturates, generally referred to as "downers" or "goofballs," are the most widely used depressants. They are pre-

scribed to reduce tension and anxiety and to induce sleep. Persons not only develop tolerance for barbiturates, but over a period of time they become physically dependent on them so that withdrawal of the drug produces severe illness. In fact, withdrawal from barbiturates is more severe and likely to cause death than withdrawal from heroin (Goode, 1972:153). Excessive doses can lead to psychotic episodes, impaired judgment, and even death. Overdoses of barbiturates are frequently involved in suicide attempts. Barbiturates are used not only for medical purposes but for recreational use. Some persons regulate their mood by using both barbiturates and amphetamines either alternately or simultaneously (for a discussion of "uppers" and "downers," see Smith and Wesson, 1973). Since their effects are similar to alcohol, it is not surprising that many regular users of barbiturates are or have in the past been regular users of alcohol (National Commission on Marihuana and Drug Abuse, 1973:160).

Mind-Expanding drugs

The new drugs that are sweeping across college campuses are called hallucinogens or "psychotomimetics" ("mimicking" madness). These terms are revealing in that they imply that the drugs typically produce hallucinations, delusions, or psychotic episodes. A less pejorative term, "mind-expanding drugs," will be used to refer to psychedelic and hallucinogenic drugs. Included in this classification are synthetic compounds such as LSD, STP, and DMT and naturally occurring substances like mescaline, peyote, and psilocybin. Mind-expanding drugs are classified as dangerous drugs, but one does not become physically dependent on them (President's Commission, 1967b:5), although prolonged usage may produce tolerance (Bureau of Narcotics and Dangerous Drugs, 1969:18).

If a single series of events could be isolated that marks the genesis of the "psychedelic revolution," it would probably be the experiments of Dr. Timothy Leary and his colleague Dr. Richard Alpert at Harvard University in the early 1960s. Their psychological experiments were canceled, and Leary and Alpert were fired for allegedly "turning on" hundreds of students to psilocybin and a new, synthetic substance called LSD. The furor created by these experiments led to restrictive legislation designed to control the manufacture, sale, and possession of LSD (Geller and Boas, 1971: 171–177). The legislation came quickly, long before the effects of the drug were clearly established. Even today there is substantial disagreement over its effects. One of the most common effects attributed to LSD, however, is genetic damage. In the late 1960s the media gave much publicity to findings from a study by Cohen (1967) and his associates—it was reported that LSD produces chromosome breakage. The study, unfortunately, did not control for intervening variables (Goode, 1972:115–116). While the evidence is far from conclusive, recent investigations question the legitimacy of these claims (BNDD, 1969:19; Weil, 1973:44–46). A study based on extensive review of almost 100 scientific papers concluded: "We believe that pure LSD ingested in moderate dosages does not produce chromosome damage detectable by available methods" (Dihotsky et al., 1971:439). These researchers also found no evidence of LSD causing birth defects. Earlier studies had failed to control for significant factors such as the purity of the drug (most street acid is contaminated), dosage level, frequency of use, and the point during a pregnancy when LSD was ingested (Goode, 1972:116–117). Much of the damage attributed to LSD may result from impurities or from other drugs. However, even when chromosome breakage occurs, it does not necessarily imply fetal damage or birth defects. The crucial question is whether, when all other factors are held constant, mothers who take pure LSD are any more likely to have birth defects than mothers who do not take it (Goode, 1972:117).

One difficulty in evaluating the effects of LSD is that "evidence" is presented by two hostile camps. Our government agencies have traditionally sought to "prove" that LSD and other drugs have negative effects. Persons who are turned on by mind-expanding drugs, on the other hand, are blind to negative effects, seeking to proselytize and gain new converts (Weil, 1973:6). The negative effects that have been documented by Establishment agencies should therefore be interpreted with extreme caution. The President's Commission Task Force Report on Narcotics and Drug Abuse (the title itself reveals a bias) cites the following dangers of LSD: "(1) Prolonged psychosis; (2) acting out of character disorders and homosexual impulses; (3) suicidal inclinations; (4) activation of previously latent psychosis; and (5) reappearance of the drug's effects weeks or even months after use" (1967b:5). LSD alters perception; colors become brighter and more intense, and objects may waver or appear distorted (BNDD, 1969:11). Some of the more extreme reactions are dizziness, nausea, dilation of the pupils, visual aberrations, and improved auditory capacity (National Commission on Marihuana and Drug Abuse, 1973: 163). Emotional states may fluctuate between extreme "highs" and extreme "lows." Sometimes what psychiatrists term "false hallucinations" are experienced,[2] "where the individual may see something but at the same time he also knows his perception doesn't have a basis in external reality" (BNDD, 1969:11). Some persons undoubtedly suffer "false hallucinations" and psychotic episodes while under the influence of LSD, but it is misleading to conclude that these conditions are caused by the psychoactive properties of the drug. First, it is important to note that only persons who have bad trips generally come to the attention of psychiatrists and hospitals. Without a sample of all LSD users one cannot determine the incidence of psychosis or psychotic episodes among them. Second, individuals who already have psychiatric problems are perhaps more likely to experiment

[2] One cannot help but wonder how a "false hallucination" differs from normal perception. Proponents of mind-expanding drugs would argue that acid enables us to see the world as it really is.

with LSD, so that LSD use may be a consequence rather than a cause of mental disorders. Third, since one seldom ingests pure LSD, many of its negative effects may result from impurities or from other drugs (e.g., most LSD is "cut" with amphetamine). Finally, one should bear in mind that the number of bad trips is a small proportion of the total number of trips. ". . . on a sheerly statistical basis the chances that the LSD user will experience a psychotic episode requiring psychiatric or medical treatment are relatively slim" (Goode, 1972:114). Available evidence also indicates that it is one of the least toxic of all drugs (Weil, 1973:48).

While there is considerable controversy over the effects of LSD, there is agreement on at least one point—LSD is a powerful drug. Its effects may be beneficial or detrimental, depending on a number of factors including the dosage, quality and purity of the drug, the conditions under which it is taken, and the mental condition of the user. These factors ultimately determine whether one has a good or a bad trip on acid.

Although LSD is a synthetic compound produced in the laboratory, it is derived from a natural substance, lysergic acid, found in ergot, a parasitic fungus of rye (BNDD, 1969:31). Peyote and mescaline are older but less potent drugs. "Peyote is the hallucinogenic substance obtained from the button-shaped growths of a cactus plant found growing wild in the arid regions of Mexico. Mescaline is a natural alkaloid, which occurs in the same plant" (President's Commission, 1967b:5). Peyote and mescaline have been used in religious rites by various North American Indian tribes. Psilocybin is a similar substance found in a mushroom fungus. The Mexican *hongos* (mushrooms), which first introduced Timothy Leary to mind-expanding drugs (Geller and Boas, 1971:162–163), were used by the Aztecs in religious ceremonies (BNDD, 1969:9).

Marijuana

Marijuana, or *Cannabis sativa*, is much less powerful than the mind-expanding drugs, although its effects are somewhat similar. Written accounts of *cannabis*, an intoxicant produced from the Indian hemp plant, date more than 4000 years (Geller and Boas, 1969:3). Marijuana was widely used for medicinal purposes and as an intoxicant in the East and Near East, but it was not until the 1910s and 1920s that it was introduced into the United States on a large scale by Mexican laborers. Accustomed to smoking regularly, they brought *cannabis* across the border and planted it for their own consumption (Geller and Boas, 1971:14).

Since marijuana is not a single uniform substance, its effects vary considerably according to the potency and psychoactive properties of the material smoked. When the drug is used at a typical social level, it is accompanied by few, if any, adverse effects. Among the more common physiological effects are accelerated pulse rate, reddening of the eyes, and dryness of the mouth and throat (NIMH, 1972:19). Marijuana smokers frequently report increased hunger, but smoking does not appear to lower blood sugar (NIMH, 1972:19). No major neurological disorders have been uncovered, although there appears to be "a small decrease in leg, hand and finger strength at higher dosages" (NIMH, 1971:10). From the standpoint of lethality, marijuana is one of the safest drugs. There are no confirmed deaths resulting from the use of marijuana even at a very high dosage (National Commission on Marihuana, 1972:83; NIMH, 1972:21). Perhaps more significant are the subjective effects of *cannabis*. Typical effects are the apparent slowing down of time, a distortion of space, a feeling of euphoria and good will, the dulling of attention, laughter, and increased suggestibility (NIMH, 1971:8). Less common symptoms are dizziness, a feeling of lightness, and nausea. Under high doses thought distortions, hallucinations, and paranoid thinking may occur (NIMH, 1972:24–26). Acute psychotic episodes occur infrequently and usually at high doses. The most important and consistent finding, however, is that *"users overwhelmingly describe their marijuana experience in favorable and pleasurable terms*; in short, they like what they feel" (Goode, 1972:51, 53).

It is difficult to generalize about the effects of marijuana, since they vary according to the drug's strength and quality, the experience of the smoker, the psychological characteristics of the smoker, and the situational context within which smoking takes place. One of the most critical factors is the experience of the smoker. The naïve smoker is more likely to experience negative effects. A group of Harvard researchers (Weil, Zinberg, and Nelsen, 1968) found that after smoking marijuana, naïve subjects generally showed decrements in performance on tests that measured motor skills and the capacity for sustained attention, whereas chronic smokers improved their performance. The naïve subjects also reported few of the subjective effects reported by the chronic smokers. Other studies have shown that experienced smokers are able to get high on a very low dosage or even on placebos, dummy marijuana cigarettes (NIMH, 1972:208). In another experiment subjects who smoked marijuana in a group setting reported more and a greater variety of subjective effects than those who smoked it alone (NIMH, 1972:209). These findings are consistent with the subcultural emphasis placed on smoking as a shared group experience. Marijuana produces ambiguous physical stimuli that are interpreted positively by the subculture of smokers. Howard Becker, in a classic study of marijuana, suggests that if a person is to become a regular, recreational user, he must first learn the technique of smoking, to perceive the effects, and to define the effects as pleasurable (Becker, 1966:41–58). This learning takes places within a group setting as the novice is guided by more experienced smokers who help him to define marijuana smoking as a pleasurable experience.

VOLUME OF DRUG USE

Reliable data on the volume of drug use are difficult to obtain. Perhaps the most comprehensive survey of drug use to date was conducted by the

National Commission on Marihuana and Drug Abuse (1973). The findings of the commission suggest that our society is not opposed to all drug
taking, but rather to the use of certain drugs by certain segments of the
population (1973:42). By far the most widely used mind-altering drug
is alcohol. Alcohol sales gross over $24 billion per year (1973:42). Over
half of the adults eighteen and older and about one-fourth of the youth
(twelve to seventeen) had consumed alcoholic beverages in the week preceding the survey (1973:44). Beer was the most popular alcoholic bever-
age both among adults and youth. Cigarette smoking was also extremely
prevalent; 38 percent of the adults and 17 percent of the youth are current
smokers. Americans also consume large quantities of proprietary (over-
the-counter) and ethical (prescription) psychoactive drugs. Over half of
the adults (56 percent) and one-fifth of the youth have had experience
with at least one of the many sedatives, tranquilizers, and stimulants that
are available (1973:50).

Marijuana is undoubtedly the most popular of the illicit recreational
drugs; it is the basic staple of the drug subculture (Davis, 1968:159). The
National Commission on Marihuana (1972:32) estimates from survey data
that 24 million Americans have tried marijuana and that 8 million are
current users (Associated Press, 1972). The use of marijuana appears to
be most prevalent among the young and the college educated. ". . . those
who have tried or used marihuana at least once, termed ever-users, are
heavily concentrated in the 16–25 age bracket. Of all the ever-users, about
half are in this group" (National Commission on Marihuana and Drug
Abuse, 1972:33). A Gallup survey (1972) showed that the proportion
of college students who had ever tried marijuana increased from 5 percent
in 1967 to 51 percent in 1971. More recent figures suggest, however, that
the use of marijuana may have reached a peak and started to level off
(National Commission on Marihuana and Drug Abuse, 1973:64). The
proportion of adults who had ever used marijuana was 15 percent in 1971
and 16 percent in 1972, whereas the proportion of youth who were ever-
users was 14 percent in both years. One of the most significant findings
of the study is that the illegality of the drug does not seem to be a major
deterrent to its use. Only 3 percent of the nonusing adults and 8 percent
of the nonusing youth say that they would try marijuana if it were legal
and available (1973:64).

The use of LSD and other mind-expanding drugs also appears to be on
the increase, particularly among college students. In 1967, 1 percent of the
college students interviewed had tried hallucinogens, but by 1971, 18
percent had tried them (Gallup, 1972). Yet when the entire population
is considered, only a fraction have tried LSD or a comparable hallucinogen.
Less than 5 percent of both adults and youth in the National Commission
(1973:68) survey have tried a hallucinogen. Moreover, only 1.2 percent
of the adults and 2.5 percent of the youth would try LSD if it were legal
and available. Experience with cocaine is even more limited; it is expensive
and not readily obtained. Approximately 3 percent of the adults and 1.5

percent of the youth have used cocaine. Among those who have not tried cocaine, 1 percent of the adults and 3 percent of the youth indicate that they would try cocaine if it were legalized and available (1973:69).

The popular press and many concerned citizens believe that we are currently in the midst of a heroin epidemic. Nonetheless, of all the drugs surveyed by the National Commission (1973:69) heroin had the lowest rate of incidence. Heroin had been tried by 1.3 percent of the adults and 0.6 percent of the youth. It is not surprising, therefore, that few of those who have not tried heroin (less than 1 percent) would try the drug even if it were legal and available. Since most persons who try heroin do not become dependent on the drug, figures concerning incidence of ever-use tell us little about the number of heroin-dependent persons. The Drug Enforcement Administration (DEA) keeps a file of active opiate users. At the middle of 1973, there were 95,897 active narcotics addicts listed, most of them heroin addicts (1973a:16). Since these figures are based on known addicts, usually those who come to the attention of the police, they undoubtedly underestimate the total number. A more realistic estimate by the DEA places the figure in excess of 600,000 (1973a:16).

It is somewhat ironic then that those drugs that receive the greatest social disapproval, whose use is assumed to take on epidemic proportions, are in reality used with much less frequency than approved drugs. "Although the use of illicit drugs tends to arouse the greatest public clamor and concern, it is, with the exception of marihuana use, a relatively uncommon occurrence when measured against other types of drug experience" (National Commission on Marihuana and Drug Abuse, 1973:63).

DRUGS AND CRIME

Part of the rationale behind the "war on drugs" is that drug use leads to crime. The so-called drug fiend is depicted as a violent animal who will resort to any means in order to maintain his habit. About 90 percent of the American public believes that heroin is directly related to crime, and "more than half of all adults and about two-thirds of our youth believe that marihuana users often commit crime to buy more of the drug and that they 'often commit crimes that they would not otherwise commit' " (National Commission on Marihuana and Drug Abuse, 1973:154). Data showing that areas with high rates of addiction have high rates of crime and delinquency have been used to support these views (O'Donnell, 1966: 374). Addiction is associated with crime, but the crimes of addicts are typically drug violations or property offenses, not crimes of violence (O'Donnell, 1966:380; President's Commission, 1967b:10). A recent study of arrest charges found that "users" (as determined by urine samples and questionnaires) of all drug substances were less likely than "nonusers" to be involved in crimes of violence (BNDD, 1971:383).

There are a number of factors that predispose the drug dependent person to crime. First, he comes into contact with members of a criminal subculture in obtaining illegal drugs. Second, although addiction is not a crime, possession of drugs and of drug-related paraphernalia such as needles and syringes are crimes in many states. Third, vagrancy statutes and other laws prohibit convicted addicts from associating with other addicts or to be in a place where illegal drugs are held (President's Commission, 1967b: 10). Finally, and most critically, the addict turns to selling drugs or to fund-raising crimes in order to maintain a supply of drugs. The relationship between drug dependence and crime, however, is not a direct causal relationship. Drugs per se do not cause crime, but the fact that they can only be obtained in an illicit market and at a high cost does. Persons who use heroin in this country are necessarily criminals (Weil, 1973:40). In Britain, where addicts can obtain drugs legally and at a modest price, the relationship between crime and addiction does not appear (Schur, 1964: 64–75). If anything, addicts in Britain appear to commit fewer crimes after they become dependent on drugs than before they were addicts (Goode, 1972:217).

Although heroin dependence is associated with crime, there is little evidence linking other drugs to crime. One study, for example, concluded that "crime associated with hallucinogen use appears to have been minimal" (Blum, 1967a:28). Some persons argue that marijuana leads to crime and base their argument on unverified reports by law-enforcement officials that criminal offenders are frequently regular users of marijuana. Much of the "marijuana hoax" (Ginsberg, 1966) can be traced to Harry Anslinger, Director of the Bureau of Narcotics for thirty-two years, who perpetuated the view that marijuana smokers are rapists and murderers (Anslinger and Oursler, 1961:38). Such propaganda led to the passage of the Marijuana Tax Act in 1937. This act, patterned after the Harrison Act, sought to control the use of marijuana by registering and taxing legitimate transactions and imposing penalities on the illicit sale and purchase of the drug (President's Commission, 1967b:12). Today it is clear that marijuana is not a cause of crime, and that millions of law-abiding Americans use it regularly (National Commission on Marihuana and Drug Abuse, 1972: 77). Marijuana tends to reduce aggression and probably decreases rather than increases the probability of violent behavior (National Commission on Marihuana and Drug Abuse, 1972:73).

TYPES OF DRUG USERS

Traditionally drug use has been associated with the more disadvantaged segments of society. In the past heroin dependence and marijuana smoking were reportedly seldom found outside of working-class and lower-class neighborhoods (Goode, 1973:160), with the exception of certain fringe groups such as jazz musicians and artists.[3] Today drug use cuts across racial, ethnic, and economic groups, although there is variation in the types of drugs used by these groups. Heroin and other opiates are still more common in the lower class, especially among persons who live in urban ghettos, but they are increasingly moving out of the ghettos and into the suburbs and campuses (Goode, 1972:160).[4] The "typical" heroin addict, nonetheless, is a black male in his twenties who resides in an urban slum (DEA, 1973b:21–23). The use of mind-expanding drugs, amphetamines, and barbiturates, on the other hand, is more common among whites and among the better educated (National Commission on Marihuana and Drug Abuse, 1973:52). Marijuana and other mind-expanding drugs are especially prevalent among young, college-educated persons (National Commission on Marihuana and Drug Abuse, 1972:33).

In discussing drugs it is important to distinguish between drug "users" and drug "offenders." Offenders use drugs that are defined as problematic by people in power, and offenders come from the less powerful segments of society, disproportionately from among the poor, the young, blacks, Puerto Ricans, and other minorities. This section focuses on drug users rather than offenders. Three fairly distinctive types of users are isolated and discussed: (1) "normal" drug users, (2) mainliners, and (3) mind-expanding drug users.

"Normal" drug users

Despite our concern with the drug problem and our condemnation of drug fiends and freaks, the United States is in a very real sense a drug-oriented society:

Stimulants, depressants, tranquilizers, sleeping pills, and any other variety of chemical compound that can cause or change a mood, have been absorbed into the nation's pharmacopoeia. Copping pills, swallowing capsules, downing tablets have become a national habit. Apart from the seventy million American consumers of alcohol . . . another fifteen million take amphetamine (speed); thirty million use barbiturates (sleeping pills); twelve million use tranquilizers; while an untold number of youngsters sniff glue, drink codeine-based cough medicine, and will try any new mind-altering substance that comes along (Geller and Boas, 1971:233).

Drug use takes various forms, ranging from the "coffee freak" to the heroin addict. It would be incorrect to say that American society is anti-drug, for we condone and even encourage the use of many drugs in many

---

[3] This is, however, a cyclical pattern. Before the turn of the century when opiate drugs were readily available, opiate-dependent persons were predominantly white and middle-class (Goode, 1972:160).

[4] Levels of addiction have traditionally been high among certain middle-class occupational groups. Physicians are particularly predisposed toward addiction (Winick, 1961; Blum, 1967b:49).

from one individual to the next. Because of this uniformity, the property of addition (and subtraction) is meaningful for interval scales. Breaking down this property into component elements, we have

1. Commutative property: If $x + y = z$, then $y + x = z$.
2. If $x = x'$ and $0 < y$, then $x' < x + y$.
3. Axiom of equals: If $x = x'$ and $y = y'$, then $x + y = x' + y'$.
4. Associative property: $x + (y + x) = (x + y) + x$.[5]

Another illustration of an interval scale is the centigrade temperature scale. The difference between $1°$ C and $2°$ C is equivalent to the difference between $95°$ C and $96°$ C. This equivalence may be established with reference to the number of calories of heat required to change a standard substance—say, water—from $1°$ C to $2°$ C, compared to the number of calories required to change the same amount of water from $95°$ C to $96°$ C: in *both* cases it takes 1 calorie per cubic centimeter. All four of the above aspects of the additivity property apply to this scale, as the reader can check by substituting temperatures for the letters. For example, suppose we had four jars of equal size, each with the same amount of water, and suppose the temperatures of the water in the jars are $10°$ (x), $10°$ (x'), $90°$ (y), and $90°$ (y'). Then according to the axiom of equals, if we add x to y ($10° + 90°$), the result will be the same as if we add x' to y' ($10° + 90°$). In this way, we corroborate the idea that the centigrade scale of temperature possesses interval properties.

Ratio scales have all of the properties of nominal, ordinal, and interval scales and, in addition, an absolute zero point so that multiplication and division become meaningful operations. We cannot, for example, say that $30°$ C is three times as warm as $10°$ C because this interval scale has an arbitrary zero point, the temperature at which water freezes. In the Kelvin scale, however, temperature may be interpreted directly by the motion of molecules. That motion is three times as rapid at $30°$ K as at $10°$ K. At $0°$ K, a temperature that can only be approached, molecules are completely motionless. With the ratio scale, we are at last able to apply the power of a great deal of mathematics to social science data.

To illustrate what ratio scales can enable the investigator to do, let us turn to Figure 6-5. It is based on a study[6] of 30 U.S. Navy seamen of

[5] This listing comes from Virginia Senders, *Measurement and Statistics* (New York: Oxford, U. P., 1958), pp. 60–62.

[6] This study, along with several similar ones, is described by Robert L. Hamblin in "Ratio Measurement and Sociological Theory: A Critical Analysis," unpublished manuscript, (St. Louis: Department of Sociology, Washington U., 1966). Further illustrations of this approach are contained in Robert L. Hamblin, David Buckholdt, Daniel Ferritor, Martin Kozloff, and Lois Blackwell, *The Humanization Process* (New York: Wiley-Interscience, 1971), especially pp. 271–86.

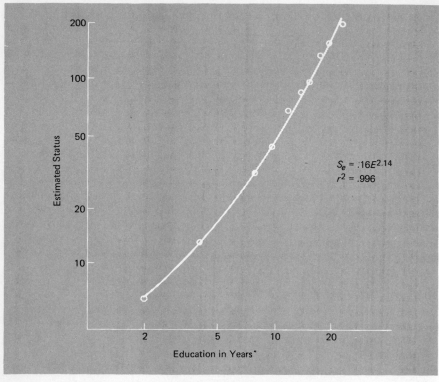

Figure 6-5.
A Ratio Scale of Status.

lower middle and working class backgrounds from the East Coast who responded to questions such as the following:

> If a college graduate has 100 units of status, how much status would a plumber have? a janitor? an architect? . . . How much status would a man have who completed the fourth grade? A doctor's degree? High school?

If S_e refers to status based on a knowledge of education, with E referring to the amount of education in years, then we can accurately estimate the status accorded to a given level of education:

$$S_e = .16E^{2.14}, \text{ with } r^2 = .996.$$

The formula is known as a "power function" and has the same form as a number of findings by S. S. Stevens in the field of psychophysics. The measurement technique used is known as "magnitude estimation."

If we examine Figure 6-5 we shall note the very close fit of the curve to the data. A measure of the degree of fit is r^2, which is the square of the correlation coefficient r and is known as the explained variance (see Chapter 12 for further details). The maximum closeness of fit is 1.0, and the minimum is 0. This degree of explained variance (.996) compares with average figures of approximately .10 for a series of published studies in the *American Sociological Review*.[7] The closeness of relationship achieved between these two variables—status and education—is analogous to the unusually wide spread of percentages in Table 2-4 of the medical student study. Here, then, is a beginning to the fulfillment of the promise held out by ratio scales: movement toward the achievement of accurate prediction. Yet for all this, let us bear firmly in mind the temporal and spatial limitations of this mechanistic approach along with its failure to confront the dynamics of investigator effect.

6.3   Data Construction Procedures

In the first part of this section I shall contrast formist data collection with pragmatist data construction, following this with a brief introduction to each of the major methods used by social researchers for constructing their data.

Formist Data Collection and Pragmatist Data Construction

Among the various modes of data collection or construction, let us pay particular attention to the experiment, especially as conceived of by John Stuart Mill. One reason for doing this is pragmatic: the experiment has played a far more important role in the history of the development of the physical sciences—our best examples of the possibilities of the scientific method—than any other technique. As for sociology, although survey techniques are the major ones used, surveys generally are analyzed by treating them as rough approximations to experimental situations. Thus, it is the methods of experimentation, especially as formulated by John Stuart Mill, that constitute the sociologist's ideal type of procedure for data collection or construction.

---

[7] L. K. Miller, "Determinacy versus Risk," mimeographed, (St. Louis: Social Science Institute, Washington U., N.D.). For studies of competition, Miller and Robert Hamblin found that explained variance averaged .06 under conditions of independence and .40 under conditions of task interdependence; see "Interdependence, Differential Rewarding, and Productivity," *American Sociological Review*. **28** (October 1963), pp. 768–78.

Mills' first experimental canon is the *method of agreement:* "If two or more instances of the phenomenon under investigation have only one circumstance in common, the circumstance in which alone all the instances agree is the cause (or effect) of the given phenomenon."[8] Let us apply this canon to the aging and adjustment study, as described in Section 2.1, using the experiment as an ideal type for guiding survey analysis, as is common practice. The "phenomenon under investigation" is the maladjustment of aged individuals, and the "circumstance in common" that this phenomenon has is role change, such as retirement, widowhood, or a shift to a self-identification as old. Then, according to the method of agreement, we may conclude that role change is the cause or effect of maladjustment, and we opt for the former because it seems to make more sense. All this is not altogether fair either to Mill or to modern formist techniques of survey analysis, although it does—I believe—convey the thrust of both.[9]

To understand the formist nature of this canon, let us apply to it the principles of identity, contradiction, and excluded middle, contrasting them with a pragmatist approach. When we define the research problem as, "What *is* the relation between role change and adjustment?" we employ the principle of identity, assuming that a relationship exists for all time rather than being subject to variation in time and space. According to the principle of contradiction, role change cannot function *both* as the cause or effect of maladjustment *and* as a factor irrelevant to maladjustment. But according to the pragmatist perspective, the situation varies for time and place and is a matter of degree: in some situations, role change plays a greater role, and in other situations a lesser role. As for the principle of the excluded middle, it states that we must choose between these two situations: *either* role change is the cause or effect of maladjustment, *or* it is not. In the pragmatist view, however, it might be *a* cause, and its influence would be a matter of degree rather than an all-or-none phenomenon.

Another approach to contrasting the formist and pragmatist orientations to Mill's method of agreement is to contrast the formist image of scientific theory (Figure 3-1) with the pragmatist image (Figure 6-1). Temporally, we have in the formist contrast between a plane of truth and a plane of observation a vision of causal relationships (signified by the lines connecting the points in the plane of truth) hovering above and eternally fixed.

[8] Quoted in Morris R. Cohen and Ernest Nagel, *An Introduction to Logic and the Scientific Method* (New York: Harcourt, 1934), p. 251. From John Stuart Mill, *A System of Logic,* Vol. 1 (New York: Harper, 1891).

[9] Mill does state in his method of agreement that there must be *only one* circumstance in common before we can draw conclusions about causality, but it would be easy to find more than one circumstance in common for any set of situations (e.g., all the situations are being thought about by the experimenter). Also, nowadays investigators do not speak of a single cause but rather of multiple causation, or multiple relationships. Nevertheless, the over-all influence of this canon seems, presently, to push for an either-or mode of thinking.

In the pragmatist view, by contrast, the levels of water within the various loops are in continual flux. Spatially, Mill concentrates his attention on only one causal relationship at a time, attempting to exclude all other factors, whereas the thrust of the pragmatist view is to take into account many factors simultaneously.

Mill puts forward other canons of experimental inquiry, including the method of difference, the method of concomitant variations, and the method of residues. In each case, the canon embodies a formist as distinct from a pragmatist world view and has come to be the basis for a great deal of current techniques for data collection. By viewing these methods from a pragmatist position, we gain orientations for going beyond them.

The Experiment, Simulation, Observation, Surveys, and Available Data: An Introduction

Let us now approach the experiment from a different direction, attempting to understand its strengths and not merely its limitations. Temporally, it gets us beyond a static view to a focus on a situation at several points in time. Spatially, we must at least be able to integrate our knowledge of two situations: a situation at one point in time, and the changed situation at a second point in time. In addition, the investigator cannot afford to separate himself from his environment but must take an active role in shaping that environment. All that a pragmatist approach requires is that, instead of stopping with the present achievements of experimental methods—which may be traced back to methods developed hundreds of years ago—we continue to move in the same directions they represent.

For example, the classical experiment has been conceived of as something that takes place over a very small time interval, under carefully controlled conditions, with the experimenter focusing only on those changes that he consciously and deliberately introduces so as to examine their impact. We might also think of experiments as taking place over long periods of time, in naturalistic settings, with the investigator attempting to take into account the full range of ways in which he affects the research process. With this approach we can include both experiments that take place under controlled conditions over small time intervals and natural experiments, like the disappearance of the dinosaur or the New Deal.

Simulation, or gaming, techniques are similar to the experiment in their emphasis on the active role of the investigator in creating his research situation. These techniques help him to create the kinds of information that enable him to learn things about the temporal and spatial aspects of this situation that he would not ordinarily learn. Temporally, the researcher does not limit himself narrowly to, say, to points in time, but can collect data generated by his simulation over a large number of points in time, giving him a better opportunity to understand the nature of the processes involved. Spatially, his simulation, or game, is a system of rules that may be related in complex ways. This contrasts with the general approach to experiments, where factors are seen as relatively independent from one another unless proven otherwise.

But there is a loss as well as a gain when we move from the experiment to simulation. Techniques for dealing with the complexity and dynamism of a simulation are largely undeveloped. As a result, what is learned from any given simulation tends to be unimpressive. With the experiment, we may learn something definite, but it may be a very trivial learning experience. With simulation, we have the opportunity to learn a great deal, but we have difficulty with developing the research tools that can help us achieve this. Indeed, the same may be said of extending the experiment to encompass more of the complexity of the naturalistic setting as well as longer time spans. However, by working with *both* experimental and simulation approaches, we can remedy to some extent the deficiencies of each.

When we take up observational procedures, it would appear that the investigator no longer takes an active role in shaping the research situation, but I do not believe that this view is valid. What he does to shape that situation no longer is in the forefront of his consciousness, but the shaping occurs nevertheless. Whatever his personality and whatever his perspectives and whatever the temporal and spatial setting of the research situation, there are multitudes of ways in which he affects not only that situation but the final conclusions he draws. According to the pragmatist framework, if we are to understand a given phenomenon, we must study not only that phenomenon but also the research context—including ourselves—within which we are attempting to understand that phenomenon. This double procedure can be extended to all modes of data construction, including the experiment. In a sense, then, all modes are experimental—whether consciously or unconsciously—and unless we devise ways of assessing those forces that are not deliberately introduced into the research situation but that do in fact operate there, we will be unable to achieve a valid interpretation of the results of our investigation.

Observational procedures are far more unobtrusive than experiments or simulations, and we thus have the opportunity to employ them in all kinds of naturalistic situations as well as in controlled settings. However, these procedures pose the vital problem of interpretation: How are we to assess the meaning of a given observation? If we attempt to do this in a narrow way, without regard to construct validity or theory, then I believe that the problem cannot be solved. However, when we put together this kind of information with other kinds—both from theory and from other data construction procedures—then progress can be made.

The survey is by far the most widely used of the sociologist's empirical tools. If we believe that what goes on in the mind of the individual is an important phenomenon, then we cannot afford to neglect this mode of data collection. By using other methods as well, we have access to *both* thoughts and behavior. And we can make use of the results of mechanistic analyses of surveys to gain insight into the behavior investigated as well as to learn how to apply mechanistic analyses to observational situations.

The collection of available data, such as documents, previous surveys, and materials from the mass media, is an approach that is hardly utilized in comparison to the survey. If we take the pragmatist perspective seriously, then data along the time continuum is essential. And if the survey is sometimes used for its convenience as compared to extended periods of participant observation—as in the case of anthropological field investigations—how much more convenient is it to make use of a library? Recently a new phenomenon has made its appearance and provides further opportunities for integration: the data bank. Most survey data collected by social scientists are very incompletely analyzed. The data from thousands of such studies await the social scientist's analyses in huge data banks.

6.4   Summary

In the foregoing we are making a transition from our previous paradigmatic and theoretical focus within the context of defining problems to procedures for the construction of the kinds of data that bear on the problem that has been defined. Here, we see that we cannot afford to abandon our concerns with paradigms and theories but must, instead, apply these approaches to the measurement context. Paradigmatically, an orientation to the measurement process based on a pragmatist image seems to make more sense for the social researcher than one based on a formist image, since the former includes the advantages of the latter and also allows for a more complex and dynamic approach to phenomena. Table 6-1 summarizes these differences. Theoretically, degree of precision must be seen in relation to reliability and validity; also, construct validation procedures—which incorporate criterion validation and face validation—are in order because of their theoretical breadth.

Once we have the kind of sense of proportion where measurement is not the tail that wags the dog of research, we can turn our attention to developing the kinds of scales of measurement most appropriate for the theoretical distance we have travelled on a given problem. As we move from nominal to ordinal to interval to ratio scales, we incorporate more mathematical properties within our scale and are thus able to develop the kind of theory that moves closer to prediction. Scales of measurement are based on procedures for the construction of data. Five such procedures are introduced: the experiment, the simulation, the observation, the survey, and the analysis of available data. Each one is to a degree experimental in character—in the sense that the researcher cannot avoid an active

Table 6-1

Formism and Pragmatism in Measurement and Scaling

Formism	Pragmatism
Static view of phenomena	Dynamic view of phenomena
The uncovering of truths does little to suggest further directions	Knowledge points toward the importance of obtaining more knowledge
Spatial narrowness: exclusion of contextual phenomena from consideration	Spatial breadth: opening up to a widening range of phenomena
The scientist is seen as a passive observer of phenomena	The scientist is seen as changing reality through his actions
Criterion validity emphasized	Construct validity emphasized
Nominal scales used	Nominal, ordinal, interval and ratio scales used
Reliability isolated from validity	Reliability associated with validity
Precision an end in itself	Precision related to reliability and validity
Research question: What *is* the relationship between role change and adjustment?	Research question: What is the relationship between role change and adjustment for a given research situation?
Data collection	Data construction
Single method of data collection	Multiple methods of data construction
One causal relationship emphasized	Multiple causal relationships treated simultaneously
Factors seen as relatively independent of one another unless proven otherwise	Factors seen as intimately interrelated and interacting

role—and each provides information that can supplement what can be obtained from using the others.

Exercises

1. Apply the pragmatist metaphor for scientific theory (Figure 6-1) to a piece of sociological research, contrasting it with the formist metaphor (Figure 3-1). Can you obtain any further insights into the study? Does this comparison suggest any directions for further research?

2. Suppose it is true that most of our measurements—scientific and personal—are quite invalid, that is, there is a great gap between the actual level of water and our perception of that level. What could we do in such a situation to move ever closer to more valid measurements?

3. Select any given piece of sociological theory and pay attention to the major concepts or variables under discussion. Which ones are treated as nominal scales, which as ordinal scales, and which as interval and ratio scales? Explain your reasoning for each assessment you make.

4. Treat some major current or historical effort at societal change as an experiment, and briefly summarize what you have learned from it. Now analyze your summary: To what extent were the principles of identity, contradiction, and the excluded middle implied? To what extent did you assume the method of agreement?

Annotated References

HUDSON, LIAM. *The Cult of the Fact.* New York: Harper and Row, Publishers, Torchbooks, 1972. Subtitled "A Psychologist's Autobiographical Critique of His Discipline," this book probes deeply into the limitations of a narrow, atemporal, and nonhumanistic approach to psychological research. Hudson directs us to look closely at the presuppositions of the observer if we wish to understand the data he collects.

KAPLAN, ABRAHAM. "Pragmatism" and "Analytic Philosophy," in *The New World of Philosophy.* New York: Random House, Inc., Vintage Books, 1961. As in the case of the Hudson book, further exploration in the area of measurement and scaling can be aided by a better understanding of the world view surrounding a given approach to measurement. Kaplan provides us with two contrasting world views that I have discussed under the labels of pragmatism and formism.

SELLIN, THORSTEN, AND MARVIN E. WOLFGANG. *The Measurement of Delinquency.* New York: John Wiley & Sons, Inc., 1964. The authors use magnitude estimation techniques to develop ratio scales for the seriousness of offenses as well as other dimensions. They demonstrate some of the potential of the ratio scale approach as well as specific procedures for utilizing it.

chapter 7
The Experiment

This chapter begins with a discussion of the experiment in historical perspective, going back to Galileo and John Stuart Mill and then forward, taking up contrasts among the biostatistical orientation, the efforts of F. Stuart Chapin to introduce the experiment into sociology, the recent surge of interest in evaluative research, and the problem of experimenter effect. This section is followed by the presentation of a number of experimental designs, which gives the reader a systematic view of the structure of various kinds of experiments. In the final section, we deal with the experimental attitude, which is a perspective that can be used within the context of any type of research whatsoever.

7.1 Historical Perspective

To understand the present situation with regard to experimental procedures, it is essential for us to go back sufficiently far in history to be able to contrast the formist approach of John Stuart Mill with the mechanistic orientation of physicists like Galileo. The current social science view of the experiment derives more from the former than the latter. The problem this poses for the social science experimenter is a serious one: He is not using, as he thinks he is, the basic approach that has worked so effectively in the history of the physical sciences, and it becomes quite difficult for him to face up to the failures of his procedures in coping with, say, the evaluation of the effectiveness of a complex social program. In this section, I shall begin with this contrast between Mill and Galileo, referring also to their modern counterparts in the biostatistical approach and the mathematical modeling orientation, respectively. The work of F. Stuart Chapin and others to use the experiment as a device for confronting complex social situations constitutes another part of this history, and its modern counterpart is the current effort to perform evaluative research with experimental tools. A third part is the Roethlisberger and Dickson Western Electric study, with its discovery of the "Hawthorne effect," followed by a recent focus on experimenter effect within experimental psychology and a current centering within sociology on the politics of social research.

Mill and Galileo

In Section 6.3 I discussed the formist aspects of Mill's first experimental canon, the method of agreement. Mill's *method of difference* also embodies these formist aspects: "If an instance in which the phenomenon under investigation occurs, and an instance in which it does not occur, have every circumstance in common save one, that one occurring in the former, the circumstances in which alone the two instances differ is the effect, or the cause, or an indispensable part of the cause, of the phenomenon."[1] To illustrate with the aging and adjustment study, the phenomenon under investigation is the maladjustment ("occurs") and adjustment ("does not occur") of aged individuals; the "circumstance" that tends to occur more in the former case than in the latter is role change, and we thus infer a causal relationship between role change and maladjustment. This example would be closer to recent ideas of the experiment if the experimenter himself introduced a change into one group of individuals (the experimental group) and withheld that change from a group presumed to be equivalent (the control group). The change that the investigator introduces is designated the "experimental treatment." By following the same kind of reasoning as was used in Section 6.3, we can locate the principles of identity, contradiction, and the excluded middle within this canon as well as within the canon of agreement.

If Mill's approach is based on logic, then Galileo's[2] centers on mathematics. But mathematics alone is insufficient for the physicist who wishes to make use of mathematics: he must also deal with ratio scale measurements. This type of measurement contrasts with the nominal scales that Mill used in his illustrations: phenomena either occur or they do not occur, and circumstances either occur or they do not occur.

For example, in Galileo's inclined plane experiment he hypothesized that the distance (D) that a ball rolls down an inclined plane will increase as a function of the square of the time it takes to roll down (T). Thus, $D = AT^2$, with A being the acceleration constant. His ratio scale of distance was produced by marking off his inclined plane into 16 equally spaced cutting points, and his ratio scale of time was measured by a water clock in which equal weights of water were assumed to produce equal units of time. In this way, he predicted the distance a ball rolled from his knowledge of A and T and the formula for a variety of inclined planes, each with an acceleration constant appropriate for its angle of inclination.

The Mill approach has its modern counterpart in the focus on a combination of statistical tests of hypotheses with the idea of randomization. It is based in good measure on the work of Pearson, Fisher, Yates, and

---

[1] Quoted in Morris R. Cohen and Ernest Nagel, *An Introduction to Logic and the Scientific Method* (New York: Harcourt, 1934), p. 256. From John Stuart Mill, *A System of Logic,* Vol. 1 (New York: Harper, 1891).

[2] See Galileo Galilei, *Two New Sciences* (Evanston, Ill.: Northwestern U.P., 1946).

Gosset.[3] Randomization, as used in the social sciences, is a procedure for assigning available subjects to the experimental and control groups in such a way that they become more alike in certain respects as the size of the sample increases. If this were to be done in the aging and adjustment study, we might use a table of random numbers (see p. 297) to select those individuals who will experience role changes (the experimental group) and those who will not (the control group). We would then assign role changes to the former and not the latter group and would follow this up with statistical tests of significance (see Chapter 12) to learn if any resulting difference between these two groups could have easily occurred on the basis of chance alone. Of course, we would not want to do this, since it would involve forcibly retiring some individuals and killing the spouses of others.

The modern counterpart of the Galilean approach within sociology is the focus on ratio scales and mathematical modeling, as illustrated by the work of Robert Hamblin.[4] An active approach on the part of the experimenter is essential for obtaining accurate measurement, as illustrated by the inclined plane experiment. For example, Hamblin works with his observers for a sufficient length of time to teach them how to think in ratio terms, and how to do so reliably. On this basis, the emphasis is on the statement of theoretical relationships in mathematical terms, as it was for Galileo with his $D = AT^2$. Mathematics is also the basis for the biostatistical approach to the experiment, but it is a different kind of mathematics, more formist than mechanist. The emphasis is on a dichotomy, as in the statistical testing within the aging and adjustment study: Is it likely that the observed difference between the adjusted and the maladjusted with respect to role change is based on chance alone, or is this unlikely? There is no concern with ratio measurement or with a statement of theory in mathematical terms.

A problem with both of these approaches is that they have not yet produced the kinds of results in research that have been the basis for theoretical breakthroughs in social science. As a result, many of their proponents have undergone disillusionment. Campbell and Stanley illustrate such feelings in their widely used description of experimental and quasi-experimental designs, which follows the biostatistical tradition:

> This chapter is committed to the experiment. . . . a wave of enthusiasm for experimentation dominated the field of education in the Thorndike era, perhaps reaching its apex in the 1920s. And this enthusiasm gave

[3] See, for example, Karl Pearson, *The Grammar of Science* (London: Black, 1900), and R. A. Fisher, *Statistical Methods and Scientific Inference* (London: Oliver and Boyd, 1956).

[4] Robert L. Hamblin, "Ratio Measurement and Sociological Theory: A Critical Analysis," unpublished manuscript, (St. Louis: Department of Sociology, Washington U., 1966). See also Hamblin et al., *The Humanization Process* (New York: Wiley-Interscience, 1971).

way to . . . a wave of pessimism, dating back to perhaps 1935. . . . the defections from experimentation to essay writing . . . have frequently occurred in persons well trained in the experimental tradition.

. . . we may anticipate that most experiments will be disappointing. We must somehow inoculate young experimenters against this effect, and in general must justify experimentation on more pessimistic grounds—not as a panacea, but rather as the only available route to cumulative progress. We must instill in our students the expectation of tedium and disappointment and the duty of thorough persistence, by now so well achieved in the biological and physical sciences. We must expand our students' vow of poverty to include not only the willingness to accept poverty of finances, but also a poverty of experimental results.[5]

Here, Campbell and Stanley advise an acceptance, rather than a questioning, of the experimental approach, despite its limited results, thus encouraging the researcher to stay within a formist paradigm.

The Experiment in Sociology

Whereas Campbell and Stanley represent the tradition of experimentation in psychology and education, F. Stuart Chapin represents that tradition as it has appeared in sociology.[6] How is the sociologist to use society as the chemist works with his chemicals? How can he possibly manipulate or control individuals or groups as the physical scientist controls inanimate objects? Chapin began with the concept of the "natural experiment," where he rejected the idea that the experimenter must actively hold human beings in a viselike grip. If the function of the laboratory is to create similar but contrasting situations, then human beings are generating experiments all the time. A number of other social scientists have adopted a similar viewpoint. Margaret Mead regarded the contrast between Samoan culture and our own with regard to adolescent behavior as providing this kind of experiment.[7] Lundberg[8] has referred to New Harmony and Brook Farm as examples of social experimentation.

The natural experiment has also come under criticism from sociologists. For example, Lundberg has pointed out—without denying the great suggestive value of such research—that the conditions of the experiment are not subject to the manipulation of the observer, and that there are too many varied factors present to permit valid conclusions.[9] Perhaps in re-

---

[5] Donald T. Campbell and Julian C. Stanley, *Experimental and Quasi-Experimental Designs for Research* (Chicago: Rand McNally, 1966).

[6] F. Stuart Chapin, *Experimental Designs in Sociological Research* (New York: Harper, 1955). For an overview of the Chapin approach, see Ernest Greenwood, *Experimental Sociology* (New York: King's Crown Press, 1945).

[7] Margaret Mead, *Coming of Age in Samoa* (New York: Morrow, 1928).

[8] George A. Lundberg, *Social Research: A Study in Methods of Gathering Data,* 2nd ed. (New York: McKay, 1942).

[9] Ibid., p. 56.

sponse to such criticism, Chapin developed the concept of the "ex post facto" experiment. Here, once again, he conceived of this approach as one that does not require the experimenter to actively manipulate the changes under investigation. In addition, he conceived the idea that the experimenter could mentally manipulate such factors and thus achieve a degree of actual control. For example, if one wishes to measure the impact of social status on, say, political attitudes, one cannot begin with equivalent groups and alter the status of members of one group in the laboratory, but one can select two groups that differ in status and proceed to match them on a variety of important characteristics, such as religion. As one continues to match on more characteristics, the number of individuals who remain so matched diminishes, but in addition the groups become more and more equivalent. As a result, the investigator moves closer and closer to Mill's requirement within the method of difference: that the groups are equivalent in all respects save one. Thus, for example, in the aging and adjustment study one would select two groups differing in role changes but equivalent in other important respects.

If the natural experiment—as well as the ex post facto experiment—opens up to the experimenter a world of phenomena for sociological investigation, moving him to extend his work to deal with occurrences extending over long time periods and involving complex relationships among variables, it also makes it more difficult to deal with such complexity. Indeed, this approach to the experiment has come under very severe criticism by those operating close to the laboratory tradition of experimentation. For example, Campbell and Stanley write:

> we judge the analysis a misleading one. . . . The mode of thinking employed and the errors involved are recurrent in educational research also. . . .
>
> In one typical ex post facto study . . . the X [treatment variable] was high school education (particularly finishing high school) and the Os [observations] dealt with success and community adjustment ten years later, as judged from information obtained in individual interviews. The matching in this case was done from records retained in the high school files. . . . Initially the data showed those completing high school to have been more successful but also to have had higher marks in grammar school, higher parental occupations, younger ages, better neighborhoods, etc. Thus these antecedents might have caused both completion of high school and later success. Did the schooling have any additional effect over and above the head start provided by these background factors? Chapin's "solution" to this question was to examine subsets of students matched on all these background factors but differing in completion of high school. The addition of each matching factor reduced in turn the posttest discrepancy between the X and no-X groups, but when all matching was done, a significant difference remained. Chapin concluded, although cautiously, that education had an effect. . . .

He had seriously *under*matched. . . . Greenwood refers to . . . the fact of self-selection of exposure or nonexposure. Exposure is a lawful product of numerous antecedents. In the case of dropping out of high school before completion, we know that there are innumerable determinants beyond the six upon which matching was done. We can with great assurance surmise that most of these will have a similar effect upon later success.[10]

What Campbell and Stanley have in mind by this seemingly devastating criticism of the ex post facto experiment is the inadequacy of matching as compared to randomization, which moves the experimenter toward the achievement of groups that have equivalent characteristics with respect to *all* factors, measured and unmeasured. What they fail to give its due, however, is the extent to which Chapin opens up the experiment so that it can become a tool for a great deal of sociologial investigation. Indeed, it has been but a short step—which would be judged very harshly by Campbell and Stanley—from the Chapin ex post facto experiment to the modes of analysis commonly used to deal with survey or other observational data. In fairness to Campbell and Stanley, they do not hold fast to the necessity of achieving the laboratory ideal. Indeed, they distinguish between "true experimental designs" and "quasi-experimental designs," based largely on the presence or absence of randomization procedures, and they encourage researchers to use the latter when the former is not possible. But what does the sociologist have to look forward to if he did limit his inquiries to those for which he could achieve an experimental design, whether quasi or true? Disappointment and a poverty of experimental results? Second-class citizenship through use of quasi-experimental, as distinct from true experimental, designs?

Before leaving Campbell and Stanley, let us focus on a significant contribution they have made to our understanding of the nature of the experiment, a distinction between "internal validity" and "external validity":

> *Internal validity* is the basic minimum without which any experiment is uninterpretable: Did in fact the experimental treatments make a difference in this specific experimental instance? *External validity* asks the question of *generalizability:* To what populations, settings, treatment variables, and measurement variables can this effect be generalized?[11]

These types of validity have to do with the validity of propositions and not directly with measurement validity, which was discussed in Section 6.1. Campbell and Stanley are following the tradition of psychological research by claiming that it is more important to understand what is going on in the experiment (internal validity) than to be able to apply experimental

[10] Campbell and Stanley, op. cit., pp. 70–72.
[11] Ibid., p. 5.

findings widely outside of the experimental situation (external validity). For example, they would be far less concerned with Chapin's loss of cases (from 2,127 to 46) in the ex post facto experiment discussed above than with the nonequivalence of his experimental and control groups. And they would also be far less concerned with sampling error—the basis for the statistical tests used in surveys, to be discussed in Chapter 12—than with the gross internal invalidity of survey analysis.

As we move to recent times, we find that the same kind of problem-solving interests that motivated Chapin and his students are involved in a current emphasis on evaluative research, that is, on research designed to assess the impact of some program or planned effort to produce change or solve some problem. And it should not be surprising that current experience with the difficulties involved in such research, both with respect to aiding the agencies involved and with respect to contributing to social science knowledge, has produced considerable disenchantment with the experimental approach. For example, Weiss and Rein draw the following conclusions on the basis of their work on the evaluation of a Model Cities program:

> The purpose of this paper is to call into question the easy assumption that experimental design is always the best way to decide whether action-programs are having desirable effects. It is for the most part an essay in destructive criticism. . . .
>
> There is much work to be done in the development of a nonexperimental methodology for evaluation research. Our argument is that this work is justified; that there is need for a more qualitative, process-oriented approach. The way to develop the methodology, we believe, is to begin working in it: to undertake evaluation research, when the action-program requires it, which is concerned with what form the action-program actually took, and with the details of its interaction with its surroundings, from which may be formed as inductive assessment of its consequences.[12]

Experimenter Effect

Three fundamental problems with the experimental method as it is used in social research are (1) temporally, the difficult of coping with lengthy time periods such as are involved in the social changes associated with natural settings, (2) spatially, the difficulty of dealing with complex systems of factors such as occur in those settings, and (3) the interaction between whatever the experimenter does and the phenomena he is investigating. The first two of these have been discussed above. The third problem—as with the first and second—is not unique to social science. In quantum physics, for example, the process of observation necessitates the

---

[12] Robert S. Weiss and Martin Rein, "The Evaluation of Broad-Aim Programs: A Cautionary Case and a Moral," in Francis G. Caro (ed.), *Readings in Evaluation Research* (New York: Russell Sage Foundation, 1971), pp. 295–96.

bombardment of the observed particles with photons of light, thus changing their position and velocity. The resultant quandary as to the original position and velocity of the particles is referred to as the Heisenberg principle of indeterminacy. In microbiology it is difficult to investigate most phenomena in vivo, that is, in the live organism. However, procedures used for in vitro investigation, like staining, alter the nature of the organism. Indeed, the organism is no longer an organism when it is being studied in vitro.

In Section 1.2 I discussed the phenomenon of investigator effect, referring to the Hawthorne Experiment, from which derives the concept of the Hawthorne effect. I also referred to recent studies by Robert Rosenthal demonstrating the ease with which the experimenter affects his subjects, including even animal subjects. Within sociology, phenomenological concerns—such as within ethnomethodology, the sociology of knowledge, and the sociology of science—have combined with growing distrust of "establishment science" to raise similar kinds of questions:[13] What axes would the researcher like to grind? Whom is he working for? How does he distort what he observes? How reflexive is he so that he can understand his impact on the investigation? Is it possible for him to be objective? Can he maintain a value-neutral stance? What's in it for him? To the researcher who is convinced that existing methods are objective, such questions are sacrilegious.

If the first two problems—time and space—were not enough to overturn our view of the efficacy of the experiment, the three problems together create an overwhelming case for such questioning. No longer are problems encountered only outside of the laboratory: it is the internal validity of the most sophisticated laboratory designs that is now at stake. As we shall see in Section 7.2, even when the experimenter incorporates a number of control groups along with randomization procedures into his design, the degree to which he can successfully deal with experimenter effect is questionable. And if the internal validity of the most sophisticated experimental research undertaken in the past is in serious doubt, how much more in jeopardy are the less sophisticated designs and, of course, all the other modes of data collection and analysis, since they tend to be patterned after the logic of the experiment? To put the matter in other words, social research seems to be experiencing a paradigm shift from the direction of data collection as well as from other directions. All of the accumulated data from the social sciences can now be seen from a perspective that opens up a major source of invalidity.

In my view, we are witnessing not a death blow to *any* scientific approach to human behavior but the birth of a far more effective scientific approach than has been used heretofore. The problems we are encounter-

[13] See for example Gideon Sjoberg (ed.), *Ethics, Politics, and Social Research* (Cambridge, Mass.: Schenkman, 1967).

ing force us to reconsider all of the fundamental questions we thought had already been answered satisfactorily. To what extent are we in trouble because our measurement procedures produce indexes or scales with little measurement validity? To what extent does lack of measurement validity—as indicated by low construct validity—suggest an inadequate theoretical framework? To what extent does an inadequate theoretical framework suggest an inadequate paradigm? By probing back to such fundamentals, we create the possibility of altering our paradigm, theory, and measurement validity and, as a result, create the basis for effective experimental (and other data collection) procedures. In Section 7.2, "Experimental Design," I shall introduce paradigmatic, theoretical, and measurement considerations.

7.2 Experimental Design

In Sections 6.3 and 7.1 I discussed the formist basis for the experiment, referring in particular to John Stuart Mill's methods of agreement and difference. Let us now trace the implications of Mill's logic of the experiment as it is evidenced in the work of Campbell and Stanley:

> The "validity" of the experiment becomes one of the relative credibility of rival theories: the theory that X had an effect versus the theories of causation involving the uncontrolled factors. If several sets of differences can all be explained by the single hypothesis that X had an effect, while several separate uncontrolled-variable effects must be hypothesized, a different one for each observed difference, then the effect of X becomes the most tenable. . . .
> . . . Related to [the above] . . . is the assumption that, in cases of ignorance, a main effect of one variable is to be judged more likely than the interaction of two other variables; or, more generally, that main effects are more likely than interactions. In the extreme form, we can note that if every highest-order interaction is significant, if every effect is specific to certain values on all other potential treatment dimensions, then a science is not possible. If we are ever able to generalize, it is because the great bulk of potential determining factors can be disregarded.[14]

Campbell and Stanley here reveal aspects of the paradigm on which the modern general approach to experimentation rests. In each of the above paragraphs, they seem to be arguing that in the case of a simple or a complex explanation of phenomena, simplicity is to be chosen over complexity (the principle of Occam's razor). For Campbell and Stanley, this principle enables the experimenter to dismiss the tenability of alternative interpreta-

---

[14] Campbell and Stanley, op. cit., pp. 36–37.

tions of his results that involve a variety of uncontrolled variables. It also leads him to assume that variables work generally in isolation from one another (main effects), as distinct from in interaction with one another (interaction effects). And what if phenomena are actually interrelated in complex ways, as the weight of social science knowledge seems to confirm? According to Campbell and Stanley, "then a science is not possible." We might revise their conclusion to read, "then a science based on formist assumptions alone is not possible." According to the pragmatist paradigm, for example, we begin with the assumption that all phenomena are in direct or indirect interaction, as distinct from an assumption giving priority to the isolation of variables. This includes both uncontrolled variables and those that are explicitly taken into account. Of course, there are times when it will be convenient to use the formist paradigm to achieve simplification.

Moving from a paradigmatic analysis to a theoretical one, in discussions of experimental design there is almost no treatment of the relationship between social science theory and the experiment. Just as experimenters tend to assume that variables work in isolation from one another in nature—not realizing that such an assumption may be an artifact of their own formist conceptual process—so do they also tend to assume that theory and data collection procedures do not interact with one another. The kinds of illustrations that tend to be used are trivial from a theoretical perspective, reflecting this lack of high standards for theory. Let me here refer to the second edition of this book as an illustration, an edition that I thought gave theory its due more than other books:

> Suppose that the plan of parents to send their children to college is the phenomenon under investigation. . . .We may then compare a group of parents exposed to the film on the importance of college with one that is not. . . . Let us assume that the only difference between these groups is whether or not they were exposed to the film. Then, according to the method of difference, the decision to send children to college is either a cause or an effect of seeing the film. Because the decision is made subsequent to the showing of the film, the conclusion (following Mill) is that the decision is the effect of seeing the film.[15]

Perhaps I along with others writing about these things considered theory important in the abstract but failed to see exactly how this kind of atheoretical research design ruins the experiment. Suppose, however, that one's theory—along with the paradigm within which it is embedded—shapes the validity of one's measurement procedures within the experiment. Suppose, for example, that poor theory will give us a picture of the height of the water in the beaker (Figure 6-2) that is very far from its actual height. Suppose that the process by which theory produces valid measurement is

[15] Bernard S. Phillips, *Social Research: Strategy and Tactics,* 2nd ed. (New York: Macmillan, 1971), p. 105.

via construct validation, and that the construct validity for measurements taken within the kind of atheoretical experiment just described is very low.

In the remainder of this section I will briefly describe ten experimental designs. In each case, I will assume that the design can be no more effective than the paradigm, theory, and measurement on which it is based. Since all of these designs come from formist tradition, I will outline limitations in the designs stemming from that tradition. Yet despite these limitations, I am convinced that the designs are worthy of serious study and have genuine utility. To go beyond where we are, we must first become familiar with where we are.

The One-Shot Case Study

X   O

In presenting this experimental design and the ones to follow, I am using Campbell and Stanley's classification designs and notation, where X represents the exposure of a group to the experimental treatment or experimental variable, O refers to the observational or measurement process, and R refers to the employment of randomization procedures in the selection of subjects.[16] As in the case of the preceding discussions, I shall focus on three sources of error: temporal, spatial, and investigator-related. Each design will be discussed in two ways: first, more or less from a formist perspective, centering on how it deals with these sources of error, and second, from a pragmatist framework, focusing on a paradigmatic, theoretical, and measurement analysis.

Thinking illustratively in terms of the evaluation of a complex social program such as a Model Cities program, the one-shot case study includes only observations after the study is completed. Temporally, there is no "before" measurement to go along with this "after" measurement, as in the case of the before-after design with a single group (O   X   O). As a result, there are problems of both memory and selective perception. In addition, there may be attempts at deliberate distortion so as to put the program in a more favorable light. Spatially, there is no comparison or control group, and thus we cannot employ Mill's method of difference, the foundation of experimental procedure. We can attempt to deal with temporal problems by using retrospective questions and whatever other devices are available for reconstructing the situation prior to the introduction of the Model Cities program, thus trying to approximate the O   X   O design. Finally, at least we are not beset by an important source of investigator effect—the effect of the first observational procedure on the second—since

[16] Campbell and Stanley, op. cit.

we take our observations only at one point in time within the one-shot case study.

And now viewing this design from a pragmatist perspective, the key problem that influences how much is learned is not the design itself—which is the worst one possible from the formist framework—but the degree to which the researcher's theory and measurement devices are up to coping with an extremely complex and changing set of phenomena (pragmatist world view). For example, from the formist perspective investigator effect is not a problem in this design, but that conclusion does not take into account the complexities and dynamism within any given observational situation. Television cameras need not be *repeatedly* placed before a group of people in order for them to have effects both on those being taped and on those working the cameras. As for the temporal and spatial difficulties that the formist sees in this design, those difficulties are also present in greater measure in the more sophisticated designs *to the degree that the investigator does not understand and cannot monitor what is going on.* For example, how can we ever select a control group, even with the aid of randomization procedures, that is equivalent to the experimental group in every important respect if interactions with unmeasured variables and with the experimenter are the rule rather than the exception? But with sufficient theoretical knowledge of the dynamics of the situation, we can inaugurate the kinds of measurement that will successively (as research continues) help us to monitor more and more of what is going on.

The One-Group Pretest-Posttest Design

$$O_1 \quad X \quad O_2$$

Temporally, this design has the advantage of providing us with a base measure, prior to the inauguration of the program, against which we can compare our "after," or O_2, measurement. This is no mean accomplishment. However, we must be wary of several sources of temporal error: historical changes having nothing to do with the program, maturational changes in the subjects that would have occurred regardless of the program, and changes in the measuring instruments (e.g., the attitudes of observers who are rating the subjects). Spatially, we are in an excellent situation, since we are comparing a group with itself and not with another group that might differ from it in a great many unknown ways. Finally, there is a serious problem of experimenter effect, that is, the possible impact of O_1 on O_2.

From the pragmatist view, this design—granting that it is no better than the theory and measurement procedures that are involved—offers very significant opportunities for effective research not provided by the one-shot study. If phenomena are not static but, rather, are in continual flux, how are we to measure such flux if not by studies such as this? For the formist, phenomena are seen as relatively static, so that a randomized experiment involving a control group and taking place only at one point in time generally is seen in a much more favorable light than this design. However, such experiments cannot monitor changes in the way that the one-group pretest-posttest can. Also, if uncontrolled variables are a problem—as they are in a complex view of the world—then the kinds of control achieved by dealing with the same group of individuals (versus two different groups, even if randomization is used) cover a great deal of ground. As for investigator effect, this is admittedly an important problem associated with this design. But it is also a vital problem associated with *every* design—even the ones with a number of control groups—to the degree that we don't have a good enough theoretical understanding of the research situation to monitor the variety of subtle and complex ways in which the experimenter interacts with his subjects and with himself.

The Static Group Comparison

$$X \quad O_1$$
$$O_2$$

In this design, a group exposed to the treatment is compared with a group not exposed to it; for example, a model city might be compared with a nonmodel city. Observations are taken after the completion of the program. The method of difference is the basic logic behind this design: observed differences between the two cities are attributed to the program, on the assumption that the two cities are equivalent. Temporally, we have the same kind of problem as in the one-shot case study: there are no base observations, and attempts to get retrospective data face problems with regard to memory, selective perception, and deliberate distortion or bias. Spatially, we do have a comparison group, but anyone who has ever attempted to match groups—let alone cities—must realize the difficulties involved. Investigator effect is not viewed as a serious problem because observations are not taken sequentially.

From the pragmatist framework, any one situation is quite difficult to understand, and there is nothing automatically advantageous about comparing one complex situation with another. Granting that we may succeed in matching them on a number of factors, what counts more than anything else are the processes involved. Such matching can be done with regard to similar processes only to the degree that we understand the nature of those processes. Even then, however, phenomena are sufficiently complex so that we cannot expect to develop equivalent groups, even if randomization were involved. As for investigator effect, dealing with two situations or groups compounds the problems. For example, the role of the researchers might be seen in quite different ways in the two cities.

The Pretest-Posttest Control Group Design

$$R \quad O_1 \quad X \quad O_2$$
$$R \quad O_3 \qquad O_4$$

This is the most widely known experimental design and is also designated as the "classical" design, perhaps because of its direct relationship to Mill's method of difference. Randomization procedures are used to determine which individuals undergo the experimental treatment and which do not, thus producing near-equivalent groups. Observations are taken initially and then after the introduction of the treatment, and any difference between the changes undergone by the two groups is attributed to that treatment. In this design, the advantages of the one-group pretest-posttest design are combined with those of the static group comparison, and additional improvements are involved. Temporally, we have direct measures of change, not only for the experimental group but also for the control group. Spatially, randomization procedures give the investigator control over all factors, measured and unmeasured, producing essentially equivalent groups. There still remains, however, the problem of investigator effect, since the pretest may interact with the posttest.

From a pragmatist standpoint, how can it be that this design's contributions to theory and problem-solving have been so sparse if it is as good as it is supposed to be? The operation seems to be quite successful, only the patient is dying. I need not at this point reiterate the various comments I have made on the three previous designs, comments pointing up the failure of such designs *by themselves* to give the investigator control over the complex forces operating within the experimental situation. Thus, for example, we might question the presumed equivalence of the two groups. To provide a new illustration of what I mean, within the formist view there is very little consideration given to the individual within a given group, whether experimental or control. For the pragmatist, this represents a gross form of stereotyping, a Procrustean bed forcing us to neglect existing complexities. By paying attention to them, however, we will have to face up to the necessity of developing improved designs based on more profound theoretical knowledge.

The Solomon Four-Group Design

$$
\begin{array}{lllll}
R & O_1 & X & O_2 & (1) \\
R & O_3 & & O_4 & (2) \\
R & & X & O_5 & (3) \\
R & & & O_6 & (4)
\end{array}
$$

This extension of the classical design is aimed at controlling for investigator effect as well as for the interaction between the pretest and the experimental treatment. For example, we may estimate the pretest measurement for group (3) by averaging that for groups (1) and (2), since the four groups are chosen by randomization procedures. The difference between that estimated pretest and the posttest, O_5, cannot be due either to the sensitizing effects of the pretest or to any interaction between pretest and treatment, since no pretest was used. As a result, we may attribute that difference to the treatment alone. Similarly, we may obtain an estimate for the pretest for group (4), with a comparison between the changes occurring in group (2) and group (4) constituting a measure of the influence of the pretest alone. Finally, if we follow Mill's *methods of residues,*[17] we can obtain an estimate of the interaction between pretest and treatment. Since we already have estimates for the effect of the pretest alone and for the treatment alone, if we compare the sum of those effects with an effect that includes those two as well as possible interaction effects— namely, the difference between O_1 and O_2 in group (1)—we can estimate the degree of interaction between pretest and treatment.

The pragmatist would say that the reader should not be misled by the excellent logic of this and other sophisticated designs into thinking that the result must necessarily be excellent research. Such experiments may—and usually are—conceived of in quite nontheoretical ways, for example, testing for the impact of seeing a given movie without conceptualizing that treatment so that it meshes with the major theories in the social sciences. Then the result will be a set of experimental and control groups where we know very little about the actual processes involved, for example, about the degree to which the groups are actually equivalent. Further, how much will we know about the particular situation of each individual in the various groups?

[17] Cohen and Nagel op. cit., p. 264. The method is: "Subduct from any phenomenon such part as is known by previous inductions to be the effect of certain antecedents, and the residue of the phenomenon is the effect of the remaining antecedents."

The Posttest-Only Control Group Design

$$R \quad X \quad O_1$$
$$R \qquad\;\; O_2$$

This is similar to the classical design, except that there is no direct pre-test measure here to check for the equivalence of experimental and control groups. However, since randomization is being used here, such pretest measures are not essential. According to Campbell and Stanley, this design is underused in education, perhaps because of a lack of awareness of the effectiveness of randomization procedures. One feature of this design is that, since there is no pretest, there is no possibility of an interaction between pretest and treatment. In addition, only half as many groups are involved as in the Solomon four-group design.

While this design may appear to be preferable from a formist perspective to the classical design (as it is to Campbell and Stanley), this is not the case from a pragmatist perspective. Here, it is change that is the essential phenomenon to be observed and probed, and the posttest-only control group design does not focus on change. For the pragmatist, the effect of utilizing randomization procedures is not the creation of equivalent groups, since such a creation depends on a degree of theoretical understanding that is rare or nonexistent at this time. Furthermore, the classical design enables the researcher to investigate the nature of his impact on his subjects, even if he is not able to control for it, whereas the posttest-only control group design does not give him this opportunity.

The Nonequivalent Control Group Design

$$O_1 \quad X \quad O_2$$
$$O_3 \qquad\;\; O_4$$

This is the same as the classical design, except that the experimental group and the control group are matched but not equated through randomization. Because of this lack, Campbell and Stanley designate it as one of the quasi-experimental designs. For them, it represents an improvement over the first three designs discussed in this section, all of which they regard as "pre-experimental." It is able to achieve—although to a lesser degree—the same kinds of things achieved by the classical design, and it is beset by the same problems as that design.

For the pragmatist, there is no such sharp distinction between pre-experimental, quasi-experimental, and true experimental designs. It is not so much the design that determines the effectiveness of the results but the level of theory and the validity of measurement one is able to bring to bear within any given design. For example, this design might achieve far more than the Solomon four-group design if it is based on a better theoretical perspective. In neither case will the experimenter be able to achieve equivalent groups, but superior theory will at least give him insight into the various things occurring within the experiment.

The Time-Series Experiment

$$O_1 \quad O_2 \quad O_3 \quad O_4 \quad X \quad O_5 \quad O_6 \quad O_7 \quad O_8$$

For Campbell and Stanley, this is another quasi-experimental design, but it represents an improvement over the pre-experimental one-group pretest-posttest design. It is essential for the experimenter to specify in advance the nature of X as well as how long he expects X to take before its effects are manifested. Otherwise, one may simply succeed in taking advantage of chance occurrences by locating evidence for whatever one believes to be true. However, with such careful specification in advance, the key problem one must be concerned with is the effects of historical factors extraneous to the experimental situation, factors that might occur simultaneous to the introduction of X.

For the pragmatist, this is a very important design. Given the complexity and dynamism of phenomena, it is difficult to understand anything that occurs. This is why profound theory and valid measurement play so vital a role in any given experiment: they help the experimenter to penetrate deeply into a given situation. With an extended time series, the experimenter has the opportunity to get ever deepening insight into a given group or given individuals. Also, it is change that is the central phenomenon under investigation, and time-series data are best for this purpose.

The Randomized-Groups Design

$$
\begin{array}{llll}
R & O_1 & X_1 & O_2 \\
R & O_3 & X_2 & O_4 \\
R & O_5 & & O_6
\end{array}
$$

The preceding designs have dealt with the experimental treatments in an either-or fashion, based on the dichotomous approach of Mill's method of difference. However, Mill also put forward a *method of concomitant variations:* "Whatever phenomenon varies in any manner, whenever another phenomenon varies in some particular manner, is either a cause or an effect of that phenomenon, or is connected with it through some fact of causation."[18] Instead of simply contrasting the presence of a given treatment in the experimental group with the absence of that treatment in the control group, we can have any number of experimental groups, each with a different degree or level of the treatment. Within this design, we may or may not wish to retain a control group that represents a complete absence of the treatment.

From the pragmatist viewpoint, such a design is most welcome, since it represents a push beyond formism. By contrasting this design with the others, we can gain insight into the tremendous oversimplification involved in the approach to measurement within the other designs: all that was required is nominal scale measurement of the treatment variables. Even this design does not require ratio scale measurement, without which it would be difficult to develop the kinds of sophisticated theoretical models that employ much of the power of mathematics. It should be noted that what I have just discussed for the treatment variable also holds true for the pretest and posttest measurements: in the preceding designs, all that has been required is nominal scale measurement.

The Factorial Design

$$
\begin{array}{llll}
R & O_1 & Xa_1b_1 & O_2 & (1) \\
R & O_3 & Xa_1b_2 & O_4 & (2) \\
R & O_5 & Xa_2b_1 & O_6 & (3) \\
R & O_7 & Xa_2b_2 & O_8 & (4)
\end{array}
$$

For the first time we are considering a design with two, as distinct from one, independent variables—X_a and X_b—each with two different levels or degrees. Each of the four resulting combinations of the type of independent variable and its level constitutes a separate experimental condition. In this way, for example, we can combine groups (1) and (2) and compare them with groups (3) and (4) to secure a contrast between the two levels of variable a (a_1 and a_2). Or we can combine groups (1) and (3) and compare them with groups (2) and (4) to contrast b_1 with b_2. In this way, several different hypotheses can be tested within the same experiment. In addition, it is also possible to test for interaction effects within this design.

Viewed from a pragmatist framework, this design represents an im-

[18] Ibid., pp. 261–62.

portant step forward in dealing with the complexity of phenomena because it deals with more than one hypothesis simultaneously and because one can also investigate the interaction among treatments. Nevertheless, this is still only one small step forward in the face of vast complexity. And even if we are permitted here to deal with a number of levels for a given variable, there is no clear call to move toward ratio scales: simple dichotomous nominal scales will still enable the investigator to use this design. The fundamental assumptions behind this experimental design remain formist: that main effects are much more likely than interaction effects, and that the vast number of uncontrolled variables and relationships does not interfere with the results.

There are a great many other experimental designs that cannot be treated here. For example, there is the Latin-square design, where each subject is exposed to a number of different treatments in a systematically varied order, thus providing that the total number of subjects are available for each treatment. There are many variations of the factorial design and the randomized-groups design, and there are designs that combine the features of several of the designs discussed here. It would be fair to say, however, that all these additional designs incorporate the same formist perspective as the designs discussed here. In Section 7.3 we shall have occasion once more to regain a general approach, as in 7.1. We are left with the problem of how to make the most of the designs available, yet how to avoid being captured by those tools presently available.

7.3   The Experimental Attitude

In the foregoing section I made use of a pragmatist perspective to point up some of the limitations of a formist approach to experimental design. My focus was on temporal factors, spatial factors, and investigator effects. I attempted to show how complex is the research situation and, relative to that complexity, how puny is the degree of control achieved by even the most sophisticated designs. Yet what conclusions should we then draw? Should we abandon such designs in favor of more qualitative approaches, as Weiss and Rein seem to suggest for the evaluation of "broad-aim programs"? Should we adhere to them, along with their implicit formist paradigm, since we have yet to invent designs that have been definitely proven to be more effective?

I believe that a more fruitful alternative is available to us, one that involves an extension of the experimental idea. To explore it, we must first pick up the threads from Section 7.1, with its analysis of a variety of approaches to the experiment. In addition, we must obtain an overview of the various experimental designs presented in Section 7.2: What are the most important things for us to learn from them? Finally, it is essential to be both constructive and concrete. Criticism is most valuable when it yields viable alternatives, and when those alternatives are clear-cut.

In reviewing Section 7.1, I find a range of paradigmatic orientations to the experiment. There is the mechanistic approach of Galileo and Hamblin and the formism of Mill and Campbell and Stanley. There is the organicism of Chapin and Weiss and Rein, who attempted to apply an experimental approach to the complex and changing environment. There is the pragmatism involved in the studies of experimenter effect and the recent questioning within sociology of the possibility of value neutrality. But neither can each of the researchers involved be so easily dismissed with a label, for that would be only a formist analysis of their contributions. Mill himself, for all his formism, had a vision of mechanism in his method of concomitant variations, and he also revealed an awareness of the existence of multiple causation. Campbell and Stanley reveal mechanistic and pragmatist overtones in much of their work, and they want others to cope with complex phenomena via quasi experiments if true experiments cannot be performed. The sociological questioning of value neutrality is being undertaken by individuals who retain a deep commitment to organicism.

Looking at Section 7.2 to obtain a view of the forest of experimental design in addition to the trees, three major directions come to view: temporal concerns, spatial concerns, and a focus on the impact of the researcher. Temporally, the very concept of an X implies some alteration over time undergone by phenomena. Also, a great many of the designs focus on phenomena occurring over at least two points in time. The contrast between the experimental and the control group is based on the experimenter's knowledge of the time sequence of his actions: when he introduces a treatment, he knows that it was not introduced at a prior time through self-selection or some other process. Spatially, all the designs involve an attempt to get beyond only one situation to compare it with one or more other situations. Finally, these designs involve a very active role for the researcher. He does not merely stand back and observe: he constructs the research situation.

My central point here is that it is possible to carry forward these temporal, spatial, and investigator concerns that form the heart of experimental design and at the same time incorporate formist, mechanistic, organicist, and pragmatist orientations. This is possible through the development of an experimental attitude. Such an attitude is a specific tool, but it is not chained to any highly specific rules for experimentation. It carries forward a sense of problem, as discussed in Part Two, into the arena of data construction, enabling the investigator to complete his feedback cycle (Figure 1-1). It is also much broader than scientific investigation per se as most individuals have come to view it: it involves the basic process of human communication or even communication by any organism, as pictured in Figure 1-2. If the importance of a metaphorical and cybernetic perspective was the theme of Part Two, then the importance of an experimental attitude *in addition to* those perspectives is the theme of the remainder of this book. Indeed, we might well see the two interacting in an upward positive loop.

What, then, are the concrete tools open to the investigator as he moves toward the construction of data? I am suggesting that he must begin with the kinds of tools that alert him to the complexity and dynamism of phenomena: paradigmatic, theoretical, and experimental perspectives. These tools will help him to probe his own fundamental behavior as well as that of those he studies. In this way, they will alert him to the immense gap between his view of where the water is and where it actually is, helping him to create the kinds of measurement that incorporate these tools.

But more specifically what is the investigator to actually do? The foregoing will alert him not only to the limitations of existing experimental designs but also to the need for utilizing other modes of data construction in addition. In Chapters 8–11 we take up such other modes. Yet such an awareness of limitations should not deter him from using the admittedly imperfect tools provided by existing experimental designs.

7.4 Summary

The experiment moves the researcher from the context of discovery into the context of verification and thus enables him to complete the loop that is essential to the scientific process. Historically, experimental procedure has not developed in such a way that it has gone much beyond Mill's canons of agreement, difference, and residues, which incorporate a formist paradigm and do not encourage the investigator to bring to bear on the research process the kind of theory that departs from that paradigm. This approach to the experiment is associated with the kinds of experimental results in the social sciences that have not contributed greatly to the further development of theory. In other words, the discovery-verification loop does not seem to be snowballing in an upward positive loop.

By applying both a formist and a pragmatist approach to each of the various experimental designs, we have a direction for taking seriously both the context of verification and the context of discovery. This procedure can thus be applied to: (1) the one-shot case study, (2) the one-group pretest-posttest design, (3) the static group comparison, (4) the pretest-posttest control group design, (5) the Solomon four-group design, (6) the posttest-only control group design, (7) the nonequivalent control group design, (8) the time-series experiment, (9) the randomized-groups design, and (10) the factorial design. In this way, the researcher can combine an experimental attitude, which incorporates a focus on the context of verification, with a commitment to the importance of paradigms and theory.

Exercises

1. Use the metaphorical and cybernetic tools discussed in previous chapters—for example, Model 1 of Human Development, presented in Section 5.5—to gain insight into any change described in Section 7.1, "Historical Perspective," then (1) define a system and an environment, (2) define a continuum for each, (3) define points along each continuum in a rough way ("calibration"), (4) take into account other factors, such as *A* and *B*, and (5) analyze the dynamic behavior of your model in comparison to the verbal discussion in Section 7.1.

2. Review the preceding chapter on measurement and scaling. Take one of the approaches to the experiment discussed in Section 7.1 and mention specific ways it fails to take into account the considerations discussed in that chapter?

3. Using a single individual in place of a group, perform a brief experiment with one of the designs discussed in Section 7.2. Begin by defining a simple problem and constructing an instrument for data collection. If randomization is required, follow the procedures outlined on page 159.

4. Interpret what you have done or—alternatively—interpret the published results of any experiment. What have you learned that you believe represents important knowledge? What have you learned about the limitations and possibilities of the experimental approach?

Annotated References

GREENWOOD, ERNEST. *Experimental Sociology.* New York: King's Crown Press, 1945. Greenwood's discussions of many different sociological views of the experiment, his exploration of the problems the experimenter encounters, and his efforts to convey the possibilities of the ex post facto experiment are still meaningful to a discipline that has only partially recognized the importance of the experimental attitude.

ROSENTHAL, ROBERT. *Experimenter Effects in Behavioral Research.* New York: Appleton-Century-Crofts, 1966. This compilation of research on the impact of the experimenter on the research project is revolutionary in its implications for the importance of drastically altering our view of the experiment in particular and the research process in general.

SJOBERG, GIDEON, AND ROGER NETT. *A Methodology for Social Research.* New York: Harper and Row, Publishers, Inc., 1968. The authors apply the sociology of knowledge to the area of social research. They see the researcher's theoretical commitment as influencing every aspect of the research process: selection of a topic, statement of the problem, selection of the research procedures, construction of data, analysis of results, and dissemination of findings.

chapter 8

Simulation and Computer Simulation

A simulation is an analogue of something else, usually some relatively complex situation. The researcher creates the simulation, just as he creates an experimental situation, and because of this he is in an excellent position to understand the rules governing the simulation. His purpose is not confined to the simulation itself, but to the situation that it is simulating: can it help him to achieve greater insight into that situation, given that the simulation lays bare a great many of the forces involved in that situation? Thus, a simulation is a kind of metaphor, only it is a metaphor that has been put to work in structuring human behavior. As with any metaphor, it can be quite suggestive, and it can also be misleading. For example, a group of individuals simulating international relations by playing the roles of heads of state can suggest modes of relationship we might not have conceived of without the simulation, and they might also mislead us into applying to international relations perspectives that only apply to a small group situation. It all depends on how effective the theory is that goes into the structuring of the simulation.

A computer simulation—an approach based on the cybernetic ideas of Section 3.2—is also an analogue of some situation that the investigator wishes to understand, only this time the analogue is sufficiently systematic—whether logically or mathematically—for him to program it on a computer. The computer operates as a logic machine, generating the logical implications of the assumptions that he begins with. Both the simulation and the computer simulation generate data. In the former case, a number of rules are made explicit to, say, a group of individuals, but a great deal is left open to them. What each one decides to do, and what they do collectively, is the fundamental object of study, and constitutes the data generated by the simulation. In a computer simulation, the computer generates data describing, say, situations at later points in time given a description of the situation at an earlier time. Although it works only with the assumptions initially plugged into it, it forces the researcher to think through those assumptions in a highly systematic way, and it reveals to him consequences of those assumptions that may not have been apparent to him initially. In a sense, then, the computer simulation generates data by alerting the investigator to information that would ordinarily not be available to him.

Simulation and computer simulation represent an extension of the experimental attitude, as described in Section 7.3. Temporally, the focus is not on two points in time, the before situation and the after situation, nor is it even limited to a small number of points in time, as in the case of the time-series experiment, although it is closest to this kind of experiment. Simulation procedures encompass very large numbers of points in time, and any given number can easily be increased. Spatially, the focus within simulation is on the deliberate structuring of a great deal of a given environment for the purpose of examining the implications of that structuring. Within the experiment our focus tends to be much narrower: we select out from a given situation a relatively small number of factors that we wish to study, and we attempt to deal with all other factors in such a way that they do not interfere with the ones under investigation, e.g., by using techniques such as randomization procedures. But to the degree that the world is such that interactions among phenomena are frequent, such techniques will be inadequate, and what actually results from a given experiment may be more the result of such interactions than of the factors under consideration. With simulation however, we include a number of such interactions very directly into the study. As for the role of the researcher, it is more active in simulation in the sense that he attempts to create a more complete research environment than in the experiment, where he leaves to chance the creation of a large portion of that environment.

Despite these efforts, the degree of success of simulation is—as in the case of the experiment—quite dependent on the success of the paradigmatic, theoretical, and measurement efforts associated with it. Just because one goes out of one's way to incorporate within one's study a number of complex interrelationships among phenomena does not mean, thereby, that knowledge is advanced. One may succeed in structuring the kinds of relationships that are quite trivial and lead to no advance in knowledge. Or one may not have any more understanding of what goes on in the simulation than of whatever the simulation is supposed to be simulating, or representing. However, with the aid of paradigmatic, theoretical, and measurement tools, the investigator can learn to penetrate, more and more, the problems of effective design as well as of insightful analysis of simulations.

In Sections 8.1 and 8.2 I illustrate the general process of simulation and computer simulation, respectively. It seems that simulation and computer simulation, like all other methods of data collection, do not stand apart from the researcher's paradigm but, rather, are based on it. Section 8.3 provides an overview of simulation and computer simulation, and Section 8.4 is devoted to the system dynamics approach to computer simulation that has grown out of an engineering and physical science tradition.

This builds on previous presentations of system dynamics notation in Figures 3-4 and 5-4.

8.1 Simulation

In this section I will discuss William Gamson's *SIMSOC, Simulated Society*,[1] a simulation widely used as a teaching device in sociology courses. The simulation literature does not sharply differentiate between simulations for research and those for teaching purposes. Whatever the knowledge outputs of simulations, it has been discovered that they frequently are very successful in enlisting the interest and enthusiasm of participants, and that they can help to provide a stimulating teaching environment. This is all to the good from a research standpoint, as it indicates that the simulation is tapping important motives, and that there may be opportunities for investigating the dynamics of those motives.

In Gamson's *SIMSOC,* each individual elects to emphasize one of three goals: (1) power—to influence what happens in the society, (2) wealth—to accumulate simbucks, and (3) popularity—to become well liked by other members of the simulated society. People live in one of four regions—Red, Yellow, Blue, and Green—with some restrictions on movement from one region to the next. No more than half of the players are allowed in any region at any one time, thus simulating the difficulty within society of achieving consensus without face-to-face communication. To survive in the society, a player must obtain a subsistence certificate, and he usually does this with money obtained from employment by one of the society's basic groups: (1) BASIN, or Basic Industry, which has an over-all objective of expanding its assets and income as much as possible; (2) INNOVIN, or Innovative Industry, which has the same objective as BASIN except that there is greater risk of loss as well as greater possibilities for gain; (3) POP, Party of the People, which emphasizes individual autonomy and decentralization, and which attempts to mobilize members of the society to work for party programs and contribute to the party; (4) SOP, Society Party, which emphasizes centralized planning and coordination; (5) EMPIN, Employee Interests, which attempts to provide individuals who are not heads of basic groups (the seven listed here) with adequate subsistence and a fair share of wealth; (6) JUDCO, Judicial Council, which tries to clarify and interpret the rules of the society; and (7) MASMED, Mass Media, which attempts to keep the society informed about important events.

According to the rules, the head of any of these seven groups (usually selected by the instructor at random) may hire and fire others on any terms

[1] William A. Gamson, *SIMSOC, Simulated Society: Participant's Manual* (New York: Free Press, 1969).

he wishes and for any reasons and may raise or lower salaries at his own discretion at any time; he may be removed only by the unanimous consent of all members of his group. In addition to these individuals who control employment and salaries, there are a number of individuals who own subsistence or travel agencies and have the power to determine the terms under which they will dispense subsistence tickets and travel tickets. The instructor, or simulator, may decide to concentrate power in a few hands by designating the heads of the different groups to be agency owners as well, perhaps even owning both types of agency. Such power may be regionally dispersed, or crosscut, so that a region or regions do not emerge with more power than others, or the power may be superimposed so that there are deprived regions and surplus power regions.

The degree of scarcity prevailing in the society may also be varied by increasing or decreasing the number of subsistence and travel tickets available. According to Gamson, this tends to affect the intensity of the conflict generated by the simulation. There are also many features of the rules themselves that build in scarcity. For example, there are four national indicators that measure the general effectiveness and health of the society as a whole (food and energy supply, standard of living, social cohesion, and public commitment). These indicators automatically decline 10% from one session to the next unless there are sufficiently high investments in public programs to raise them, and the result is to lower the income available to all the heads of groups. Another illustration is the possibility of being arrested by the police force, with the police simulating, in this game, the existence of force (whether legitimated or not) in the society. All it takes is enough simbucks to set up a police force that can arrest others or protect specified individuals from arrest. More generally, the rules of the game are fixed, and this represents an important source of scarcity. As Gamson puts it, "the rules of the game in the Manual are like the laws of nature which this society lives under. You can't change them, even if everyone in the society wants to."[2]

According to Gamson, SIMSOC avoids having a programmed quality, where the constraints of the environment are so overwhelming that the player's choices are more apparent than real:

> SIMSOC, however, is a different type of game. The environment it attempts to simulate produces dilemmas or problems for the players rather than forces which determine their behavior. There are many alternative ways of playing it that will, in some sense, "work" perfectly well. The environment is minimally "programmed" to channel their behavior in a particular fashion. . . . A major design problem has been that of keeping forces in balance—forces between conflict and common interest, for

---

[2] Gamson, *SIMSOC, Simulated Society: Instructor's Manual* (New York: Free Press, 1969), p. 12.

example—so that no single course of action appears obvious or best for all players.[3]

There are many other features of SIMSOC that I cannot deal with in this brief space; in general, they help to create more complex situations for the participant to face, such as the rule that the instructor may announce the occurrence of special events affecting the society. But the foregoing is enough to sketch the essentials. A key question for us to consider here is: How can SIMSOC produce the kinds of data that are the basis for insights into human behavior? There is also the more general question: How can any simulation produce such insights?

Two important functions of a simulation for the social scientist are (1) to yield insight into the nature of the "rules" that govern the phenomena being simulated, and (2) to yield directions for altering those rules so as to create more effective functioning. These two functions are closely related. One must generally first understand a situation before he is in a position to alter it in a direction of his choice. Furthermore, it is through efforts at alteration that one gains further understanding of the rules. Gamson makes a similar point:

> The use of games for teaching seems to me to be most successful when the students are asked to make the jump from player to simulator. As players they accept certain constraints which are given in the rules and use resources to achieve certain objectives specified or suggested by the rules. When the students become simulators, the *rules themselves* become the resources and they can manipulate these resources—hypothetically or actually—to see whether the resulting process will take the form which they believe it will. Developing simulations is too enjoyable and valuable a learning experience to be hoarded by professors.[4]

Thus, the simulation provides a kind of laboratory situation that lays bare many of the rules of human behavior, making it easier to understand the way they function as well as how to change them.

A serious problem for the achievement of these functions is the simulator's own degree of paradigmatic, theoretical, and measurement knowledge. For example, suppose he believes—as Gamson does—that "the [SIMSOC] environment is minimally 'programmed' to channel their [individuals'] behavior in a particular fashion." Suppose he does not recognize the formist structuring he achieves by inducing individuals to choose *either* power *or* wealth *or* popularity, to choose *either* the Red region *or* the Yellow *or* the Blue *or* the Green, by selecting different individuals as heads for his seven basic groups, and by sharply differentiating the functions of these

[3] Ibid., p. 2.
[4] Gamson, "Simsoc: Establishing Social Order in a Simulated Society," in Michael Inbar and Clarice S. Stoll (eds.), *Simulation and Gaming in Social Science* (New York: Free Press, 1972), p. 68.

groups. Suppose he fails to recognize the severe scarcities in the simulated society that give it a deterministic flavor like that of the mechanistic paradigm, with rules that can never be altered, with individuals staying with fixed goals, with fewer subsistence and travel tickets than individuals need and desire, and with virtual dictators governing—or at least having the potential to govern—the various aspects of life. Suppose that he un-wittingly constructs an organicist environment where the individual's welfare is very largely determined by his success in relating to other individuals—such as employers, subsistence ticket agents, and travel ticket agents—and where there is very little elaboration of processes within the individual relative to processes within the environment.

An understanding of society includes an understanding *both* of the way it is and of the ways it might be, and is thus heavily dependent on a knowledge of social change. To gain such insights, it is essential for us to simulate a wide range of possibilities. If we are unaware of our own paradigmatic assumptions, we will not be able to produce such a range. Furthermore, we will think that we are in fact producing such a range, since we will not be aware of the extent to which we are imposing constraints, just as a fish is unaware of the constraints imposed by a watery existence. Gamson's simulation carries us a good distance in probing the nature of industrial society, but it is limited by his own paradigmatic assumptions, from which follow his theoretical orientations and simulation procedures.

8.2 Computer Simulation

Let us now move to an examination of computer simulation in the context of a particular study by John and Jeanne Gullahorn, "Computer Simulation of Role Conflict Resolution."[5] The Gullahorns began with the questionnaire data that had resulted from a study of labor union leaders and attempted to simulate the processes that produced that data. They did this by (1) making a series of theoretical assumptions about how the individual makes a decision in a role conflict situation, (2) proceeding to develop a computer program incorporating these assumptions, (3) making predictions about the behavior of "simulated individuals," that is, sets of numbers that had been created largely by random processes and that reflected forces involved in the role conflict situation, and (4) checking the accuracy of these predictions against the questionnaire data.

The questionnaire items were preceded by an introduction that set the stage for the role conflict situation:

> Assume that you are an officer of the Employees' Club, which is largely supported by the company. You believe strongly in the union and attend

[5] John T. and Jeanne E. Gullahorn, "Computer Applications in Social Science," *American Sociological Review*, **30** (June 1965), pp. 353–65.

meetings regularly. Your fellow workers have chosen you to be their Chief Steward, and you wonder whether you should resign from the club office so that you can devote your time to the job of Chief Steward. *You really haven't time to do both jobs well.* You feel responsible for the continued success of a program which you have started for the club, and at the same time you feel obligated to do a good job as Chief Steward.[6]

This was followed by more specific information about particular situations involving choices, such as:

In each of the following situations, please check the appropriate space to indicate the action you would be most likely to take. An officer of the company tells you that if you continue your good work in the Employees' Club it may lead to a management position. What if—

	I would be most likely to do the following		
	Resign from club office	Retain both positions	Resign from position of chief steward
1. Both the union executive committee and the people you represent as Chief Steward want you to keep the club office.	19*	44	37
2. The executive committee wants you to keep the club office—the people you represent want you to serve as steward.	42	36	22
3. The executive committee wants you to serve as steward—the people you represent want you to keep the club office.	29	39	32
4. Both the executive committee and the people you represent want you to serve as steward.[7]	61	24	15

* The numbers are the percentages of responses in each category, with the total number of respondents (N) being 148.

The Gullahorns assumed that the union leaders' choices were a product of their moral commitment to each role and reference group pressures.

[6] Ibid., p. 357.
[7] Ibid.

Three reference groups were involved: (1) the people they represented, (2) the union executive committee, and (3) the management. Moral and reference group commitments were combined into overall measures of the total value of retaining the Chief Stewardship (V1) and the total value of retaining the Employees' Club office (V3). The assumption made followed Homans' concepts of cost and profit, incorporating principles from Skinnerian psychology and classical economics. It is also an application of a mechanistic paradigm, with choices seen as a product of forces, and is similar to the model of occupational choice (see Section 2.2).

The computer simulation flow diagram designed to simulate the labor union leaders' process of choice on the questionnaire appears in Figure 8-1.[8] We might think of each simulated respondent as simply a set of numbers grouped together in, say, a given location. The flow diagram embodies a series of assumptions about how those numbers interact (or how the individual functions) without addressing the problem of changes in the numbers, and yields choices by each simulated respondent that are the same as those in the questionnaire. The simulated choices are then compared with the actual choices on such criteria as the per cent answering each item in a given way, thus indicating whether the simulation is able to reproduce the distribution of responses that actually occurred.

In examining Figure 8-1, the first eight boxes constitute a short-cut decision procedure, which comes into play only in the minority of cases where the individual's moral commitment to one role or the other is extreme, resulting in uniform choices for all questions (Box 5 or 6 or 8), regardless of the special circumstances involved in each question. In Box 1 a location for the simulated respondent is selected, and numbers representing his moral commitments to the Chief Stewardship and the Employees' Club are assigned to that location in Box 2. This is achieved by a random number generator through a process similar to an individual's use of a table of random numbers; it is known as a "Monte Carlo" technique. In Box 3 the computer calculates whether or not the moral commitment to the Chief Stewardship is very high; the .81 weighting was selected because the original questionnaire data showed that 19 per cent of respondents were so committed to the stewardship that they would resign from the Employees' Club, even if both the union executive committee and the people they represented as Chief Steward wanted them to remain in the club. In the case of such extreme commitment (a "yes" for Box 3), it is then determined if there also exists an extreme commitment to the Employees' Club. If there is such a commitment ("yes" for Box 4), it is predicted in Box 5 that the simulated respondent will vote to retain both positions for all items in the questionnaire; if not ("no" for Box 4), Box 6 predicts a uniform vote to resign from the club on all items. If there is no extreme commitment to the stewardship ("no" in Box 3), but there is one to the club

[8] Ibid., p. 360.

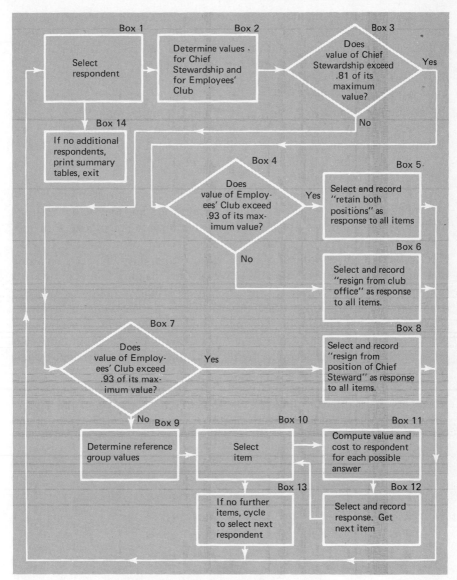

Figure 8-1.
Flow Diagram for Simulation of Role Conflict Resolution.

("yes" in Box 7), then a uniform response to resign the stewardship is predicted for all items (Box 8).

In most cases, however, such extreme moral commitments were not involved ("no" in Box 3 and "no" in Box 7), and the flow moves to Box 9, where a Monte Carlo procedure assigned numbers to each simulated respondent reflecting the relative importance of the three reference groups: the people represented, the executive committee, and the management. These numbers were combined with simulated moral commitments of each respondent to yield total scores for V1 (value of retaining the Chief Stewardship) and V3 (value of retaining the Employees' Club office). The decision procedure referred to in Boxes 11 and 12 may be understood by examining Figure 8-2. Where V1 is much greater than V3 ("yes" in Boxes A and B), Box C is predicted for the item in question. Where V3 is much greater than V1 ("no" in Box A and "yes" in Box E), Box F is predicted. In the intermediate situation where V1 and V3 are not very far apart, Box D is predicted.

The Gullahorns succeed in obtaining a very close correspondence between the behavior of their simulated respondents and the actual respondents. At this point, we are faced with evaluating the significance of this achievement. It lays bare a possible process that could have produced choice behavior by a number of individuals, a possibility that rests on a fair amount of social science literature. We are not dealing here simply with a number of relatively isolated factors that contribute or fail to contribute to a given effect: rather, it is a complex pattern of factors that is involved. Furthermore, the Gullahorns are not simply emerging with formist statements that certain factors are related to others: they are coming up with close correlations and accurate predictions, similar to the mechanistic approach of the medical student study.

Yet let us see these successes within a larger perspective. For all of the closeness of relationship between the value commitments and the preferences for medical fields in the medical student study, the key issue of the

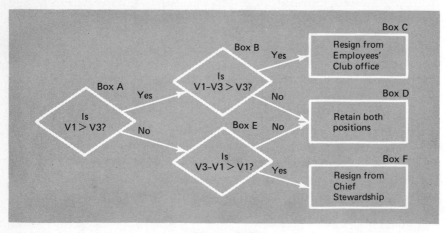

Figure 8-2.
Flow Diagram for Boxes 11 and 12.

forces producing *changes* in values and beliefs was not faced: once these things were given, I proceeded to predict preferences. Similarly, the Gullahorns do not address this vital issue of changes in values. Their work is not based on data obtained at more than one point in time, and this handicaps the possibilities of dealing with change. In the simulation, it is Monte Carlo techniques that produce the moral commitments as well as the relative importance of the reference groups, but a temporal perspective might yield an understanding of the process producing changes in these values.

And what of the substance of the findings: the mechanistic paradigm to the effect that people seek to maximize goal fulfillment? I might comment here in a manner similar to my reaction to SIMSOC: Even if we grant that this generally describes human behavior fairly well, human behavior is plastic. The way it is is not necessarily the way it might be, and it is the responsibility of the investigator to explore the full range of possibilities as well as the processes that would produce the various alternatives. Here, the researcher who is committed to a mechanistic paradigm is severely handicapped in how much of this range he is able to explore. He will have difficulty in exploring what he cannot see, or is not aware of, and he will perceive only a portion of that range. The Gullahorns,[9] for example, structure the individual's behavior as the product of fixed internal forces (moral commitments) as well as fixed external forces (commitment to reference groups).

8.3 Overview

Simulation and computer simulation are relatively new approaches to data collection. To the student, simulation may appear to be interesting but frivolous, and computer simulation may seem esoteric and inconsequential. The above illustrations may have done little to alter such views. They are not atypical of other efforts to use simulation and computer simulation in social science. The strengths of simulation and computer simulation lie in their potential for dealing with the temporal and spatial dimensions as well as with the role of the investigator. Both techniques are open to the complex patterning of behavior spatially, and represent a step beyond the experiment—with its focus on the operation of pure factors in isolation from one another—in this respect. Temporally, it is a process that is under the microscope more than simply behavior at several different points in time. And there is wider scope here for the part played by the

[9] John T. and Jeanne E. Gullahorn, "Computer Simulation of Role Conflict Resolution," in John M. Dutton and William H. Starbuck (eds.), *Computer Simulation of Human Behavior* (New York: Wiley, 1971), p. 355.

investigator in that he more consciously constructs a great deal of the situation and, as a result, tends to be more aware of the impact of his role.

Why, then, haven't these techniques been more widely utilized over the past decade? Most important, I believe, is their newness, for most of the illustrations have evolved only within the past decade. As with any new technique, there are problems both of education and of legitimation. In addition, there are also some serious weaknesses associated with simulation and computer simulation. They can be no better than the investigator's assumptions, theory, and measurement techniques. In these respects, those who simulate tend to be neither better nor worse than others. Consequently, their results lack the effectiveness that would enable us to label them as the shiny new wave of the future.

Simulation procedures—like Gamson's SIMSOC—suffer from the same kinds of problems that are involved in the field, as distinct from the laboratory, experiment. A great many things are going on simultaneously, and it is only somewhat easier to understand the forces operating in this situation than in situations in everyday life. Furthermore, since the researcher's role is even more active than in the experimental situation, the effects he induces are far-reaching, and it is essential that he have an understanding of their nature.

As for computer simulation, a serious problem here is a dependence on the kinds of mathematics used in statistical analysis or in econometrics as distinct from the kinds stemming from the physical science and engineering tradition. The former tends to produce simulations in the formist tradition. For example, the Gullahorns' simulation is one incorporating a yes-no logic of decision making. The latter, by contrast, tends to push the investigator to develop ratio scales and toward the mechanistic, organicist, and pragmatist paradigms. It is this kind of approach—one that can also be extended to noncomputer simulation—that is our topic in Section 8.4.

8.4   System Dynamics: An Approach to Mechanistic, Organicist, and Pragmatist Modeling

When I dipped into some calculus as an undergraduate, no one ever said explicitly that this was a tool limited to use in the physical sciences and engineering, but all the examples we used cried out that this was the case. Other experiences told me the same story: students and professors who knew about calculus tended to know very little about the social sciences, and vice versa. The situation now is not the same as it once was. More important, it is changing rapidly in the direction of applying the tools of the calculus to social science problems. And since calculus deals with instantaneous rates of change, or flows (the differential calculus), as well as accumulations (the integral calculus), it provides the basis for theories of change, whether in the inanimate or the animate world.

Yet for all its power, the differential equations—which combine differential and integral calculus—incorporate the limitations of a mechanistic world view, or paradigm. To begin with, there is a deterministic flavor carried over from the formist distinction between truth and falsehood: one expects to determine the equations that, once and for all, correctly describe the situation. It is the same as in algebra: when $y = 3x^2 + 6$, we have defined y for all time. Yet the world may be a far more complex and dynamic place than can be described once and for all by *any* set of differential equations, no matter how numerous or complex. Another major limitation of the calculus is the mathematical skills required to set up and solve complex systems of differential equations, skills that are not common even among mathematicians. Are these limitations associated with the calculus, then, insuperable?

With the advent of the electronic computer, and with the development of the computer simulation procedures known as system dynamics,[10] such problems are becoming less and less formidable. In short, these new tools go far beyond simply enabling us to easily set up and solve the equivalent of complex sets of differential equations, for that would still leave us squarely within the mechanistic paradigm. These tools are sufficiently flexible so that it is quite easy to change the model with changes in the situation; we need not view any part of the model as fixed for all time. In this way, we can move toward an organicist paradigm. And beyond this, the investigator need not divorce himself from the modeling process. Indeed, he can make the development of his own cybernetic intuition central to his simulation work, thus operating within a pragmatist paradigm, by utilizing the third cybernetics.

In the remainder of Section 8.4 I shall present an extremely simple illustration of the system dynamics approach. My purpose here is not to present a realistic example but to give the reader a basis for a thorough understanding of the methodology involved. To understand the approach thoroughly, one must be able to do by hand what the computer does with its program, and I hope to enable the reader to accomplish this. This approach already has been illustrated in previous chapters in a less technical way (Sections 3.2 and 5.5). I begin by defining a problem paradigmatically and theoretically, continue with a discussion of model structure and model

---

[10] For a nontechnical illustration of the techniques of system dynamics, see Donella H. Meadows et al., *The Limits to Growth* (New York: Universe Books, 1972). A more technical introduction to these techniques, centering on a social science illustration, is to be found in "From Beaker Metaphor to a Dynamic Mathematical Model of Human Development" (developed by the author in collaboration with Peter M. Senge), in Bernard S. Phillips, *Worlds of the Future: Exercises in the Sociological Imagination* (Columbus: Merrill, 1972), pp. 268–330. The most thorough over-all explanation of system dynamics is Jay W. Forrester, *Principles of Systems* (Cambridge, Mass.: Wright-Allen Press, 1968). Other major applications of the approach by Forrester are *Industrial Dynamics* (Cambridge, Mass.: M.I.T. Press, 1961), *Urban Dynamics* (Cambridge, Mass.: M.I.T. Press, 1969), and *World Dynamics* (Cambridge, Mass.: Wright-Allen Press, 1971).

behavior, and end with a discussion of the implications of this approach. This is an exercise in theory construction, and I would like to simplify things here by not dealing with the relationship between a computer simulation and data collected to test the simulation.

Definition of the Problem

My central focus here will be on an exploration of the mechanistic paradigm. I am hoping that this exercise, simple as it is, will enable us to understand that paradigm more thoroughly and, thus, will help us to increase our insight into the organicist and pragmatist world views that build on that paradigm. More concretely, I want to deal with the personality dynamics of the individual when he is involved in choice behavior, such as has been discussed in the context of the occupational choice study (Section 4.2) and the Gullahorns' computer simulation of role conflict resolution (Section 8.2). In particular, I want to explore the mechanistic conception of human behavior as a set of forces or levels of aspiration associated with a set of choices, or decisions, geared to fulfill those forces. All of this has implications beyond personality dynamics. For example, Davies' theory of revolution—as presented in Figure 4-4—combines the levels of aspiration of individuals within a given social unit into "expected need satisfaction," which, as a result, becomes a social force. In addition, he combines the various individuals' choices, or decisions, into "actual need satisfaction." For Davies, it is the gap between expected and actual need satisfaction that is crucial to understanding the genesis of revolution.

To utilize system dynamics, it is essential that these two concepts be conceived of along continua, whether it is the individual's or the group's expected and actual need satisfaction we are thinking of. Here, we may apply the beaker metaphor (Figure 3-3) to the situation as a device for helping us to achieve this. Let us picture expected need satisfaction as the height of the beaker and actual need satisfaction as the level of the water. If we, then, conceive of each concept (expected and actual need satisfaction) as rising or falling by degrees—as we can—and if that concept is meaningful and important to us, then we have achieved this gradational approach. Note that here we are shifting from a formist view of choice as a selection among a number of alternatives to a mechanistic view of choice as representing a degree of need satisfaction. This view is similar to that in the occupational choice study, where preference for field of medicine was predicted on the basis of the *degree* to which value commitments could be satisfied in a given field. It is also similar to the Gullahorns' predictions of role conflict resolution on the basis of the *degree* of social profit or loss involved in a given choice.

To be able to think in terms of degree is not easy to learn, especially since almost all of our language pushes us to think formistically. In Section 3.1 I discussed some of the problems involved in formist thought as it is generated by ordinary language and scientific language. What is required are not simply continua but meaningful and important continua, that is, continua that are interwoven with theories and paradigms. Once again, we cannot escape the relation between theory and research. The continuum is not an end in itself but a means to larger ends. We have many continua that can be used, such as amount of money or chronological age or amount of education, but those continua are not necessarily of vital theoretical importance. There are other kinds of continua that are more difficult to measure because of their less tangible nature, such as degree of value commitment or subjective age or intellectual development, which probably are far more important because of their potential links with so much more of human behavior.

In order to get very far with defining the problem, we need to think in terms of a concrete situation, located in time and space, that we wish to explain. The context I select is a classroom situation. In particular, I am thinking of a class I teach, Sociology of the Future. My expected need satisfaction, or level of aspiration, has to do both with my own learning in the course and with the effectiveness of my teaching; my aspiration is such that I wish to continually improve in both areas. My actual need satisfaction, however, is not up to that level of aspiration. Perhaps, then, the computer simulation can shed light on this gap between aspiration and achievement.

Before proceeding to the technical structure of the model, I might distinguish three different theoretical perspectives that might be taken, corresponding to the mechanistic, organicist, and pragmatist paradigms. Mechanistically, we might conceive of my class performance, or actual need satisfaction, as a product of my level of aspiration, that is, we might see behavior as a product of forces without exploring the genesis of those forces. From an organicist perspective, we might look to the class as a reference group for the instructor and, thus, as exerting pressures on his behavior, and we might, further, see the nature of those pressures as in flux. In addition, the organicist approach would inquire into the factors producing this flux. However, because organicism builds on mechanism only to a limited degree, there would tend to be no clear-cut dimension from a less to a more desirable situation along which that flux would be viewed. Within the pragmatist approach, there would be concern both with external and internal pressures on the instructor, there would be a similar view of the situation as one of continuing flux, and there would also tend to be one or more definite dimensions along which to view such change.

Model Structure

Having begun to define the problem, the remaining steps within the computer simulation follow logically from that definition. Let me begin by distinguishing between model structure and model dynamics. The model structure is the pattern of relationships among the elements of the model, just as the social structure is the pattern of relationships among individuals or groups. Model dynamics refers to the behavior produced by the model, seen graphically along various continua, just as everyday behavior is largely a product of social structure. Two of the elements of the model structure are the Aspiration Level (*AL*) and the Level of Achievement (*LA*). The system dynamics approach also calls for inflows and outflows, just as the level of water in a beaker comes from somewhere and might drain to somewhere else, and these two additional elements of the model are designated Rate of Achievement (*RA*) and Achievement Aging Rate (*AAR*). The model is pictured in Figure 8-3.

The solid arrows in Figure 8-3 designate actual flows that remove a quantity of something from one place and deposit it in another; for example, the solid arrow from Level of Achievement to the sink below Achievement Aging Rate lowers the Level of Achievement. However, the broken arrow from Level of Achievement up to Rate of Achievement represents information feedback, similar to the information one obtains while filling a glass with water from a faucet when one looks at the level of water in the glass, and this does not transfer a quantity from one place to another.

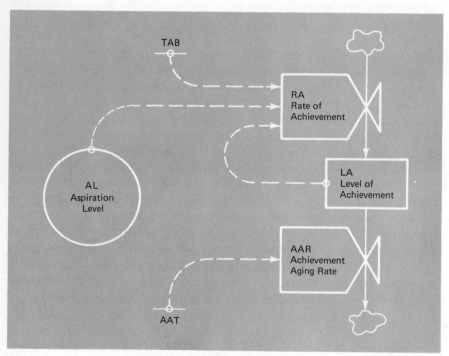

Figure 8-3.
Model Structure: Level of Aspiration and Achievement.

Two elements of the model not discussed previously are *TAB,* or Time for Achievement Buildup, and *AAT,* or Achievement Aging Time. These two constants both convey the assumption that things do not occur instantaneously, but instead take place over some finite time interval. In the classroom situation, for example, it takes time to accomplish effective teaching and learning. Similarly, there is an interval from one class session to another, and the process of forgetting over time is represented by the Achievement Aging Time as well as the Achievement Aging Rate.

The equation for the Rate of Achievement (*RA*) is

$$RA = \frac{AL - LA}{TAB}.$$

In words, Rate of Achievement is equal to the gap between Aspiration Level and Level of Achievement divided by the Time for Achievement Buildup. Here we see the fundamental assumption behind the model: that it is this gap that constitutes the key force for increasing the Rate of Achievement. When *RA*, or the Rate of Achievement, is multiplied by a given unit of time—say *DT*—we have the total amount of inflow into the Level of Achievement during that time period. Similarly, when *AAR*, or the Achievement Aging Rate, is multiplied by the time unit *DT*, we have the total amount of outflow from the Level of Achievement. The difference between inflow and outflow constitutes the net inflow:

$$\text{Net Inflow} = (DT)(RA - AAR).$$

This understanding of net inflow is the basis for the formula for Level of Achievement. Let us think of the simulation as taking place over a number of discrete time intervals where the beginning of each interval (the same as the end of the previous interval) constitutes a point in time. The Level of Achievement (*LA*) at any point in time *K* is based on the Level of Achievement at the previous point *J* incremented by the Net Inflow over the interval between J and K:

$$LA.K = LA.J + (DT)(RA.JK - AAR.JK).$$

Thus far, the formulas for Rate of Achievement (*RA*) and Level of Achievement (*LA*) have been specified. One additional formula remains, that for the Achievement Aging Rate (AAR). We might assume that this rate constitutes a decay of the Level of Achievement and, thus, depends on how high that level is. In addition, since AAR is a rate, it should take into account the Achievement Aging Time, AAT, or else the decay would be instantaneous. Thus, we have

$$AAR = LA/AAT.$$

These formulae, along with other information, are incorporated into the computer program, which reads as follows:

```
A    AL.K = 10 + STEP(10,5)
R    RA.KL = (AL.K — LA.K)/TAB
C    TAB = 2
L    LA.K = LA.J + (DT)(RA.JK — AAR.JK)
N    LA = AL*5/7
R    AAR.KL = LA.K/AAT
C    AAT = 5
PRINT  AL,LA,RA,AAR
PLOT  AL = A,LA = L,RA = R,AAR = Z
SPEC  DT=1/LENGTH=20/PRTPER=1/PLTPER=1
```

Each line of the program, except for the last three, which specify the nature of the output, is preceded by a letter that identifies it as a rate (R), a level (L), an auxiliary (A), which functions as a component of a rate but is specified for ease of understanding, a constant (C), or an initial or starting value (N). All of the rate and level equations specify time points and time intervals, with the present time point being represented by K, the preceding point by J, and the next time point by L. The computer calculates everything for a given K and then repeats the process for the next time point by redefining J, K, and L, doing this for as many time points as are called for. The first line of the program calls for an Aspiration Level of 10, which is then incremented 10 units after a time interval of 5 (days). The constants Time for Achievement Buildup and Achievement Aging Time are set at 2 and 5, respectively, with the idea that decay occurs more slowly than the buildup process. The initial value for the Level of Achievement is taken as 5/7 of the Aspiration Level so that the system could begin with the Level of Achievement at equilibrium, enabling us to better understand any changes in it. The PRINT line specifies the four factors for which we desire numerical values to be printed over the period of time under investigation: AL, LA, RA, and AAR. The PLOT line specifies the abbreviations to be used for each of these factors when the computer plots a graph of changes in these factors. The SPEC, or specification, line determines the general format for printing and plotting: DT specifies the computation time interval, which may be less than the printperiod (PRTPER) and plotperiod (PLTPER) but never greater, and LENGTH determines the total number of time units (e.g., days) over which the simulation is to take place.

Model Behavior

Perhaps the key problem for the student of computer simulation is the mystery associated with the process, especially since he tends to begin with a sense of awe and frequently of fear in relation to this powerful instrument. To penetrate this mystery, I shall not bother to use the computer to determine the dynamic behavior of this aspiration-achievement model. Rather, I shall perform all calculations by hand. Of course, this is a much more time-consuming process. Also, in the case of complex models, it is not very practical because of the amount of time that would be involved in hand calculations. But for present purposes, this approach will enable us to understand the operations of the computer.

We shall calculate for two kinds of output, just as the computer does: a numerical output (printing) and a graphical output (plotting). What is required for the numerical output is a calculation of the values of each of the four factors—AL, LA, RA, and AAR—for each time unit (e.g., day) over the total length of 20 (days). In Table 8-1 I have listed these calculations, made by hand. Let me now explain the calculation process. At the beginning of the simulation, where $t = 0$, the Aspiration Level is at 10 units; it will remain there until the fifth day, when it moves to 20 and continues there for the remainder of the simulation. This was assumed in a rather arbitrary fashion so as to simulate a situation where, after a static period, aspiration moves up sharply and suddenly and then remains at the higher level. I wanted to explore the implications of this for the other factors.

When this jump in aspiration occurs on day 5, it does not instantaneously alter LA, the Level of Achievement, much as an instantaneous opening of a tap does not change the level of water in a beaker under the tap. At the moment under consideration (K), the Level of Achievement is determined by the sum of two factors: LA.J, or the Level of Achievement the previous day (7.14), and the Net Inflow during the period from J to K. We can determine that Net Inflow by examining the difference between RA.KL (column 4) and AAR.KL (column 5) for the *fourth* day; by looking at that preceding day, we in effect are converting a "KL" period to a "JK" period, in the same manner as the computer would do the calculation. Actually, this difference betwen the fourth and fifth columns must be multiplied by DT to determine Net Inflow, but since DT is 1 in this example, we can ignore it. Since $1.43 - 1.43 = 0$, we add nothing to

Table 8-1

Calculations for the Simulation of Level of
Aspiration and Achievement

t (days)	AL Aspiration Level	LA.K = LA.J + (1) (RA.JK− AAR.JK) Level of Achievement	RA.KL = (AL−LA.K)/2 Rate of Achievement	AAR.KL = LA.K/5 Achievement Aging Rate
0	10	7.14	1.43	1.43
1	10	7.14	1.43	1.43
2	10	7.14	1.43	1.43
3	10	7.14	1.43	1.43
4	10	7.14	1.43	1.43
5	20	7.14	6.43	1.43
6	20	12.14	3.93	2.43
7	20	13.64	3.18	2.73
8	20	14.09	2.95	2.82
9	20	14.22	2.89	2.84
10	20	14.27	2.86	2.85
11	20	14.28	2.86	2.86
12	20	14.28	2.86	2.86
13	20	14.28	2.86	2.86
.	.	.	.	.
.	.	.	.	.
20	20	14.28	2.86	2.86

LA.J to obtain LA.K, and LA.K remains unchanged from the fourth to the fifth day.

What does change, however, as a result of this sudden increase in Aspiration Level is RA.KL, or the Rate of Achievement between the fifth and sixth days, since this is based on the gap between the Aspiration Level (now at 20) and the Level of Achievement (still at 7.14). That gap, which is 12.86, must be divided by the Time for Achievement Buildup, which has been set at 2, and the result is that RA.KL = 6.43. This change in the Rate of Achievement occurs, then, because that rate is tied to the Aspiration Level, but this is not the case for the Achievement Aging Rate, which is tied to the Level of Achievement. Since there has been no change in LA.K during the fifth day, neither will there be a change in AAR.KL, which is calculated by dividing LA.K by 5, which is the constant assumed for the Achievement Aging Rate.

On day 6 we obtain a dramatic increase in the Level of Achievement, from 7.14 to 12.14, based on a Net Inflow of 5, which is the difference between the Rate of Achievement and the Achievement Aging Rate on the fourth day. However, the new Rate of Achievement (RA.KL) falls because the gap between aspiration and achievement is lessened due to the dramatic rise in achievement and the maintenance of aspiration at 20. The new Achievement Aging Rate, by contrast, rises, since it is directly proportional to a level of achievement that is higher. These trends continue on subsequent days: Level of Achievement continues to rise, only ever more slowly, since its increase is based on a Net Inflow Rate that is diminishing. And the Net Inflow Rate continues to decrease because the Rate of Achievement continues to decline because of the narrowing gap between aspiration and achievement, while at the same time the Achievement Aging Rate continues to rise because of the increasing—albeit slowly—Level of Achievement. At day 11 an equilibrium is once again reached—and maintained indefinitely—when the declining Rate of Achievement reaches the same value (2.86) as the rising Achievement Aging Rate, thus producing a Net Inflow Rate of zero.

Table 8-1 may now be used as the basis for graphing the model behavior of Aspiration Level, Level of Achievement, Rate of Achievement, and Achievement Aging Rate. The results are shown in Figure 8-4. On the

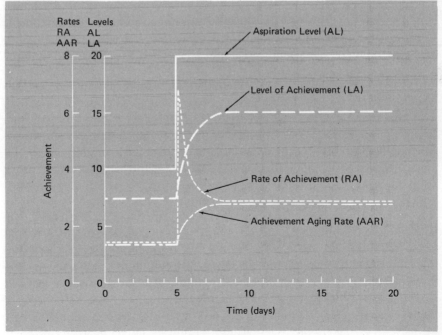

Figure 8-4.
Model Behavior: Level of Aspiration and Achievement.

abscissa, or X-axis, we have time in days, with 20 days in all and a calibration for each day. There are two different kinds of calibration for the ordinate, or Y-axis: there is a scale representing both the Aspiration Level and the Level of Achievement, going from 0 to 20; and there is a scale for the Rate of Achievement and the Achievement Aging Rate, which goes from 0 to 8. Here we see a repeat of what has just been discussed, only we can see more clearly what is happening in a graph. During the first five days we have an equilibrium situation: Aspiration Level is maintained at 10, Level of Achievement is maintained at 7.14, and the two rates are maintained at 1.43. On the fifth day Rate of Achievement goes up dramatically and then goes down almost as dramatically to meet the Achievement Aging Rate, which was coming up gradually. At the same time, we have a rapid increase in Level of Achievement after the fifth day, but this increase turns out to be a negative loop which asymptotically moves toward equilibrium at a level of 14.28, an equilibrium achieved at the same time (day 11) that the two rates meet to produce a Net Inflow of zero.

Implications

This modeling approach is sufficiently flexible so that it can be useful for three world views: mechanism, organicism, and pragmatism. Mechanistically, it should be obvious to the reader that the foregoing discussion has depended on an emphasis on the continuum, and that we have made a good deal of use of mathematical thinking. As a result, we are able to describe more of the complexities and dynamism in any given situation than with a formist approach. We should be aware that it is a large transition for the mind to move into a gradational mode of thinking, and we should also be aware of how much of our thought is nongradational. In addition, there is a focus here on processes of accumulation or integration along a given dimension or continuum, a focus that is also present in engineering applications of the differential equations. Such an approach builds on the power of ordinary language and carries it further. However formist it might be, language does manage to enable us to bind time and space to a degree, to pull past and future situations into the momentary situation. The cumulative approach resulting from an emphasis on the continuum and on accumulation does this also, only to a greater degree, for it pushes us to think of each situation in relation to an infinite series of situations, stretching into the past and future along that continuum. Also, the separation of levels from rates pushes us to think in a most dynamic way.

But just as in the case of the experiment, our paradigm here limits us in certain ways. For example, with a mechanistic paradigm we would tend to view all of the specific relationships within the model structure as fixed, and we would avoid seeking to learn under what conditions we can have an upward positive loop. Thinking in terms of concrete material things rather than intangibles, it would be difficult for us to conceive of levels that continue to rise unless there are flows from other levels, and not simply information flows. We would not tend to inquire, for example, as to the conditions that would produce a continuing increase in Aspiration Level. Neither would we tend to explore the conditions that might continually reduce the Achievement Aging Rate or increase the Rate of Achievement. Thus, the kind of model behavior illustrated in Figure 8-4 would mesh with our sense of the way the universe works and the only way in which it can work.

From an organicist perspective we might see phenomena as changing to a much greater degree, as in the case of Davies' concepts of expected need satisfaction and actual need satisfaction. We could also make use of the mechanistic idea of the continuum so that we would be able to view such changes along particular dimensions. However, we would still be faced with the problem of how such changes occur. In the Davies context, we would have difficulty in understanding the conditions that enable expected need satisfaction to pull actual need satisfaction up along with it, in contrast to a situation where actual need satisfaction pulls down expected need satisfaction. Our answers would tend to be based on an outward view: in the classroom situation, we would see the student's or the teacher's reference groups as the major basis for his raising or lowering his aspiration (in addition to his actual need satisfaction).

A pragmatist perspective would alert us both to the teacher's personality as a major source of what is occurring as well as to our own world view and theory as one specific lens through which we are viewing and constructing what we see. Bringing to bear my own personal teaching experience, the teacher who is *primarily* concerned with the reactions of the student will too easily lower his aspirations in the case of failure. I recall, for example, a teaching situation where I had great difficulty during a week of teaching in demonstrating to students in my Sociology of the Future class the techniques for doing a particular exercise that required them to apply a cybernetic perspective to Polak's *The Image of the Future*.[11] I was so convinced of the importance of the exercise that, despite all of the negative feedback, I maintained my aspiration level the following week and succeeded in helping students pull themselves up to doing the exercise and finding it meaningful. Within this pragmatist perspective the tension between individual and group can be more easily maintained and can help the investigator to probe the complexities of how to achieve a continuing rise in expected need satisfaction along with actual need satisfaction. In addition, there is a focus on the role of the investigator. The crucial question is not, as in the organicist tradition, how can I develop a model to explain a given situation. Rather, it is how can I teach myself to think

[11] Fred Polak, *The Image of the Future* (San Francisco: Jossey-Bass, 1973).

in a more complex way so that I can understand a given situation. Yet a pragmatist orientation is, by itself, not nearly as powerful a research tool as an orientation stemming from pragmatism combined with organicism, mechanism, and formism.

8.5 Summary

Techniques of simulation and computer simulation carry forward the experimental attitude to the point where the researcher employs his theoretical framework as a tool in the construction of the research situation. The two approaches vary in the degree to which they structure that situation: computer simulation functions as a logic machine, grinding out the implications of an initial theory, whereas simulation, or gaming, techniques allow participants a range of options within the framework of a set of rules. Both succeed in generating information on the nature of processes by dealing with many different points in time. Yet despite the potential of these techniques, they are limited by the investigator's awareness of the paradigm and theory he is using to structure the simulation.

One method of computer simulation that appears to be particularly promising for the social scientist is system dynamics. By incorporating a vital part of the physical science tradition in the form of the differential equations, system dynamics is well designed to deal with rapid change as well as accumulation in the form of upward or downward positive loops. Here again, the investigator remains a prisoner of his degree of knowledge of his own paradigm. Although system dynamics has functioned primarily within the mechanistic paradigm, it is well suited to the organicist and pragmatist paradigms as well.

Exercises

1. Develop a research design that combines experimental and simulation techniques for data collection. How do the two kinds of data supplement each other?

2. Play Gamson's SIMSOC, using a system of record keeping (such as note-taking, tape recordings, and observation by nonparticipants) to keep track of what is going one. Now try to analyze this record. Try the procedure once more, only this time define a problem you are vitally interested in investigating (based on your earlier session with SIMSOC), and focus your data around that problem. Can you gain more insight into the dynamics of the game in this latter way?

3. Write a modification of the computer program listed on page 196, changing the first line, the two constants, the initial condition (N), and

the specification line. Now calculate a revised Table 8-1 and a revised Figure 8-4.

4. Compare the model structure and behavior described in Section 8.4 with the model of the aging process described in Section 5.5. How do they differ? How are they similar? Try to apply the model of Section 5.5 to the classroom situation discussed in this chapter: does this give you any additional insights?

Annotated References

DUTTON, JOHN M., AND WILLIAM H. STARBUCK (eds.). *Computer Simulation of Human Behavior*. New York: John Wiley & Sons, Inc., 1971. The authors have pulled together thirty-four illustrations of computer simulation and added a number of pieces that help the reader to find his way around. The major sections are: introduction, individuals, individuals who interact, individuals who aggregate (including the Gullahorns' study), individuals who aggregate and interact, and methodological issues.

INBAR, MICHAEL, AND CLARICE S. STOLL. *Simulation and Gaming in Social Science*. New York: The Free Press, 1972. This book, modeled after Hammond's *Sociologists at Work,* presents twelve case studies of simulation and computer simulation—including SIMSOC—along with explanatory material.

RASER, JOHN R. *Simulation and Society: An Exploration of Scientific Gaming*. Boston: Allyn & Bacon, Inc., 1969. This is a concise and penetrating discussion of the nature of noncomputer and computer simulation. It is informed by a broad background of knowledge of the social sciences.

chapter *9*

Interviews, Questionnaires, and Surveys

Interviews and questionnaires are the most widely used methods of data construction in sociology, perhaps for reasons analogous to the importance of speech and writing in human communication. Through these techniques the social researcher endeavors to probe not only the goals and beliefs of the individual but also the values and norms of groups. In addition, the investigator is interested in patterns of interaction as well as other kinds of observable behavior, and these instruments can provide him with important information here as well. Further, in these ways we are able to transcend—far more than in the experiment or noncomputer simulation—the limitations of the time period over which the research takes place, inquiring into the distant past as well as the distant future.

Chapter 9 is divided into two parts, one about measurement and scaling and the other about various aspects of interview, questionnaire, and survey techniques. In Chapter 6 we discussed some fundamental ideas about the nature of measurement and scaling, but it remains to move from those ideas to more concrete procedures and illustrations. Historically, it is within the survey context that most knowledge about measurement and scaling has developed. As for the survey itself—using this term generically to include particular techniques of interviewing and questionnaire construction—it is essential that we explore its liabilities as well as its assets. If progress in social research has not been rapid enough to respond to the pressures of societal problems, then survey techniques must certainly carry a major portion of the responsibility for that failure.

9.1 Measurement and Scaling in the Survey

As we delve into the mysteries of particular scaling techniques used by survey researchers, let us not lose sight of our over-all direction: to see such procedures as possible paths for helping us to obtain information feedback on problems we have defined of theoretical and paradigmatic importance. Every specific procedure embodies within itself not merely a theoretical framework but a paradigmatic world view. By probing scaling procedures, we gain additional theoretical and paradigmatic insights, and as a result we are able to understand the shortcomings of existing measurement procedures. More important, we can develop approaches for going beyond those shortcomings. I shall take up in this section four procedures: Likert-type scaling (including the technique of summated ratings), Guttman scaling, Thurstone scaling, and magnitude estimation. As devices for improving precision, these scaling techniques are not better than the degree of measurement reliability and validity involved, and the latter is, of course, based on how well a measurement participates in, and contributes to, our theoretical and paradigmatic framework.

Likert-Type Scaling

A single item often is inadequate for the accurate measurement of a given variable. A set of items—properly selected and analyzed—frequently will yield greater precision, that is, will help us to move further along the continuum from nominal to ordinal to interval to ratio scale. Also, it is frequently the case that a greater degree of reliability and validity can be developed for a scale constructed from a set of items than for a single item. This is particularly important, since the precision of a scale cannot help us without a comparable degree of reliability and validity.

Likert-type scales—also called summated rating scales—are very easy to develop and make good intuitive sense. Indeed, there would be a good chance that if the reader were asked to devise a simple way to combine a number of questionnaire items into a scale that gives the items equal weight, he would hit on this procedure. To explain the procedure, I will use as an illustration a set of eight items from the questionnaire to be discussed in Section 9.2 (the same one that has been the basis for preceding illustrations of pragmatist research).

GENERAL ATTITUDES

Do you agree or disagree with each of the following statements?
CIRCLE THE ANSWER THAT BEST APPLIES.

8. The ordinary man should depend on the experts to tell him the best ways of doing things.
   1. Disagree [1]
   2. Not sure [0]
   3. Agree [0]

9. I frequently mix business with pleasure.
   1. Disagree [0]
   2. Not sure [0]
   3. Agree [1]

10. Man's intelligence is fixed at birth, and there is nothing that he can do to change it.
    1. Disagree [1]
    2. Not sure [0]
    3. Agree [0]

11. It's good for a person to think about the past and the future.	1. Disagree	[0]
	2. Not sure	[0]
	3. Agree	[1]
12. Nowadays, it's possible for an ordinary person to rise very far in life.	1. Disagree	[0]
	2. Not sure	[0]
	3. Agree	[1]
13. I try to do things that are too difficult for me to do so that I'll learn things I don't know.	1. Disagree	[0]
	2. Not sure	[0]
	3. Agree	[1]
14. I usually compare my work to the work of others rather than to the work I have done in the past.	1. Disagree	[1]
	2. Not sure	[0]
	3. Agree	[0]
15. When I'm in a new situation I usually think about what others expect of me more than what I expect of others.	1. Disagree	[1]
	2. Not sure	[0]
	3. Agree	[0]

These questions are designed to get at a broad dimension: the degree to which the individual believes in a pragmatist paradigm. For example, an individual who depends on the experts or who compares his work mainly to others or who thinks largely about what others expect of him is outer-oriented; one who does not mix business with pleasure or think about the past and the future sees his roles in a formist way; and one who feels that his intelligence is fixed and that he cannot rise very far and who does not try to learn to do difficult things is not very developmental. By combining all of these questions into a scale, we are able to take into account a number of different aspects of the pragmatist world view.

The numbers in brackets at the right-hand side of each question do not appear on the actual questionnaire. They constitute a weighting of 1 for a pragmatist response and 0 for a less pragmatist response. I could equally well have attempted to differentiate three different weights for each question, but I am sufficiently unsure about what "not sure" might mean to different respondents that I decided to combine those responses with the less pragmatist ones. To give each respondent a total score on this scale of pragmatist attitudes, I simply add his scores on all of the eight items. Thus, an individual at the lowest end of the scale would have a zero, and an individual at the highest end an eight.

Rensis Likert has developed a more elaborate technique for obtaining summated ratings,[1] a technique that may easily be modified so that it can be adapted to any particular research situation:

1. There are five categories for responses: "strongly agree," "agree," "undecided," "disagree," and "strongly disagree."

[1] Gardner Murphy and Rensis Likert, *Public Opinion and the Individual* (New York: Harper, 1937).

2. Statements are classified into those that are favorable and those that are unfavorable, and approximately the same number of each type is utilized.

3. For the favorable statements, the weights given to "strongly agree," "agree," "undecided," "disagree," and "strongly disagree" are 4, 3, 2, 1, and 0, respectively. For unfavorable statements, the weights are 0, 1, 2, 3, and 4, respectively. Thus, agreement with favorable statements and disagreement with unfavorable statements are treated as equivalent.

4. A large number of statements are given to a group of respondents who are representative of those for whom the questionnaire is being constructed.

5. The responses are analyzed to determine which items discriminate best between the high-scoring individuals (on the scale as a whole) and the low scorers, and those items to which high scorers and low scorers respond similarly are eliminated. This is known as an *item analysis*.

The idea behind (2) is to avoid giving the respondent any hint as to the researcher's own opinions. However, this is not completely possible because what one researcher defines as an extreme item might be defined by another researcher as a very moderate item. As for (4), Likert is using a criterion validity approach (see Section 6.1), with a pretest group used as a criterion for the one he is interested in. One problem here is a lack of explicit consideration of theoretical relationships, as would occur with an orientation to construct validity. An alternative approach would be to put in whatever time would be necessary in prior work with a small sample of the group one is interested to test hypotheses; such work would simultaneously test for construct validity, as in the case of the pretest of Section 2.4. Concerning (5), one problem is that the researcher's own paradigm may stand in the way of his developing items that achieve substantial discrimination, since his paradigm may agree with that of most of the respondents. The remedy here is the researcher's awareness of his own assumptions as compared to those of his respondents.

Guttman Scaling[2]

One problem with the Likert-type, or summated, scale stems from the fact that the items are weighted equally. Suppose, for example, that item

---

[2] The most thorough treatment of Guttman scaling is contained in the original volume that presented it: Samuel A. Stouffer, Louis Guttman, Edward A. Suchman, Paul F. Lazarsfeld, Shirley A. Star, and John A. Clausen, *Measurement and Prediction* (Princeton, N.J.: Princeton U. P., 1950). This is one of a series of four volumes on the American soldier in World War II. For additional perspectives, see Matilda and John Riley and Jackson Toby, *Sociological Studies in Scale Analysis* (New Brunswick, N.J.: Rutgers U. P., 1954).

10 is far more important than the others, and that if an individual thinks his intelligence is fixed, this indicates a very negative orientation to pragmatism, despite pragmatist responses on several other questions. The Guttman approach constitutes an effort to calibrate a scale, just as we might calibrate a thermometer: we strive to arrange the items along a continuum from low to high. Also, the technique incorporates procedures for testing whether the axioms for simple order (Section 6.2) are satisfied by any scale we produce.

For example, the third axiom for simple order was:

(3) If $x < y$ and $y < z$, then $x < z$.

In the example used previously, if basketball team x loses more than half of the time to team y, and team y tends to lose to team z, then team x must also tend to lose to team z for this axiom to be satisfied. Let us now apply this approach to the pragmatist items just discussed. Figure 9-1 displays hypothetical relationships among these items that would enable us to assess whether this axiom is satisfied. Just as in the case of the Likert-type scale, a 1 is a pragmatist response and a nonpragmatist response is 0. To provide a simple illustration, I have assumed that the questionnaire items from 8 to 15 are also in the correct order for calibrating a scale of pragmatism, with 8 being at the pragmatist end and 15 at the nonpragmatist end. According to this purely hypothetical assumption, only 10% of respondents are pragmatist for item 8; but if a respondent is pragmatist on this extreme item, he will also be pragmatist on all of the other items.

Groupings of Respondents					Item Number				
Scale Type	%	8	9	10	11	12	13	14	15
A	10	1	1	1	1	1	1	1	1
B	10	0	1	1	1	1	1	1	1
C	10	0	0	1	1	1	1	1	1
D	10	0	0	0	1	1	1	1	1
E	10	0	0	0	0	1	1	1	1
F	10	0	0	0	0	0	1	1	1
G	10	0	0	0	0	0	0	1	1
H	10	0	0	0	0	0	0	0	1
I	20	0	0	0	0	0	0	0	0
Cumulative % "1"		10	20	30	40	50	60	70	80

Figure 9-1.
Item Response Patterns for Guttman Scaling.

Thus, the A group of respondents are extremely pragmatist. The B group responds pragmatically on all questions except 8. Combining the two groups, we could say that 20% of respondents answer either 8 or 9 in a pragmatist way. As we continue down the rows we find the same patterns repeated: individuals who respond in a pragmatist way on an extreme item will also respond in that way on all less extreme items.

In relation to the third axiom for simple order, let us focus on whether individuals in the different scale types satisfy this axiom. I shall define "precedes," or "$<$" between two scale types, or categories, as follows: A precedes B if there are more individuals who are pragmatist on 9 but not 8 than the number of individuals who are pragmatist on 8 but not 9. In Figure 9-1, there are no individuals who are pragmatist on 8 but not 9, but 10% of the sample are pragmatist on 9 but not 8, thus indicating that A $<$ B. The same is true for the relation between B and C: B $<$ C. Now, we may also observe that the transitive relationship holds: A $<$ C, since there are no individuals who are pragmatist on 8 but not 10, but 10% of the sample are pragmatist on 10 but not 8. Pursuing this approach, we would find that A $<$ B $<$ C $<$ D $<$ E $<$ F $<$ G $<$ H $<$ I, and that the relationships are transitive up and down the line. As for the first and second axioms for simple order, these specify that we must not define distinct scale types unless we can also distinguish between them on this criterion of precedence, and that in a situation where we can make such a distinction, we should also treat the individuals as located within distinct types. These axioms are also satisfied if the third axiom is satisfied, since all of the scale types are distinguished from one another and a precedence relation occurs between any pair.

The significance of the Guttman scaling approach is that it provides procedures enabling the researcher to test for the existence of a simple order among a set of items, thus helping him to move from nominal scales to ordinal scales. He might even desire to see whether such a scale has more mathematical properties than those he tested for, perhaps using it as he would a ratio scale and testing it for construct validity. If it does not work in this way, then he might work further with the scale, perhaps using magnitude estimation procedures to develop his ordinal scale into a ratio scale. Thus, Guttman scaling enables the investigator to take an important step forward in incorporating mathematical properties within his measurements. As a result, it paves the way for formulating his theory in mathematical or cybernetic terms.

Guttman scaling procedures have undergone two technological transformations. In the "old days," following the appearance of *The American Soldier* volumes (such as *Measurement and Prediction*) in the late forties and in 1950, a "scalogram board"—described in Volume 4[3]—was used.

---

[3] Volume 4 is the *Measurement and Prediction* book cited above.

A next step was the use of electrical-mechanical data processing equipment, such as the IBM counter-sorter, which could process a much larger number of respondents more rapidly than the scalogram board, which had to be used with a sample of respondents. Most recently, we have the development of Guttman scaling programs for electronic computers, and it is possible to perform highly complex scaling procedures on ever larger samples in a matter of minutes, once the data has been made available to the computer. As in the case of computer simulation, what is most important is that the researcher understand the essential operations, regardless of which technology he is employing. I shall list these in order of occurrence:

1. Select or construct those items that you wish to scale. According to Guttman the most important task within the entire scaling process is a conceptual one, and no mechanical procedure can substitute for it. A primary consideration here is construct validity: does the set of items point toward a concept that is enmeshed in a system of relationships with other important concepts? Without such construct validity, a scale may satisfy the axioms for simple order and yet have little utility. The more clearcut are one's assumptions and theory, the easier it is to construct a meaningful set of scalable items.

2. Dichotomize each of the items in your scale, deciding which responses should receive a 1 and which should receive a 0, just as with the pragmatist attitude scale.

3. Calculate the percentage of respondents in the entire sample who are in the 1 category for each item. This is analogous to the "Cumulative %" row at the bottom of Figure 9-1. Arrange the items in order from the one with the smallest percentage in the 1 category to the one with the largest, as in Figure 9-1.

4. Revise your definitions of 1 and 0 (cutting points) and/or eliminate some items to help you achieve unique scale types with definite precedence relations among them by developing a spread in the percentage of respondents in the 1 category for each item. In the pragmatist attitude scale for example, you might define some of the "not sure" responses as 1 rather than 0, or you might decide to eliminate one of a pair of items when both yield about the same percentage of respondents in the 1 category. There is nothing holy about the particular procedures used to form the scale. The most important test for the scale is the test for construct validity. If it does well there, we shall of course become much more particular about how to improve the scale and fussier about our procedures.

5. Obtain the distribution of responses within each of the perfect scale types (shown in Figure 9-1) as well as within each of the nonscale

types (e.g., 1, 1, 1, 0, 1, 1, 1, 1). This can be a time-consuming operation, especially if there are more than four or five items in the scale, since there are so many possible nonscale types. With an IBM counter-sorter, thé procedure would be to sort one item into its 1 and 0 piles, then to sort each of these piles into 1 and 0 piles on the basis of the second item, resulting in four piles, and continuing this procedure for each subsequent item. Figure 9-2 illustrates the sorting procedure for a four-item scale. Note the five perfect scale types (S): 1111, 0111, 0011, 0001, and 0000. All the other emerging categories are nonscale types (N).

6. Test for scalability by calculating the "coefficient of reproducibility."[4] This coefficient measures the degree of accuracy with which we are able to reproduce the responses of individuals if we know only the perfect scale type closest to their response patterns. It is calculated as follows:

$$\text{Coefficient of Reproducibility} = 1 - \frac{\text{No. of errors}}{\text{No. of questions} \times \text{No. of respondents}}.$$

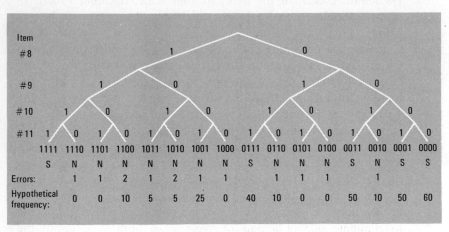

Item																
#8				1								0			
#9		1				0				1				0		
#10	1		0		1		0		1		0		1		0	
#11	1 0	1 0	1 0	1 0	1 0	1 0	1 0	1 0								
	1111	1110	1101	1100	1011	1010	1001	1000	0111	0110	0101	0100	0011	0010	0001	0000
	S	N	N	N	N	N	N	N	S	N	N	N	S	N	S	S
Errors:		1	1	2	1	2	1	1		1	1	1		1		
Hypothetical frequency:	0	0	10	5	5	25	0	40	10	0	0	50	10	50	60	

Figure 9-2.
Sorting Schema for Guttman Scaling.

[4] A more rigorous procedure for counting errors is presented by W. H. Goodenough in "A Technique for Scale Analysis," *Educational and Psychological Measurement,* **4** (1944), pp. 179–90. For a statistical test that takes some of the arbitrariness out of the requirement of .90, see Leon Festinger, "The Treatment of Qualitative Data by 'Scale Analysis,'" *Psychological Bulletin,* **44** (1947), pp. 149–61. See also Louis Guttman's reply in "On Festinger's Evaluation of Scale Analysis," *Psychological Bulletin,* **44** (1947), pp. 451–65.

An error is defined as a departure from the nearest perfect scale type. Thus, for example, the pattern 1101 contains only one error, since it could be changed to the perfect scale type 1111 by changing the 0 to a 1. On the other hand, the pattern 1100 contains two errors because we would have to either change both 1's to 0's or both 0's to 1's. In calculating the number of errors, we must multiply the number of errors associated with a given nonscale type by the number of respondents in that nonscale type, and we must then sum the errors for all of the nonscale types.

To illustrate the calculation of the coefficient of reproducibility, let us use the frequencies (bottom row) from the hypothetical four-item scale of Figure 9-2. Adding the frequencies in that row, the total number of respondents comes to 265. As for the number of errors, we must add the following (going from left to right): 1×0, 1×0, 2×10, 1×5, and so on. The resulting total number of errors comes to 80, and applying the formula for the coefficient of reproducibility, we have

$$\text{Coefficient of Reproducibility} = 1 - \frac{80}{4 \times 265} = 1 - .08 = .92.$$

A coefficient of reproducibility of .90 or more is generally considered to constitute evidence for the "scalability" of the scale, that is, evidence for ordinality.

7. Assign scores to each of the items and proceed to test for construct validity. For example, the number of 1's in a given perfect scale type can be counted, as in the summated rating technique. For the nonscale types, one can assign to a given type the same score as its closest perfect scale type, or one might wish to cut corners and simply count the number of 1's, as in the case of the perfect scale types. It would also be useful to give a unique score to each of the nonscale types so that it could be analyzed further. In testing for construct validity one is, at the same time, using the scale in analyzing one's data by relating it to other measurements.

8. On the basis of the results of the construct validity analysis, the investigator may wish to improve his scale. He might begin by picking out the nonscale types that contain the largest numbers of respondents and attempting to discover what factors produced those types by cross-tabulation of membership in a given nonscale type with other items or scales in the questionnaire. He might also wish to move from an ordinal scale to an interval scale via Thurstone scaling or to a ratio scale by developing procedures for mag-

nitude estimation.[5] Descriptions of both techniques follow in this section.

Thurstone Scaling

The Thurstone method of equal-appearing intervals[6] constitutes an effort to go beyond the development of a set of items satisfying the axioms of simple order so as to produce an interval scale, that is, one where the distances between scores are meaningful. Although there are severe limitations to the procedure—to be discussed subsequently—the approach is highly instructive.

1. Choose the concept or variable you would like to measure and proceed to construct or gather together many statements bearing on the concept. In the original description of the method, 130 statements were used developing a scale for measuring attitudes toward the church.

2. Obtain the cooperation of as many judges as possible—perhaps fifteen or more—in rating each statement with reference to its degree of "favorableness" or "unfavorableness." In the original study, each judge was given a large number of cards, each of which contained a statement to be rated. In addition, each judge was given a set of eleven cards containing the letters *A* to *K* arranged as follows:

Unfavorable				Neutral					Favorable	
A	*B*	*C*	*D*	*E*	*F*	*G*	*H*	*I*	*J*	*K*

Each judge was asked to sort the statement cards into the eleven piles represented by the lettered cards, separating them on the basis of their varying degrees of favorableness or unfavorableness.

3. Judgments from those judges believed to have sorted carelessly are omitted. Statements receiving widely different ratings from different judges are eliminated.

4. Each of the remaining statements is given a scale value corresponding to the median, or middle, position to which it is assigned by the judges. Here, pile A is designated with a score of 1, pile B with 2, and the remaining piles with scores that increase to 11 for pile K.

[5] For a technique of scale analysis—the "scale discrimination technique"—that incorporates some of the techniques developed by Likert and Thurstone, see A. L. Edwards and F. P. Kilpatrick, "Scale Analysis and the Measurement of Social Attitudes," *Psychometrika,* **13** (1948), pp. 99–114.

[6] L. L. Thurstone and E. J. Chave, *The Measurement of Attitude* (Chicago: U. of Chicago, 1929).

5. A final selection of about twenty items is made with the aim of obtaining an even spread from A to K. Preference is given to items with the highest degree of agreement among the judges. Thus, for example, an item placed in piles D, E, F, G, and H would be rejected in favor of one placed only in E, F, and G, other things being equal. An alternate form of the scale may also be constructed as a means of testing for reliability.

The value of this approach lies in its careful attempt to develop a series of items that enable the investigator to place individuals along an interval scale with reference to some continuum. Granting the imperfection of all procedures, the Thurstone techniques are such that a great deal of agreement among judges may be obtained provided that they are motivated to do their work with care and provided that the overall concept and the particular items are constructed with perceptiveness. There are also fundamental problems with the approach. As distinct from Guttman scaling, no clear-cut tests are used to assess whether the resulting scale satisfies the axioms for interval scales. Also, the judges are not the same as the respondents, and it is possible that the two groups might greatly differ in their evaluations of the various items. In addition, Thurstone is adopting the formist emphasis on criterion validity—with his establishment of the separate group of judges as the basis for his criterion—and is neglecting construct validity. How good a given scale is should be determined pragmatically, on the basis of what it can do for our theoretical understanding, and this is only achieved in small measure when a criterion validity approach is used exclusively.

One approach to remedying these deficiencies is to make the respondents the judges, as in the case of Guttman scaling. Here, the problem of differences between judges and respondents is eliminated. The researcher might also work hard with respondents, teaching them to do careful work, thus perhaps helping to achieve a more precise interval scale. A stumbling block to such a procedure is the presence of an organicist paradigm within the researcher, leading him to think of himself as a passive observer more than as an active creator of data. Thus, he would hesitate to take an active teaching role. Such a role, as we shall shortly see, is essential in the case of magnitude estimation procedures. Within a pragmatist paradigm, the researcher assumes that the data are in large measure shaped by himself, and he seeks to uncover the forces involved in that shaping.

Magnitude Estimation

If ratio scales are so important as a basis for bringing to bear on social research the powerful tools of mathematics and cybernetics, what is holding up the social scientist in developing them? Perhaps the major problem—as in the case of making respondents into judges in the Thurstone scaling technique—is the researcher's organicist paradigm. Ratio scaling procedures call for a very active role on his part, analogous to his role in simulation procedures: he must create or structure a situation so as to enable his respondents to "think ratio." If he believes that this constitutes interference with "the truth," defined as what emerges from passive observation, then he will not adopt such a role. However, since a passive role also involves investigator effect, their is little justification for it as a standard operating procedure. From a pragmatist perspective, ratio scales will not appear from our environment if we just wait for them to come: we must learn to construct them. The techniques are available, and they await a willing spirit.

In Section 6.2, especially Figure 6-5, I presented a brief illustration of magnitude estimation, a procedure for the construction of ratio scales. There are many illustrations of this procedure in the psychophysical literature, but its use in the social psychological or sociological literature is as

---

FORM 1

Number: ____

Date: _____   Interviewer: _____   Observer: _____

If a college graduate has 100 units of status, what would be the status of a man—

who is a:		*who makes each year:*	
Insurance salesman:	____	$1,500	____
Executive: large corporation	____	$3,000	____
Plumber:	____	$4,500	____
Garbage truck owner:	____	$6,000	____
Architect:	____	$8,800	____
Surgeon:	____	$12,000	____
University professor:	____	$18,000	____
Fishboat owner:	____	$26,000	____
Shoeshine man:	____	$38,000	____
County judge:	____	$54,000	____
Carpenter:	____	$78,000	____
Tenant farmer:	____	$110,000	____
School teacher:	____		
Atomic physicist:	____		

who has completed (just) . . .

2nd grade	____	High school	____
4th grade	____	College	100
8th grade	____	A doctor's degree	____
		4 years specialization beyond doctorate	____

yet quite sparse.[7] The Hamblin illustration from Section 6.2—which deals with the construction of a ratio scale of status—was presented along with a detailed discussion of the magnitude estimation techniques involved in developing that scale. The basic instrument Hamblin used was the interview schedule as shown on the preceding page.[8]

What was crucial for Hamblin in his investigations was not the above instrument alone but, rather, that instrument in the context of a series of procedures designed to teach respondents to think in ratio terms. The training process is vital for Hamblin: he maintains that "ten sets of estimates from well-trained observers are better than 100 sets from untrained or confused observers." His instructions for setting up such training are:

1. Interview observers individually. Start by teaching them how to estimate magnitudes using numbers. Using an unlined paper with 9 dots printed 1.3, 2, 4, 5.5, 8, 11, 14, and 19 centimeters from the bottom, give the following instruction:
"We'll start by teaching you how to use numbers to measure things. I want you to judge how far these dots are from the bottom of this paper. If this dot (point to the 4 cm dot) is 100 units from the bottom of the paper, how far from the bottom of the paper is this dot? (Point to the 8 cm dot) This dot? (Point to the 2 cm dot)"
If the observer gives numbers that approximate the appropriate ratios, have him give the distance estimates for the other dots. If the observer gives numbers that are badly out of ratio (for example, a 110 instead of approximately 200 for the 8 cm dot and a 90 instead of around 50 for the 2 cm dot), proceed as follows:
"Is this (8 cm) dot a third as far, half as far, twice as far, three times as far, or four times as far as this (4 cm) dot?" The observer will usually reply, "Twice as far."
"If it is twice as far, and this first dot is 100 units from the bottom, then how many units is this second dot from the bottom?". . . .
2. Once the distance estimates are completed, plot the data on logarithmic coordinates [as in Figure 6-5, with the observer's estimates on the Y-axis and the distances on the X-axis]. . . .
3. "Where are you from?" "————." "In your home town you probably noticed that some people were looked up to, others were looked down on—in other words that people were given a different amount of prestige, respect, or status. This could be due to many things, income, dress, education, occupation, one's home, one's looks, one's car, etc. Today, however, I want you to estimate the status of a number of individuals on the

---

[7] In sociology, see Robert L. Hamblin et al., *The Humanization Process* (New York: Wiley-Interscience, 1971), and T. Sellin and M. E. Wolfgang, *The Measurement of Delinquency* (New York: Wiley, 1964). For a review of the literature by a leading contributor to the technique, see S. S. Stevens, "Psychophysics and Social Scaling" (Morristown, N.J.: General Learning Press, 1972).
[8] Robert L. Hamblin, "Ratio Measurement and Sociological Theory: A Critical Analysis," unpublished manuscript (St. Louis: Department of Sociology, Washington U., 1966), p. 78.

basis of one item of information: their occupation, their income, or their education. Let us assume that a college graduate has 100 units of status. If another individual has twice as much status in your judgment, give him a 200 . . . If a man has no status at all give him a zero. Okay?"

Using Form 1 [see above] and filling in the blanks with numbers as you go, proceed with the questions, such as the following: "If a college graduate has 100 units of status, how much status would a plumber have? a janitor? a railroad engineer? How much status would a man have who makes $54,000 per year? $8,800? $1,500? How much status would a man have who completed the fourth grade? A doctor's degree? High school?"

4. At least once, when you are about half through, check on ratios . . . If there is any question even, it is better to start again, perhaps after going through the instructions a second time. . . .

5. If additional series of estimates are taken from an observer, let him rest periodically, about 2 minutes for every 10 minutes of estimations. Keep good eye contact, show continued interest, and he will ordinarily respond accordingly. You may give the observer previous estimates when he asks, but usually he will not ask if you sit so he *cannot* see the numbers you have written down. . . .

6. Usually 30 sets of estimations are desirable; 2 sets from 15 observers or 1 set from 30. Remember, however, it is accuracy and not the amount of data that counts most.[9]

Hamblin has come a long way from the organicist paradigm of the passive interviewer or observer. His procedures include a means for testing the degree to which his respondents are in fact making estimates on a ratio scale. For Hamblin, it is possible for almost everyone to learn to think in this way if sufficient care is taken to teach him. One problem is that many of us have learned, as a result of responding to numerous questionnaires, to learn to think in other ways, such as in ordinal or interval terms. However, those experiences can also serve as a prelude to thinking in ratio terms, since a ratio scale includes both ordinal and interval characteristics. A far more serious problem is that the formist paradigm embodied in language, culture, and personalities structures our thinking largely in nominal scale terms, and it takes some learning to make the transition to thinking in ratio scale terms.

9.2 The Survey

Survey techniques generally are thought of more as an art than a science, but perhaps both should be involved. Perhaps we should bring to bear on survey research procedures whatever scientific knowledge we have about human behavior. Perhaps, also, we should recognize the present limitations

---

[9] Ibid., pp. 72–76.

of that knowledge, and learn as much as we can by becoming familiar with techniques used in the past. In this section we take up three major topics: survey design, degree of structure, and interviewing techniques.

Survey Design

Before getting too deeply into specific procedures, we must remind ourselves of the importance of the definition of the problem, which involves bringing to bear our paradigmatic and theoretical perspectives on the research situation and, in addition, involves our developing—motivationally—a sense of problem about what we wish to do. It is this definition of the problem, along with continuing redefinitions of it as we move along the research process, that makes good research possible. Without it, we are only going through the motions of research.

In this section we examine four aspects of designing surveys or planning interview or questionnaire studies: administration, one-shot and sequential data, surveys and experiments, and the ethics of survey research. Concerning administration, the survey researcher must organize many different kinds of tasks into a pattern that produces effective research; in addition to creative intellectual work, he also frequently produces an *ad hoc* research organization which generates its own set of problems. The data he generally attempts to obtain are one-shot or cross-sectional data, and as a result have many built-in limitations. By comparing survey research with experimental designs, and by combining features of both, he frequently can find solutions to his problems. He must also face general ethical issues, and by confronting them, he may also learn to improve his research instruments.

Administration. C. Wright Mills, in his *The Sociological Imagination,* argued convincingly about the dangers to creative research stemming from the development of a "bureaucratic ethos." Writing about the young social scientists who inhabit the various research bureaucracies, he states:

> I have seldom seen one of these young men, once he is well caught up, in a condition of genuine intellectual puzzlement. And I have never seen any passionate curiosity about a great problem, the sort of curiosity that compels the mind to travel anywhere and by any means, to re-make itself if necessary, in order *to find out*. These young men are less restless than methodical; less imaginative than patient; above all, they are dogmatic—in all the historical and theological meanings of the term. Some of this is of course merely part of the sorry intellectual condition of so many students now in American colleges and universities, but I do believe it is more evident among the research technicians of abstracted empiricism.
>
> They have taken up social research as a career; they have come early to an extreme specialization, and they have acquired an indifference or

a contempt for "social philosophy"—which means to them "writing books out of other books" or "merely speculating." Listening to their conversations, trying to gauge the quality of their curiosity, one finds a deadly limitation of mind. The social worlds about which so many scholars feel ignorant do not puzzle them.[10]

In this book, Mills has much to say about the dangers of specializing in the details of research techniques without the guidance of theory, designating this as "abstracted empiricism." He also indicts a concern with "grand theory" without a corresponding concern for the kinds of empirical research that would provide feedback for that theory. In his chapter on the bureaucratic ethos, he shows how narrow points of view become structured bureaucratically into research organizations, with a resulting loss of creative imagination.

If we accept Mills' ideas on the dangers of the bureaucratic ethos, what can be done about the situation? Is Mills simply suggesting that the researcher should not work within a large research organization? Or can the bureaucratic ethos creep into very small-scale projects as well? And exactly how does it generate forces antithetical to the research process? Julius Roth has a great deal to say about these questions in his article on "hired hand research," where his focus is on lower-level research employees, such as interviewers and observers:

> There is no reason to believe that a hired hand in the scientific research business will behave any different from those in other areas of productive activity. It is far more reasonable to assume that their behavior will be similar. They want to make as much money as they can. . . . They also want to avoid difficult, embarrassing, inconvenient, time-consuming situations as well as those activities which make no sense to them. (Thus, they fail to make some assigned observations or to ask some of the interview questions.) At the same time they want to give the right impression to their supervisors—at least right enough so that their material will be accepted and they will be kept on the job. (Thus, they modify or fabricate portions of the reports in order to give the boss what he *seems* to want.) They do not want to "look stupid" by asking too many questions, so they are likely to make a stab at what they think the boss wants—e.g., make a guess at a coding category rather than having it resolved through channels.
>
> Even those who start out with the notion that this is an important piece of work which they must do right will succumb to the hired hand mentality when they realize that their suggestions and criticisms are ignored, that their assignment does not allow for any imagination or creativity, that they will receive no credit for the final product, in short, that they have been hired to do somebody else's dirty work. When this

[10] C. Wright Mills, *The Sociological Imagination* (New York: Grove, 1961), p. 105.

realization has sunk in, they will no longer bother to be careful or accurate or precise. They will cut corners to save time and energy. They will fake parts of their reporting. They will not put themselves out for something in which they have no stake except in so far as extrinsic pressures force them to. . . .

I do not want to give the impression that the hired hand mentality with its attendant difficulties is simply a characteristic of the large-scale on-going research organization. We may find it at all size levels, including the academic man hiring a single student to do his research chores. . . .

From specific examples from the research world and by analogy from research on hired hands in other occupational spheres, I am convinced that research tasks carried out by hired hands are characterized, not rarely or occasionally, but *typically,* by restricted production, failure to carry out portions of the task, avoidance of the more unpleasant or difficult aspects of the research, and outright cheating. The results of research done in part or wholly by hired hands should be viewed as a dubious source for information about specific aspects of our social life or for the raw material for developing broader generalizations.[11]

According to Roth, the hired hand mentality—similar to Mills' concept of the bureaucratic ethos—has deadly effects on the quality of the research process. If Mills wrote of the dangers of becoming a research administrator, then Roth is writing of the dangers of having research underlings. But what, then, is to be done? Both Mills and Roth imply the general nature of their answers: that research must be done in such a way that it is meaningful and important to the researcher, whether he be a research director or a research employee. Employees must be encouraged to contribute their own ideas, and the approach to research must be sufficiently flexible so that those ideas can be taken seriously. Research directors must never become so involved in the hack-work aspects of administration that they lose sight of the prior importance of their responsibility for creative work. Is it possible to do this on a practical basis? I believe so, but it will become a reality only to the extent that we face up to the severe criticisms being leveled at the way research is generally conducted, and to the extent that we become convinced that the present situation is, generally, intolerable. In other words, we must define the bureaucratic ethos and the hired hand mentality as problem if we are to find ways of resolving them.

One-Shot and Sequential Data. As if these problems in survey work are not enough, there is this: almost all surveys are one-shot efforts at data collection, that is, data are collected only at one point in time. And if social and personality change is central to understanding human behavior, how much can we learn from the survey? One possible response to this

[11] Julius A. Roth, "Hired Hand Research," *American Sociologist,* **1** (August 1966), 190–96; reprinted in Norman K. Denzin (ed.), *Sociological Methods: A Sourcebook* (Chicago: Aldine, 1970), pp. 547, 549, 555.

problem might be the panel study, which involves restudies of the same individuals at a number of points in time. But panel studies are quite rare in sociological research, perhaps because of the time involved, perhaps because of the loss of participants, perhaps because of the expense, perhaps because of a general lack of conviction as to their importance, or perhaps for a combination of these reasons. So we are left with the present state of things: the sociologist recognizes, on the one hand, the importance of social change, yet on the other hand he does research in such a way that it becomes difficult for him to learn about change.

One way out of this dilemma—although it is only a very partial solution—is the use of retrospective and prospective questions in the survey. As a matter of fact, it is here that the survey method possesses advantages over some others. Granting that all of us easily distort past and future to meet the needs of the present situation, we can still learn a good deal from such questions. The following illustration is taken from the same questionnaire that has been used to illustrate the pragmatist approach:

AREAS OF YOUR LIFE: PAST, PRESENT AND FUTURE
For each of these areas of your life, rate your PAST, PRESENT, and EXPECTED FUTURE level of satisfaction. For example: For "Your family relationships," circle either "high," "medium," or "low" in the PAST column according to your preference; then circle your choice in the PRESENT column and your choice in the FUTURE column. Do the same for each of the other areas of your life ("Your leisure time activities," etc.)

	PAST	PRESENT	EXPECTED FUTURE
16. Satisfaction with— Your family relationships	1. high 2. medium 3. low	1. high 2. medium 3. low	1. high 2. medium 3. low
17. Satisfaction with— Your leisure time activities (including friendships)	1. high 2. medium 3. low	1. high 2. medium 3. low	1. high 2. medium 3. low
18. Satisfaction with— Your housing situation and neighborhood location	1. high 2. medium 3. low	1. high 2. medium 3. low	1. high 2. medium 3. low
19. Satisfaction with— Your health	1. high 2. medium 3. low	1. high 2. medium 3. low	1. high 2. medium 3. low
20. Satisfaction with— Your work (If retired or planning to retire, take into account your attitude toward retirement)	1. high 2. medium 3. low	1. high 2. medium 3. low	1. high 2. medium 3. low

With questions of this type, the survey researcher can at least begin to get some ideas about ongoing processes. This series of items also bears on the pragmatist orientation, which is a developmental one. An individual who sees himself as staying at the same levels in the future as he is now, or who sees himself as moving downward, tends to have less of a developmental orientation than an individual who sees himself as improving in general.

There are many other things that the survey researcher can do to deal with the temporal dimension. He can begin with his definition of his research problem, defining his theoretical framework so that time is taken more seriously. He can focus more attention on panel study designs, perhaps shortening the time period involved between one wave and the next so as to make this approach more practical, or perhaps dealing with a much smaller sample of respondents for the same reason. He can begin to focus attention on the time sequence involved during a given interview or questionnaire-response period, paying particular attention to the order of questions as well as the sequence of behaviors of the interviewer or of the individual administering the questionnaire. He can continue to develop his techniques for the analysis of survey data so as to improve his ability to make temporal inferences. He can use other techniques for data collection in addition to the survey, techniques that obtain data at a series of points in time.

Survey, Experiment, and Simulation[12]. From a formist perspective, the relevant question for this section is to explain the similarities and differences among these three techniques for data collection. From a pragmatist perspective, the focus is on ways of combining these procedures so that each builds on the others. Chapter 6, "Measurement and Data Construction," sets forth a general framework: that every mode of data collection is an experiment in the sense that the researcher changes the phenomena he observes. Chapter 7, "The Experiment," introduces the concept of experimental attitude, which is an orientation to developing an upward positive loop within the research process based on a powerful concern for the active testing of theoretical ideas. Chapter 8, "Simulation and Computer Simulation," illustrates the potential of these new techniques for dealing with change, especially to the degree that the investigator abandons a formist or even mechanistic paradigm and moves to a pragmatist one.

If the concept of an experimental attitude is valuable in enabling the investigator to be alert to learning about the ways in which he changes the situations he observes, then we might also conceive of a "gaming perspective" as helping him to be aware of the way in which he plays games

[12] For a comparison of experimental and survey approaches, see Carl I. Hovland, "Reconciling Conflicting Results Derived from Experimental and Survey Studies of Attitude Change," *American Psychologist,* **14** (1959), pp. 8–17.

in his social research experiences. He constructs research environments, and if he understands the rules of these games, he can reconstruct them. What term shall we use to refer to a survey approach? We might refer to this as a "cognitive perspective," for the survey researcher wants most of all to understand the thought processes of those he studies. These three approaches can be applied both to the researcher and to those he studies: we can examine the ways in which others "play games" and alter the situations they are in through their efforts to observe phenomena, and we can look at the researcher's own thought processes. The researcher can, then, apply all three—an experimental, a gaming, and a cognitive perspective—to any given research situation.

The Ethics of Survey Research. If we refer back to Roth's description of hired hand research, we have a context for discussing important ethical issues. Roth was concerned with the effects of bureaucratic treatment of research workers on the research process, and he found them to be quite destructive. Mills also was concerned with the same kind of issue, and his over-all conclusion was that the bureaucratic ethos—embodied, for example, in the social structure of the large research organization—makes creative and productive research most difficult. We have, then, two illustrations that link ethics to research effectiveness, regardless of any humanistic reasons for questioning a bureaucratic ethos or hired hand research.

What kind of ethical stance are Mills and Roth advocating? Roth gives us some clues in the following passage about how a research director might relate to his assistants:

> Through a series of discussions, general agreement is reached about the nature of the study and the manner in which it might be conducted. Some division of labor is agreed upon in these discussions. However, none of the field workers is held to any particular tasks or foci of interest. Each is allowed to pursue his data collection as he thinks best within the larger framework, although the field workers exchange information frequently and make new agreements so that they can benefit from each other's experience.[13]

Instead of hierarchy and a rigid division of labor—the characteristics of bureaucratic organizations—we have equalitarian relationships and the communication of information. Suppose we now extend this nonbureaucratic ethos to the relations between the survey researcher and his respondents. It would call for two-way communication between the two on an equalitarian basis, and it would rule out the researcher's using or manipulating his respondents to achieve private purposes that in no way help his respondents.

[13] Roth, op. cit., p. 550.

Such an extension of a nonbureaucratic ethos to the interviewer-respondent relationship may be justifiable not only on humanistic grounds but also on the grounds of producing effective and creative research. From a reflexive standpoint, it enables the researcher to learn about himself, since the respondent also functions in part as an interviewer within a two-way communication process; such learning is essential for the researcher if he is to deal with investigator effects. From an experimental perspective, the researcher is no longer in the position of structuring the research encounter within the mold of his own paradigm and theory alone: he must open up to a much greater degree to the testing of his ideas against alternative paradigms and theories. And from a developmental standpoint, whatever new molds he constructs are continually being opened up through additional research encounters.

Types of Survey Structure: Rigidity and Flexibility

If we look carefully at the controversies surrounding any given research procedure, we will discover a battle between fundamental world views, or paradigms, as well. Take for example the question of the degree of rigidity or flexibility within the interview situation. Should the interviewer use standard wording for all questions so that every respondent will receive the identical stimulus and differences among the respondents will not be (supposedly) a product of anything done by the interviewer? Implicit within such advice is a formist view of human behavior, following along the lines of Mill's method of difference: differences among respondents will be inferred to be a product of their different attitudes if all other factors are held constant.

What are the drawbacks of such an approach? We might start with the implications of the hired hand mentality that would be imposed on interviewers who felt very uncomfortable with this procedure: we might obtain "restricted production, failure to carry out portions of the task, avoidance of the more unpleasant or difficult aspects of the research, and outright cheating," and this might be the rule more than the exception. What about the impact of such behavior on the respondent? What would the reader's reaction be to an interviewer who volunteered no spontaneous words but read everything, and who answered all questions in an obviously memorized way? I know that my own reaction to a telephone interviewer who tried to do this with me was quite negative. I resented talking to someone whom I considered to be acting more like a machine than a human being. Why should I give up my own time if no human contact was involved? I resented the hired hand mentality or the bureaucratic ethos carried over into the interviewer-respondent relationship.

Is the best alternative to this kind of rigidity a flexibility that allows each participant in the research process to structure things completely on his own? Should the researcher avoid giving any definite instructions to his assistants, and should his assistants avoid giving definite instructions to the respondents? Carried to its extreme, such an approach would eliminate all uniform research instruments such as questionnaires and interview schedules. The investigator would not be able to construct Likert-type and Guttman scales, let alone perform Thurstone scaling and magnitude estimation. Although Roth leans in this direction more than in the direction of structure, I do not think he had this in mind. He does maintain that general agreement should be reached about the nature of the study and the manner in which it might be conducted, and such agreement could easily include the common acceptance of particular research instruments. For Roth, if there is to be a particular structure, it must be reached on the basis of common consent rather than be imposed by some on others.

There appears to be a vital issue that Roth does not face: the degree to which a researcher is a prisoner of his own paradigm. If I work with a group of interviewers who are formist to the core, then I may avoid inducing in them a hired hand mentality by joining them in their formist ways. But would that result in productive research, or only in happy research workers? Roth begins to get at the problem when he talks about the importance of communication among the researchers. To the extent that such communication works in my illustration, it could open up the paradigmatic differences between myself and the interviewers, leading to a broader research perspective than any one of us had initially.

Interview situations are always structured in one way or another, and the crucial question for the investigator is to develop the kind of structure most conducive to the construction of important information. Part of this involves the kinds of relationships among the research staff where each individual finds his own work meaningful. In addition, however, there is the relationship between respondent and interviewer to consider: that must be meaningful as well. An extremely rigid approach would tend to militate against this for most respondents. An interviewer who felt free to be spontaneous might also produce a rigid structure for the respondent to the degree that the interviewer himself was a prisoner of, say, a formist paradigm. What I am suggesting is that a more genuine spontaneity or freedom on the part of the interviewer is based on self-knowledge and, in particular, knowledge of the limitations of his own paradigm. To the extent that he has such knowledge, he will be in a better position to construct an interview situation that is more meaningful for the respondent. For example, he will be more likely to see the interview situation as a learning experience for himself, and this will tend to have favorable implications for the respondent.

There are specific issues within the survey relating to the type of survey structure. For example, there is the question of the relative merits of the questionnaire and the interview, taking into account the greater potential flexibility of the interview. There are so many other factors involved in a research project (e.g., the adequacy of the definition of the problem) that affect its success that this particular decision is not crucial in itself. It is all too easy for the researcher to lose flexibility by setting up a hierarchy of methods, with one method considered to be good and others to be bad. One result of this is to discourage research. The potential researcher who has neither the time nor the money to engage in an interviewing project may be dissuaded from engaging in any research because he has heard negative things about the questionnaire.

Another specific issue has to do with the choice between fixed-alternative questions, such as those presented earlier in this chapter, and open, or open-ended, questions, such as "Why did you do—?" or "What do you like most about—?" or "How do you feel about—?" or "What do you think you will do about—?" Such open questions are generally more difficult to analyze, depending on how clear the researcher is about his theory and how well he has worked out measurement procedures. On the other hand, they constitute a useful device for enabling the researcher to learn things he did not anticipate in his fixed-alternative questions. It seems to me that the important question for most research situations is not *whether* to have any questions of one type or the other but *what proportion* of each type makes the most sense for a given research context. Also, rather than accept each type as a given, the researcher might design his survey so as to shed light on the various forces surrounding a respondent's answers to questions of each type.

Interviewing Techniques

Standardized, Semistandardized, and Unstandardized Interviews. Just as there are open and fixed-alternative questions in the questionnaire, so are there standardized, semistandardized, and unstandardized approaches to interviewing.[14] The issues in the interviewing context are very much the same as in the questionnaire context: How can a uniform analysis of the data be made if each interviewer is free to do what he wishes? On the other hand, how can a respondent be motivated to do a good job if he is dealing with a wooden interviewer who does not relate to him personally for fear of affecting the respondent's answers?

One way of looking at the types of interview is from the perspective of the contexts of justification and discovery. The unstandardized approach gives the interviewer the greatest flexibility to follow up things he learns within the interview process. The standardized approach gives him the kinds of uniform responses that make it easier for him to analyze his results. But my statements here indicate mere tendencies. The actual situation within which any given mode of interviewing takes place is a highly complex one, and the technique that the interviewer is conscious of having

[14] For three articles on interviewer-repondent interaction, see Denzin, op. cit., pp. 185–209.

adopted is only one small part of the picture. Thus, an unstandardized approach may produce little in the context of discovery if the interviewer is guided by inadequate theory or has poor self-knowledge. Similarly, a standardized interview may not be productive for the same or other reasons.

The semistandardized interview is based on an attempt to achieve the best of both worlds. One approach is for the interviewer to have a number of specific questions to ask but, in addition, the freedom to follow up whatever he thinks important in his own way. He may perform such follow-up during the interview within the context of particular questions and/or after the formal phase of the interview is over. In many situations, respondents who feel inhibited by the question-and-answer situation open up very well after the interviewer puts down his interview schedule and pen and relates to the respondent in a more qualitarian, or everyday, way.

Taking notes is not necessarily the best way of recording the results of an interview. For many situations, this might inhibit the respondent greatly, perhaps resulting more than anything else in responses based on what the respondent thinks the interviewer expects. The same holds for reading questions from an interview schedule. Of course, one could not manage a standardized interview without being able to read and record, but nonstandardized interviews and some kinds of semistandardized interviews would be possible. Another alternative for recording is the tape recorder, which should be considered only if the time and expense involved in transcribing is taken into account. A great many respondents would not be deterred in the least by having their interviews taped, although one could not easily plan to do this for all respondents. A tape provides, of course, the exact words of the respondent along with those of the interviewer, in addition to many intangible factors of human communication. Some taped interviews might prove highly suggestive to a researcher whose source of data for most of his interviews is a written protocol.

One particular kind of semistandardized interview is the "focused interview,"[15] which focuses on the effects of a given phenomenon experienced by the respondent. In the context of experimental design, this would also be considered a one-shot case study, or an X O pre-experimental design (Section 7.2). The interviewer comes to the interview situation with a list of topics based on his previous study of the phenomenon in question. His knowledge of that phenomenon helps him to direct his questioning so as to discover the difference between the way he viewed it and the way the respondent viewed it. His ability to discover the kinds of distortions in the respondent's perceptions, and the reasons for those distortions, is based on his ability to understand his own distortions. There is a close relationship between the focused interview and the historian's oral history, which provides detailed interviews focused on phenomena experienced by the

[15] Robert K. Merton et al., *The Focused Interview* (New York: Free Press, 1956).

respondents. For example, Studs Terkel's *Hard Times: An Oral History of the Great Depression* includes 162 different points of view about the Depression from people who lived through it. The focus here is not on an event of quite short duration, as in the focused interview, but rather on a process that stretched over many years.

Some Severe Problems. To understand more clearly why it is that choices among the foregoing types of interviews create only one of the important forces within the interview situation, we must probe the dynamics of that situation more deeply. Let me begin by raising a number of issues. Why should a respondent consent to be interviewed in the first place? What does he get out of it? To what extent does he automatically try to conform to what he thinks the interviewer wants to hear? Under what conditions does he deliberately lie? How well equipped is he to answer the questions asked, taking into account his memory and his understanding of what the questions call for? How well does he understand the interviewer's questions? To what extent does his behavior change from one part of the interview to the next? Would he react differently with different interviewers?

These are only a few questions touching on the complexity of the interview situation. There are very few answers to such questions, and the result is that the interview situation is largely an unknown phenomenon. For example, we have learned from studies of experiments that experimenters generally influence their subjects in covert and powerful ways. If this is the case for the experiment, where investigators generally try to keep to a minimum their interaction with subjects, how much more true must it be in the interview situation? In that situation, one of the factors researchers suspect is operating in a powerful way is the "social desirability variable."[16] In one questionnaire study, personality trait items were rated by respondents who were asked to judge the traits in terms of whether they considered them desirable or undesirable in others. A different group of individuals was then asked to indicate whether the items were characteristic of themselves. A close relationship was found between the social desirability of a given item and the probability of its appearance among the self-ratings. Generalizing from this study to the interview situation, much that the interviewee says may be strongly influenced by his conception of the social desirability of saying it.

We might also delve into the ability and willingness of the respondent to give information. We must, first, be wary of an organicist paradigm, which tends to lead the researcher to believe that whatever he observes outside of himself is the truth. If his own ideas are suspect, why shouldn't the ideas of others be at least equally suspect? Respondents differ greatly

---

[16] Allen L. Edwards, "The Relationship Between the Judged Desirability of a Trait and the Probability That the Trait Will Be Endorsed," *Journal of Applied Psychology*, **37** (1953), pp. 90–93.

in their memory, their understanding of questions, their emphasis on the social desirability variable, their interest in a given study, what they get out of being interviewed, and many other things as well, just as do interviewers. In a sense, each interview is a study in itself.

Projective Techniques and Other Indirect Methods. One approach that deals with at least some of these complexities is the use of projective techniques and other indirect methods for obtaining information from respondents. Such procedures are based on the assumption that factors not in the awareness of the respondent may have important effects on his behavior. They represent an attempt to obtain the kinds of data that a respondent may be unable or unwilling to reveal. There are, of course, important ethical questions involved in such procedures. Do they not constitute an invasion of privacy? What right does the interviewer have to obtain information without the knowledge and consent of the respondent? Such questions involve a number of additional considerations. For example, is the interviewer—or the study director—giving anything to the respondent in return for his time and efforts? How valuable is what the researcher gives to the respondent? How trivial or important is the information the researcher obtains? To what extent does the researcher alert the respondent to what he is doing and to the results of his analysis? To summarize, such ethical issues are no easier to resolve than the question of how to understand the complexity of the interview situation itself.

Projective techniques are data collection methods that involve the presentation of relatively unstructured stimuli to the respondent. It is assumed that, because the stimuli are unstructured, the respondent will be required to organize or structure them and will, in the process, reveal important aspects of his own personality and behavior. Although these techniques were originally utilized in clinical situations, they are presently being applied in research situations. With the Rorschach Test, for example, subjects are presented with a series of cards, each of which has a different picture of an ink blot, and are asked, "What might this be?" Another example of a commonly used projective technique is the Thematic Apperception Test, or TAT, in which the respondent is asked to tell a story about each of a series of pictures. The ink blots and pictures constitute the relatively unstructured stimuli, and the respondent's answers to the questions represent his structuring of the stimuli.

Projective techniques vary in the degree to which the stimuli are unstructured. The Sentence Completion Test is generally more structured than either the Rorschach Test or the Thematic Apperception Test. By "structured" I mean commonly understood or shared perceptions as to the nature of the stimulus. In the Sentence Completion Test the respondent is asked to complete a series of sentences (for example, "My favorite _____";

"John's father made him _____"). Because the stimuli consist of words rather than ink blots of pictures, the investigator can focus attention on particular phenomena he is interested in exploring.

Another type of projective technique has to do with asking the respondent to play one or more roles. This technique is called *psychodrama* if he plays himself, *sociodrama* if he acts out the roles of others. Here the respondent is removed from the paper-and-pencil situation, and he has relatively little opportunity to prepare an answer he thinks would have social desirability. If the interviewer himself adopts a role that complements that adopted by the respondent, he has the opportunity to subject the respondent to sequences of stimuli and to investigate the dynamics of his behavior.

Other indirect methods are more structured than projective techniques and consequently tend to have a higher degree of reliability. In the error-choice method, for example, respondents are asked to choose among different possible answers to a factual question (such as "What is the salary of the average psychiatrist?"). All the answers provided are incorrect, and the direction of the error a respondent makes is used as a measure of his values, attitudes, or expectations. Another relatively structured indirect test is the information test, which is based on the premise that the amount and kind of information an individual possesses about a given subject are related to his values and expectations. Consequently, information questions may be used as indirect measures of these factors.

Projective techniques and indirect methods have come under severe criticism because of the lack of demonstration of their criterion validity and their poor face validity. Campbell, for example, states that the literature is almost devoid of evidence indicating that indirect questions provide more valid data than information produced by direct questions.[17] Part of the problem is that the researchers who use these techniques tend to be clinically oriented and tend not to be concerned with testing for reliability or validity. As a result of such criticism, interest in using such procedures is not widespread. Yet if there are problems with validating projective tests and indirect methods, are there not equally severe problems with all other modes of measurement? As I have tried to indicate in this chapter and the preceding ones, our methods of measurement are put forward within highly complex human situations, and our general failure to understand the dynamics of those situations from a theoretical perspective produces poor construct validity for *all* of our measurement procedures. If this is the situation, there is no reason to hold some procedures in particularly low esteem, especially—as in the case of projective tests and indirect methods—if they offer a different approach.

---

[17] Donald T. Campbell, "The Indirect Assessment of Social Attitudes," *Psychological Bulletin,* **47** (1950), pp. 15–38.

9.3 Summary

What can be said to summarize this chapter? What is the nature of the cognitive perspective of the survey as distinct from an experimental or gaming (simulation) perspective? Let us think of a cognitive orientation, or perspective, as a kind of "head simulation": as outlined in Section 1.1, the researcher (or any individual) goes through a covert rehearsal process mentally. He then acts on his environment to collect or construct data (experimental perspective), or as a lay individual, he communicates. To the extent that he adopts a gaming perspective, he is able to construct social systems—not just in his head but externally—that simulate more complex or more realistic social contexts. With all of these tools for collecting data, the researcher is in a far better position to understand the vast unknowns of human behavior than with only one of them at a time. One of the lessons of this chapter is the enormity of those unknowns relative to our present knowledge. Yet with these three perspectives—along with the nonverbal and historical orientations to be discussed in Chapters 10 and 11—he should be able to make rapid progress provided that he does not lose sight of the importance of bringing to the surface his paradigmatic and theoretical frameworks.

Exercises

1. Follow the procedures outlined in Section 9.1 to construct a four-item Guttman scale, based on four questions that might be dictated to a class of students. What is the coefficient of reproducibility? Does the order in which the questions scale, as well as the nature of the largest nonscale types, give you any insight into the variable you are attempting to measure?

2. Apply the technique of magnitude estimation outlined in Section 9.1 to three individuals, using Form 1 to obtain their ratings of the relative status of various occupations, income levels, and educational attainments. Is it possible for you to teach others to think in ratio terms with respect to the status dimension? What lessons have you learned about how to do this effectively?

3. Relative to Exercise 1, interview several of the individuals who provided you with their responses, using a semistandardized approach. What can you learn about the way each one structured the situation within which he provided his responses? Do you detect the operation of the social desirability variable?

4. Do the same for Exercise 2, only this time use either a standardized or an unstandardized approach.

Annotated References

GORDON, RAYMOND L. *Interviewing: Strategy, Techniques, and Tactics.* Homewood, Ill.: Dorsey Press, 1969. Also: Stephen A. Richardson et al. *Interviewing: Its Forms and Functions.* New York: Basic Books, Inc., Publishers, 1965. These books, written from the perspectives of cross-cultural and social psychological backgrounds, respectively, convey a great deal of the experiences that social scientists have had with the interviewing process.

JAY, MARTIN. *The Dialectical Imagination: A History of the Frankfurt School and the Institute of Social Research.* Boston: Little, Brown and Company, 1973. This study of a major group of thinkers in the social sciences illustrates that interviewing combined with an array of other approaches can produce excellent scholarship. Jay never loses sight of his over-all approach, his definition of the problem: to portray the genesis and dynamics and complex relationships of the Frankfurt School and the Institute, relating them to the world-historical situation.

RILEY, MATILDA WHITE, AND JOHN W. RILEY, JR., AND JACKSON TOBY. *Sociological Studies in Scale Analysis.* New Brunswick, N.J.: Rutgers University Press, 1954. The authors present, in addition to discussions of the procedures of the Guttman approach to scale analysis, a series of innovative ideas and techniques for extending the Guttman approach to a wide range of phenomena.

chapter 10
Observation

What can techniques of observation possibly add to those procedures for data collection already discussed? With an experimental, gaming (simulation), and cognitive orientation, is not the investigator well equipped to do his job? Observation yields the kind of emphasis on the nonverbal aspects of human behavior that is not provided by a cognitive orientation, and—together with a cognitive orientation—it alerts the investigator to the impact of process or change in ways not sufficiently covered by the experiment and simulation. Through experiments and gaming, the researcher centers on the construction of an environment, whereas it is by means of cognitive and nonverbal measurement procedures that he is able to focus on the implications of that environment for human beings. This is not to say that what we discover through interviewing and observation does not also involve the construction of a given environment, nor should it imply that there is no assessment of impacts within the context of experimental and simulation procedures. The difference, rather, is one of degree. The symmetry between these two pairs of data collection techniques is analogous to that between defining a research problem and interpreting the results of the study: the former provides a framework that launches the scientist on his voyage of exploration, and the latter centers on charting his path.

This chapter is divided into two parts: observation in the field and observation in the laboratory. Not so long ago researchers commonly believed that the latter situation is much better understood and more carefully controlled than the former. Now, doubts about this difference are widespread. How, then, are they to be distinguished? One way is in terms of the degree to which the researcher *consciously* constructs procedures for assessing what is going on. Unconscious structuring goes on in both laboratory and field, of course, and the key to understanding such structuring lies in a knowledge of one's paradigms and theory. Laboratory and field observation techniques are to one another, then, as the experiment is to the interview: on a continuum with respect to emphasis on construction and assessment. The observer in the laboratory and the experimenter concentrate on consciously constructing a portion of the research situation, whereas the field observer and the interviewer focus on assessing whatever is going on.

10.1 Field Observation

In this section I would like to accomplish two general things: to introduce the subject with an overview of its nature, and to provide a detailed illustration by discussing one particular research project I am familiar with. The overview is intended to alert the reader to the type of thinking by sociologists that has been associated with this approach, and the illustration is designed to introduce him to the flavor—perhaps even the excitement—of this kind of investigation.

In Section 1.1 I referred to three stages in American orientations to methodology: a pre-World War I period emphasizing social reformism and qualitative research, a post-World War I period that questioned the focus on personal documents in *The Polish Peasant* and encompassed the burgeoning of quantitative research techniques, and the present-day situation in which the fruitfulness of the latter for the development of social science or the solution of societal problems is under serious examination. Present-day controversies about social research methods reflect a more general division within academia and society between the two cultures of the humanities and the sciences. The concept of triangulation, which I take up initially, constitutes an approach to building bridges across these cultures. My second topic—roles, games, and objectivity—employs some sociological concepts to help us penetrate more deeply into some of the complexities of field observation as well as a central methodological issue associated with it. The research illustration that follows constitutes an application of these ideas.

Triangulation

Norman Denzin describes triangulation in this way:

> In addition to the use of multiple methods, there are at least three other varieties of triangulation. *Theoretical triangulation* involves the use of several different perspectives in the analysis of the same set of data. *Data triangulation* attempts to gather observations with multiple sampling strategies. . . . *Investigator triangulation* is the use of more than one observer in the field situation.[1]

As suggested at the beginning of this chapter, the multiple methods of experiment and simulation, on the one hand, and survey and observation, on the other, focus respectively on the conscious structuring of the research situation and on assessing the impact of whatever structures exist, thus giving him a wide range of information. To theoretical triangulation—

[1] Norman K. Denzin (ed.)., *Sociological Methods: A Sourcebook* (Chicago: Aldine, 1970), p. 472.

which might be illustrated by discussions in Chapter 4 of structural-functionalism, conflict theory, social exchange theory, symbolic interactionism, and phenomenology—we can add "paradigmatic triangulation." It is too easy for a variety of theories to represent the same paradigm, thus not providing the triangulation expected, without explicit consideration of the paradigm behind a given theory. In all of these ways—as well as through data and investigator triangulation—the researcher recognizes the limitations of any given research procedure and moves toward an integration of knowledge.

If we accept the importance of triangulation in the abstract, what specific implications does this have for our behavior as social researchers? For one thing, we might avoid an overdependence on the survey in sociology. For another, we might not rely exclusively on the kinds of methods discussed in Chapters 7, 8, and 9, namely, methods that are "obtrusive" in that they alert people under investigation to the fact that research is taking place. In their book on *Unobtrusive Measures,* Webb, Campbell, Schwartz, and Seechrest call for the use of the kinds of methods discussed in this chapter and the next:

> Today, some 90 per cent of social science research is based upon interviews and questionnaires. We lament this overdependence upon a single, fallible method. . . .
> In sampling the range of alternative approaches, we examine their weaknesses, too. The flaws are serious and give insight into why we do depend so much upon the interview. But the issue is not choosing among individual methods. Rather it is the necessity for a multiple operationism, a collection of methods combined to avoid sharing the same weaknesses. The goal of this monograph is not to replace the interview but to supplement and cross-validate it with measures that do not require the cooperation of a respondent and that do not themselves contaminate the response.
> Here are some samples. . . .
> The floor tiles around the hatching-chick exhibit at Chicago's Museum of Science and Industry must be replaced every six weeks. Tiles in other parts of the museum need not be replaced for years. The selective erosion of tiles, indexed by the replacement rate, is a measure of the relative popularity of exhibits. . . .
> The degree of fear induced by a ghost-story-telling session can be measured by noting the shrinking diameter of a circle of seated children.
> Chinese jade dealers have used the pupil dilation of their customers as a measure of the client's interest in particular stones. . . .
> Library withdrawals were used to demonstrate the effect of the introduction of television into a community. Fiction titles dropped, nonfiction titles were unaffected. . . .
> The child's interest in Christmas was demonstrated by distortions in the size of Santa Claus drawings.

Racial attitudes in two colleges were compared by noting the degree of clustering of Negroes and whites in lecture halls.[2]

In using such methods, we should realize the limitations of even unobtrusive, or "nonreactive," measures. For one thing, even if the method itself does not intrude on the subject, a great many other things do, things that are part of his everyday situation. What matters is how good any measurement is—unobtrusive or not—in monitoring these forces, and this is a question of construct validity. For another thing, even the use of methods that are unobtrusive to others necessarily intrudes the researcher's own perspectives on how he defines his problem, how he obtains measurement, and how he interprets his results. There is no way of avoiding this intrusion, but he can learn about its nature by probing those perspectives. Also, triangulation might be achieved through other investigators with quite different perspectives.

How does the researcher develop his abilities along these lines? Perhaps most important, I believe, is for him to tear down the wall separating his research behavior and his everyday behavior and to learn to become more reflexive in both. If "the unexamined life is not worth living," then there are good humanistic reasons for doing this, but there are research reasons as well. One cannot expect to go through most of one's experiences oblivious to the complex relationships between the things one observes and the forces producing them and suddenly, when one is in a research context, become extremely perceptive about such relationships. Every moment of life provides the would-be researcher with an opportunity for developing the keenness of his observational tools, to the extent that he learns to see relationships between the scientific method (Figure 1-1) and human interaction (Figure 1-2). Books like those by Arthur Conan Doyle can help in this quest. Sherlock Holmes is a master of observational technique. But we can improve on him to the degree that our theory provides us with more profound assumptions about human behavior than he was able to make.

Roles, Games, and Objectivity

If the research situation is as complex and dynamic as previous chapters have indicated, and if existing theoretical and methodological tools are inadequate to the purpose of achieving deep understanding, what alternatives do we have? One is to discount such criticism, blinding ourselves to our limitations. Another is to become disenchanted and perhaps cynical. Neither of these alternatives produces effective research. A third is to continue to triangulate, remaining confident that this will produce important

[2] Eugene J. Webb, Donald T. Campbell, Richard D. Schwartz, and Lee Sechrest, *Unobtrusive Measures* (Chicago: Rand McNally, 1966), pp. 1–2.

results and at the time remaining perceptive about the actual level of the water in the research beaker. In this spirit, let us pull together two theoretical concepts—"role" and "game"—and see to what extent such a union can help us to penetrate a key problem in field research: the degree to which a participant in life can also be a scientific observer of his experiences. Does he develop goals as a participant that prevent him from seeing those experiences scientifically? Can he be objective about them?

Let us begin with the gaming, or simulation, idea, as discussed in Chapters 3 and 8, adding to it the view of the survey (Chapter 9) as a head simulation. Out of this material emerges the concept of a game as a system of rules—let us now include roles as well—that can be changed by the game players, depending on their degree of knowledge of the rules and roles. For example, it would be difficult for them to change the game in other than a superficial manner if the paradigm on which the roles are based is unknown to them. Now let us make the big jump and conceive of all human behavior from this gaming perspective, trying simultaneously to rid ourselves of some stereotypes we have about games. In this view, the game is not necessarily a win-lose proposition: such social structures of a formist type constitute only one kind of game. Neither is the game necessarily a repetitive phenomenon: formist games, based on the A-is-A principle, are of this type, but not organicist or pragmatist games. Nor is a game necessarily a trivial exercise, or a bowl of cherries: it can also lie at the heart of human nature, and it may be our own ascetic and humorless spirit that tends to reject its importance.

To apply these ideas to the field observation context, one important idea from methodological literature on this subject is that the researcher—willy-nilly—works from within the context of some role. The advice to him goes something like this: Don't be a "complete participant" and "go native," because then you'll lose your scientific objectivity. On the other hand, don't be a "complete observer," because then you'll isolate yourself and lose rapport with the people you're studying. Although it is difficult, be either a participant who doesn't lose objectivity or an observer who doesn't lose rapport.

Implicit in this advice is an assumption that a somewhat detached, or disinterested, approach to participation is valuable for the research process, enabling the investigator to see what is going on with somewhat different eyes than those of other participants. Such a disinterested approach is not necessarily either more scientific or less scientific: what matters is the researcher's *understanding* of the roles he plays and their impact on himself and those he studies. A detached investigator and one who goes native can both miss the impact of their particular roles on the research situation, and both can fail to understand what is going on. But whatever the researcher does, he is playing *some* role: he does not have the choice of viewing behavior from Mt. Olympus or from the vantage point of the Greek chorus. If he is alive, he is a player of games. As a scientist, he can choose to become curious about the rules governing those games. And the game of detachment is at least as complex as the game of going native: in the former, one is committed to science, whereas in the latter one is committed to other things.

By learning the rules of the game one also begins to learn how to change those rules. This gives the field researcher choices: he need not simply allow his research role to emerge, all the time watching the situation helplessly: he can participate more actively in creating that role. But a researcher is not a superman, and controlling one's research role involves such things as knowledge of one's own personality. Yet the researcher can work up to this over a period of time, just as any human being can. Not only can he learn to shape his own role to a very great degree but he can also learn to shape the games that are being played in the field situation. And if he can shape them, he can also allow them to be shaped by others. Whichever he does, his insights into the genesis of human behavior will be much greater. And to the degree that these insights focus on his own behavior, he is becoming more objective than a detached observer who fails to understand that he is playing the game of detachment.

An Illustration: The 1968 French Student Revolt[3]

One aspect of triangulation is investigator triangulation, for example, the use of more than one observer of a given phenomenon. A key function that scientific communication is supposed to have is to enable members of the scientific community to replicate, or repeat, one another's work. But such repetition may not carry us very far beyond our presently inadequate knowledge. Here we come up against a serious limitation of the triangulation concept: it is quite formist in its implication that the "truth" lies somewhere, and that it is the job of the scientist to locate it. It is an orientation that is similar to the formist distinction between the plane of truth and the plane of observation: our observations supposedly help us, by triangulation, to locate the correct point in the plane of truth. If we shift, then, to seeing triangulation as a way of filling our beaker of knowledge higher and higher, then we have a pragmatist basis for analyzing investigator triangulation.

From this perspective, how can the observations of one investigator lead to the *substantial development* of the ideas of another investigator? For one thing, he might take into account differences in the research situation and explain resulting modifications of the observations in terms of these differences. The greater the differences in the research situation that can be explained, the wider the applicability of the theoretical perspective in

---

[3] David Volodia Stratman, "The 1968 French Student Revolt: A Study of Modern Political Delinquency," Ph.D dissertation, Boston University, 1970.

question. And if we are dealing with differences in paradigms—if, for example, one investigator is pragmatist and another is organicist—then investigator triangulation can produce a great increment of knowledge. The typical problem of trivial replication is, I believe, a result of near identity in the paradigms of the investigators. The present illustration, however, presents a much different situation: an investigator who not only challenges existing paradigms in research and theory but in society as well. Let us, then, proceed to test the idea that this might be a useful approach to triangulation.

David Stratman, in his observational study of the French student revolt of 1968, was particularly interested in exploring the genesis of "political delinquency." He begins by pointing up major assumptions within the prevailing focus on success and opportunity, as developed by Merton, Cloward, Ohlin, Miller, and others:[4]

(1) success-goals, as a composite product of dominant subsystems in the social structure, are unconditionally or faithfully accepted by each social category where they are directed; (2) hence, success-goals are always social products manufactured *for* and unalterably *by* the target-social-category.[5]

Within this framework, the key explanation for delinquency is the degree of opportunity, or the availability of means, for achieving these success goals. But the researcher who accepts this paradigm for political delinquency, according to Stratman, blinds himself to the possibility that others do not necessarily accept the dominant subsystem's success goals so readily. Indeed, they might go so far as to substitute an alternate set of success goals of their own. In such an eventuality, societal attempts to repress their delinquency will be viewed—in their eyes—as the delinquency of society with reference to their own alternative success goals.

Stratman illustrates the dangers of accepting the Merton-Cloward-Ohlin-Miller paradigm for the research process:

Characteristic, and of particular interest for our analysis of success-goal categories, are the findings of an impressive survey research (280,000 respondents) carried out in France and published in May, 1967, one year before the outbreak of the French Student Revolt.

The respondents, French boys and girls betwen 15 and 24, were asked to outline the criteria for social success. The choices were indicative of the ideological paradigm of the researchers, excluding possibilities of response which might have been dissonant with the prevalent conventional success-goal categories.

[4] See for example Richard Cloward and Lloyd Ohlin, *Delinquency and Opportunity: A Theory of Delinquent Gangs* (New York: Free Press, 1960).
[5] Stratman, op. cit., p. 2.

Once the respondents were permitted to make choices *only* within the limits of *acceptable* categories, it is of little surprise to learn the principal "finding" of the research team:

"The young Frenchman thinks of getting married early, but is careful not to have children before securing the means of bringing them up correctly. His number one objective is professional 'reussite.' Awaiting, the young man saves to buy an automobile, the young female for her dowry. The youth are interested in the problems of the day but do not request earlier admission to the political life: 72% believe that the voting age should not be lowered under 21. He does not think of war in the near future and believes that industrial efficiency, internal order, and the cohesion of the people will determine the future of France."

The anachronisms—think of alleged obsession with dowry, flat refusal to enter political arena before 21, emphasis on internal harmony and order—are, in retrospect, shocking.[6]

Stratman is here pointing up perhaps the major problem standing in the way of effective research: the researcher's blindness to the limitations of his own paradigms. As another illustration of the same kind of thing, he cites a questionnaire item formulated by Mizruchi and his coworkers to uncover success goals: "Could you list, in order of importance, those things which you believe to be signs of success in our society? (1) Owning your own home, (2) Having lots of money, (3) Having a good education, (4) Having lots of friends, (5) Having people look up to you, and (6) Having a good, steady job."[7] For the political delinquent participating in the French Student Revolt, these are not the major success goals.

If Stratman does not accept the success-opportunity paradigm, what is his own choice? He distinguishes between achieving a goal and showing what can be achieved, stating that political success may encompass the demonstration of the possibility and potentiality for success. He maintains that it is a major accomplishment to demonstrate that it is possible to fight City Hall and to shatter the myth of the invincibility of the De Gaulle regime. Stratman's view here parallels that of Daniel Cohn-Bendit—the leading figure in the French student revolt—who maintained that the revolt had proved untrue the myth that nothing can be done about the regime. What we have here is a paradigm that differs from the mechanistic one in which the major force in society is seen as the thrust to fulfill given goals, as in the occupational choice study (Section 2.2) or the role conflict computer simulation study (Section 8.2). By contrast, we have a developmental approach corresponding to an organicist or pragmatist perspective: there is an emphasis on opening doors to future goal fulfillment. Also, there is an iconoclastic emphasis. The shattering of myths is seen as im-

[6] Ibid., pp. 4–5. The quote is from "Libre Blanc de jeunesse."
[7] Quoted in Stratman, op. cit., p. 6. From Ephraim H. Mizruchi, *Success and Opportunity* (New York: Free Press, 1964).

portant work. Finally, there is a Dionysian element in Stratman's approach, as he indicates in his summation when he maintains that he undertook the study "gladly and with light heart," as well as in his numerous metaphors (e.g., "Martyral success," "Trojan Horse," "Dionysian Movement," "Cadmean Victory").

All of the foregoing discussion of the prevailing mechanistic paradigm for understanding delinquency and an alternative paradigm has definite implications for observational research procedures. Given his alternative paradigm, how did it affect Stratman's observational procedures? Over-all, Stratman succeeds in uncovering the kinds of data that would be missed to a great extent by a researcher operating within a mechanistic paradigm. He unearths the demythologizing nature of the revolt as well as its Dionysian character. He sees it as a "producer of fiestas, joy, poetry and drama, vigorous inter-personal relations, all pervaded by a genuine collective atmosphere of erotic and ideative shower." To illustrate, he collected a large number of Dionysian graffiti, which includes these:

Kiss your love without dropping your gun
Make love and begin again   Odéon

I have something to say, but I don't know what   Censier

You'll end up dying from comfort   Hall Grand Amphi, Nanterre

"See Nanterre and live"
Go die in Naples with the Club Mediteranee   Amphi, Music, Nanterre

Creativity
Spontaneity
Life   Censier

My desires are reality   C 24, Nanterre

Friends, you can make love in Political Science,
    not just in the fields.   Mvt. 22 Mars, Hall Political Sciences

The perspective of enjoying tomorrow never comforts me
    in the boredom of today.   Stairway C 1 èr étage, Nanterre

Art is dead, let's free our daily lives   Sorbonne

When people realize that they are bored,
    they stop being bored.   Sorbonne

Look at yourselves. You're sad   (The rebels) Sorbonne

We want: the structures to be at man's service and not man
    at the structures service.
We want to have the pleasure of living and not the pain
    of living.   Odéon

The Bourgeoisie has no other pleasure than
    degrading them all (pleasures).   Fac. of Law Assas.[8]

[8] Ibid., pp. 240–45.

We in the West tend to stereotype the Dionysian orientation as one which sacrifices tomorrow for today, perhaps because we are so ready to sacrifice today for tomorrow. Yet these graffiti do not indicate any such orientation: today is important, and tomorrow is important as well. There is not simply an interest in enjoyment or happiness ("You'll end up dying from comfort") : there is a focus on creating something better, on development, on dedication. There is not the mechanistic orientation to fulfilling precise goals ("I have something to say, but I don't know what"). Many of the graffiti focus on emotional expression, sexual or otherwise. The emphasis is on active rather than passive expression. There is a great deal of iconoclasm ("Art is dead, let's free our lives," "Go die in Naples with the Club Mediteranee," "Look at yourselves. You're sad," "The Bourgeoisie has no other pleasure than degrading them all (pleasures)").

Stratman summarizes his conclusions as follows:

> The present study of the French Student Revolt has tried to visit and check for usefulness the foundations of a series of concepts lacking good accreditation in sociological thought [a variety of metaphors coined by Stratman]. We did so gladly and with light heart, believing that the "desacralisation" feature of modern student movements ought to be paralleled by "anomalous" rather than "normal" scientific work. The disaffection of the French student with the traditional historical values, i.e., the great destiny of the Great Nation, the traditional dreams of the Empire and of successive republics, the tricolor and Marseillaise, Maxim, the cancan, Moulin Rouge, Champs Elysee coffee shops, national monuments, even Dada and Aragon, Louvre and Versaille, is deep and irreversible. . . .
>
> This author thinks that the monotony hypothesis sharply illuminates the dreary sub-existence of the post-industrial man and the effervescent pursuit of joy, pathos, drama, radiated by the modern political delinquent. It explains the apparent lack of *telos,* the uncontrollable orgastic trepidations of the student revolt. It accounts for the situation of unpredictability because the modern "normal" researcher defines the condition of acute monotony "normal" and fails to detect the syndrome of emerging student revolution. . . .
>
> The exuberant spirit of the French student revolt was more than an effort to reach the ebullience of sensate joys, allegoric imagination, unharnessed thought—as many of the posters, graffiti, poems, slogans, cartoons tell us. It was not only a search but an expression of the revolutionary *homo ludens.*[9]

The kind of triangulation that opens up new areas of understanding—which, I believe, this piece of work illustrates—is not easily achieved, for the investigator's paradigm must be distinct from the paradigms of pre-

[9] Ibid., pp. 231–32.

vious investigators. It is not simply a question of his research orientation: it is a matter of his personality and way of life as well. The research process and the process of living are in interaction, regardless of how much we try to compartmentalize them. Stratman's view of the French student revolt as exemplifying *homo ludens* is related to utilizing the concepts of roles and games to analyze human behavior. Was the revolt merely a drama, a game, a sexual release of libido? Was it a serious affair? Or was it both? According to Stratman, the researcher deeply involved in normal research—accepting, say, formist or mechanistic paradigms—would miss the *homo ludens* aspects of the revolt. And if he failed to see its dramaturgical aspects, he would also fail to see its realistic significance.

10.2 Laboratory Observation

Introduction

The distinction between field and laboratory observational procedures is also the distinction between two social science traditions: that of the anthropologist and that of the experimental psychologist. The field observer typically enters the research situation for an extended period of time and participates to some degree in the situations he observes. Usually, he does not limit his investigation to collecting data on a specific list of topics he has decided on in advance. Although he will focus on some things and will have some explicit ideas about what he wants to achieve in advance of entering the field, he generally likes to leave the field observation situation open to new directions on the basis of whatever he learns in the field. He frequently uses a number of informants, who have access to information not readily available to himself, to give him the benefit of their experiences. He tends to look down on "artificial" situations, such as experiments, because they depart so much from the naturalistic conditions he observes. He also tends to see surveys as relatively superficial in comparison to the range of information and the extended period of investigation that tend to characterize field observation.

The laboratory tradition tends to be a formist one. There are explicit hypotheses with which the researcher begins, and he generally sticks with them throughout the investigation. He works with his subjects for a limited period of time. He attempts to control, insofar as he can, the research conditions. He usually does not engage in any extensive interviewing of his subjects, but tends to rely on what they do or say under the predetermined conditions. He frequently makes use of statistical tests in his analysis of the data to help him evaluate whether or not his hypotheses are correct. He tends to be suspicious of the degree of knowledge that can be obtained in naturalistic situations because of the lack of control of relevant factors that exists under such conditions. He also tends to be suspicious of survey data because of its heavy reliance on verbal, as distinct from nonverbal, data.

The emerging interest in the triangulation of research procedures is based on an assumption that each technique has serious limitations as well as important strengths. The field situation is not as natural as it might look, nor is the investigator as spontaneous and free as he thinks he is. He affects the situation he observes in a great many ways, and he tends to have little understanding or control over the ways in which he does so. Also, the investigator is himself a prisoner of his own unrecognized paradigms and will tend to obtain whatever data fit those paradigms. Neither is the laboratory situation as controlled as it might appear to be. Most of us tend to be overly impressed with technological gadgetry and lose sight of the degree to which such gadgetry effectively monitors the complex and intangible forces operating within the laboratory situation. There is, in particular, the phenomenon of investigator effect, which tends to operate powerfully in the laboratory. And there are also, as in the field situation, limitations induced by the nature of the investigator's paradigm.

As a concrete illustration of the problems involved in both approaches, let us take up the observational technique of video-taping. On the one hand, it allows the investigator to go out into the field, obtaining data in naturalistic settings. On the other hand, it has effects on those settings far beyond those that would be induced by an individual walking into them without such equipment. The observational record video tape can produce goes far beyond the fallible memory of an observer, beyond what he could obtain with pencil and paper, and beyond what he could do with a tape recorder. Yet how are such data to be analzed? What are their significance? To what extent have they been influenced by the video-taping itself? Was there only an initial effect of the video-taping process—one that was gradually eliminated—or a continuing effect? Was the investigator seen as a kind of Peeping Tom or as someone doing useful research work or as someone making a movie?

If we are to take triangulation seriously as a way of meeting the complexities of human behavior with an approach that does justice to that complexity, then we must do two things at once. We must, on the one hand, learn whatever we can about available techniques and make full use of them, with the idea that each additional technique helps us to probe areas we would not be able to reach otherwise. In addition, we must focus the searchlight of investigation on the technique itself and on ourselves as users of the technique. This reflexive approach is essential if we are to take seriously the phenomenon of investigator effect, if we are to take heed of the structuring achieved by any technique, and if we are to give recognition to the ways in which the investigator's paradigms and theoretical perspectives shape every aspect of the research process. Video-taping opens up to the social researcher techniques of observation that, potentially, can carry his understanding of human behavior a great distance. But that potential can be realized only to the degree that the technique and its user are subjects of investigation.

An Illustration: Criticism and Interaction[10]

This research project on criticism and interaction, undertaken by Stephanie Hughes, probes some aspects of the interaction process that go on in face-to-face situations. It is based on a distinction between "negative criticism" and "rounded criticism." The negative critic seizes on the deficiencies of what has been said or done, whereas the rounded critic achieves balance by dealing with both weaknesses and strengths. Hughes' general hypothesis is that rounded criticism can produce a better communication process and more effective collaboration on joint tasks than negative criticism.

If her aims had been limited to these, she would not have done the kind of research that attempted to take a large step in the direction of the development of better technologies for human communication. In a sense, she already knew the answers to those questions on the basis of her personal experience. She might have obtained additional confirmation of that knowledge, but would that have been worth the two-year effort involved in the project? Her aspiration for knowledge that went beyond those questions, knowledge that could be applied, was high. Given that aspiration, what occurred was a project that ended in unanticipated ways. She began with an over-all assumption that the tradition of laboratory research would enable her to fulfill that aspiration. During the research process, she underwent a profound disillusionment, after having pushed those techniques very far, with the strengths of that tradition. By the completion of the project, she converted that disillusionment to a balanced understanding of the weaknesses and strengths involved in controlled observational procedures.

Hughes' research design centered on collaboration with a research partner who worked, successively, with thirty-six female participants with the task of inventing, using a particular principle, a game to be played with a set of dominoes. These principles—such as "tossing the dominoes" or "matching the dominoes"—varied in level of difficulty, based on the assessments of five judges. Each of eighteen different principles was used twice, with the easier and more difficult principles distributed so as to counterbalance each other. The design called for the research partner to use negative criticism with half of the participants and rounded criticism with the other half, and within this limitation, to follow her inclinations freely, to strive to develop the best game possible, and to develop her own problem-solving skills to the utmost. The design also insured that the first

[10] Stephanie Krahn Downs Hughes, "Criticism and Interaction," Ph.D. dissertation, Boston University, 1973.

time a new principle was used was not associated, disproportionately, with a particular form of criticism. Invention of the game took up about twenty minutes. During an additional twenty minutes, the participant responded to written questions about the game invention session. A final period of fifty minutes or so was used to orally debrief the participant about the session, and included playing back a tape recording of the session. "Clinicking" (discussion) sessions between the researcher and the partner took place periodically.

An array of instruments for data collection were used, and these produced measurements for twenty-five variables. Personal data sheets provided information on academic and family background. Suggestion-criticism-coping sequence forms, filled in by both researcher and partner, attempted to assess the chronological sequence of events (e.g., ignored criticism, argued against criticism, ignored suggestion, argued against suggestion, argued for suggestion, built on suggestion, accepted suggestion, tabled suggestion, dismissed suggestion). Game summary write-ups were prepared by each participant in conjunction with the research partner, as were task accomplishment assessment sheets. Reaction sheets, filled out by all participants, centered on degree of interest in continuing the session and in working with someone in a similar manner in the future. Participants also completed a 16-item questionnaire designed to yield a scale of interest in social acceptance and a scale of competitiveness. A semantic differential[11] format was used to assess how participants felt about competitiveness and about collaborativeness. Session-review-with-participant forms were used to

---

[11] The semantic differential technique is a method used for probing the underlying meaning that a given concept has for an individual or group. It was introduced by Charles E. Osgood, George J. Suci, and Percy H. Tannenbaum in *The Measurement of Meaning* (Urbana, Ill.: U. of Illinois, 1957). This procedure was used in the Hughes study by asking participants to fill out questionnaires like the following:

Put a check at a point along each line to describe how you feel when you are *competing to win something*.

	Extremely					Extremely	
		Moderately			Moderately		
			Slightly		Slightly		
				Neutral			
clean	____	____	____	____	____	____	____	dirty
deep	____	____	____	____	____	____	____	shallow
ugly	____	____	____	____	____	____	____	beautiful
strong	____	____	____	____	____	____	____	weak
foul	____	____	____	____	____	____	____	fragrant

Osgood and his co-workers have emphasized that the meaning of concepts for respondents seems to involve evaluation, potency, and activity. Individuals tend to judge or evaluate concepts according to such polar adjectives as good-bad, nice-awful, and beautiful-ugly. Potency may be indicated by strong-weak, large-small, and heavy-light, whereas activity may be indicated by fast-slow, active-passive, and sharp-dull. The method itself is more general than these specific factors isolated in the initial studies, and Hughes is adapting it to her own purposes.

codify data emerging from the debriefing sessions with participants. Participant feelings over time—concerning her relationships with the partner, her contribution to the game, and the partner's contribution—were measured on grids with a time axis and another axis varying from "unfriendly" or "highly dissatisfied" to "friendly" or "highly satisfied." Session review wrap-up forms focused on the participant's reactions to the kind of criticism she received. Debriefing forms that divided a game-invention session into four time periods codified supplementary information on the debriefing sessions.

In a study of this level of complexity, it is not possible to do more than provide a brief and impressionistic sketch of a few of its aspects in a limited number of pages. A large number of specific hypotheses bearing on the differences between negative and rounded criticism were studied, and generally, the data bore out the researcher's ideas about the impact of the one versus the other. But this did not satisfy the researcher's original level of aspiration, namely, for much deeper knowledge of the genesis and subtleties and impact of the criticism process than she started with. She developed a number of approaches in an attempt to satisfy that level of aspiration. One of them was to focus on the "interaction stream" between partner and participant. This approach is conveyed in the following illustration:

Let's look now at a typical example of how rounded criticism is managed. It shall again be a composite illustration, but this time based heavily on case #28R. One of the pair draws a principle and reads it aloud: "Forming letters with the dominoes." As the tape and timer are started, the people push the dominoes around on the table. After exchanging a few humorous comments about regressing to childhood, the participant makes a specific suggestion. "The object could be for each person to form a letter out of the squares with a certain number, like this." She indicates the "T" she formed of "5's." The partner studies the "T" for a moment and then gives her criticism. "Yeah, using the numbers un-babyfies it. It gives us a system. But I don't think there are enough of any numbers to make complicated letters, like B." The participant responds by modifying the notion: "Yah, well we could use the whole domino—what it adds up to—and the half besides." The partner makes a "B" that way and then makes her criticism: "You do have more to work with. And the adding makes it more educational. It's too bad these ends hanging out mess up the letter."

The participant defends her idea, and begins to question the partner about it: "That doesn't bother me much. Can you think of . . . ?" Suddenly enthusiastic, the partner builds, saying "Hey, it could be they have to substract the ends from what all the dots *in* the letter add up to." The participant agrees and builds further: "Sure, and the next guy could start his letter from any of those ends and get points for it." The partner critiques: "Yes, that gives us a link between players. I think this scoring system is a little fuzzy, though." The pair goes on to work out the scoring system and the other elements of the game in the time remaining.[12]

Despite these efforts, which do yield greater insight into the dynamics of the interaction process, the results are still a far cry from the kind of insight that the researcher is after. She reveals her aspiration in a paragraph in the final chapter:

> It is conceivable that children can be raised in an environment—a reality can be constructed—in which aggressive impulses regularly find expression in noninjurious and functional activities—encouraged by a host of norms, one of which is rounded criticism. Socialized in this way, they would have not only greater inclination but more tools to be proactively collaborative. The long-held hope of "making peace"—between individuals, classes, races, religions, states and nations—would have more foundation.[13]

Against this aspiration, Hughes discovered that a number of important things were going on in the research sessions that she could not monitor adequately or control. Most important, there was the personality of the partner, which could not be controlled adequately by instructions to give negative criticism in one instance and rounded in another. If the partner liked a given participant and yet was supposed to give negative criticism, there were numerous ways in which such criticism could be softened without the partner being aware of the process. And even if sessions between researcher and partner revealed what was going on, the partner herself was not in complete control of her behavior in subsequent sessions. In addition to the personality of the partner, there was the personality of the participant. Despite all the efforts at measurement, how much of the complexity of given participant's personality was revealed? The researcher, in an attempt to fill in some missing ground at the beginning of the project, developed her own observational rating of the level of "sympatico" of each participant. Those with high scores appeared to the researcher to be particularly self-confident, trusting, inquisitive, and interested in the project. Those with the lowest scores appeared to lack these qualities and to be somewhat defensive and self-conscious.

In addition to theoretical conclusions, Hughes draws methodological ones as well on the basis of the problems she encountered in a complex study that was partly experimental, partly observational, and partly a survey:

> All of the above mentioned are problems fairly common to projects put in the context of verification. Because of sociologists' aspirations to be "scientific," they have been so conceived. Since "hard science"

---

[12] Hughes, op. cit., pp. 237–38.
[13] Ibid., p. 251.

is concerned with quantitative data and statistical analysis, the positivistic sociologist has wanted to produce numbers. But sociologists must face certain realizations. Social phenomena are in constant flux and are considerably more complex than complex physical phenomena. Careful measurement of some miniscule detail, isolated and stopped to allow the measurement, has not had much impact, nor has careful measurement of large social system dynamics, segregated, balanced and controlled to allow the measurement. When the richness of a social process rises from a catalytic combination of factors, it impoverishes the inquiry to study those factors in isolation one from another. And while insight into the functioning of such a process is developing, to arbitrarily settle on a classification system for a fullblown enumeration is self-defeating.[14]

There appears to be no set of procedures already codified that can fulfill the level of aspiration with which this study was conceived, but perhaps that itself is a major finding of the study. One can pile on measurement upon measurement, one can triangulate with different methods of data collection, one can go beyond formist modes of research, and still one has a long way to go. In her concluding section, Hughes discusses the possibility that rounded criticism can continue to move deeper and deeper, both negatively and positively, likened to a pendulum swinging in increasing arcs. We might see, for example, the negative arc as the questioning of an individual's paradigm from the perspective of an alternate paradigm, and we might see the positive arc as the presentation of such an alternate paradigm. Hughes herself refers to something similar in her concluding chapter when she speaks of a need "to legitimize reflexive study as a tool for inquiry in the context of discovery." Yet none of this should be taken to belittle the importance of the context of verification. If careful quantitative measurements of trivial details are unnecessary, then careful quantitative measurements of important theoretical variables are crucial.

Applying the lessons from the Stratman study of the French student revolt, to what extent does Hughes approach her study with a paradigm that is almost identical with that of previous investigators in this area? Does she, by contrast, work from a distinct paradigm that might be expected to produce nontrivial investigator triangulation? Figure 10-1 illustrates the way rounded criticism (2) contrasts both with (1) positive criticism (where agreement between A and B is emphasized) and (3) negative criticism (where disagreement between A and B is emphasized). These latter two forms of interaction tend to produce a static situation: A and B can choose to maintain their stances in an all-or-none manner. By contrast, within rounded criticism each is encouraged by the existence of the overlapping area C to see the situation from the perspective of the other, thus tending to yield the kind of development of personal perspective characteristic of a pragmatist paradigm.

[14] Ibid., p. 257–58.

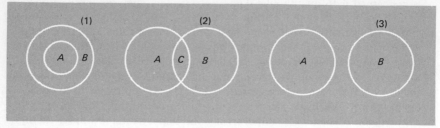

Figure 10-1.
Positive, Rounded, and Negative Criticism.

The two studies can be seen to be related in another way as well. Figure 10-1 (2) illustrates the structure of a metaphor as well as the structure of rounded criticism: take A to be the sticks supporting a chair, B to be a human leg, and C to be the growth in meaning attached to both chair sticks and human legs when we speak of the "leg of a chair." For Stratman, the researcher can too easily miss the Dionysian aspects of human behavior because of his ascetic heritage, neglecting to see *homo ludens* or gamelike behavior. A game is a kind of metaphor where a correspondence is drawn between real life and the game. Both games and metaphors are important bases for the socialization process and perhaps for human development generally. They also mesh with a researcher's concern for both the context of discovery and the context of verification.

10.3   Summary

Like other methods of data collection, techniques of observation require the support of theoretical and paradigmatic knowledge in order to define a research problem and lay a firm basis for data collection procedures. Without such knowledge, the researcher has little basis for knowing how to go about taking his observations or how to assess his observations after they are taken. This is just as important for field observations as it is for laboratory observations, although it is commonly thought that a theoretical framework is important primarily in relatively structured settings like the laboratory. In field situations we tend to be less conscious of the ways in which we, as investigators, are structuring the research situation, but we are structuring it nonetheless.

As we continue to discuss additional methods of data construction, it becomes apparent that each one has something unique to offer the investigator. For example, observational procedures give him an extended ability—beyond the more cognitively oriented survey techniques—to assess many different kinds of nonverbal behavior. They help to free him from dependence on verbal behavior and thus to depart from the "rational man" assumption that verbal behavior can predict nonverbal behavior. The concept of triangulation, as applied to different research techniques, points us toward a research approach that can capture the advantages of a variety of procedures. Thus, we can learn to develop a research orientation that is experimental, gaming, cognitive, and nonverbal.

Exercises

1. Using the fundamental perspectives and paradigm employed by Stratman, observe the Dionysian aspects of some leisure time activity in comparison to those of a given classroom. What are the differences? How well have you been able to adopt Stratman's paradigm?

2. Apply field observation techniques in family or friendship situations. What role are you assuming? To what degree do you feel role conflict? Do you feel that you are in control of the role you are assuming? Can you gain insights beyond those you already have? Is it important for you to define a problem?

3 and 4. Apply controlled observational procedures within the foregoing contexts, centering on some question of interest that has emerged from the preceding exercises. Before proceeding, define the problem so as to bring to bear relevant social science knowledge. Take Hughes' advice about not letting the details of your procedures get in the way of what is going on.

Annotated References

DENZIN, NORMAN K. (ed.). *Sociological Methods: A Sourcebook*. Chicago: Aldine Publishing Company, 1970. Contains three articles on participant observation, three on the life history method, two on the naturalistic perspective, and four on research triangulation.

LIEBOW, ELLIOT. *Tally's Corner: A Study of Negro Streetcorner Men*. Boston: Little, Brown and Company, 1967. Liebow presents the results of a field observation study in the anthropological tradition that has become somewhat of a classic in a short time. In an appendix, "A Field Experience in Retrospect," he centers on the methods involved.

WEBB, EUGENE J., DONALD T. CAMPBELL, RICHARD D. SCHWARTZ, AND LEE SECHREST. *Unobtrusive Measures*. Chicago: Rand McNally & Co., 1966. The chapter on simple observation deals with such topics as exterior physical signs, expressive movement, physical location, conversation sampling, and time sampling. Other chapters include a controversial one on "contrived observation: hidden hardware and control."

chapter 11
Available Data

11.1 Introduction: The Historical Approach

It is all too easy for the sociologist to neglect the rich resources of knowledge embodied in data that has been collected in the past. In his eagerness to make new discoveries, he may also focus on new data, assuming that old data can be of little use to him. Yet just because data have been used or analyzed previously is insufficient reason to believe that those data have been well understood. Indeed, our division of labor almost guarantees that such data will have been looked at from a narrow perspective. The question is always an open one: how are we to understand the dynamics of human behavior that are embodied in any set of available data? This question becomes more pertinent as we begin to realize—as illustrated in the preceding chapters on data construction—how little of the dynamics and complexity of the human behavior encompassed by even our most sophisticated research designs we understand.

The historian tends to be very interested in such information, since for him it holds the keys to an understanding of the past. The sociologist, who generally is more interested in understanding the present, can easily overlook the degree to which the past is embodied in the present. As a result, he may emphasize taking samples of data from one relatively narrow time period—the present. Yet if human behavior is a function, to a great extent, of temporal and spatial contexts, then such samples are quite limited. To think that, somehow, an analysis of the present can explain human behavior for all time illustrates a mechanistic paradigm: the nature of human beings, having been determined once and for all, requires observation at only one point in time. But much of the body of sociological knowledge suggest a more change-oriented paradigm.

Another reason for the sociologist to be concerned with available information on the past is that he is now in a better position than ever before to contribute to an understanding of the past and, thereby, of the present as well. If the experimental orientation is a useful one, then the observer of data also constructs in part the data he observes. Our knowledge of history, then, is partly a function of the knowledge we bring to bear on history. If we assume that we are now in a better position than ever before to bring social science knowledge to bear on past situations, then our understanding of those situations should also improve as a result. History is being rewritten all the time. Every historical event—such as the development of the industrial revolution—is only minimally understood relative to the kinds of understandings that await us.

But we cannot proceed very far in an effort to deal with available data without exploring the nature of data. What are data? The very terms I have used in posing this question—the "nature of data" and the use of "are"—imply a static and rather formist perspective: that data exist out there, unchangeable in form, waiting to be interpreted, and that different investigators would arrive at the same conclusions. This approach implies the formist distinction between the plain of truth and the plane of observation, with data existing on the plane of observation, and with truth being unaffected by spatial or temporal contexts. It is very difficult to think of knowledge in any other way than this, since this paradigm is so deeply embedded within our way of life and processes of thought.

Yet there are alternatives to this, as illustrated by the pragmatist paradigm. We can see truth, or the validity of statements about phenomena, as referring to the levels of water in a variety of beakers, as illustrated in Figures 6-1 and 6-2. In this view, truth itself does not change with the viewer: there is a truth that it is possible for all viewers to learn to accept, a truth that explains the partial experiences of every observer. Science is possible, then, in the sense that we might expect that a community of scientists can—through mutual communication—progress on the road to ever greater knowledge. Having said this, we must recognize how far any given scientist's perception may be from an understanding of where the water really is, especially if he has little awareness of how much he himself participates in constructing the image he sees. Thus, the apparent truth will change drastically with the viewer, and it is only through increasing knowledge that we can expect an increasing convergence between apparent truth and truth.

These abstract ideas have very concrete implications for the investigation of available data. If any investigator's vision of where the water is will be hampered by the narrowness of his frame of reference—especially by his failure to be reflexive—then we can go far beyond the knowledge of the past that has been handed down to us by the various specialists who have studied the past, provided that we can bring to bear a wider frame of reference. All of the studies and data handed down become to an extent mysteries, to be explored anew, since the apparent truths handed down may differ widely from the actual truths. A key implication of this approach, then, is to open up new possibilities, to raise the level of aspiration of the modern investigator by showing him opportunities that are quite feasible for him to undertake, opportunities that he would not otherwise undertake in deference to the experts of the past and to his own limited knowledge. This is what I mean by the "historical perspective" that an interest in available data can teach us, just as the modes of data construction discussed previously teach us experimental, gaming, cognitive, and nonverbal perspectives.

All of these perspectives extend far beyond the limits to which they are usually assigned within the scientific research process, suggesting once again the relationship between scientific research and human communication, as pictured in Figures 1-1 and 1-2. To the degree that we segregate the two, such perspectives can be legitimately applied only by bona fide scientists in bona fide scientific research projects. However, because such scientists will attempt to apply them only during a minute portion of their lives, they will be unable to learn them very well, since for the nonscientific portion of their lives—almost all of their experiences—they will be learning quite different perspectives. To learn these perspectives effectively, the scientist must use them in more and more of his life, working in areas where he is no longer defined as a scientist or expert. Of course, if he can operate in such areas, so can others.

In this way, all phenomena are opened up to the research process, as contrasted with the very narrow range of phenomena that occur within defined research projects and are being investigated by those defined as scientists. The scientist's everyday experiences become data, and so do the everyday experiences of everyone else. Without such an opening up, imagine how much potentially useful data from human experiences are lost to the scientific process—perhaps 99.999999 per cent or more. Every organization, every professional, every human being, each day has numerous experimental and observational experiences—using these terms broadly to include the full range of data construction and data collection techniques—that fail to contribute to our systematic knowledge of human behavior because they are not defined as scientific experiences.

Yet to open up this almost unimaginably rich source of data to scientific exploration will require considerable effort, and perhaps we had best think of proceeding one step at a time. If the scientist can master the experimental, gaming, cognitive, nonverbal, and historical orientations within the context of research projects, then he can learn to do so within the context of his everyday life experiences. And to the extent that he is able to do this, he will be able to teach others to do it as well: to teach the teacher or the physician or the social worker or the engineer to view their professional—and, later, their everyday—behavior from experimental, gaming, cognitive, nonverbal, and historical perspectives, and to communicate whatever knowledge they attain as a result so that the codification of scientific knowledge can be accelerated.

In this chapter I take up a quantitative and a qualitative illustration of a historical approach, that is, an illustration of an emphasis on available data. These illustrations both involve discussions of procedures for the analysis of data, a topic that has been reserved for Part Four of this book. Yet it is not possible to segregate the various parts of the research process so neatly. Indeed, we have had to take into account considerations relating to analysis in each chapter. In this chapter, however, even more than in the preceding ones on data construction, analysis is emphasized.

11.2 A Quantitative Illustration: Social Science Data Banks

Of all the quantitative social science research that has been performed up to this point in time, a proportion has found its way into data archives, or data banks, many of which are easily accessible to any researcher. The challenge this poses to the modern researcher is considerable: by using whatever theories and research procedures he can, how much can he add to the insights of previous researchers? For example, suppose that most researchers work within a formist framework, and that they tend to see most portions of, say, a questionnaire or interview schedule as separated from one another. Then the analytic procedures they would follow would, correspondingly, segregate different parts of the questionnaire: some tables would deal with some parts of the instrument, and other tables with other parts. There would be little analysis that would utilize a theoretical perspective to pull together a great deal of the questionnaire or interview schedule simultaneously. If this were the situation, a researcher with another paradigm—say, a mechanistic one—would be in a position to integrate the data in ways that had not been done previously. For him, the data, embodying many man-hours of research, provides an open door to testing and developing his own theoretical ideas. And if there are hundreds and hundreds of studies readily available for analysis, then in a relatively short time he can gain a vast amount of information.

I believe that my example in the above paragraph does represent the existential situation of the modern researcher. To the degree that his own paradigm—along with the theory and methodology that would be associated with it—departs from a formist one—vast opportunities for doing original and important research are available, and they require only a small fraction of the research effort that is generally required. He might perform something on the order of twenty projects in the amount of time that would normally be required for one, and his expenses for the twenty would be quite low. I will illustrate the approach in this section by employing an organicist paradigm and by applying organicist theory and methodology to data collected in the Almond and Verba Five-Nation Study.[1] These data were available to me through the Inter-University Consortium for Political Research.[2]

[1] See Gabriel A. Almond and Sidney Verba, *The Civic Culture* (Boston: Little, Brown, 1965).

[2] Access to these data is obtained through university membership in the consortium at a cost of several thousand dollars per year. Tapes of a large number of studies

The context for this study was a course in research methods required of graduate students entering the Boston University Department of Sociology. I wanted to present an illustration of techniques for analyzing social science data banks that would be simple and clear yet would show the possibilities available to the researcher. A first step was for me to look over the codebooks containing the detailed descriptions of the data presently available on computer tape at Boston University and to locate a study to be analyzed. I selected the Almond and Verba study because a student in a previous class—Roger Whittaker—had examined the codebook and found a great many questions in the interview schedule that covered a range of experiences that might be of interest to sociologists. Whittaker's selection, in turn, was based in part on his interests in doing comparative analyses. On the basis of his interests, he had developed some specific hypotheses and had located items in the codebook that could be used to test those hypotheses. This illustration, then, is based on that theoretical formulation.

A great deal of the Almond and Verba study centered on the subject of *Political Participation* (e.g., "Do you follow the accounts of political and governmental affairs . . . ?) in an attempt to explore those factors inducing individuals to participate in their national political processes. Whittaker located four sets of items that he saw as potentially related to political participation: (1) *Political Sense of Efficacy* (e.g., "If you made an effort to change this regulation, how likely is it that you would succeed?"), (2) *Family Participation* (e.g., "How much influence do you remember having in family decisions affecting yourself?"), (3) *School Participation* (e.g., "Did you participate . . . in running school affairs?"), and (4) *Work Participation* (e.g., "When decisions are made affecting your own work, do those in authority over you ever consult you about them . . . ?"). Whittaker's general hypothesis was that degree of participation in family, school, and job situations is related to degree of political participation and sense of political efficacy.

By defining a problem in relation to theories and paradigms, we are linking it to a very wide range of available data that has been summarized in these relatively abstract forms. Without going into the detail exemplified by the illustrations in Chapter 4, this hypothesis can be related to important bodies of sociological theory. For example, there is an implicit recognition of the importance of the phenomenon of political alienation, stemming from conflict theory. From a structural-functional viewpoint, there is a sense of the interrelationships among the various structures of society, that is, that the family, school, and occupational structures prepare the individual to take up important political functions. From social exchange

by social scientists in a variety of disciplines can be purchased for a nominal fee, and codebooks are supplied for all available studies to all members. For information, writer the consortium at Box 1248, Ann Arbor, Michigan 48106.

theory we can derive the idea that if the individual learns early in life to find his social participation rewarding, that will encourage him to find political participation rewarding later in life. As for symbolic interactionism and phenomenology, Whittaker centers his investigation on the forces that surround the decisions of the individual within the political arena; to the extent that this study is pursued beyond the brief illustration presented here, it would be essential to explore the complex and dynamic interactions among the various factors outlined as they affect any given individual. I am suggesting, then, that although these two theoretical perspectives are only indirectly illustrated in the material to be presented, they nevertheless would be important for guiding further work.

Behind Whittaker's hypothesis and behind these theoretical traditions lie certain paradigms. I see the organicist paradigm as the dominant one within the analysis to be illustrated and the pragmatist paradigm as being involved in a subsequent analysis centering on the implications of symbolic interactionism and phenomenology, with both of these analyses incorporating both formist and mechanistic assumptions. Whittaker's central concern is a comparative one: for example, how do processes differ between Mexico and the United States? Implicit in this idea—I believe—is the notion that cultures and societies have evolved in different directions and in varying degrees along these directions. Thus, the dynamics of political alienation would be a different thing in nations at different stages of the industrialization process. Depending on the stage, in part, different kinds of social structures will develop, and these in turn will tend to constrain the individual to behave in different ways.

If we limit ourselves to any one nation considered at a given stage of industrialization, then the mechanistic paradigm is involved in association with the organicist paradigm. The individual's political goals are developed through immersion in family, school, and work structures. Once he develops these goals, he is then constrained to act them out within the political arena, in much the same way as a billiard ball given an initial momentum must move unless it meets some opposing force. And if the billiard ball is given little or no momentum, as in the case of individuals who have learned to withdraw from participation, then we can expect little political movement. The formist paradigm is also involved: the analysis centers on assessing whether or not a difference in political participation exists between those who have participated in family, school, and work structures and those who have not. It is only when such a difference has been established that we can begin to explore the particular dynamics of the forces involved.

If theoretical and paradigmatic perspectives are not carried forward within the measurement process, then the result is the familiar gap between theory and method, with the theory providing irrelevant and even misleading window dressing for the study. The measurement basis for an analysis that would go beyond the formist paradigm is an approach that pulls together simultaneously a great deal of the data within the interview schedules. Mechanistically, we can conceive of adding together the various factors producing a force for participation within family, school, and work contexts, and then using this combined measure as an index of the force available for political participation. From an organicist perspective, we would see this force as varying between nations at different stages of the industrialization process. And from a pragmatist framework, we would want to pull together the many different indicators of an individual's existential situation in relation to those forces surrounding him.

In order to keep things as simple as possible for purposes of classroom presentation, I decided to focus on data from the United States sample, thus moving largely into a mechanistic paradigm. My belief was that it would be possible for the student—on the basis of an understanding of a mechanistic approach, which would give him experience in pulling together many different items within the study—to easily move beyond this paradigm on his own. For example, an organicist approach would focus on comparing nations at different stages of industrialization, and a pragmatist approach would involve integrating a great many more items bearing on more facets of the individual's life situation with the ones already discussed. One further simplification involved drawing a random sample of 310 individuals from among the almost 1,000 respondents in the U.S. study. This was due to purely technical considerations. I wanted students in the course to be able to learn how to work from remote terminals connected to the central computer, and the smaller sample made this possible. The procedure I had recommended to them was to do all of their analyses on a sizeable sample from a terminal and then to do the final runs with the entire sample working directly with the central computer. This is a convenient procedure because one can continually interact with the data on a terminal, posing many questions and obtaining many answers within a single session, whereas the central computer operation is done on an overnight basis, and the researcher cannot sequentially ask a series of questions.

The classroom exercise, in addition to illustrating the analysis of data archives, also was designed to illustrate the SPSS[3]—Statistical Package for the Social Sciences—techniques for the analysis of data. This package constitutes extremely versatile procedures for performing scaling operations, for constructing tables, and for performing different types of statistical tests and constructing various measures of degree of association. The researcher who learns how to use this package will be able to do highly sophisticated analyses in a very short time, provided of course that he has a clear-cut theoretical direction and provided that he understands the nature of the various statistical techniques that he can bring to bear.

[3] For a description of SPSS, see N. Nie, *Statistical Package for the Social Sciences* (New York: McGraw-Hill, 1970).

The analytic procedures used began with the construction of five Likert-type scales of political participation, political sense of efficacy, family participation, school participation, and work participation. To illustrate with reference to the family scale, four items were selected from the interview schedule as bearing on family participation, and the answers to each were divided into two categories: those indicating less participation and those indicating more participation. The former categories were assigned weights of 0 and the latter categories weights of 1, as follows:

	Less Participation	More Participation
How much influence do you remember having in family decisions affecting yourself?	0	1
If a decision were made that you didn't like, did you feel free to complain . . . ?	0	1
If you complained, did it make any difference in your parent's decision?	0	1
At that time do you remember ever actually complaining?	0	1

Thus, an individual who answered each question in a high-participation way could obtain a maximum score of 4, contrasting with a minimum score of 0. Seven items were incorporated into the school participation scale, producing a maximum of 7 and a minimum of 0. The work participation scale went from 3 to 0; the political participation scale ranged from 10 to 0; and the political sense of efficacy scale ranged from 6 to 0. All of this scale construction involved a series of recoding operations that could be performed from a terminal using SPSS.

The next step called for a series of cross-tabulations of one scale against another, in accordance with the hypothesized relationship between degree of participation in various social systems and degree of political participation. For example, Table 11-1 presents the results of a cross-tabulation of degree of family participation and degree of political participation. For the purpose of ease of interpretation, I simplified the scale of political participation so that it ranged from 1 (low participation, to 2 (high participation) instead of from 0 to 10. Reading across the top row, we have a range from 70% of the low family participators who are also low political participators to 33% of the high family participators who are low political participators. The second row tells the same story: 30% of the low family participators are high political participators, and this compares with 67% of the high family participators who are also high political participators.

In Chapter 12 I shall discuss statistical tests of hypothesis. At this point, I might simply indicate that a chi-square (χ^2) test indicated a statistically

Table 11-1

A Cross-Tabulation of Family Participation and
Political Participation

Political Partici- pation	Family Participation				
	Low 0	1	2	3	High 4
low 1	70%	53%	43%	44%	33%
high 2	30%	47%	57%	56%	67%
total %	100%	100%	100%	100%	100%
total N	(47)	(45)	(44)	(72)	(102)

significant relationship between these two variables at the .001 level. In words, the chances are only one in a thousand that such findings as appear in Table 11-1 could have been produced from a population (from which the sample was selected, e.g., adults in the United States at a given point in time) where no relationship between the variables existed. Because of his minute risk, we can afford to reject what is called the *null hypothesis,* namely, the hypothesis of no relationship.

Many other cross-tabulations were obtained along with statistical tests and measures of association related to each cross-tabulation. For example, a scale of political orientation was constructed by combining the scales of political participation and political sense of efficacy, and political orientation was found to be related to family and school participation (.01 and .001 levels, respectively) but not to work participation. As another illustration, a scale of social participation was constructed by combining the scales of family, school, and work participation, and social participation was found to be related to the scales of political orientation, political participation, and political sense of efficacy at the .01, .01, and .05 levels, respectively.

In the foregoing illustration, I have attempted to demonstrate how easy it is to learn to take advantage of the social science data banks available to the researcher. The analysis discussed here appears to indicate that it is possible to come up with interesting and respectable findings without a heavy investment of time and money. I believe that this illustration also indicates that efforts to combine many items into scales—thus moving beyond a formist paradigm—can prove to be fruitful. For example, the percentage range in Table 11-1 from 70% to 33% (a range of 37%) is a substantial one. It is only recently that such masses of data have become so readily available, and only recently that computer technologies have been developed for dealing easily with such data. It remains to be seen just what the implications of applying scaling techniques that enable the investigator to analyze a large portion of his instruments for data collection within the same table will prove to be. One indication of the possibilities is Table 11-2—appearing on page 268—where the percentage range is 63%.

11.3   A Qualitative Illustration: Content Analysis

In addition to quantitative data available for analysis, there are storehouses of qualitative data awaiting analysis. These are located in many places, the most important being the library. For example, there are the newspapers, periodicals, films, tapes, and video tapes produced by the various mass media. There are arrays of political, judicial, and other governmental records. There are industrial records of all kinds. There are many private documents, such as diaries. Perhaps most important, there are the millions of books that have been written. The thread running through all of this material—distinguishing it from quantitative material, such as census findings, actuarial records, and sales records, as illustrated in Section 11.2—is that it is conveyed by means of language, whether written or spoken.

Whatever the reasons, sociologists generally have not chosen to explore such material in depth. One well-known study that illustrates the potentials within the approach was Leo Lowenthal's study of biographies that appeared in *The Saturday Evening Post* and *Collier's* between 1901 and 1941.[4] Lowenthal—although he did not use these terms—was interested in tracing a shift from a mechanistic to an organicist paradigm: from "idols of production" to "idols of consumption." He divided the biographies into those written about political figures, business and professional people, and entertainers, and he compared the proportion of biographies in each of these fields occurring at different periods. He found a striking decline in the percentage of political biographies: from 46% in the 1901–1914 period to 25% during 1940–41. There was a slight decline in the percentage of business and professional figures (from 28% to 20%), and an enormous increase in the percentage of entertainers (from 26% to 55%). Within the entertainment category itself, he found a dramatic shift from 77% of the biographies dealing with entertainers from the serious arts (literature, fine arts, music, dance, theatre) during the earlier period to only 9% during the later period. Lowenthal summarizes the shift in this way:

> We called the heroes of the past "idols of production"; we feel entitled to call the present-day magazine heros "idols of consumption." Indeed, almost every one of them is directly or indirectly, related to the sphere of leisure time. . . .

[4] Leo Lowenthal, "Biographies in Popular Magazines," in William Petersen (ed.), *American Social Patterns* (Garden City, N.Y.: Doubleday, 1956), pp. 63–118.

It is neither a world of "doers" nor a world of "doing" for which the biographical curiosity of a mass public is evoked. . . .

The average man is never alone and never wants to be alone. His social and psychological birth is the community, the masses. His human destiny seems to be a life of continuous adjustment: adjustment to the world through efficiency and industriousness; and adjustment to people by exhibiting amiable and social qualities and by repressing all other traits. . . . The character image on which an affirmative judgment is passed in the biographies is that of a well-trained employee from a well-disciplined lower-middle-class family.[5]

Lowenthal illustrates the potential of content analysis for dealing with social change. It is one thing to attempt to collect, say, interview data from a given sample of individuals at a number of widely separated points in time, with all the time, difficulties, and resources involved, and it is quite another to collect data from the mass media. Here we have possibilities for the analysis of available data to provide the investigator with historical perspectives over large stretches of time in a relatively painless way. Lowenthal is dealing with a fundamental shift in paradigm that has been given many labels in addition to his own. I might call this a change from mechanism to organicism. David Riesman might label it a shift from inner direction to other direction.[6] Charles Reich might call it a transition from Consciousness I to Consciousness II.[7] Here, then, is one orientation for content analysis: to include measurements dealing with cultural paradigms.

The detailed illustration of content analysis that I wish to present centers on the analysis of cultural paradigms. It is a study that is based on a questionnaire freshly administered, as distinct from the analysis of data already available. However, I am including it because of its focus on linguistic analysis. The reader might recall that at the beginning of this section, I characterized the thread running through all available qualitative data as consisting of their communication by means of language. Although this is not a particularly startling statement, it implies that an understanding of the meanings conveyed by language is essential for the analysis of available qualitative data. Dealing with ways in which language reveals the paradigms of its users, the study to be discussed pulls together a focus on paradigms and one on linguistic analysis. The approach is analogous to the projective techniques used in surveys: the researcher may draw inferences about the respondent that the respondent himself is not aware of.

I am not claiming here that the illustration to be presented is a definitive one, but rather that it points in a very important direction. If the researcher is limited to whatever his respondents are conscious of, then this is a severe

[5] Ibid., pp. 74, 87–88, 98–99.
[6] David Riesman, *The Lonely Crowd* (New Haven: Yale, 1961).
[7] Charles A. Reich, *The Greening of America* (New York: Bantam, 1971).

restriction. However, if he can learn to probe behind the individual's distorted visions of himself, then this can be a basis for truly effective theory. And if such probing can utilize the kinds of data that surround us, so much the better.

This study was conceived by Andrew Plotkin, a graduate student at Boston University, as a way of exploring the fruitfulness of an idea for a doctoral dissertation. It was based on the assumption that paradigms may be revealed by the degree to which people relate relatively disparate experiences to one another, and by the kinds of explanations people give for these relationships. The initial plan was to administer questionnaires just prior to the arrival of the comet Kohoutek, during the period when the comet would be clearly visible, and after the comet had disappeared. The comet itself was seen as providing a kind of projective test for the individuals queried about it: explicit norms about how one should behave in relation to comets have not been developed, and thus conditions would be favorable for the individual to reveal his own paradigms. Although the comet never did become very visible to the naked eye, the first (and only) questionnaire did serve its purpose in its attempt to illustrate the possibility of deriving paradigms from linguistic analysis.

Respondents were asked questions modeled after some of the questions in the study of the aging process (see Sections 2.4, 9.1, and 9.2):

> In each of the following questions two experiences are named. Please decide if they have anything in common. In the blank spaces provided *before* each of the questions, write "1" if you think the experiences mentioned have *nothing* in common, write "2" if you think they *might* have something in common, and write "3" if you think they *definitely* have something in common. Then in the space below each question, briefly explain your decision. . . .

_____ 1. salary you receive, people you work with:

_____ 2. feeling of doing useful work on your job, the way you spend your leisure time:

_____ 3. enjoying yourself at home, having religious beliefs:

_____ 4. the way you spend your leisure time, the flight of a comet overhead:

_____ 5. a high paying job, enjoyment at home:

_____ 6. many chances for advancement in your job, learning to solve problems:

_____ 7. getting respect because of your job, having close relationships with your family:

_____ 8. the flight of a comet overhead, enjoying your work:

The researcher's orientation was to view individuals who saw nothing in common as well as those who claimed something definitely in common as representing one kind of paradigm (let us call it formist), and individuals who claimed the experiences might have something in common as representing another kind of paradigm (for example, a pragmatist one). A formist is accustomed to seeing the world in discrete packages and to neglect considering the possibilities of other relationships than those he has been taught. A pragmatist, by contrast, would look to all kinds of interrelationships, but he would also be open to the uniqueness of any given situational context.

This analysis is based on the responses of 81 students at Boston University in November, 1973. The eight foregoing items together formed an "integration score," which measured the degree to which respondents were able to integrate disparate experiences. The scoring system was a Likert-type scale. Plotkin reasoned that respondents who indicate that two experiences have *nothing* in common are similar to those who indicate that they *definitely* have something in common. Both, according to Plotkin, are associated with a relatively closed mind, as distinct from a response that the disparate experiences *might* have something in common. Consequently, the extreme responses of "1" and "3" were both coded 1, whereas the intermediate response of "2" was not recoded. The result was that the maximum integration score for the eight items together became 16, whereas the minimum score—supposedly characteristic of the closed mind, or true believer—became 8.

Plotkin next proceeded to analyze the verbal content of the explanations that each respondent gave of the reasons for his decisions, obtaining a language score that summarized his verbal behavior. That score centered on the degree to which his verbal behavior revealed a dichotomous as distinct from a gradational orientation. For example, unmodified verbs ("if you work with garbagemen") were counted as dichotomous in comparison to modified verbs ("the harder I work"). Plotkin next developed a total score for a respondent's linguistic behavior based on the difference between the number of answers oriented in a dichotomous way (dic) and the number oriented gradationally, or dimensionally (dim): Language score = dic — dim. These language scores varied between 8 and 0 for the eight questions.

Table 11-2 presents the relationship beween integration scores and language scores for the 81 respondents. The relationship is a rather marked one. Reading across the first row, we find that fully 88% of those with low integration scores also exhibit dichotomous language, whereas 60% of those with intermediate integration scores and 25% of those with high integration scores do so. Of course, this last percentage is based on a total of only four individuals, so that we should reserve judgment as to just how striking the relationship is pending additional data.

In this analysis we can see one of the most important assets of content analysis: our ability to probe beneath the conscious beliefs of the indi-

Table 11-2
Cross-Tabulation of Integration and Linguistic Scores

| Linguistic Scores | Integration Scores | | |
	Low (8–10) %	(11–13) %	High (14–16) %
Dichotomous (3 or less)	88 (22)	60 (31)	25 (1)
Dimensional (4 or more)	12 (3)	40 (21)	75 (3)
Total	100 (25)	100 (52)	100 (4)

viduals under investigation. The result—that there is a close relationship between the structure of an individual's language and his consciously expressed beliefs—is an encouraging one for the would-be content analyst. It indicates that a great deal may be learned about the authors of linguistic content from this type of analysis without having to subject them to interview procedures. Indeed, it may well prove to be the case that such linguistic scores have more construct validity than scores based on survey data, which are more subject to investigator effects.

There are a great many other measuring procedures that could be applied to language to detect underlying paradigms, and such measures might be combined to produce measurement with increasing validity. For example, we could assess the manifest content of what is being said to determine whether it portrays individuals determining their fate or being determined by the situations they are in. Language could be examined to assess its degree of metaphorical, as distinct from literal, emphasis. The temporal and spatial ranges of phenomena could be assessed. We might determine the relative frequency of use of active and passive voice. We might monitor the relative frequency of usage of *we* in the editorial sense (when a writer means himself). We might examine to what degree a writer introduces autobiographical content.

Such techniques can help to open up the vast stores of qualitative data available to the investigator. But we need not limit ourselves to these content analysis procedures alone. Indeed, if we do so, we shall miss most of the complexity of the human behavior involved. For example, what is the relationship between changes in the *The Saturday Evening Post* and changes in society? The Lowenthal content analysis gives us only one piece of a puzzle, and we require the triangulation of this procedure and theoretical orientation with other procedures and other theoretical perspectives. Yet, let us not downgrade too much the importance of content analysis procedures. The convenience of obtaining such data in comparison to most other kinds of data is great, especially if we are taking a dynamic perspective and wish to compare phenomena over time. Also, there is the amount and variety of such data, and the lack of previous social scientific analysis of it. For example, imagine the possibilities for performing cross-cultural analyses, the analyses of widely separated eras, by means of such procedures.

11.4 Summary

In this final chapter on data construction procedures, we might do well to look back at their relationship to problem definition. It is vital to define a problem so as to build on available knowledge through the utilization of theoretical and paradigmatic understandings, but such efforts will not carry us very far unless we can obtain accurate feedback on that problem via the data we bring to bear on it. And it is through the triangulation of methods of data construction, as aided by the historical approach that the analysis of available data can help to provide, that we can obtain such feedback. Indeed, without such data it would be quite difficult to obtain feedback relative to the kinds of theoretical and paradigmatic frameworks that have temporal and spatial breadth.

Just as our ability to carry forward on a problem we have defined is dependent on the data we can muster, so is it also the case that our ability to utilize data is based on the breadth of our theoretical and paradigmatic frameworks. Data are all around us, yet we require the eyes to take note of the available opportunities. There are the thousands of studies buried in data archives where we can gain access to raw data; there are the vast numbers of published studies, each associated with the particular perspective of the author and thus open to re-examination on the basis of more comprehensive perspectives; there are the storehouses of information of all types produced in written form by the mass media and by a wide variety of commercial and specialized publishers; and there are the staggering numbers of human experiences—indeed, all of human experience—that are never codified in any formal way but that potentially could be used to advance general knowledge. All such opportunities remain unfulfilled without the kinds of theoretical and paradigmatic perspectives that recognize them as legitimate opportunities.

Exercises

1. Obtain access to a codebook for a study that has already been analyzed. Without referring to the results of that analysis or to its aims, define

a problem on which you could obtain relevant data from the study, and sketch out a possible analysis. Now, compare your problem and the analysis you would perform with what was previously done. Do you think your approach would produce insights not produced by the original study?

2. Draw out the theoretical and paradigmatic implications of the problem you defined in Exercise 1 and compare them with the theoretical and paradigmatic implications of the problem as previously defined. How different are they?

3. Apply the techniques Plotkin used, as described in Section 11.3, to analyze some of your own writing as well as the writing of, say, nine others who also complete the brief questionnaire described by Plotkin. Do your results agree with those of Plotkin?

4. Develop additional techniques for linguistic analysis along the lines sketched at the end of Section 11.3 and apply them to the data you worked with in Exercise 3. Does this change the results of your analysis in any way?

Annotated References

DENZIN, NORMAN K. (ed.). *Sociological Methods: A Sourcebook*. Chicago: Aldine Publishing, Company, 1970. This collection includes three articles on the life history method: Howard Becker's "The Relevance of Life Histories," Clifford Shaw's "The Baby Bandhouse," and "Note on the Statistical Treatment of Life-History Material" by Ruth Cavan, Philip Hauser, and Samuel Stouffer.

POLAK, FRED. *The Image of the Future*. San Francisco: Jossey-Bass, Inc., Publishers, 1973. Polak illustrates the historical perspective with a book that neither deals with social science data archives nor with systematic content analysis procedures but, nevertheless, succeeds in exposing the reader to vast amounts of information from the past that are relevant for the present and the future.

WEBB, EUGENE J., DONALD T. CAMPBELL, RICHARD D. SCHWARTZ, AND LEE SECHREST. *Unobtrusive Measures*. Chicago: Rand McNally & Co., 1966. There are two chapters on archives. "The Running Record" includes discussions of actuarial records, political and judicial records, other government records, the mass media, data transformations and indices of the running records, and over-all evaluation of running records. "The Episodic and Private Record" includes treatment of sales records, industrial and institutional records, and written documents.

part IV

Analysis and Interpretation of Data

The analysis and interpretation of data is too important a task to be left to data analysts, although it is difficult for the student of social research to attain sufficient confidence in this area to become his own man. Yet if he fails to do so, he will see all his efforts at problem definition and data construction come to nought, for the prevailing paradigms behind data analytic techniques tend to contradict those behind social science theory. The unhappy results of such conflict are conclusions that miss the problems previously defined. It is not so much that problem and conclusion are in direct contradiction: it is that the latter does not go far enough in the direction of the former. How much good does it do to be able to say with a great deal of confidence that A is related to B if we desperately need to know how these two factors are interrelated with each other and with many other factors in a given situation so that we have a basis for changing existing relationships? If we are desperately searching for clues to effective human relationships in the dark areas of human behavior, how much does it help us to be told that if we come back to the well-lit areas, we will be able to make more definitive statements? We cannot afford to do only the kind of research that neatly fits into available statistical techniques: we must shape the techniques to our own definition of the research problem. Yet we must be able to derive what we can from the available techniques.

The chapters in Part Four cover a great many technical topics, yet the logic behind each topic is exceedingly simple, and the student should be able to use these chapters as a basis for going much further in his education if he so chooses. Chapters 12 and 13 summarize the two fundamental topics of statistical analysis: testing hypotheses and correlation-regression. Here I am concerned with determining whether or not given relationships exist (Chapter 12) and going on to examine the degree and nature of those relationships (Chapter 13). In Chapter 14 I discuss a number of specialized techniques used by sociologists and other social scientists to explore relationships among a set of variables.

chapter 12
Statistical Tests of Hypotheses

Statistical procedures constitute a portion of the techniques that have been developed for the analysis of data and, thus, for bringing data to bear on the researcher's problem. They comprise approaches to making decisions about the bearing of data on the research problem. They help the investigator to become quite explicit about the basis on which he comes to a given decision, say, to conclude that evidence supports his initial hypothesis. By so doing, statistical procedures are aids to the process of scientific communication. By revealing the investigator's criteria for decision making to himself and others, they enable those who question those criteria to come up with different decisions on the basis of different criteria. Without such explicitness, we would be unable to separate the researcher from the data. With the aid of statistical methods, however, we can utilize the data while still disagreeing with the conclusions of the researcher who developed that data.

Yet it would be one-sided to plunge into an exposition of the many ways in which statistical procedures can advance the research process without first looking at the other side of the coin. Sociologists exist today in a house largely divided against itself, with statistically oriented, or quantitative, sociologists occupying one of the many corners. Now is not the time—and perhaps the time is past once and for all—to repeat all the old platitudes about the importance of both quantitative and qualitative sociology: what is required is to convince the qualitative researcher that a quantitative approach can be relevant to his own needs and that he need not succumb, in the process, to becoming a pawn of those quantitative specialists who are masters of the most esoteric of the existing techniques. What is also required is to convince the quantitatively oriented researcher that his mastery of technique can prove to be his own undoing if he allows statistical procedures to become ends in themselves, and to convince him of the importance of developing criteria as to what is and what is not of theoretical relevance.

Perhaps the problem with statistical analysis is not that it has been carried too far but rather that it has not been carried far enough, and I do not mean that we require far more esoteric procedures. If the statistical approach provides a structure within which the researcher bares certain assumptions on the basis of which he makes decisions, then perhaps we need to go still more deeply into our assumptions, down to our fundamental paradigms. From this perspective, the core of statistics is not a quantitative approach but, rather, a procedure for baring fundamental assumptions so that wise decisions about the implications of data can be made. The qualitative researcher needs to employ this procedure at least as much as the quantitative student of human behavior, especially if he naively assumes that he starts with no assumptions whatsoever but is completely open to experience. Then the statistical approach becomes a way of linking decisions about the relevance of all kinds of data—quantitative or qualitative—to explicit paradigms and theory. This approach is itself based on certain assumptions and theory.

In this chapter I shall begin with an illustration of the process of statistical testing, using the work of Plotkin described in Section 11.3 for this purpose. This will be followed by a paradigmatic analysis of the illustration in an attempt to probe the various assumptions used in the statistical testing process. Finally, I shall present an overview of the various kinds of statistical tests and their purposes, assumptions, and utility. It is my hope that a student of social research who understands the ideas in this chapter will have the basis necessary to proceed to the many excellent texts available that deal with statistical analysis for detailed understanding of how to perform the various tests.

12.1   An Illustration: Fisher's Exact Probability Test [1]

I shall begin with an overview of the illustration and then proceed with more detailed treatment of (1) the mathematics of probability involved, (2) the null hypothesis, states of nature, and types of errors, and (3) the level of significance, the region of rejection, and decision. Beginning with an overview, let us recall Plotkin's study, which cross-tabulated integration scores, based on a series of eight questions about relationships that the respondents were able to see, and linguistic scores. In his earliest work on this project, Plotkin administered his questionnaire to eight individuals and obtained the results portrayed in Table 12-1. The individuals are referred to with the letters A through H. The linguistic scores here were derived in a different way from that which Plotkin used subsequently in the study of 81 students at Boston University. Here, he centered on the use of conditional modal verbs, such as *might, could, should,* and *would.* Plotkin's hypothesis here is that integration of disparate elements is associated with the use of conditional language.

[1] See Sidney Siegel, *Nonparametric Statistics for the Behavioral Sciences* (New York: McGraw-Hill, 1956), pp. 96–104.

Table 12-1
Preliminary Listing of Data for 8 Individuals:
Linguistic Study

Individuals	A	B	C	D	E	F	G	H
Integration Scores	9	9	9	9	10	10	12	14
Conditional Language Scores	0	0	0	0	5	2	3	6

The data of Table 12-1 may be simplified by presenting it in the form of a fourfold table, as in Table 12-2. The problem that now presents itself is how to make use of such data as feedback to the original problem. Does it support the idea that the individual's paradigm (integration versus disparateness), as measured by the series of eight questions that went into the construction of the integration scores, relates to his use of conditional language? Or does it negate this idea? If the idea is supported, then we can be encouraged to probe more thoroughly into the various ways in which paradigm choices affect linguistic behavior, and we can also develop a variety of approaches to assessing linguistic behavior so as to improve our understanding of it as well as our measurement procedures. If the idea is not supported, then we would do well to re-examine both the theoretical stance that was the basis for constructing the cross-tabulation (including the paradigm behind the theory) as well as the specific measurement procedures employed. Thus, whether or not the statistical testing procedure supports the original idea or hypothesis, it contributes to knowledge: it encourages us to elaborate on an idea that shows promise, or it pushes us to rethink the idea as well as the procedures for its measurement if the idea does not work out.

Table 12-2
Preliminary Cross-Tabulation: Integration
and Conditional Language Scores

Conditional Language Scores	Integration Scores	
	9 or less	10 or more
0–1	4	0
2 or more	0	4
Total	4	4

The Mathematics of Probability[2]

As we proceed into the mathematics that will provide the basis for statistical testing, we must not lose sight of our central purpose: to decide whether or not Table 12-1 lends support, or fails to lend support, to the idea of a relationship between integration scores and conditional language scores. More specifically, we have data on eight individuals. Four of them proved to be formist (integration score of 9 or less) on the series of eight questions about relationships, and these same four individuals did not use conditional language. The other four individuals were more pragmatist in their integration scores (10 or more) and also tended to use conditional language. A statistical test, based on the mathematics of probability, will help us determine whether this association between high integration score and conditional language (or low integration score and no conditional language) could have occurred purely on the basis of chance, or whether it would be difficult to attribute the association to chance alone. In other words, are we free to pursue further the idea that formists tend to use unconditional language and pragmatists tend to use conditional language, or should we re-examine this idea and the measurement procedures along with it?

From an intuitive perspective, the probability of an event is the chance that it will occur; from a mathematical perspective, probability is a number that can be 0, 1, or any place on the continuum between 0 and 1. A probability of 0 indicates no chance that the event will occur, whereas a probability of 1 indicates certainty that the event will occur. Probabilities close to 0 suggest a slight chance, and as the probability gets closer to 1, the chances of the event occurring increase. If the chances of occurrence and nonoccurrence are equal—as are the chances of heads coming up when we toss a fair coin—the probability is .5.

Much of the mathematics of probability has to do with ways of combining probabilities so as to calculate the probability of events—say, for example, the occurrence of what is described within Table 12-1—in complex situations. To calculate the probability of obtaining two heads in two tosses of a coin, for example, we use the multiplication rule: *If* A *and* B *are two events independent of one another, the probability of getting both* A *and* B *is the product of the probability of Event* A *and the probability of Event* B. For a fair coin, with A being the event "heads on the first toss" and B the event "heads on the second toss," then the probability of A and B, or $p(A \text{ and } B)$, is equal to $.5 \times .5$, or .25. To calculate the probability of obtaining exactly one head in two tosses of a coin, we make use of the multiplication rule as well as the addition rule: *If* A *and* B *are two events mutually excluding one another, the probability of getting either* A *or* B *is equal to the sum of the probability of Event* A *and the probability*

---

[2] For a treatment of probability theory, see Samuel Goldberg, *Probability,* (Englewood-Cliffs, N.J.: Prentice-Hall, 1960).

of Event B. For a fair coin, let A be the event "heads on the first toss and tails on the second toss" (*HT*), and let B be the event "tails on the first toss and heads on the second toss" (*TH*). These two events are mutually exclusive, so that we can use the addition rule:

$$p(HT \text{ or } TH) = p(HT) + p(TH)$$

By the multiplication rule, $p(HT) = p(H) \times p(T) = .5 \times .5 = .25$, and $p(TH) = p(T) \times p(H) = .5 \times .5 = .25$. Thus, we have:

$$p(HT \text{ or } TH) = p(HT) + p(TH) = .25 + .25 = .5$$

If we consider these rules of multiplication and addition to be axioms, then one particularly useful theorem deriving from them, which enables us to calculate the probability of getting exactly r heads in N tosses of a coin, is the *binomial theorem*:

$$p(r) \quad = \quad \binom{N}{r} \quad \times \quad p(H)^r p(T)^{N-r},$$

or $\dfrac{\text{probability of}}{\text{exactly } r \text{ heads}} = \dfrac{\text{number of ways of}}{\text{getting } r \text{ heads}} \times \dfrac{\text{probability of one of the}}{\text{ways of getting } r \text{ heads.}}$

Let us illustrate this general formula with the two examples calculated above. In the first, we are calculating the probability of two heads in two tosses of a fair coin. Thus, $r = 2$, $N = 2$, $p(H) = .5$, and $p(T) = .5$. Then:

$$p(2 \text{ heads}) = \binom{2}{2} \times (.5)^2 (.5)^0.$$

Because any number taken to the power of 0 is equal to 1, we have

$$p(2 \text{ heads}) = \binom{2}{2} \times (.25)(1).$$

As for evaluating $\binom{2}{2}$, we have a general formula giving us the number of possible combinations of N things taken r at a time:

$$\frac{N!}{r!(N-r)!}.$$

Thus,

$$p(2 \text{ heads}) = \frac{2!}{2!0!}(.25).$$

To evaluate $N!$, which should be read "factorial N," we multiply $(N)(N-1)(N-2) \cdot \cdot \cdot (2)(1)$. Thus, $2! = (2)(1) = 2$. Finally,

$$p(2 \text{ heads}) = \frac{2}{(2)(1)}(.25) = .25,$$

which is in agreement with the probability previously calculated. As for the probability of exactly one head in two tosses of a coin, we have

$$p(1 \text{ head}) = \binom{2}{1} \times (.5)^1 (.5)^1 = \frac{2!}{1!1!}(.25) = 2(.25) = .50.$$

We are now very close to being able to deal with Table 12-1. Let us first transform that table into a situation we can more easily visualize. Suppose we have a jar with four old pennies and four new pennies and we choose at random four pennies from the jar. What is the probability that all four of the pennies we choose will be new pennies? This can be solved with the aid of what mathematicians call the *hypergeometric theorem*, which is another theorem based on the axioms of the rules of multiplication and addition. The components required for using the theorem are N, the total population of elements (in this case 8), r, the number of elements chosen at random (4), n_1, the number of elements of one type (4 new pennies), n_2, the number of elements of the other type (4 old pennies), and k, the number of elements of one type that are chosen (4 new pennies). This theorem gives us the probability that all four of the pennies selected at random from the jar will be new pennies, with the result being that the four pennies remaining in the jar will be old pennies. In relation to Table 12-1, if a high paradigm score has no relation to conditional language score and thus functions in a random way with regard to conditional language, then what are the chances that selecting the four individuals with high paradigm scores will also produce the four individuals with high conditional language scores (new pennies) and leave remaining the four individuals with low conditional language scores (old pennies)? According to the hypergeometric theorem, where $K = 4$:

$$p\left(\begin{array}{c}k \text{ high conditional}\\ \text{language scores}\end{array}\right) = \frac{\binom{n_1}{k}\binom{N - n_1}{r - k}}{\binom{N}{r}} = \frac{\binom{4}{4}\binom{4}{0}}{\binom{8}{4}} = \frac{(1)(1)}{\dfrac{8!}{4!4!}} = \frac{4!4!}{8!}$$

$$= \frac{1}{70} = .014.$$

Null Hypothesis, States of Nature, and Types of Error

Since we are interested in obtaining evidence for the existence of some relationship between integration scores and conditional language scores, one procedure for doing so is to begin with an assumption that no relationship exists and then to see whether such an assumption leads to an improbable state of affairs and, thus, to the likelihood that such an assumption is false. Such an assumption made for the purposes of testing its logical consequences (which negates our hypothesis that a relationship between two factors does indeed exist) is called a *null hypothesis* (H_0). In the present illustration, our null hypothesis (H_0) is that "there is no significant relationship between the integration scores and the conditional language scores of the respondents."

Let us begin by noting whether the proportion of individuals with high integration scores who also have high conditional language scores is the same as the proportion of individuals with low integration scores who also have high conditional language scores. From Table 12-1, these proportions are $4/4 = 1$ and $0/4 = 0$, respectively, so that it would seem that no statistical test is necessary to show that these two proportions are not the same. However, suppose that—in the case of pennies in the jar—it was relatively easy for us to choose four new pennies from the jar just on the basis of chance alone. The purpose of the statistical test is to make a decision about whether a relationship exists that could not easily occur on the basis of chance alone. If H_0 is that the two proportions are equal, then the *alternative hypothesis* (H_1) is that the proportion of individuals with high integration scores who also have high conditional language scores is greater than the proportion of individuals with low integration scores who also have high conditional language scores.

Whether we ultimately decide to reject H_0 in favor of H_1 or to accept H_0, it is essential to be aware of the fact that our decision may be an erroneous one. We should take into account a possible gap between our hypothesized view of the state of nature and the actual state of nature. Table 12-3 presents four logical possibilities. Two of these are correct decisions: we can accept the null hypothesis of no relationship when the state of nature is that no relationship exists, or we can reject the null hypothesis of no relationship when in fact some relationship exists. One kind of incorrect decision produces what is known as a *Type I error:* rejecting H_0 when in fact no relationship exists. The other kind of incorrect decision produces a *Type II error:* accepting H_0 when in fact a relationship exists.

Level of Significance, Region of Rejection, Decision

Before being able to come to a decision, we must decide on how great a risk we are willing to run of making a Type I error. This risk, which is the probability of making a Type I error, is called the *level of significance* (α). For example, if we set the level of significance (α) at .10, then the probability of making a Type I error—that is, the probability of rejecting a true H_0—is no more than .10. In other words, there would be no more than one chance in ten that we would be rejecting H_0 when in fact no relationship exists. If we wish to have no more than one chance in twenty of rejecting a true H_0 and risking a Type I error, then we would set $\alpha = .05$, which is a level of significance that tends to be used conventionally.

Table 12-3
Alternative Decisions and Alternative States of Nature

States of Nature	Decisions	
	Accept H_0 (no relationship)	Reject H_0 (relationship)
No relationship	Correct decision	Type I error
Relationship	Type II error	Correct decision

The level of significance (α) and the probability of Type II error (β) are inversely related to one another for a given size sample. Thus, by decreasing α we simultaneously increase β, or the probability of accepting a false H_0. In other words, we would be increasing the chances of deciding that no relationship existed when in fact one actually did exist (the state of nature). Consequently, the chances of uncovering a relationship would be decreased. On the other hand, if we decreased β and thus improved our chances of discovering relationships, we would also be increasing α, or the chances of rejecting H_0 when in fact no relationship exists. Thus, there would be a greater likelihood of coming up with false statements that certain relationships exist.

Levels of significance like .05 and .01 were originally used primarily in medical contexts where, for example, it was important to be fairly certain that some relationship exists between the use of a new drug and favorable therapeutic results. The chances of proclaiming a drug's effectiveness when in fact it is ineffective (making a Type I error) are thus reduced to no more than one in twenty or one in one hundred. However, those significance levels came to be widely used in the context of social science research as well, thus producing a sizable β for the most common sample sizes and making it difficult to uncover relationships that actually exist. In the present situation, I will set $\alpha = .10$ because I am concerned about β as well as α. Another reason for setting α at a higher than customary level is that the sample is quite small, and β increases as the sample size diminishes for a fixed α. For example, if α were set a .01 for this size sample, it would not be possible to reject H_0 no matter how extreme the sample turned out to be (e.g., four new pennies out of the sample of eight). Thus, it would not be possible to make a Type I error. However, if a relationship did indeed exist, then we would be certain to make a Type II error ($\beta = 1$), that is, we would be constrained to accept a false H_0 no matter how the sample turned out.

The *region of rejection* is the set of all the different outcomes or events that would cause us—using the decision procedure discussed above—to reject H_0. Such a region is set up in advance of looking at the data; otherwise, it is too easy to set the level of significance in such a way that the region of rejection will cause the researcher to make the decision he wanted to make in the first place. For present purposes, let us simply pretend that we do not as yet know the actual outcome of this study, as portrayed in Table 12-2. Looking at that table, let us see it as only one of many possible outcomes. Now, would such an outcome fall within the region of rejection? We have already calculated, using the hypergeometric theorem, that the probability of such a table occurring under H_0 is .014, which is considerably less than the level of significance of .10. Thus, Table 12-2 would fall within the region of rejection, since the chances of such a table occurring under H_0 would be less than .10 (only 14 in 1,000).

Would any other outcomes also fall within the region of rejection? To use the Fisher test, we must consider the row and column totals (marginals) to be fixed when making calculations for less extreme outcomes than that in Table 12.2. Let us consider this outcome:

$$\begin{matrix} 3 & 1 \\ 1 & 3 \end{matrix}.$$

Using the hypergeometric theorem, we have

$$\frac{\dbinom{4}{3}\dbinom{4}{1}}{\dbinom{8}{4}} = \frac{(4)(4)}{\dfrac{8!}{4!4!}} = .23.$$

This probability is larger than .10 and thus falls outside of the rejection region. Let us now consider the following outcome:

Conditional Language Scores	Integration Scores	
	9 or less	10 or more
0–1	0	4
2 or more	4	0

Using the hypergeometric theorem, we have:

$$\frac{\dbinom{4}{0}\dbinom{4}{4}}{\dbinom{8}{4}} = .014.$$

This appears to fall within the rejection region, yet let us not be too hasty about including it. Note that such a table would be exactly opposite to the direction of the relationship that was originally hypothesized. In such an outcome, those with high integration scores have low conditional language scores, and those with low integration scores have high conditional language scores. The Fisher exact probability test requires us to specify the direction of H_1. It is what is known as a *one-sided* test, as distinct from a *two-sided test,* where the direction need not be specified in advance. For a one-sided test, only those outcomes in the specified direction can be included within the rejection region. Thus, we cannot include the above outcome in the rejection region. Consequently, the only possible outcome falling within the rejection region is the one specified in Table 12-2. That region must not total more than .10, according to the level of significance set up for this test. It can include any number of outcomes so long as their total does not exceed .10. But it can be much less than .10, as in the present illustration.

Finally, we come to our decision. The data of Table 12-2 fall within the region of rejection, and so we reject H_0 in favor of H_1. What does this mean? The data provide some evidence in support of the original idea that formists tend to use unconditional language more than pragmatists, or that pragmatists tend to use conditional language more than formists. Thus, the statistical test gives us some evidence for the internal validity of this idea, that is, that such a relationship pertains in the situation under investigation. But what about external validity, that is, how widely this finding can be generalized outside of the particular situation under study? In Chapter 13 I shall have a good deal to say about sampling, where the issue of external validity, or representativeness, is crucial. Let us, then, forego further consideration of the external validity of this decision until Chapter 13.

12.2 Paradigmatic Analysis of Statistical Testing

Despite the extensive use of mathematics within the context of statistical testing, the dominant paradigm within this mode of analysis is a formist one. This has both advantages and limitations for the social scientist, whatever the paradigm he chooses to adopt. To understand the nature of the impact of this paradigm on the research process, we must first understand why the specific aspects of statistical testing procedures are formist, and this constitutes the first part of this section. At that point, we are in a position to proceed with discussions of the merits and limitations of this paradigm, which constitute the second and third parts of this section.

Formism Within Statistical Testing Procedures

The most obvious relation between the formist paradigm and a statistical test is the dichotomy between H_0 and H_1, around which the test revolves. In doing a statistical test, our concern is with a choice betwen accepting or rejecting H_0. If H_0 is rejected, then we tend to use this as evidence in favor of H_1. In the illustration in Section 12.1, our null hypothesis was that no relationship between integration score and conditional language score existed. When this H_0 was rejected, we did so in favor of an H_1 that specified that formists tend to use unconditional language more than pragmatists. The focus, then, is on the existence or nonexistence of a relationship between variables and not, for example, on the degree of relationship or on the nature of the particular type of relationship (e.g., its mathematical structure) involved.

We find many other indications of this formist perspective if we probe other aspects of the testing process. For example, the whole approach to the concept of probability suggests the metaphor of the contrast between the plane of truth and the plane of observation, as presented in Figure 3-1. The true probability of, say, a coin's coming up heads is seen as an unchangeable verity, much like the Platonic Idea, in contrast to the observed relative frequency of heads in a limited number of tosses of a coin. The proportion of heads in various sets of tosses—or samples—clusters around the true probability, thus illustrating the idea that there is a point on the plane of observation that corresponds to the "true" value.

From a temporal perspective, we have a static orientation to phenomena in this view of unchanging truth. We are dealing with existence or nonexistence, as distinct from changes, rates of change, acceleration, and so on. Imagine, for example, the pragmatist metaphor for viewing phenomena—as illustrated in Figure 6-1—which involves the continuing flow of water into and out of beakers and continuing change in the levels of the water. A static orientation implies also a lack of concern for time order. We can perform the Fisher test, for example, equally well on survey data taken at one point in time or on experimental data revealing changes over time. Insofar as we are satisfied with such a testing procedure, we are not motivated to explore dynamic relationships, and we will be quite happy to rely on static devices for collecting data, such as survey data obtained at one point in time.

From a spatial perspective, we have in the statistical testing process a rather narrow orientation to phenomena. Our focus within the formist metaphor is on obtaining a correspondence between a *point* in the plane of truth and a *point* in the plane of observation. Contrast this with the three levels of water in interaction with one another illustrated in Figure 6-1. The mathematics that forms the basis for statistical testing procedures has, in general, been concerned with probabiity distributions associated with isolated occurrences, as distinct from complex interrelations among phenomena. The spatial approach involved is illustrated by the multiplication and addition rules for combining probabilities. To apply the multiplication rule, we must assume that events are completely independent of one another. To apply the addition rule, we must assume that the occurrence of one event implies the nonoccurrence of another. One manifestation of the formist spatial perspective is the emphasis of statistical testing procedures on isolated hypotheses as distinct 'from interrelated sets, or systems, of hypotheses. The focus is on analysis as distinct from synthesis.

This temporal and spatial perspective has important repercussions for the kinds of phenomena that the researcher pays attention to, assuming that researchers cannot help but be influenced by the paradigms out of which their research tools are constructed. For example, there is no need to pay attention to the phenomenon of investigator effect, that is, to the impact of the researcher himself on the research process. The true probabilities hover high overhead in the plane of truth, remaining completely unaffected by the details of *which* ant-like investigators are scurrying around in the plane of observation. And even if other truths are seen as affecting the truth that is being investigated, we need not consider them in a particular investigation, since phenomena can be isolated from one another.

As another illustration, there is a failure to deal with such complexities as the interaction between individual personality and group structure, as illustrated in the study of the aging process in Section 2.4 (based on the metaphor of Figure 6-1). Statistical testing procedures are associated with the analysis of aggregates, or groups, as distinct from individuals, and this is the case in psychology as much as in sociology. Yet even within the focus on a given group, or aggregate, there tends to be little concern with the structure of that group. In order to deal with structure, we must deal with relatively complex relationships among a number of factors, and the thrust of the statistical testing procedures available is not geared to dealing with this kind of complexity.

Some Advantages of Formism

One approach to the formist, mechanistic, organicist, and pragmatist paradigms is that each one can contribute to the others, and therein—I believe—lies its utility for the social researcher. However, it is also possible to construe any paradigm as an end in itself, and this appears to be the primary source of the limitations deriving from a paradigm. I shall first center on the former way of construing formism, and then I shall focus on the latter.

In the introduction to this chapter, the statistical approach was seen as making explicit the factors that go into the scientist's decision procedures as he deals with data. It is, then, a baring of the researcher's fundamental paradigm and theory as they operate within the data analysis situation. In the first part of this section I was able to make use of this explicit nature of statistical procedures to explore the paradigmatic and theoretical implications of procedures for testing hypotheses. If such procedures were not so explicit, then the above analysis would have been far more tenuous.

What I am suggesting, then, is that this explicitness constitutes a major advantage of statistical testing procedures, provided we analyze the paradigmatic and theoretical implications of our procedures. With such explicitness, we are in a position to take into account a given investigator's data without necessarily accepting his conclusions. We can more easily come to different conclusions, since we are in a position to set up different criteria within our own procedures for decision making. For example, we might choose a different level of significance from that of the original investigator. Or we might choose a one-sided test in contrast to his two-sided test. Or we might choose a different statistical test altogether, one that functions in a more efficient way for the given situation. Thus, the statistical testing procedure can be an important aid to the process of scientific communication.

One additional aspect of the statistical approach is its orientation to the importance of data. Formism provides us with a dramatic choice between alternatives. In religion, it is between righteousness and sin, heaven and hell, God and man. In statistical testing, it is between statistical significance and statistical insignificance. The data analysis procedure becomes important in its own right. It is insufficient simply to define a problem: we must bring data to bear on that problem and, in the process, decide the fate of our preconceptions. By rejecting a null hypothesis, we lay the basis for going further with our original idea. By accepting a null hypothesis, we achieve insight into the inadequacies associated with those ideas or with the measurement procedures connected with them. In either case, we are given impetus in our movement toward increasing knowledge.

Some Disadvantages of Formism

Just as statistical testing procedures can help us to move toward increasing knowledge, they can also come to be seen as ends in themselves and thus serve as barriers to such scientific progress. Over-all, the temporal and spatial limitations associated with formism—embodied in statistical testing procedures—may be viewed not as simply a first step in moving toward a more dynamic and complex view of reality but rather as a final step. If reality is indeed dynamic and complex, then statistical tests interpreted in this way will prevent us from learning ever more about the nature of that reality. It is not the statistical tests themselves that are at fault but rather the use made of them by the investigator. Someone with a formist paradigm will, then, tend to see them as ends in themselves. However, even such an investigator can contribute markedly to the knowledge of others. Since he must be explicit in his assumptions in order to use such procedures, others can feel free to make different assumptions while still paying attention to the data he collects.

To illustrate the disadvantages, there is an over-all aura of "truth" that can easily surround the performance of statistical tests, and this aura can capture both the investigator and his audience. The investigator who is so captured can become so enamored of his accomplishment—say, the finding of statistical significant relationships—that he loses all sense of perspective. He may tend to equate statistical significance with theoretical significance, forgetting about, say, the importance of construct validity in favor of the importance of the isolated relationships he has tested. He may, thus, fail to go beyond his finding and neglect to use it as a basis for deeper explorations into complex realities. He may not remember how small a distance such a finding takes one on the road to effective knowledge.

The researcher's audience can also be captured by this aura of truth. Part of the problem is simply the impressiveness of any use of mathematics whatsoever, since most of us are aware of the power manifested by mathematics as incorporated within the physical sciences. As a result, statistical significance all too easily comes to be equated with theoretical significance. We then tend to see phenomena in the chopped-up way prescribed by the formist paradigm, and we fail to ask the kinds of questions and define the kinds of problems that would probe the interrelatedness of phenomena. We talk a good deal about social change, but by putting on the blinders of allegiance to the formist paradigm, we do very little about understanding it.

Another illustration of the disadvantages of an end-in-itself approach to statistical testing is the disenchantment with the statistical approach that it has produced. Very few of the studies that have made use of statistical testing procedures have had any major impact on fundamental sociological theories, let alone on developing the basis in knowledge for effective social technologies, and a large proportion of such studies have been viewed generally as quite trivial. As a result, many social scientists have become so cynical about the utility of statistical procedures that they refuse to remain open to their possibilities for advancing the scientific process. I see this as a most unfortunate state of affairs. Just as the end-in-itself approach to statistics carries forward a vision of this enterprise as embodying the truth, it also encourages others to view it as embodying falsehood when it fails to live up to its promises. Yet if we abandon such all-or-none assumptions, there is room for statistical testing procedures to make a useful contribution to the scientific process.

12.3   An Overview of Statistical Testing Procedures

Let us now step back from the specifics of the illustration presented in 12.1 and also attain some distance from the paradigm incorporated within testing procedures with its advantages and disadvantages. Let us move to the situation of the student of social research who must cope with a bewildering variety of statistical testing procedures. What criteria is he to use for selecting one from among this vast array? What are the implications of his choices? How is he to take into account his own particular purposes? In this section we cannot go very far with such questions, but at least we can begin to address them.

Most important, we must not lose sight of the research process as a whole in any approach we take. A statistical test can only do so much for us. It cannot make up for a problem defined in such a way that we fail to recognize our paradigmatic assumptions or the relationship between the proposed research and the existing body of theory. It cannot help us very much if our measurement procedures produce measures with little construct validity, reliability, or precision. It cannot be of much aid if our procedures for data construction fail to penetrate very deeply into the complexities of the situation investigated. Nor can it, of itself, carry us very far in the direction of the kind of knowledge that represents deep understanding or that provides the basis for effective technologies.

Taking these limitations into account and retaining our overview of the research process as a whole, we are in a much better position to make effective choices within the context of statistical testing procedures. Let us begin with the choice of *level of significance*. In the last part of Section 12.1 I contrasted the traditional approach in social science—stemming from the medical tradition—that pays attention only to the probability of Type I error (α), with an approach that gives the probability of Type II error (β) its due. This choice is related to the investigator's interest in the context of discovery (Section 1.4). By choosing to increase α, we are also choosing to emphasize the context of discovery at the expense of the context of verification. This choice depends on our over-all assessment of the state of existing knowledge. Do we feel that it is more important to be more definitive about the tentative knowledge that is floating around, or do we feel that it is more important to develop ideas that go beyond whatever tentative knowledge exists? In my own view, social science has had a history of statistical testing where β has hardly been taken into account relative to α, and that history has not been very noteworthy in its production of the kinds of statistical analyses that have shaped existing theory in important ways. In other words, I feel it might be useful at this point to test another approach to setting the level of significance.

Another choice open to the investigator is that between a one-sided test and a two-sided test, also designated as a one-tailed test and a two-tailed test. In a two-sided test, the researcher tests an H_0 of, say, no relationship against an H_1 of, say, a relationship in either direction. In a one-sided test, the researcher specifies a particular direction for H_1. If there is any theoretical reason to believe that one direction is more likely than the other, a one-sided test is preferable. It carries the investigation one step further, since it yields evidence about more than the simple fact that some relationship exists. Furthermore, assuming that the state of nature is such that the predicted direction of relationship is correct, a one-sided test generally involves a much lower probability of Type II error (β) than a two-sided test.

An additional choice involves the type of scale involved in the measurements, that is, whether the measures are nominal, ordinal, interval, or ratio. There are different kinds of tests appropriate for the different levels of measurement. For example, the Fisher exact probability test can be used with nominal scales (categorical measurement) but not with other levels of measurement. The χ^2 test[3] used for the data discussed in Section 11.2 (Table 11-1) also is designed for nominal scale data and not for higher levels of measurement. There are numerous tests designed for ordinal level data. To illustrate, if we did not convert the data of Table 12-1 to the categorical approach in Table 12-2, we could have used the Mann-Whitney U test for ordinal data (the result would have been exactly the same). The general approach that seems most appropriate is to select from those tests designed for a given level of measurement. As for which test from among a number designed for the same level, sometimes the selection can be made in favor of a test that is described as being the most efficient one. But there is a danger involved in having available a range of tests for the different levels of measurement: one tends to be satisfied with the lowest level of measurement (nominal scales), since one is able to employ statistical tests appropriate to that level. The investigator, thus, is not motivated to develop scales of measurement that are increasingly precise. Also, we should not be carried away with our assessment of the level of measurement represented by a given scale, since its conformity to that level is a matter of degree and is ever in doubt.

An investigator frequently can choose between a *parametric* and a *nonparametric* statistical test.[4] A key difference between the two types of tests is whether or not a normal distribution, or bell-shaped curve, is assumed for the population under investigation. I shall have occasion to say a good deal about sampling from populations as well as probability distributions in Chapter 13. At this point, let us only consider one major implication of this difference: it is much riskier to assume a normal distribution in dealing with small samples than large ones. Thus, the application of parametric tests to small samples generally involves considerable risk in making unwarranted assumptions. Nonparametric tests, which have become widely known to social scientists only within the past decade, have

---

[3] See Siegel, op. cit., pp. 104–11. Or see Hubert M. Blalock, Jr., *Social Statistics,* 2nd ed. (New York: McGraw-Hill, 1972), pp. 275–87.

[4] For a more detailed discussion of the difference between these two kinds of tests as well as a number of illustrations of nonparametric tests, see Blalock, op. cit., pp. 243–72.

encouraged work with small samples, since there are a variety of tests available for use with such samples. These tests also tend to be more appropriate for use with lower levels of measurement than parametric tests, and consequently have the disadvantage of failing to encourage the investigator to make his measurements more precise.

There are other important distinctions among statistical tests, some of which I will pursue in Chapters 13 and 14. For example, there are tests associated with measures of association (see Chapter 13). There are also tests associated with more complex modes of analysis than those illustrated in this chapter or the preceding one, and some discussion of these will appear in Chapter 14. At the risk of repetition, I think it fitting to return—in closing this chapter—to the point I was making at the beginning of Section 12.3. Statistical tests constitute only one tool within the research process and cannot be expected to single-handedly transform that process into a highly effective one. Yet, taking this limitation into account, the statistical approach can help that process to become highly effective by pushing the investigator to communicate his assumptions and by sensitizing him to the importance of subjecting his ideas to a dramatic empirical test.

12.4 Summary

The statistical approach can take its place alongside the experimental, gaming, cognitive, nonverbal, and historical approaches discussed in the various chapters on data construction. It helps the investigator to become explicit about his decision procedures and thus can be an important aid within the process of scientific communication. It also serves as a connecting link between the process of constructing data and that of reaching conclusions as to what has been learned within the research process, conclusions that are essential for the next round of defining the problem. Yet the researcher must be wary lest he allow statistical tools to become ends in themselves and thus lose sight of the importance of all the other aspects of the research process. Furthermore, there is a formist paradigm buried within statistical testing procedures, and this can influence the investigator to fail to ask questions that go beyond the formist paradigm. Through an awareness of such problems, the researcher moves into an excellent position to take full advantage of the wide range of statistical tests available for various kinds of situations. He can also learn to make choices as to the testing procedures most appropriate for his purposes, making decisions with respect to the level of significance, the choice of a one-sided or two-sided test, and the type of test most appropriate for the level of measurement attained. And as the researcher learns to use the statistical approach, he also moves in the direction of becoming ever more explicit about aspects of his decision procedures that previously were hidden from view.

Exercises

1. Apply the hypergeometric theorem to the situation where these numbers substitute for those in Table 12-2:

•	2	2
	2	2

Would such an outcome fall within the region of rejection for the decision procedure discussed in Section 12.1?

2. Would you reject the null hypothesis that you are dealing with a fair coin in favor of the one-sided alternative hypothesis that the probability of heads coming up is greater than that for tails if you obtained five heads in six tosses of the coin? Use the binomial theorem.

3. Do the same as for Exercise 2 above except use an alternative hypothesis that is two-sided.

4. Choose a study involving a statistical test from a social science journal. In what ways does the approach taken illustrate the advantages, and in what ways the disadvantages, of formism?

Annotated References

BLALOCK, HUBERT M., JR. *Social Statistics*. 2nd ed. New York: McGraw-Hill Book Company, 1972. This is widely recognized as *the* book for introducing students of social research, especially those from sociology, to the study of statistics. In addition to his emphasis on causal analysis and the logic of statistical inference, Blalock includes in this edition discussions of a number of nonparametric statistical tests.

BROSS, IRWIN D. J. *Design for Decision: An Introduction to Statistical Decision-Making*. New York: The Free Press, 1965. Bross helps to make the idea of statistical decision-making meaningful by embedding it within the context of human decision-making in general, that is, the process of selecting one action from a number of alternative courses of action.

PHILLIPS, DEREK L. *Abandoning Method*. San Francisco: Jossey-Bass, Inc., Publishers, 1973. A most insightful reaction to the triviality that exists in many quantitative methodological procedures. It conveys an understanding of some of the damage that is done by procedures which have become ends in themselves, where the purpose of achieving understanding is lost sight of.

13

Sampling, Correlation, and Regression

In Chapter 12 I discussed statistical tests of hypotheses while skirting the topic of sampling. Yet an understanding of the testing process is limited if we fail to see testing as a means of generalizing from a sample to a population. By discussing sampling in this chapter, I hope to give the reader a better grasp of the functions of statistical testing. And as we move beyond testing for the existence of relationships among variables, we come to be concerned with the degree and nature, or type, of the relationships involved. Correlation and regression procedures are widely used statistical techniques for assessing degree and type of relationship, respectively, thus helping us to utilize more aspects of data than were considered in Chapter 12.

An exposition of sampling, correlation, and regression techniques is useful in itself, since the student of social research will encounter them throughout the social science literature. In addition, however, I believe that it is essential for the student to probe their paradigmatic and theoretical implications, just as was done in Chapter 12 for statistical tests of hypotheses. Such probing, in my belief, lies at the core of the statistical approach, an approach that improves scientific communication by providing a framework within which the researcher reveals his decision procedures. Rather than deal with such discussions in a separate section of this chapter, I shall incorporate them within each of two sections, the first on sampling and the second on correlation and regression.

13.1 Sampling[1]

Internal and External Validity

Rather than begin our discussion of sampling in the abstract, let us proceed within the context of the Plotkin study, as presented in Table 12-2.

[1] For a more extended treatment of sampling, see Bernard Lazerwitz, "Sampling Theory and Procedures," in Hubert M. Blalock, Jr., and Ann B. Blalock (eds.), *Methodology in Social Research* (New York: McGraw-Hill, 1968), pp. 278–328.

It is obvious that the percentage of individuals with high integration scores who have high conditional language scores (100%) is greater than the percentage of individuals with low paradigm scores who have high conditional language scores (0%). But does this mean that if the study were repeated with the same individuals, assuming that they were to undergo no fundamental change in orientation, the same result would occur? Are there factors within the research situation that might vary from one data construction period to the next—say, for example, subtle changes in the mood of the researcher—and thereby affect the outcome of the study? What is being discussed here is internal validity: how well our findings apply to the particular research situation under investigation. What is at issue here is not just how complex the factors involved are but our degree of knowledge of them. And since we may assume—I believe—a relatively scant knowledge of what is going on in the research situation, internal validity is generally problematic.

External validity deals with the degree to which research findings can be generalized beyond the boundaries of the research situation. To the extent that the researcher understands what is going on, he generally wishes to apply that explanation as widely as possible beyond the research situation. Perhaps, for example, it applies to similar situations or similar individuals or similar groups. Perhaps it applies to a great deal of human behavior or even to all human behavior. One technique that researchers frequently look to for achieving external validity is *probability sampling.* Probability sampling is a method of selecting (or constructing) a subset, or sample, of units or elements from a population, or larger set, in such a way that each unit has a known probability of being included in the sample. Since these probabilities are known, it is possible—with the aid of statistical techniques—to calculate the *sampling error,* that is, the probability that the sample result differs from a result based on a census of the entire population. Using such techniques, the researcher is thus able to develop an assessment of external validity.

To the degree that we are concerned about external validity—as measured by sampling error—we will attempt to minimize such error, and an effective procedure for doing so is the utilization of large probability sampless. Yet the larger the sample, the less opportunity there is to deal with problems of internal validity. For example, we might have a crew of ten interviewers and know very little about the dynamics of each interviewer's style, much less about the context of each particular interview. And if internal validity is sacrificed, then what is the worth of trying to generalize findings that we are very uncertain of? It would seem, then, that external validity constitutes a stage beyond internal validity, and becomes important to the degree that we have achieved worthwhile results with internal validity. Consequently, the large probability sample is not necessarily a good research strategy, especially to the degree that internal validity is at issue.

In addition to the probability sample, there are various kinds of non-probability samples, and we may examine the implications of such procedures for external and internal validity. For example, there is the nonprobability sample that results when it becomes possible to collect data from only a proportion of the units designated within a probability sample, such as when a survey group is able to interview only 80 per cent of those individuals in the probability sample. There is also the quota sample, where interviewers are required to obtain specified numbers of respondents who fit into various social categories (e.g., so many white males over 50, so many black females over 50, and so forth). With quota sampling, it is left up to the interviewer which individuals he will select to fill his quota, and his tendency will be to choose those who are easiest to locate and who are consequently not among the poorest segment of the population. Another kind of nonprobability sample is the choice of individuals who are particularly well-informed about whatever the researcher wishes to know. And still another approach is the choice of extreme cases so as to provide the researcher with important contrasts. In all of the above types of nonprobability sampling procedures, there is no formula we can turn to to estimate sampling error, and consequently it is difficult to estimate external validity and thus to generalize from the sample to a wider population. Yet these approaches may offset this loss with a gain in internal validity. For one thing, such sampling procedures tend to be less expensive and to involve less time than probability sampling techniques, and thus resources that would have had to go into the sampling effort become available for dealing with internal validity problems. As another illustration, a study of knowledgeable informants may produce far more understanding per individual studied than the most rigorous probability sample. Or a study of extreme cases can point up contrasts that would be hidden within a large probability sample.

Another factor that affects internal and external validity is the size of the sample. If a sample is a probability sample, then sampling error diminishes as the size of the sample increases, thus tending to increase external validity. It is largely because of this that sociologists tend to survey large numbers of individuals, usually in the hundreds and sometimes in the thousands. The driving motive behind such efforts is the vision of using the sample as a basis for understanding the behavior of very large aggregates or social systems, perhaps even whole societies. Complex technologies for drawing probability samples of various types have been developed with this in mind.

Yet one result of this emphasis on large samples is to discourage the researcher who has time or money only for a small sample. If a study of a small sample will have little external validity, why bother? In my view, there is little justification for such an attitude. Most important, the problem of internal validity still looms very large in even the most highly controlled study, and a small sample may enable the investigator to devote his full attention to making headway there. The sociologist who alerts himself to the perspective of the experimental social psychologist will find a much greater concern with internal validity than with external validity. Another reason for working with small samples is that statistical tests can easily be applied in such situations, using nonparametric statistics. And if, in addition, the researcher uses one-sided tests and sets his significance level at .10 or higher, he will be in an excellent position to discover new relationships by lowering the probability of Type II error to levels comparable to those that apply to much larger samples where the significance level is kept low and where two-sided tests are employed.

Types of Probability Samples

Most of us are familiar with techniques for drawing a *simple random sample,* which is the most widely known of the probability sampling procedures. In this approach, each unit within the population from which the sample is to be drawn must have an equal chance of being chosen. For example, in a lottery a large number of slips of paper may be placed in a bin and thoroughly mixed, and then a sample will be drawn from the bin. Each slip is of equal size, and the thorough mixing assures that later entries have no better and no worse chance than earlier ones. Also, the individual selecting the slips has no way of knowing which ones he is selecting and so cannot act on the basis of preferences.

Social scientists frequently choose simple random samples with the aid of a table of random numbers, such as Table 13-1.[2]

Suppose, for example, that we wish to obtain a simple random sample of 10 individuals from a population of 73 individuals. We might proceed by giving each individual in the population a unique two-digit number (01, 02, 03, . . . 10, 11, . . . 72, 73). Then, we could enter the table of random numbers at a random point by closing our eyes and marking the table with a pencil. If that point is, say, closest to the fourth row and seventh column ("3"), we could proceed horizontally from left to right, and so on, recording the numbers in pairs: 34, 69, 50, 08, 37, 41, 57, 46, 01, and 29. Any number over 73 and any number that is repeated would not be counted.

Tables of random numbers are constructed by locating a natural or manmade process that generates numbers in such a way that (1) each of the ten numerals has the same probability of appearing, and (2) each subset of numerals (for example, each pair) has the same probability of appearing. These probabilities are tested by using the relative frequency of the appearance of each numeral and subset of numerals as a measurement of its probability. The digits in Table 13-1 were produced by summing

[2] Interstate Commerce Commission, *Table of 105,000 Random Decimal Digits,* Statement No. 4914, File No. 261-A-1, 1949, p. 10.

Table 13-1
Table of Random Numbers

Columns

Rows	1	2	3	4	5	6	7	8	9	10	11	12	13	14	15
1	3	5	3	4	8	8	2	8	5	4	5	5	8	4	6
2	6	1	0	7	8	5	2	4	3	3	2	2	1	8	4
3	6	6	6	8	2	2	5	4	4	2	8	3	6	6	8
4	7	3	7	7	8	6	3	4	6	9	5	0	0	8	3
5	7	4	1	5	7	4	6	0	1	2	9	7	7	6	5
6	8	2	4	5	3	1	9	5	3	2	4	9	9	8	8
7	0	1	1	3	7	8	6	1	6	8	7	8	2	5	7
8	7	3	1	6	1	4	6	0	6	1	3	0	9	4	6
9	1	8	6	0	1	1	8	1	9	8	1	9	4	6	8
10	2	5	6	2	7	6	3	1	0	7	3	0	8	0	6

ten digits, each of which had to do with a different type of information (for example, shipment weight, revenue, serial number of a car). Only the units digit of the resulting sum was retained, and this constituted the digit used for the table of random numbers.

A *stratified probability sample* is obtained by dividing the population into whatever strata are most meaningful for the research problem and then selecting, for example, a simple random sample from each stratum. For example, suppose we wished to study reactions to the women's liberation movement in our population of 73 individuals. We might, then, want to assure ourselves that the sample contains the same proportions of males and females as does the population. Thus, if there are 36 males and 37 females in the population, then we would use the table of random numbers as outlined above, only with one difference: after choosing 5 males, we would ignore all further choices of males, completing our choices of 5 females. Or, if 5 females were chosen before 5 males were chosen, we would ignore further choices of females.

This is an example of proportional stratified sampling, where the proportions of individuals in the various strata of the sample are the same as the proportions of individuals in the various strata of the population. If the investigator feels that more information is needed from one stratum of the population than from others, he may use disproportional stratified sampling techniques. For example, suppose that the attitudes of males on women's liberation are much more homogeneous than the attitudes of females, where a greater variation is expected. He might then select 6 females and 4 males, or even 8 females and 2 males, and in the final analysis weight each male's opinions more than each female's so as to secure a representative picture of the population as a whole.

Clustered probability samples are designed for relatively complex situations and are characterized by an initial sampling stage in which groupings or clusters of the units to be sampled are selected by means of a probability sample. Suppose, for example, we wish to sample all individuals of voting age within a large city. We might begin by taking a simple random sample—or a stratified random sample—of the census tracts within the city, with the tracts constituting the clusters, or groupings, of the individuals. For a second stage, we might proceed to take a simple random sample of all individuals residing within the census tracts selected in the first stage. We would need a complete list of those individuals in order to do so, and if one was not available we would have to go through the time and expense of listing every individual by going door-to-door.

However, if we used cluster sampling techniques in the second stage as well as the first, the task would be simplified. We could select a simple random sample of the city blocks within each of the census tracts selected in the first stage. Also, instead of a simple random sample in the third stage, we might utilize *systematic sampling*. With this procedure, we begin with a random starting point among the first n units and then take every nth unit. Thus, for example, suppose we wanted to sample every fifth individual. Each interviewer would be given a random number between 1 and 5, inclusive, and a technique for ordering the individuals in a given household (for example, by age). He would begin with the individual designated by his random number, then skip the next four individuals, interview the fifth, skip the next four, and so on. In this way, his skipping might sometimes carry him several households down the block, and sometimes (rarely) would produce another interview (an individual of voting age) in the same household. Although systematic sampling is more convenient than simple random sampling, one of its disadvantages is that every set of units does not have the same probability of being chosen. It is very difficult, for example, to obtain more than one individual from the same household, using the above illustration, and for some purposes it might be important that there be some instances where several members from a given household are drawn.

Sample and Population

I have deferred introducing a critique of sampling processes until this point in order to present the nature of these processes in a systematic way. However, the time has come for critical analysis. We must begin with the most fundamental questions. What are the purposes? To what extent does sampling interfere with these purposes? Are statistical tests meaningful when nonprobability samples are involved? Under what conditions are nonprobability samples to be preferred to probability samples? Are there other kinds of error than sampling error that we should be taking into account? What paradigms are implied by sampling processes? Obviously, we can do no more than make a dent in these questions, but by raising them it can at least be suggested that no aspect of sampling procedure is beyond criticism.

The paradigmatic analysis of statistical testing of Section 12.2, which elaborated on the formist aspects of such testing, applies in general to sampling procedures. The focus within sampling just as within hypothesis testing is on a contrast between a plane of truth, where the true probabilities or parameters for the population as a whole lie, and the plane of observation as represented by the sample. The result is a relatively narrow spatial perspective and a static temporal perspective. Yet for all this, probability sampling appears to show great potential for dealing with the problem of external validity by specifying the conditions under which data is selected. It offers procedures by which the researcher can avoid selecting the kind of sample that merely happens to be most convenient, or that happens to conform to his own views as to the nature of human behavior. We should keep a balanced perspective as we attempt to probe more deeply.

One place to begin is with the concept of "population." The key function of probability sampling is to enable the investigator to achieve external validity in generalizing to a population beyond the specific sample selected. Now, suppose we refuse to accept a narrow spatial view of phenomena and do not see ourselves examining an isolated hypothesis to determine how widely it holds, since we do not believe it is possible to deal with phenomena effectively in this manner. Instead, we are interested in a system of interlocking hypotheses. Also, suppose we do not accept a static temporal view where it is assumed that some relationship exists without change in the population and that it is our job to discover the nature of that reality. Instead, let us assume continuing change, and let us also assume that our own investigation contributes to that change. With this new set of assumptions, the population we are concerned with becomes a much more complex entity. How, then, is it possible to achieve external validity?

One direction is—spatially—to design one's data collection instruments so that they deal with the complex context of the phenomena under investigation. For example, an interview schedule deals primarily with verbal behavior, yet one can triangulate this procedure with others, such as observational or simulation techniques. In this way, we do not rip apart the context that explains the behavior we week to understand, for we assume that the behavior is not easily understood in isolation from that context. Another illustration is to sample units of experience within the behavior of a single individual, as distinct from assuming that a population must comprise a number of individuals. As for a temporal direction, if phenomena are assumed to be changing, then we must focus on such changes with whatever data collection instruments we use. In the survey, we can ask retrospective and prospective questions. As for observational procedures, we can conduct them over a long period of time. Experimental and simulation procedures, as well as the analysis of available data, can deal more directly with change. Thus, it is a population of changes rather than a population of static entities to which we seek to generalize.

Another aspect of sampling to consider is the relation between sampling error and other kinds of error. Sampling error is the error in measurement due to the fact that sample results vary in one respect or another from what would be true for the population as a whole. If sampling error is the only kind of measurement error involved, then the larger the probability sample we take, the smaller the error, for probability samples tend to converge on true population values. But let us recall Chapter 6, where we discussed the relationships among measurement validity, reliability, and precision. It is validity that is far more important than the others, and reliability is second in importance. Precision is important only to the degree that validity and reliability issues have been dealt with, at least to some extent. Now, our ability to deal with sampling error represents one aspect of precision. Whereas scaling deals with precision as it relates primarily to internal validity, probability sampling deals with precision as it relates primarily to external validity.

Following this reasoning, we can place sampling in perspective. If, for example, we are unconcerned with construct validity, then an elaborate sampling procedure is like tying a jet engine to a toy car. Yet if we become concerned with construct validity, then we become deeply involved with theory and with internal validity. There is no getting around it: we cannot focus on any aspect of the research process—like sampling—without dealing with every other aspect of that process. Much like the links of a chain, several poor links can destroy the effectiveness of all the other links. And we certainly cannot treat any link—such as probability sampling—as an end in itself: what kind of sampling procedure we devise depends on the total chain we are attempting to forge. And if we move away from the formist contrast between a plane of truth and a plane of observation and toward a pragmatist perspective, then we had best attempt to forge the kind of chain that deals with that complexity and dynamism.

An additional aspect of sampling that we might explore has to do with the nature of drawing a probability sample. By using a table of random numbers as a basis for drawing a simple random sample, for example, the investigator is prevented from making his choices in unknown ways that might bias the results of the analysis in some direction he desires or some direction resulting from his choice of, say, convenient procedures. Yet since that same investigator affects the research process in myriads of other ways, he has every opportunity to achieve a great deal of bias. Following sampling procedures to their logical conclusion, suppose he selected his research topic, defined his problem, selected measurement and analysis procedures, and even wrote his final report via sampling procedures: what would this produce? It is easy, for example, to imagine the outcome of a written report based on sampling words from a dictionary. But why should it be any less justifiable to sample at that stage of the research process than at an earlier stage?

One perspective on this question is to see sampling as an attempt to reduce unknown biases stemming from the investigator. However, this example illustrates that it is not possible to eliminate such bias without at the same time eliminating the intelligence of the investigator, for the sampling processes at each stage of the investigation could be produced by a computer properly programmed. But, if we recognize the importance of making use of his intelligence, can anything be done about the hidden biases involved? One approach is simply to bring the biases up to the surface. Once they are not hidden, they are no longer dangerous, because they can be taken into account as additional variables within the research process. They can be studied, just as other variables are studied.

How far have we gone with respect to the questions posed at the beginning of this discussion? Perhaps some distance with respect to a general approach, but the questions must still be answered for each particular study. Nonprobability sampling is useful along with probability sampling, especially to the degree that the former can bring to bear on the investigation the intelligence of the researcher as well as the knowledge of his respondents, and also to the degree that hidden assumptions or biases can be brought to the surface. As for the purposes of sampling, these have been related to the search for external validity, but that in turn is related to every aspect of the research process. Thus, sampling decisions cannot be isolated from the set of decisions involved in the research process as a whole. For example, it is one-sided to pay too much attention to sampling if this means a neglect of procedures for dealing with internal validity and reliability. Are statistical tests meaningful when used with nonprobability samples? It would be ridiculous to say either yes or no: many researchers have found them meaningful as a pragmatic means of locating relationships that should be explored further, while many more insist that statistical tests have no meaning unless used within the context of probability sampling. I believe that the rules of the game of science should not be decided by methodologists, but should emerge from those techniques that effectively fulfill the aims of science. I also believe that the rules of the game are in continual flux as we learn to improve our techniques.

13.2   Correlation and Regression [3]

In this section I shall touch on some techniques that are designed to go beyond the question of whether or not a given relationship between

[3] A detailed discussion of correlation and regression procedures is contained in Hubert M. Blalock, Jr., *Social Statistics*, 2nd ed. (New York: McGraw-Hill, 1972), pp. 361–470.

variables exists. Correlational techniques explore the degree of relationship between variables, and regression techniques aim at predicting a given variable from one or more other variables by constructing an equation specifying the nature, or type, of relationship involved. In this section I shall begin with a discussion of regression, since the most commonly used correlational techniques are based on an understanding of regression, and then I shall proceed with correlation. I shall once again include a paradigmatic analysis of these techniques.

Regression

It is frequently said that the aims of science are explanation and prediction; the focus of regression is on the latter. Beyond passive prediction lies active control. The scientist wishes, for good or ill, to be in a position to shape his environment, and understanding and prediction help him to do this. All this undoubtedly conjures up visions of the evil scientist who seeks to control the physical world and even the behavior of human beings. Yet there is another way of looking at things. The environment, physical and human, is rapidly moving in ways that often run counter to human goals. It is not only ecological disasters, wars, racism, poverty, mental illness, crime, and the like that we have great difficulty in dealing with but also less dramatic things like human happiness and the ability of one human being to communicate with another. From this perspective, the scientist is presently quite helpless, along with everyone else. If there are ways out of our dilemmas, then perhaps the methods of science can point in the appropriate directions. And if the scientist is so bold as to attempt to apply correlational and regression techniques to human phenomena, then he is moving in a direction that may prove to be most beneficial. And if these techniques turn out to be quite limited, then at least we shall have made some progress from the effort and learned some lessons.

Most work with regression deals with the prediction of one variable on the basis of another variable, and almost all of this work centers on "linear regression" and uses "least squares" techniques for the calculation of the equation used for predictions. I shall proceed by presenting an illustration of the technique and follow this with a discussion of the implications and limitations of this approach. In the event that the reader has not read between the lines of the foregoing paragraph, I will state my general orientation. Regression techniques constitute an attempt to do something very important, for prediction is an important basis for the development of further understanding as well as for the construction of social technologies. Yet in the face of the complexities and dynamism of human behavior, linear regression is presently a noble failure, based on assumptions that the world is much simpler than it turns out to be. On the other hand, alternative assumptions can be the basis for a far more effective use of regression techniques, and these can thus constitute an important tool on the road to ever better analytic procedures.

I am selecting for this illustration the data from Table 2-4, which presents the relationship between resultant goal commitments and the percentage who gave favorable ratings to a given field of medicine within the occupational choice study. In Table 13-2 these data are presented within a format that simplifies the calculation of both the "least squares regression line" and the "Pearson r," or "product-moment correlation coefficient."

To understand the nature of linear regression, we must go back to the algebra of the line. In graphing the equation, $y = 1 + 2x$, we have a specific illustration of the general equation for the line, $y = a + bx$. y is what is known as a function of x: for each value that x takes on, there is a corresponding value for y. This is illustrated in Figure 13-1. Thus, for example, the point $x = -2$ is paired with $y = -3$, and so on. In the general equation for the line, $y = a + bx$, b is the slope and a is the y-intercept. In Figure 13-1, we can see the line intercepting the y-axis where $y = 1$. The slope is a measure of the angle the line makes with the x-axis; it is 0 for horizontal lines, 1 or -1 for lines hitting the x-axis at $45°$ angles, and approaches ∞ or $-\infty$ as a line gets closer to the vertical position. It may be calculated from a knowledge of the location of any two points on the line by dividing the difference between their y-coordinates by the difference between their x-coordinates. Thus, for the points $(2, 5)$ and $(1, 3)$ in Figure 13-1, we may calculate the slope as follows: $(5 - 3)/(2 - 1)$, or $2/1$, or 2.

Let us now attempt to graph the linear function for the X, Y data in Table 13-2, proceeding in the same way. In Figure 13-2, a key difference between the graph in Figure 13-2 and the one in Figure 13-1 is that the points are not all on the line. The line is the best estimate of the location of these pairs, using the least squares criterion. According to this criterion, the sum of the squares of the vertical deviations of the points from the line is minimized. As an added attraction, the sum of these deviations is zero. We may approximate this line for data that are quite linear (as in

Table 13-2
Schema for Performing Regression and Correlation Calculations

X	Y	XY	X²	Y²
1	86	86	1	7,396
2	71	142	4	5,041
3	60	180	9	3,600
4	44	176	16	1,936
5	37	185	25	1,369
6	17	102	36	289
$\Sigma X = 21$	$\Sigma Y = 315$	$\Sigma XY = 871$	$\Sigma X^2 = 91$	$\Sigma Y^2 = 19{,}631$

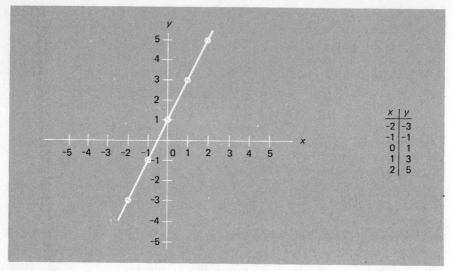

Figure 13-1.
A Linear Function: $y = 1 + 2x$.

Figure 13-2) simply by drawing a line where negative and positive deviations appear to balance one another. The formulas for calculating b and a, derived by means of the calculus, are

$$a = \bar{Y} - b\bar{X} = \frac{\Sigma Y}{N} - \frac{b\Sigma X}{N} = \frac{\Sigma Y - b\Sigma X}{N}.$$

$$b = \frac{\Sigma(X - \bar{X})(Y - \bar{Y})}{\Sigma(X - \bar{X})^2} = \frac{N\Sigma XY - (\Sigma X)(\Sigma Y)}{N\Sigma X^2 - (\Sigma X)^2}.$$

To calculate the regression line, we substitute the values for ΣX, ΣY, ΣXY, and ΣX^2 from Table 13-2, taking $N = 6$ (6 points). Thus:

$$b = \frac{6(871) - (21)(315)}{6(91) - (21)^2} = -13.23.$$

$$a = \frac{315 + 13.23(21)}{6} = 98.8.$$

Thus, the regression line is: $Y = a + bX = 98.8 - 13.23X$.

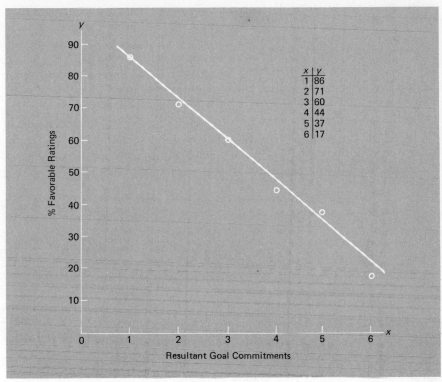

Figure 13-2.
Regression of "Favorite Ratings" on "Resultant Goal Commitments."

Correlation

There are a variety of different ways of assessing the degree of relation between X and Y. For example, we can simply look at the spread of percentages in a table if it has the form of Table 2-4. This spread of 69% can then be compared with the spread in other similar tables and used as a rough way of comparing the degree of association in the various tables. The most widely used method was developed by Karl Pearson and measures the amount of deviation around the least squares regression line. The formula for r is

$$r \text{ (or } r_{xy}) = \frac{\Sigma(X - \bar{X})(Y - \bar{Y})}{\sqrt{[\Sigma(X - \bar{X})^2][\Sigma(Y - \bar{Y})^2]}}$$

$$= \frac{N\Sigma XY - (\Sigma X)(\Sigma Y)}{\sqrt{[N\Sigma X^2 - (\Sigma X)^2][N\Sigma Y^2 - (\Sigma Y)^2]}}.$$

By applying this formula to a set of points, then, we emerge with a measure of the degree to which the points deviate from the least squares regression line. As for the properties of r, it takes on values between -1 and 1, inclusive. An r of 0 indicates zero correlation, or degree of association. The closer r is to 1 or -1, the greater is the degree of positive or negative correlation. A positive correlation is associated with a line of positive slope, and a negative correlation is associated with a line of negative slope. A more stringent procedure for assessing degree of association is to calculate the *coefficient of determination* by squaring r. Thus, if we square an r of .50, we end up with a coefficient of determination of .25.

Let us, then, perform the calculation for r, using the data from Table 13-2:

$$r = \frac{6(871) - (21)(315)}{\sqrt{[6(91) - (21)^2][6(19,631 - (315)^2]}} = -.99.$$

Even using the more stringent coefficient of determination, the result is a negative relationship that can hardly get any more negative ($r^2 = .98$). In other words, the least squares regression lines passes very close to the set of points on the graph, and we can use it to predict the Y coordinate corresponding to any given X coordinate quite effectively. For example, if $X = 2$, then the regression line predicts that $Y = 98.0 - 13.23(2) = 72.3$, which is close to the actual value of 71.

Although they are rarely used, techniques for measuring *nonlinear correlation* have been developed that assess the closeness of fit of data to *nonlinear regression* equations. These equations can take on a vast variety of different forms. One common curve is the *exponential equation, $Y = e^x$*, where $e = 2.718 \ldots$, the base of the natural logarithms. In Figure 13-3 we see the behavior of Y for a very simple exponential equation. As X becomes more and more negative, Y approaches 0, since $e^{-x} = 1/e^x$. When $X = 0$, $Y = 1$, since any number taken to the zero power is, by definition, 1. And as X becomes more and more positive, Y approaches infinity. It is beyond the scope of this book to deal with the various methods of assessing degree of correlation in relation to the exponential equation or other nonlinear equations, although one very simple technique involving very little mathematics is simply to plot the data carefully on graph paper, measure the vertical distances of points from the curve, and sum the squares of these distances.[4]

---

[4] For another way of going beyond the simplicity of linear regression and correlation, one which centers on feedback relationships over time, see Jay W. Forrester, *Principles of Systems,* 2nd preliminary ed. (Cambridge, Mass.: Wright-Allen Press, 1969).

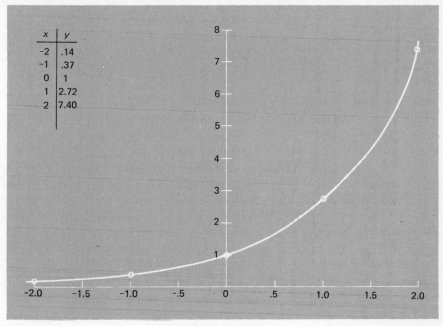

x	y
-2	.14
-1	.37
0	1
1	2.72
2	7.40

Figure 13-3.
The Exponential Equation.

In addition to the Pearson r, which is most meaningful to the degree that we are dealing with ratio scales, there are many kinds of correlation coefficients designed specifically for ordinal measurement. Two particularly well-known examples are Spearman's r_s and Kendall's tau (τ). Neither of these approaches starts with a regression line, as does the technique for measuring Pearson r. Tests for statistical significance have been devised for all of these measures of correlation so that, for example, we can test whether or not a correlation is significantly different from zero, thus arriving at an alternative way of testing a null hypothesis of no relationship between two variables.

Thus far we have been discussing correlation techniques involving the relationship between two variables. More complex techniques have been developed for dealing with correlations involving a number of variables simultaneously. Most of these techniques represent an extension of the considerations taken up in the previous discussion of Pearson r. For example, *multiple correlation* constitutes an assessment of degree of deviation from a *multiple regression* line. In multiple regression, the researcher is interested in predicting one dependent variable from any number of independent variables. Such an equation is illustrated by the following equation, which is directly analogous to the equation for the line:

$$Y = a + b_1X_1 + b_2X_2 + \cdots + b_kX_k.$$

As for multiple correlation (R), what we do is once again analogous to simple correlation procedures. Where only two independent variables are involved, for example, we sum the square of the deviations (vertically) from the least squares plane. *Partial correlation* procedures[5] measure the degree of relationship between a dependent variable Y and any one of the independent variables involved in a multiple regression equation, all the while partialling out the effects of (or controlling for) one or more other independent variables. For example, in $r_{ij.k}$ we measure the degree of relationship between i and j, controlling on k. The sociologist has generally preferred the kinds of techniques to be discussed in Chapter 14 over partial correlation techniques in attempting to achieve this objective, for such procedures are simpler and involve fewer assumptions about the level of precision of the measurements involved (e.g., whether nominal, ordinal, interval, or ratio).

Paradigmatic and Theoretical Implications

As a general statement, what was said in Chapter 12 about the paradigmatic and theoretical implications of statistical testing also applies to correlation and regression. One key difference is that correlation and regression techniques are based on a mechanistic paradigm as well as a formist one, whereas statistical testing involves the mechanistic paradigm to a lesser degree. The focus of the latter is much more on a yes-no question, whereas the former is deeply involved with the mathematics of the relationships among phenomena.

One approach to exploring these implications is to begin with a particular context, that of the occupational choice study, which is the basis for the discussions of mechanism in Section 2.2 and is also the basis for the illustrations of correlation and regression procedures in the previous parts of this section. Suppose that all we knew was that a statistically significant relationship exists between resultant goal commitment for a given field of medicine and the student's preference or lack of preference for that field. This would be at least a start in understanding the forces involved, but it would not carry us very far. A great many other factors could also be discovered that are significantly (from a statistical significance perspective) related to preference for a given field. How would we assess the relative

[5] A nontechnical treatment of the uses of partial correlation is contained in Hubert M. Blalock, Jr., *Causal Inferences in Nonexperimental Research* (New York: Norton, 1972).

importance of this variety of factors so as to learn the best directions in which to proceed?

With the aid of correlation and regression techniques, we are able to compare these relationships with one another with reference to the *degree* of relationship associated with each. This does not imply that we therefore deal only with those relationships manifesting high correlations and forget the rest, but at least it gives us more of a sense of priority. If we have an r of .99 for the relationship between resultant goal commitments and percentage of favorable ratings, and if we have r's of the order of .15, .20, and .25 for a host of other factors (as is far more typical of the kinds of correlations that obtain in social science), then we had best focus a great deal of attention on the r of .99. This can be seen even more dramatically when we deal with coefficients of determination, for the four coefficients are .98, .02, .04, and .06, respectively.

Yet for all this, how far have we actually come in our efforts to understand the phenomena in question, even given such a high coefficient of determination? In my belief, we have taken only a very tiny step forward. What can we do with our regression line and high coefficient of determination? For example, what do we know about the actual fields of medicine that the students eventually entered? What can we say about the substantial proportions of students who were unfavorable to medical fields for which they had high resultant goal commitments (for example, the 29% of preference ratings that went in the opposite direction predicted by a resultant goal commitment score of 2)? Perhaps most important, what have we learned about the forces that *change* resultant goal commitments in one direction or another?

The central limitations of correlation and regression procedures are associated with their static temporal approach and spatial narrowness, just as in the case of a great many other procedures evaluated in this book. To perform regression and correlation, including multiple and partial correlation calculations, we need not have data at different points in time. The "predictions" we attempt to make are not predictions as used in the ordinary sense of the term, where we think of some future time in relation to a present time, but only specifications of functions that relate one variable to another. Perhaps the greatest danger of the availability of such techniques is that this does not encourage us to ask more difficult questions, and to take the difficult road necessary to begin to answer them. How does occupational preference change from one point in time to the next? How do resultant goal commitments change over time?

Along with this static temporal orientation is a spatial narrowness. For example, almost all the preceding discussion of correlation and regression has been about the relationship between two variables, and this relationship has been conceived of in an extremely simple—namely, a linear—manner. From all the evidence from the social sciences that I have been able to assess, I find little support for such simplicity in any aspect of human behavior. Human interaction, for example, is a two-way street, where changes feed back and forth on one another and where complex contexts involving many factors must be taken into account. The focus of both the simple and the advanced techniques of regression and correlation, however, is to chop up this complexity into bits and pieces, to assume that other factors than those explicitly dealt with do not affect the result, to control, or partial out, variables when such controls can hide the complex web of interrelationships involved, to assume that the world of phenomena comes in separate and independent packages.

Yet all this is not to say that techniques of correlation and regression are of little use—far from it. For example, if coefficients of determination were calculated for all of the relevant tables in all of the social science journals, then we would begin to face up to how little we have accomplished thus far. We can use techniques of multiple and partial correlation effectively to the degree that they are based on effective measurement and effective theory. All of these procedures, if used to a much greater extent than they are used presently, can indeed carry social science further. Yet let us also be on guard lest the means become the end. Let us also face up to the static temporal perspectives and narrow spatial perspectives that they foster.

13.3   Summary

The topic of sampling deals with the process of making decisions about which phenomena to study. A central issue involved has to do with our relative emphasis on external validity and internal validity. If external validity is important, then we would want to choose a sample in such a way that we are able to generalize our findings to a larger population. Of course, for such generalizations to be meaningful it is essential that the findings we wish to generalize have a fair degree of internal validity. There are a variety of types of probability samples that help the researcher achieve external validity, such as simple random samples, stratified probability samples, clustered probability samples, and systematic samples. Yet, taking all this into account, it is essential never to lose sight of the research process as a whole, including the paradigmatic and theoretical implications of our approach to internal and external validity and sampling.

Regression and correlation procedures enable the investigator to go beyond the question of whether or not a given relationship exists to an examination of the degree and type of relationship involved. Among the techniques available to the researcher are nonlinear correlation and regression, multiple correlation and regression, and partial correlation. All of these techniques fall largely within the mechanistic paradigm and, as a result, incorporate some of the power of mathematics. This enables them to go beyond in various respects the formist paradigm implied by tests of hypotheses. However, they also carry with them a relatively static temporal orientation and a spatial narrowness, and it is thus essential to bear these limitations in mind if we are to utilize such procedures effectively.

Exercises

1. Using Table 13-1 as your table of random numbers, draw a simple random sample of 10 days of the year, dealing with the table numbers in groups of 3 and designating each day with a number from 001 to 365.
2. From Table 11-1 calculate the least squares linear regression of the percentage with high political participation on the scale of family participation.
3. Calculate the correlation coefficient associated with the regression line of Exercise 2.
4. Select any journal article utilizing Pearsonian regression or correlation techniques and discuss the relation between the theory and the implicit assumptions behind these techniques.

Annotated Bibliography

BLALOCK, HUBERT M., JR. *Causal Inferences in Nonexperimental Research.* New York: W. W. Norton & Company, Inc., 1972. For the student who has at least some idea of the nature of correlation and regression, Blalock provides a largely nontechnical discussion that can carry his understanding much further.

BLALOCK, HUBERT M., JR. (ed.). *Causal Models in the Social Sciences.* Chicago: Aldine Publishing Company, 1971. Although a great many of the articles here are highly technical, there are many that are much less so. What is particularly valuable here are the insights that can be gained from work outside of sociology, such as that in econometrics.

LAZERWITZ, BERNARD. "Sampling Theory and Procedures," in Hubert M. Blalock, Jr., and Ann B. Blalock (eds.). *Methodology in Social Research.* New York: McGraw-Hill Book Company, pp. 278–328. Lazerwitz discusses the various types of sampling and balances his material with illustrations from sociological survey work. For a still more detailed treatment, see Leslie Kish. *Survey Sampling.* New York: John Wiley & Sons, Inc., 1965.

chapter 14
Multivariate Causal Analysis

It is not enough to be able to state that a relationship exists between factor *a* and factor *b*, or to be able to say that the relationship is a close one, or even that we can "predict" b from a. The social scientist wishes to achieve deep understanding of phenomena, and he tends to associate such understanding with causal understanding. For many years he has hesitated to mention the concepts of "cause" and "effect" because it was felt that they were too far-reaching and therefore unscientific. After all, we can never be certain that one factor is the cause of another; all we can know is that factors are related. Rather than go out on a limb, the social scientist has preferred to remain cautious. Yet there is a new approach to causality that is coming to the fore. Although we can never be certain about cause and effect, we do not live from one minute to the next without making numerous causal assumptions. And if we do this in everyday life, why not in science? Also, it is the search for causal relationships that is perhaps the fundamental basis for scientific inquiry. Why try to hide this fact from view? We are learning, then, to place social science inquiry within the framework of causal analysis. However, in keeping with the tentative nature of science, we need never assume certainty about any given cause-effect relationship.

There are two major traditions of causal analysis that have been developing in sociology: the cross-tabulational and the correlational. The cross-tabulational tradition developed in the context of the analysis of survey data as sociologists endeavored to make sense out of the findings that emerged. It is a largely nonmathematical tradition, although it is associated with statistical testing of hypotheses. The correlational tradition is of much more recent origin and is more mathematical. It too tends to be associated with the analysis of survey data. However, instead of a focus on the frequency distribution of one variable within categories of another, the focus here is on the correlations manifested by a set of variables. In this chapter I shall discuss each of these traditions in turn and, in addition, explore their paradigmatic implications.

14.1 The Cross-Tabulational Tradition

Whereas the earliest approaches to cross-tabulation dealt with the relationships between pairs of variables, it came to be realized that other factors must be brought into the picture for an adequate understanding of the situation. A major emphasis came to be placed on three-variable analysis. For example, suppose factor *a* is related to factor *b* because factor *c* causes both *a* and *b*. In such a situation, we say that the relationship between *a* and *b* is *spurious*. In another situation, *a* and *b* are interrelated because *a* causes *c*, which in turn causes *b*. Here, *c* is designated as an *intervening variable*. In a third situation, an initial relationship between *a* and *b* may be stronger within one category of the third variable *c* and weaker within another category of *c*. Here, we speak of the *specification* of the relationship. In this section I take up each of these three situations and conclude with a paradigmatic analysis of some aspects of the cross-tabulational tradition.

Spurious Relationships

I will make use of a hypothetical illustration in order to clarify the nature of the relationships involved. Let us begin, then, with a relationship between the number of fire engines (*x*) present at a given fire and the amount of damage (*y*) produced by the fire. This relationship is illustrated in Table 14-1. Of the fires involving two or more fire engines 59% produced damage of $10,000 or more, whereas only 30% of the fires involving one fire engine produced that amount of damage. This relationship can be tested for statistical significance. Let us employ a commonly used test, the

Table 14-1

[*xy*]: Relationship Between Number of Fire Engines (*x*) and Amount of Damage (*y*)

Amount of Damage	Number of Fire Engines	
	1 (%)	2 or more (%)
$10,000 or more	30	59
Under $10,000	70	41
Total	100	100
	(1,500)	(700)

t test for the significance of differences between proportions.[1] The null hypothesis (H_0) is that P_1, the proportion of fires involving two or more fire engines producing damage of $10,000 or more, is equal to P_2, the proportion of fires involving one fire engine producing this amount of damage. As for the alternative hypothesis, H_1: P_1 is greater than P_2. Setting the level of significance at .10, we find that the relationship is statistically significant (actually, it's significant at the .001 level).

Of course, it is absurd to think of this relationship as a causal one. Obviously, more fire engines do not cause increased damage. This is the type of finding that encourages further probing: How are we to explain this relationship? Survey analysts proceed by doing a three-variable analysis, introducing third variables that might explain what is going on. One useful technique is to control on this third variable, that is, to examine the relationship between the other two variables within each of two categories of the control variable. This is illustrated in Table 14-2, where the third variable (*t*) is the number of alarms.

In analyzing Table 14-2, let us begin by treating it as two distinct tables relating number of fire engines (*x*) to amount of damage (*y*): one table dealing only with one-alarm fires, and the other with two-to-three alarm fires. In looking at these two tables, we may note that—within each one—there is no relationship between *x* and *y*, in contrast to the situation depicted in Table 14-1. But how are we to explain the contrast between Table

Table 14-2
[*xy;t*]: Relationship Between Number of Fire Engines (*x*) and Amount of Damage (*y*), Controlling on Number of Alarms (*t*)

| | 1-Alarm Fire | | 2–3 Alarm Fire | |
	2 or More Fire Engines (%)	1 Fire Engine (%)	2 or More Fire Engines (%)	1 Fire Engine (%)
$10,000 or more	5	5	80	80
Under $10,000	95	95	20	20
Total	100	100	100	100
	(200)	(1,000)	(500)	(500)

[1] For a very useful table enabling the researcher to perform such tests very rapidly, see Vernon Davies, "A Rapid Method for Determining the Significance of the Difference Between Two Percentages," Stations Circular 151, rev. July 1962 (Pullman, Wash.: Washington Agricultural Experiment Stations, Washington State U.).

14-2 and 14-1? Suppose that the relationship among *x*, *y*, and *t* are as follows:

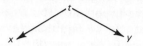

Then by controlling on *t*, we also eliminate the basis for the relationship between *x* and *y*, and thus that relationship disappears, as in Table 14-2. In order for this to occur, we should expect *t* and *x* to be related, and also *t* and *y*. Tables 14-3 and 14-4 depict these two relationships. As we

Table 14-3
[*tx*]: Relationship Between Number of Alarms (*t*) and Number of Fire Engines (*X*)

Number of Fire Engines	1-Alarm Fire (%)	2–3 Alarm Fire (%)
2 or more	17	50
1	83	50
Total	100	100
	(1,200)	(1,000)

Table 14-4
[*ty*]: Relationship Between Number of Alarms (*t*) and Amount of Damage (*y*)

Amount of Damage	1-Alarm Fire (%)	2–3 Alarm Fire (%)
$10,000 or more	5	80
Under $10,000	95	20
Total	100	100
	(1,200)	(1,000)

might have expected, the number of alarms (t) is related to the number of fire engines (x), and it is also related to the amount of damage (y).

Just what is happening in all of the foregoing? A relationship between two variables, x and y, is shown to be spurious because a third variable, t, is related both to x and to y. Furthermore, when we control on this third variable, the relationship between x and y disappears. Prior to controlling on this variable, we were able to obtain a relationship between x and y because both x and y were correlated with t. When we control on t, however, we remove the effect of this correlation, and the result is the elimination of that relationship between x and y.

An Intervening Variable

Another possible set of relationships among x, t, and y is $x \rightarrow t \rightarrow y$. Here, t intervenes between x and y, and is designated as an intervening variable. If you ignore time order, then the relationships here are the same as in the spurious case: in both, x is related to t, t is related to y, and x is not directly related to y but is indirectly related to y through t. And also in both, when we control on t, the relationship between x and y disappears. How, then, can we tell the difference between these two situations? If we are dealing with survey data collected only at one point in time, then we must rely on the nature of the variables. For example, we can assume that the number of alarms (t) precedes both the number of fire engines and the amount of damage.

We can illustrate the intervening variable situation with the same data used to illustrate the spurious relationship because of the similarity of these two situations. Let us designate x as race, y as IQ score, and t as degree of education. Tables 14-5, 14-6, 14-7, and 14-8 parallel the preceding four tables, incorporating the same cross-tabulations. The key difference has to do with the time order of the variables: t comes in between x and y

Table 14-5
[xy]: Relationship Between Race (X) and IQ Score (y)

IQ Score	Black (%)	White (%)
100 or more	30	59
Under 100	70	41
Total	100	100
	(1,500)	(700)

Table 14-6

[xy,t]: Relationship Between Race (X) and IQ Score (y),
Controlling on Degree of Education (t)

IQ Score	Not a High School Graduate		High School Graduate or More	
	White (%)	Black (%)	White (%)	Black (%)
100 or more	5	5	80	80
Under 100	95	95	20	20
Total	100	100	100	100
	(200)	(1,000)	(500)	(500)

Table 14-7

[tx]: Relationship Between Degree of Education
(t) and Race (X)

Race	Not a High School Graduate (%)	High School Graduate or More (%)
White	17	50
Black	83	50
Total	100	100
	(1,200)	(1,000)

instead of preceding both x and y. To the extent that the relationship between x and y is mediated only through t, we should see that relationship disappear when we control on t, just as in the case of the spurious relationship.

From Table 14-5 we see a relationship between race (x) and IQ (y). When we control on education (t) in Table 14-6, this relationship disappears. From Tables 14-7 and 14-8 we see that education (t) is related to race (x) as well as to IQ (y). Thus, t acts as an intervening variable. We can explain the relationship between race and IQ by showing that it is the relationship between x and t and between y and t that produces the relationship between x and y.

Table 14-8

[*ty*]: Relationship Between Degree of Education (*t*)
and IQ Score (*y*)

IQ Score	Not a High School Graduate (%)	High School Graduate or More (%)
100 or more	5	80
Under 100	95	20
Total	100	100
	(1,200)	(1,000)

Of course, it should be understood that these hypothetical tables are designed to make interpretations especially simple. For example, there is no ambiguity in the data presented: either there is a clear-cut relationship, or there is no relationship. Also, from our general knowledge of the nature of the variables involved, we can make inferences about the time order of their occurrence. In actual research, however, the data are rarely as unambiguous and the time order is rarely so obvious.

Specification

Specification is usually not a dramatic process. We start with a simple relationship between two variables and then introduce a third. By controlling on the third variable, the initial relationship does not disappear, as in the cases of spurious relationships or intervening variables. However, our understanding of how that relationship works changes as we examine the three-variable table. For example, the relationship could be maintained or be intensified within one category of the control variable while being eliminated within the other category.

This may be illustrated with data I collected in one of my classes a number of years ago. I was interested in the relationship between motivation, as expressed by interest in a class assignment and by how close to the front of the room a student sits, and performance, as measured by grade. I began with assessing the relationship between expressed interest in a class assignment (x) and grade (y), as presented in Table 14-9. The result was quite definite: x and y are related (H_0 that $P_1 = P_2$ is rejected in favor of H_1 that P_1 is greater than P_2, .10 level).

How will our understanding of this result be specified when we introduce the variable of seating position (t)? Let us try it and see. Table 14-10 presents the relationship between x and y, controlling on t. We find that,

Table 14-9

[xy] : Relationship Between Interest in a Class
Assignment (X) and Grade (y)

Grade	Interested (%)	Not Interested (%)
B— or higher	58	25
C+ or lower	42	75
Total	100	100
	(19)	(24)

Table 14-10

[xy;t] : Relationship Between Degree of Interest in Assignment
(X) and Grade (y), Controlling on Seating Position (t)

	Rows 1–3		Rows 4–15	
Grade	Interested N	Not Interested N	Interested N	Not Interested N
B— or higher	8	4	3	2
C+ or lower	3	7	5	11
Total	11	11	8	13

if we were to consider this as two separate tables, the relationship in the left-hand table is statistically significant but not the relationship in the right-hand table.[2]

What does this add to our knowledge? One interpretation is that where one sits is a behavioral manifestation of motivation, and that those who *both* express interest in a class assignment *and* sit up front have a higher degree of motivation that those who simply express interest. On the other hand, those who express interest but who fail to sit near the front may have relatively little motivation (the word is not the deed) and, thus, exhibit little contrast with those expressing no interest in the class assignment.

[2] The test used on the left-hand table was the chi-square test corrected for continuity; see Sidney Siegel, *Nonparametric Statistics for the Behavioral Sciences* (New York: McGraw-Hill, 1956), pp. 104–11.

Paradigmatic Analysis

Let us bring to bear a paradigmatic analysis of the cross-tabulational tradition by using Tables 14-9 and 14-10 as illustrative of that tradition. This analysis centers on the merits and demerits of the formist paradigm. Here, there is the implicit distinction between the plane of truth and the plane of observation. Statistical relationships are mere observations, whereas causal arrows come from the plane of truth. The task of the social scientist is seen, then, as moving from one to the other, but never with absolute certainty that any diagram of causal arrows is in fact the truth.

As for strengths, we have the drama of a finding that a given relationship exists or even that it does not exist. In Table 14-9, the existence of a relationship is demonstrated. In Table 14-10, we see that relationship disappear within one category of the control variable while being maintained in the other. Since it is data that enable us to achieve this drama, data thereby become quite important. This is, after all, part of the statistical approach: respect for the importance of data as providing an essential feedback for theory. The other part of this approach has to do with a baring of the assumptions one rests on in order to come to research decisions, such as the rejection of a null hypothesis. Here, the cross-tabulational tradition is intertwined with the statistical testing tradition, so that this second aspect of the statistical approach also is involved.

These strengths, however, also imply weaknesses, since they do not go far enough. Although some assumptions are bared, others are not. And the key to uncovering such assumptions is to pay attention to the data stemming from the researcher's own behavior as well as from the behavior of those he observes. For example, in Table 14-10 we have the separation of three variables: grade, degree of interest in an assignment, and seating position. The analysis centers on a separating out of the effects of degree of interest and seating position on grade. However, there is no focus on synthesis within the formist paradigm. To show what I mean, we might have seen both interest and seating position as dealing with the motivational dimension and given individuals scores of 0, 1, or 2 depending on their illustrating neither, one, or both of these motivational factors. The way this might look is presented in Table 14-11. Note that there is a very wide percentage spread involved here, although I didn't want to put the percentages in the table because of the small numbers involved: 73% of those with the greatest motivational commitment received a B— or higher, 37% of those with a moderate motivational commitment, and only 15% of those with the lowest motivational commitment. Combining two variables along a single dimension may illustrate a mechanistic, organicist, or pragmatist paradigm, but it tends to be alien to the formist perspective.

Another serious weakness of the cross-tabulational tradition is that causal arrows are seen as going in one direction or in the other, but not

Table 14-11
Motivational Commitment and Grade

	Motivational Commitment		
	2	1	0
Grade	N	N	N
B— or higher	8	7	2
C+ or lower	3	12	11
Total	11	19	13

in both directions at once. I remember working with the late Edward A. Suchman in the early 1960's on analyzing a series of studies that linked contact between majority and minority group members and prejudice. I asked him how appropriate it would be to study the ways in which prejudice affected contact. He agreed that this too was an important effect, but he maintained that the present study was focusing on prejudice as a dependent variable and had no room for considering it as an independent variable as well. By failing to see things working in feedback relations, a great deal of realism is thereby lost. Also, we tend to see things in an all-or-none way rather than as matters of degree: one either is motivationally committed, or one is not.

Suppose we wanted to learn how to increase the student's motivational commitment. Seeing commitment as an independent variable does not help us here: we must learn to see it as a dependent variable. But what does it depend on? Grade? Perhaps. But there must be other factors as well. One major problem with the cross-tabulational approach is that it deals with only a few factors simultaneously, and that it is embedded within a paradigm that resists the combining of multiple factors into scales. For example, we might want to combine motivational commitment in a wide variety of areas of life. And we also might want to combine "grade," or effectiveness, in many areas of life. In this way, we might get insight into the sources of motivational commitment, but we would also be stepping outside of the formist paradigm.

Another problem of the cross-tabulational tradition stems from the very successes it has achieved in its three-variable analyses. Through its ability to learn important things about time order—e.g., the conditions under which relationships are spurious or there is an intervening variable—the limitations of data collected at only one point in time tend to be ignored. In this respect, the cross-tabulational tradition, the correlational tradition, and the statistical testing tradition all point in the same static direction:

they do not require data collected at a number of points in time. Thus, their very success also produces a failure to go further. I am assuming here that phenomena are sufficiently dynamic so that a failure to deal with sequential data leads, at some point, to a serious limitation in our understanding.

14.2   The Correlational Tradition

Although psychology has incorporated a correlational tradition for many decades, it is only within the past decade or two that sociology has developed such a tradition as well. Much of psychology's interest in correlation stems from the influence of factor analysis techniques, which have been and are widely used in that discipline in the testing or measurement of various types of abilities and aptitudes. Fruchter describes factor analysis as follows: "A basic assumption of factor analysis is that a battery of intercorrelated variables has common factors running through it and that the scores of an individual can be represented more economically in terms of these reference factors. An individual's score on a test is dependent upon two things: the particular abilities assessed by the test, and the amount of each of these abilities possessed by the examinee."[3] A "battery of intercorrelated variables" means that each variable is correlated with every other variable.

The factor analyst begins with a set of intercorrelations among a number of variables and, by means of a series of mathematical procedures, produces a number of common factors. Within the context of testing, each factor represents a particular ability assessed by the set of tests. Each test is viewed as assessing this ability to a greater or lesser degree; the index of this degree is called the *factor loading* of the test. For example, a given test may have the maximum loading of 1.0 on a given factor and loadings of 0.0 on the remaining factors, indicating that it provides the best possible measure of that one factor and useless measures of other factors. Another test might have a factor loading of 0.5 on several factors—providing fairly good measures—and 0.0 on the remaining ones. Let us designate a test's various factor loadings as $a_1, a_2, a_3, a_4, \ldots$. If we then designate the amount of each of these various abilities in an individual's possession as $x_1, x_2, x_3, x_4, \ldots$, then that individual's score (s) on a given test may be calculated as follows:

$$s = a_1x_1 + a_2x_2 + a_3x_3 + a_4x_4 + \cdots$$

[3] Benjamin Fruchter, *Introduction to Factor Analysis* (New York: Van Nostrand, 1954), p. 44.

As it became easier to perform factor analyses with the advent of the computer, sociologists more frequently utilized these techniques. But there were other reasons as well for making use of correlation coefficients. For example, the limitations of statistical testing were coming to be better understood, especially the idea that the level of significance is not a good measure of the degree of relationship.

However, perhaps the most influential force in the recent upsurge of interest in correlation by sociologists derives from long-standing efforts within the cross-tabulational tradition. There, it will be recalled, a major thrust has been to develop the causal arrows linking sets of three variables by examining the relationship between two of them while controlling on the third. Now, there is a simple way of achieving the same kind of result within the correlational literature: perform partial correlations. For example, the correlation between variables i and j while controlling on variable k is

$$r_{ij \cdot k} = \frac{r_{ij} - (r_{ik})(r_{jk})}{\sqrt{1 - r_{ik}^2}\,\sqrt{1 - r_{jk}^2}}.$$

Thus, with a bit of manipulation of the unpartialled correlations—also called zero-order correlations—we can produce partial correlations.

Let us now see how we can make use of partial correlation to investigate the causal relationships among sets of three variables. In Figure 14-1, four different causal situations are illustrated.[4] We should recognize (1) and (2) from our discussions in Section 14.1: (1) illustrates the case of an intervening variable, and (2) illustrates a spurious relationship. According to correlational theory, in the case of (1) and (2) we have the following tendency:

$$r_{xy} = r_{xt}r_{ty}.$$

As for (3) and (4), also according to correlational theory, we have this tendency:

$$r_{ty} = r_{xt}r_{xy}.$$

[4] This approach derives from the work of Simon and Blalock. See Herbert A. Simon, "Spurious Correlation: A Causal Interpretation," *Journal of the American Statistical Association,* **49** (1954), pp. 467–79; and see Hubert M. Blalock, Jr., *Causal Inferences in Nonexperimental Research* (New York: Norton, 1972).

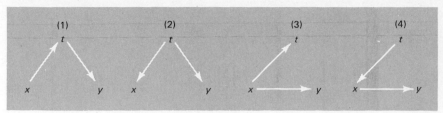

Figure 14-1.

Some Causal Relationships Among: x, y, and t.

These are stated as tendencies because of the sampling fluctuation that is to be expected from r's based on samples; the relationships would be definite were the entire population to be represented.

What is all this leading up to relative to causal interpretations? Simply that the partial correlation can be an effective device for assessing the nature of a set of causal relationships. Let us begin with (1) and (2). If it is true that $r_{xy} = r_{xt}r_{ty}$, then $r_{xy} - r_{xt}r_{ty} = 0$. But this is the numerator of the partial $r_{xy \cdot t}$. This can be checked by substituting in the above formula for $r_{ij \cdot k}$. Thus, if the numerator is zero, the partial as a whole is zero. Just as in the case of the cross-tabulational literature, these techniques by themselves do not indicate whether it is the spurious relationship situation or the intervening variable situation, but nevertheless they do alert us to these two situations in the event that the relevant partial correlation is close to zero. As for (3) and (4), the situation here is quite analogous to the preceding one. Here, we are dealing with the partial $r_{ty \cdot x}$. If we can assume that $r_{ty} = r_{xt}r_{xy}$, then the numerator of the partial will be zero, and the partial as a whole will be zero.

What kinds of assumptions are the basis for this approach to causal analysis? For one thing, there are no two-way arrows, indicating no two-way causation. Another is that y is uniformly seen as a dependent variable, and not as an independent variable. Another major assumption is that all uncontrolled variables have essentially a random effect on x, y, and t. The system of three variables is, in this sense, seen as a closed system. Finally, and perhaps most important, there is the big question of measurement error. Partial correlations are not only subject to sampling error; they are subject to measurement error as well. Blalock illustrates the relationship between sampling and nonsampling error in Figure 14-2.[5] Thus, nonsampling error may be much more important than sampling error. In my own view, I would suggest that it is typical for nonsampling error to be a far greater proportion of the total error than is even suggested in this diagram. Nonsampling error deals, for example, with such questions as

[5] Hubert M. Blalock, Jr., *Social Statistics*, 2nd ed. (New York: McGraw-Hill, 1972), p. 529.

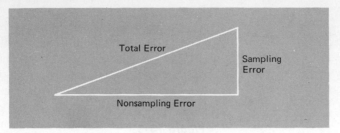

Figure 14-2.
Sampling and Nonsampling Error.

the validity and reliability of measurement, questions that lead back to paradigmatic and theoretical considerations.

The foregoing constitutes an introduction to a rapidly developing body of literature on causal analysis. Much of this literature centers on the concept of "recursive model," which involves one-way causation and is handled by "recursive equations." With such equations we no longer focus on a single dependent variable, such as y in the foregoing discussion, but rather on more complex situations. Also, the equations are set up in such a way that two-way causation does not take place. Here is an illustration of a system of four recursive equations;[6] note that the y terminology for the dependent variable is abandoned:

$$X_1 = e_1.$$
$$X_2 = b_{21}X_1 + e_2.$$
$$X_3 = b_{31}X_1 + b_{32}X_2 + e_3.$$
$$X_4 = b_{41}X_1 + b_{42}X_2 + b_{43}X_3 + e_4.$$

Here, we assume that none of the later variables affects the preceding ones, but that the preceding variables affect the later ones. For example, X_4 is affected by X_1, X_2, and X_3, but it does not in turn affect X_1, X_2, or X_3. The e_1, e_2, e_3, and e_4 terms are error, or disturbance, terms representing the effects of all omitted variables. The b's function as in the multiple regression equation discussed in Chapter 13, where we are predicting X_2 or X_3 or X_4 instead of Y. The notation "b_{21}" indicates that we are predicting X_2 with the aid of X_1; "b_{42}" indicates that we are predicting X_4 with the aid of X_2; and so forth.

A modification of this simple recursive model is what is known as a "block recursive system." In such a more complex system, which involves

[6] Hubert M. Blalock, Jr. (ed.), *Causal Models in the Social Sciences* (Chicago: Aldine, 1971), p. 2.

what is known as "simultaneous equation techniques," sets, or blocks, of variables are recursively related. However, reciprocal causation is allowed within blocks. Because of the additional complexity that this introduces, ordinary least squares estimating procedures are no longer appropriate, as they are in the simple recursive system. In such complex systems, there frequently are too many unknowns to be able to estimate the equations of the system, in which case we refer to the system as being underidentified. We can also have a situation of overidentification, where we have to choose the best method of estimation from among a number of alternatives, and a situation of exact identification. The overidentification situation has the advantage that multiple predictions can be made from the excess variables, thus providing us with additional information in situations where we are uncertain about the nature of the equations, much as triangulation techniques work in obtaining accurate measurement.

One assumption associated with simple recursive systems is that the error, or disturbance, terms are uncorrelated with the independent variables in each equation as well as with each other. What is being assumed, then, is that all unmeasured variables are uncorrelated in these ways. In addition, by examining each equation we can see the assumptions of additivity and linearity in the relations among each set of independent variables and its dependent variable. This is directly analogous to the additivity and linearity assumptions involved in factor analysis.

One approach to causal model building has taken on the name of *path analysis*. It too is based on recursive systems of equations. It involves a type of regression analysis, just as do the procedures involved in the foregoing discussion. A central tool here is the *path coefficient,* which is a standardized partial slope in the case of simple causal models involving one-way causation. It is calculated as follows:

$$\beta_{ij \cdot k} = b_{ij \cdot k} \frac{s_j}{s_i}.$$

$b_{ij \cdot k}$ is a partial slope, where variable i is predicted from variable j, controlling on variable k. Also, s_j and s_i are the standard deviations of variables j and i, respectively. The standard deviation of a given variable X is calculated as follows:

$$s = \sqrt{\frac{\Sigma(X_i - \bar{X})^2}{N}} = \sqrt{\frac{\Sigma X^2}{N} - \left(\frac{\Sigma X}{N}\right)^2}.$$

In another formula, we can see the relationship of the path coefficient to the partial correlation coefficient:

$$\beta_{ij \cdot k} = \frac{r_{ij} - r_{ik} r_{jk}}{1 - r_{jk}^2}.$$

Note that the numerator of the path coefficient is identical to the numerator of the corresponding partial correlation coefficient. Thus, we can use path coefficients in the exploration of causal relationships just as we used partial correlation coefficients, since this numerator can become zero just like the partial correlation coefficient numerator.

What can be said in relation to a paradigmatic analysis of the correlational tradition that I have not already said in the context of discussions of statistical testing, correlation and regression, and the cross-tabulational tradition? Very little, I believe. As tools for analysis become ever more elaborate—and the ones discussed here are only an introduction to those that have already been developed—it seems that the danger of the researcher losing his sense of perspective tends to increase geometrically, or perhaps even exponentially. The more complex tools require a substantial investment in time in order to master them. At that point, one tends to lose touch with work that does not require such tools, communicating primarily with others using those tools. In this way, a critical perspective toward those tools tends to be lost, and one centers on the details of how they are to be used. Yet the over-all case for such tools tends to remain unproven. I believe that what is required to make this case is nothing less than exciting or fruitful theory emerging from such analyses.

There is little question that the recursive model approach moves the researcher in the direction of situations more complex than those involving simply one dependent variable, and it helps us to understand something of the nature of this complexity. Yet let us not forget the host of simplifying assumptions that go along with this approach—e.g., the lack of two-way causation, the assumption that we are dealing with a closed system where all other unmeasured variables are uncorrelated with the independent variables in each equation, and the assumption that the relation between the set of independent variables and the dependent variable for each equation is additive and linear. How realistic is this in the light of social science theory? I suspect that it is not realistic at all.

Yet why, then, are such assumptions made? I suspect that the key reasons have to do with the limitations of mathematics. For example, one of the major reasons for assuming that only one-way causation exists—thus providing the basis for setting up recursive systems—is to make it easy to estimate the various coefficients by using least squares procedures. But is this a good enough reason? Isn't it much like looking for the lost coin under the light because one cannot see in the dark where the coin was dropped?

Suppose, however, that the darkness itself is produced by unquestioning allegiance to a mechanistic paradigm, where one never questions the limitations of mathematics? Suppose that light can be produced in the dark areas by shifting to a cybernetic paradigm, where mathematics is used as far as it goes, but where one need not adopt unrealistic assumptions. Obviously, the case for such an approach is yet to be thoroughly established, and it would be ridiculous to abandon a critical perspective toward it. Thus, the researcher would do well to utilize the correlational tradition insofar as it proves helpful, bearing in mind its limitations.

14.3 Summary

The cross-tabulational tradition and, more recently, the correlational tradition have produced powerful technical tools for the analysis of data. The cross-tabulational tradition, emerging from the context of survey research, has led to ways of understanding causal relationships among sets of three variables. We are able to develop evidence about spurious relationships and intervening variables as well as about the specification of relationships. This approach to analysis carries with it the strengths and weaknesses of the formist tradition. So long as we are aware of its limitations, we are in a position to utilize it as an important tool for social research.

The correlational tradition developed largely from the influence of psychological testing procedures along with the rapid development of mathematical statistics. It includes factor analysis, one of the earliest techniques developed, and has expanded into a variety of additional highly specialized procedures. Some of these are particularly useful for serving the growing interests of social researchers in the analysis of complex causal relationships. Partial correlation is one important technique that can yield information analogous to that deriving from three-variable analysis within the cross-tabulational tradition. Most recently, path analytic techniques have been developed that are a type of regression approach in their emphasis. These procedures are most useful additions to the tools of the social researcher, provided that he becomes aware of the limiting assumptions they incorporate and works toward the ability to deal with more realistic assumptions.

Exercises

1. Construct your own illustration of a spurious relationship. Do you understand intuitively why the relationship is spurious?

2. In Section 14.1, t intervenes between x and y. Now, suppose we discover another variable (u) that intervenes between x and t. For example, u might be the emphasis on achievement fostered within the home environment. Assume that education (t) is completely determined by this variable. Now construct some tables you think would show the relationships among these four variables.

3. Using methods from the correlational tradition, draw the relationships among these four variables. Which partial correlation coefficient or coefficients would you expect to be zero?

4. Do a paradigmatic analysis of your work in Exercises 2 and 3, critically evaluating its limitations.

Annotated Bibliography

GLASER, BARNEY G., AND ANSELM L. STRAUSS. *The Discovery of Grounded Theory*. Chicago: Aldine Publishing Company, 1967. Glaser and Strauss center on qualitative research procedures. Throughout, their focus is on the context of discovery. For example, they claim that typical procedures for the analysis of survey data are so one-sided in favor of verification that much is lost.

ROSENBERG, MORRIS. *The Logic of Survey Analysis*. New York: Basic Books, Inc., Publishers, 1968. In treating the procedures for analyzing survey data in depth, Rosenberg deals with such topics as extraneous and component variables, intervening and antecedent variables, suppressor and distorter variables, conditional relationships, conjoint influence, specification, clarification, description, and interpretation.

VAN DE GEER, JOHN P. *Introduction to Multivariate Analysis for the Social Sciences*. San Francisco: W. H. Freeman & Co., Publishers, 1971. The book is divided into two parts: introduction to matrix algebra and techniques of multivariate analysis. The author lays the mathematical basis within the first part for dealing with a variety of complex topics in the second part, including simple regression and correlation, multiple and partial correlation, partial correlation analysis and path analysis, factor analysis, and nonrecursive linear models.

part V

Scientific Communication

What happens to the results of scientific investigations? All too often, very little. Given the high degree of specialization within each discipline, it is too easy to bury the results of research within very narrow communication channels. The readers of one journal may know very little of what is going on in journals in neighboring subdisciplines, let alone in other disciplines. In this way, assumptions can be protected from the views of those who might start from different assumptions. Is this communication, or is it a failure to communicate?

I believe that it is both. At one level, individuals with common assumptions are carrying forward the implications of those assumptions. At another level, however, it constitutes a failure to confront those assumptions with alternative ones. For example, one way of confronting any discipline with alternatives is to face up to efforts to deal with important problems, problems that do not know the boundaries of any given discipline. Here, then, is one way to structure the questioning of fundamental scientific assumptions, or paradigms: structure efforts to communicate between the two cultures of the scientists and the technologists. But if a status hierarchy is maintained between the two, then neither one will be interested in seriously questioning his own paradigm. The scientist will "already be in possession of creative truth," and will need the technologist merely to spread the word. And the technologist, who will be convinced of the inadequacy of scientific knowledge, will be certain that he is doing the only relevant thing in his search for solutions. And in the process, both will preserve their own narrow assumptions, protecting themselves from more effective knowledge.

The problem of communication between scientist and technologist illustrates the general problem of communication. How is it possible for the scientist—or anyone—to become convinced of the inadequacy of his own *knowledge and of the possibility of moving toward improving that knowledge? How do all of us learn to move from playing a truth game to playing a knowledge game, from playing exclusively a game of verifying our own beliefs to playing discovery as well as verification? Here we might return to the approach outlined in Chapter 1—reflexive, interdisciplinary, developmental—to provide the broad outline of an answer.*

If we are not sufficiently aware of the difficulties and inadequacies within present communication processes—if we think the level of the water of communication is actually much higher than it really is—then there will be little sense of problem with respect to communication. We will pound out our articles, books, and lectures, assuming that someone out there is not only listening but also understands, can act on the basis of that understanding, and has the will to act. This self-examination is, I believe, well fostered by an interdisciplinary approach. In the example just given, it is the technologist with different assumptions from those of the scientist who is in an excellent position to help him become aware of just how effective his communication process is. It is also the student of dramatic and literary communication who is in an excellent position to point up the limitations of scientific communication in reaching people where their feelings are and not only where their heads are.

All this is not done overnight, and should we desire quick solutions, let us be prepared for rapid discouragement. The social scientist is not educated to think in these broad communicative ways, and the humanist is not educated to his scientific responsibilities. Yet now more than ever—given the scope of the problems faced by societies—we need to open up communication channels. Scientist, humanist, and technologist must somehow find ways, one step at a time in a developmental fashion, to incorporate knowledge from others' experiences. Perhaps such communication will show the way toward a scientific method that is both humanistic and effective.

chapter 15

Information
Feedback

The problem of communication between the two cultures of
the humanities and the sciences is a piece of a larger problem: four-way
communication among the humanities, the social sciences, the physical
sciences, and the technologies. Such communication is also the basis of
growth within a given discipline. For example, it is a scientific method
incorporating the theory of the social sciences, paradigmatic perspectives
from philosophy, the mathematical tradition of the physical sciences, and
the humanistic and expressive perspectives of the humanities that can effectively advance any given social science. Yet how do we move toward such
communication?

I believe that our most important task in this final chapter is to illustrate
the importance, indeed the necessity, for the student of a discipline like
sociology to widen his horizons if he hopes to make more rapid progress
in understanding society and in dealing with societal problems. There will
be three parts to this chapter, with each corresponding to contributions
to sociology that can come from the humanities, the sciences, and the technologies, respectively. From the humanities, I have selected ideas emerging
from Isaac Asimov's *Foundation* trilogy, ideas that I believe have paradigmatic significance for the student of sociology. From the physical science
tradition, I have selected something very profound and little known from
the foundations of mathematics—Gödel's Proof—which has implications
for our understanding of the socialization process and the context of discovery. As for the technological tradition, I have selected a sociological
analysis of efforts to put knowledge to work in industrial and governmental
organizational operations, an analysis that is suggestive for the general
student of sociology.

15.1   Isaac Asimov's Foundation Trilogy [1]

What does the student of sociology have to learn from literature? In
my view, it is exactly where his own education is weakest that he stands

[1] Isaac Asimov, *Foundation, Foundation and Empire,* and *Second Foundation*
(New York: Avon Books, 1966, 1966, 1964).

to gain. For example, literature tends to be holistic and contextual and oriented to taking sequences into account. Also, it is very frequently concerned with the intricacies of personalities and the way they function in particular settings. In addition, literature is much more concerned with metaphor than is social science, thus helping the reader to make leaps from one context to another. By contrast, and this is by no means harmful in and of itself, social science focuses on the abstract, attempting to move from the particular to the general. Also, it tends to be analytical, closely examining relationships between one part of a system and another. On the whole, social science centers far more on the context of verification and literature on the context of discovery. To put the two together is like the achievement of triangulation in research methods: each provides some insights that the other does not. Are we, as sociologists, less scientific by opening our minds to the literary disciplines? Only, perhaps, if we think that discovery and metaphor have no place in science.

I want to make use of Asimov's holism and sense of context and history and personality by bringing it to bear on a central problem that sociologists still find quite problematic: the nature of the forces within the continuing industrial revolution. But what can the nonspecialist possibly add to the knowledge of the specialist here? I simply request that the reader withhold judgment. In my view, the nonspecialist has a great deal to offer: a sense of the process as a whole as it works in concrete settings, and a presentation of the process within an imaginative view that penetrates deeply into the vital forces involved, avoiding the distractions that a too close knowledge of detail often provides.

Let us center on a parallel between the shift from a preindustrial to an industrial era in Europe and one that Asimov describes as occurring thousands and thousands of years in the future during a period when the Galactic Empire is crumbling and something new is developing out on the periphery of the galaxy. It is not at all any actual events that are important but, rather, the processes involved. What stages does this new Foundation, beginning on the planet Terminus at the periphery of the galaxy, pass through, and why? There is a shift from a religious era to a trader and merchant prince era, corresponding to the European middle-class revolution. What are some of the forces involved in the shift? And perhaps most important, what insights does this yield about the shifts we are now going through from an industrial to a post industrial world?

To understand the parallel involved, we must use concepts rather metaporically. For example, "religion" usually connotes—to the Western ear—something not quite naturalistic. Yet the religion introduced by Asimov in his first chapter on "the psychohistorians" is entirely secular. Hari Seldon is the founder of the Foundation, a group of scientists and others who dedicate themselves to shorten what they have mathematically calculated will be a thirty-thousand-year dark age following the fall of the

Empire to a period of only one thousand years. Seldon's approach combines the development of mathematics, history, and psychology, or more properly, social science. Instead of attempting to obtain accurate predictions for individuals, he predicts for masses and for social structures. The Foundation, then, comes to be dedicated single-mindedly to saving the galaxy from this dark age—in a parallel to the Judaic-Christian dedication to spiritual salvation. Purportedly, the Foundation group is to achieve its ends by the compilation of a massive Encyclopedia that will preserve the heritage of civilization, much as the Church attempted to do during the Middle Ages in Western Europe.

The Foundation trilogy centers on the early part of this one-thousand-year history, when the Empire is decaying and the repercussions of this are being felt throughout the galaxy. Seldon predicts a series of crises—or "Seldon crises" as they came to be known—during which there is a high probability that the power of the Foundation will continue to increase as the power of the Empire continues to ebb. A solution for one period of time, however, is not a solution for another period, for the forces afoot in the galaxy and the ways in which they are structured in relation to one another continue to change over the years. During each of the early Seldon crises, an image of Seldon appears in the "time vault" with some sage words of advice recorded many years previously. During the first crisis, for example, Seldon has this to say:

> The Encyclopedia Foundation, to begin with, is a fraud, and always has been! . . .
>
> It has served its purpose, since by it we extracted an imperial charter from the Emperor, by it we attracted the hundred thousand humans necessary for our scheme, and by it we managed to keep them preoccupied while events shaped themselves. . . .
>
> This, by the way, is a rather straightforward crisis . . . To reduce it to its fundamentals, it is this: You are a planet suddenly cut off from the still-civilized centers of the Galaxy, and threatened by your stronger neighbors . . . You are an island of atomic power in a growing ocean of more primitive energy; but are helpless despite that, because of your lack of metals.[2]

What, then, is the solution to this first Seldon crisis? Let us turn to the analysis by Salvor Hardin, the first Mayor of the Foundation, who looks back on that crisis from the perspective of thirty years beyond it:

> The temptation was great to muster what force we could and put up a fight . . . What I did, instead, was to visit the three other kingdoms, one by one; point out to each that to allow the secret of atomic power to fall into the hands of Anacreon was the quickest way of cutting their

[2] Isaac Asimov, *Foundation,* pp. 68–70.

own throats; and suggest gently that they do the obvious thing. That was all. One month after the Anacreonian force had landed on Terminus, their king received a joint ultimatum from his three neighbors. In seven days, the last Anacreonian was off Terminus. . . .
That was the time to begin all-out prevention of war. I played them one against the other. I helped each in turn. I offered them science, trade, education, scientific medicine. It made Terminus of more value to them as a flourishing world than as a military prize. It worked for thirty years.[3]

What caused the decline and fall of the Empire, whether the Galactic Empire or the Roman Empire of western history? What forces were at work in the genesis of the newly emerging power known as the Foundation or, in history, the industrial revolution? A major message of this piece of literature is not its definitive answers but its opening up of a series of questions. We are dealing here with a focus on the context of discovery. Literature maintains its ability to communicate effectively largely, perhaps, because of this open-endedness. Seldon may think he has most of the answers, but the fascination of the novel lies in the drama of new questions being posed for which the old answers are no longer satisfactory. This drama also is produced by the focus on metaphor, as distinct from less contextual abstractions: a metaphor creates an overlapping of two phenomena that suggests relationships that ordinarily would not occur to the reader. Indeed, this is exactly what we are discussing now: a metaphor relating part of the history of western civilization with the "history" of the Galactic Empire.

I would like to suggest then, a parallel between the two in the phenomenon of the upward positive loop. In Figure 15-1(a), we have a union of two forces that together were involved in the origins of the industrial revolution in Western society: religious legitimation of the Protestant ethic—built on the Jewish ethic—of hard work. The internal arrows indicate dynamic behavior: a continuing expansion as distinct from a levelling off. Thus, there is room for a development of one factor to affect the further development of the other factor, as would occur in an upward positive loop. For example, harder work produces greater conviction as to religious salvation, which in turn encourages still harder work, and so on. Or, in the case of galactic history, production of the encyclopedia produces greater conviction of the fulfillment of the Seldon Plan, and so on.

Yet, as Seldon predicted, a solution for one stage in history is not necessarily a solution for the next stage. In Figure 15-2 we have one difference in the situation: an increasing secularization. The result is the upward negative loop for each of the variables, as indicated by the decelerating arrows. If religious salvation, for example, comes to be less of a force, then the

---

[3] Ibid., pp. 76–77.

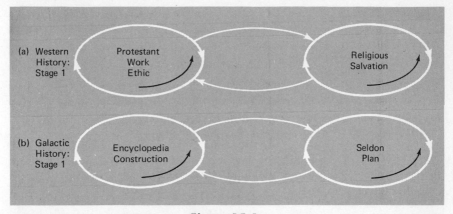

Figure 15-1.
The Industrial Revolution: Stage 1.

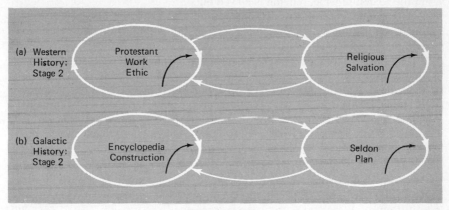

Figure 15-2.
The Industrial Revolution: Stage 2.

sacred aspects of the work ethic—the idea of work as a religious calling—lose part of their force. Similarly, if the Seldon plan becomes less of a religious dogma, then rigid ways of achieving that plan—the construction of an encyclopedia—also become less important. But in their place—with respect to both western history and galactic history—rise new solutions to these problems, solutions involving secularization. In Figure 15-3 we see a third stage of history, where work becomes more secularized, losing its religious trappings, and participates directly in economic productivity and the development of political power. As the Foundation continues to develop, it sheds more and more of the religious trappings of a priesthood that had been used to spread and keep control over its atomic power

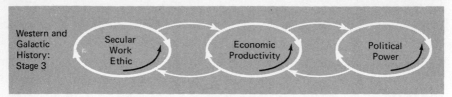

Figure 15-3.
The Industrial Revolution: Stage 3.

secrets. Hober Mallow, a trader and merchant prince of a later day, exemplifies the new approach:

> "There are some things I *didn't* tell Sutt [a religious leader] right now. He tried to control the Foundation itself by religious forces as he controlled the outer worlds, and he failed,—which is the surest sign that in the Seldon scheme, religion is played out.
> "Economic control worked differently . . . If Korell prospered with our trade, so did we. If Korellian factories fail without our trade . . . so will our factories fail. . . ."
> "So then," said Jael, "you're establishing a plutocracy . . . Then what of the future?"
> Mallow lifted his gloomy face, and exclaimed fiercely, "What business of mine is the future? . . . There will be other crises in the time to come when money power has become as dead a force as religion is now. Let my successors solve those new problems, as I have solved the one of today."[4]

Mallow is referring to a next stage of history such as might be seen in Figure 15-4, where the secular economic ethic loses its developmental force, and a negative loop ensues between a materialistic ethic and the quality of life. All of these four stages of history—Western or Galac-

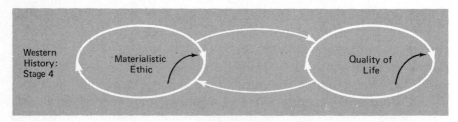

Figure 15-4.
The Industrial Revolution: Stage 4.

[4] Ibid., pp. 199–200.

tic—have in common the same general process. A developmental orientation in one factor tends to be associated with the same in another factor,
with the two moving together in an upward positive loop. However, once
a factor is no longer seen as moving in a desired direction, it closes down
on itself and fosters a closing down of associated factors.

The same idea has been put forward in other language by Fred Polak
in his *The Image of the Future,*[5] a book very much in the spirit of recent
sociological views on the social construction of reality. The Judaic-Christian
formist tradition also provided a powerful vision of a future, of an Other,
beyond where preindustrial man was. That vision provided religious, economic, and political bases for movement toward that future. Man's problem in Stage 4 is that our image of the future has played out, and no new
approach to imaging has survived both the sacred and the secular "Death
of God." What is required, then, is a Stage 5 of Western history where
some kind of postindustrial ethic is related to quality of life in an upward
positive loop.

15.2   Gödel's Proof[6]

From the humanities we move to the world of mathematics and, in particular, to a proof first published in 1931 in a German scientific periodical
by a young Czech mathematician of twenty-five, a proof entitled "On
Formally Undecidable Propositions of *Principia Mathematica* and Related
Systems." It was on the basis of this paper, which caused a stir that has
by no means yet subsided in the world of mathematicians, that Kurt Gödel
was invited to join the Institute for Advanced Study at Princeton and later
received an honorary degree from Harvard University citing his proof as
one of the most important advances in logic in modern times.

My purpose in discussing Gödel's Proof is simply to demonstrate how
seemingly esoteric material from disciplines very far removed from sociology can add greatly to the sociologists's knowledge, and how he can no
longer afford to isolate himself from such knowledge. If he continues to
do so, then he lengthens considerably the time it will take to make important advances in his own field, repeating mistakes that need not be repeated and failing to see directions that he would otherwise be alerted
to by other disciplines.

Obviously, a few pages does not suffice to go deeply into the history
of the foundations of mathematics, just as we were not able to penetrate
very far into the dynamics of the industrial revolution in the preceding

[5] Fred Polak, *The Image of the Future* (San Francisco: Jossey-Bass, 1973).

[6] The principle ideas on which this discussion is based are presented by Ernest
Nagel and James R. Newman, "Gödel's Proof," *Scientific American* (June 1956), re-
printed in *Mathematics in the Modern World, Readings from Scientific American*
(San Francisco: Freeman, 1968), pp. 221–30.

section. Yet by focusing on one or two central ideas, I may at least be able to do some illustrating. My focus, then, will be on the relations between logic and mathematics. In a sense, we have already been discussing this relationship in the context of contrasting formism and mechanism. A direction of the discussion will be the limitations of logic in contrast to the limitations of mathematics and, more generally, the limitations of language. Perhaps this is simply another way of showing that mechanism goes further than formism in at least some respects.

The heart of the matter is the relationship between formal logic and arithmetic. For formal logic, let us begin to think in terms familiar to most readers, namely, Euclidean geometry, with its axioms, or postulates, and its theorems strictly derivable from those assumptions and a series of definitions. One of the great advances within the history of logic was the extension to non-Euclidean spaces. In this way, the approach became much more formal; it no longer depended on intuitive notions as to the nature of space but could be dealt with in the abstract. A further advance along these lines was the development of symbolic logic by George Boole in the 19th century, providing a uniform system of symbols that could be used for stating logical relationships like "not" ($\sim$), "or" ($\vee$). "If . . . then" ($\supset$), "There is an . . ." [∃], and so on.

Two further developments leading up to Gödel's Proof were Alfred North Whitehead and Bertrand Russell's *Principia Mathematica* and David Hilbert's program for the complete formalization of mathematics. The *Principia,* published in 1910, attempted to demonstrate that mathematics is an extension of logic by supplying a system of symbols—following up on the work of Boole—permitting all statements of pure mathematics to be codified in a standard manner. In addition, it stated explicitly most of the rules of formal logic that are employed in mathematical proofs. For example, let us begin with a translation of the Aristotelian syllogism into the language of Boolean symbolic logic:

All gentlemen are polite.	$g \subset p$
No bankers are polite.	$b \subset \bar{p}$
No gentlemen are bankers.	$\therefore g \subset \bar{b}$

One of the basic propositions from the *Principia* is

$(p \vee p) \supset p$ if either p is true or p is true, then p is true.

This is called the "principle of tautology," and is analogous to the Aristotelian principle of identity, that A is A. This proposition is a part of what is called the elementary logic of propositions, or the "sentential calculus." It is based on a two-valued logic—that is, it is formist—in that the truth-value of a proposition is assumed to be restricted to either "truth" or "falsity." Thus, it accepts the classical "Law of the Excluded Middle." There is, in contrast to this kind of logic, a three valued logic, and there are even *n*-valued logics.

The sentential calculus, of which the above illustration is a part, codifies a small portion of formal logic. It illustrates a mathematical system for which the objectives of David Hilbert's theory of proof are fully realized. Without going into Hilbert's complex work to any extent, we might at least consider his aim: to use the axiomatic method in order to place mathematics on a more consistent basis, that is, to formalize mathematics. Thus, Hilbert was much impressed by the advances in this direction made by the *Principia*. Hilbert proceeded to regard mathematical expressions as simply empty signs, drained of all meaning, and to contrast these expressions with *metamathematics,* that is, with statements about mathematics. Thus, the expression $2 + 3 = 5$ is a mathematical statement, for it is constructed entirely out of elementary mathematical signs. But the statement "$2 + 3 = 5'$ is an arithmetical formula" belongs to metamathematics because it describes a string of mathematical signs. An absolute proof of the consistency of arithmetic, then, would show, by metamathematical procedures that two contradictory formulas cannot *both* be derived from the axioms for arithmetic by valid rules of inference.

But the *Principia* codifies only a fragment of formal logic. The question remains: Is it possible to develop a formalized system embracing the whole of arithmetic that can be proved consistent in the sense of Hilbert's program? It is at this point that Gödel's ingenious and startling proof becomes relevant. In his 1931 paper he clearly demonstrated the impossibility of carrying through Hilbert's program: All efforts to prove arithmetic to be free from contradictions are doomed to failure. This was foreshadowed by a whole series of paradoxes that have been part of the history of mathematics and philosophy, paradoxes pointing up contradictions within ordinary language and logic. For example, there is the barber paradox. Assume that in a certain village there is a barber who shaves all and only those men who do not shave themselves. Does the barber shave himself? If he is one of those men who do not shave themselves, then he does shave himself, since he shaves all those who do not shave themselves. Starting the other way around, if he is one of those who shave themselves, then he does not shave himself. What are we to conclude, other than that paradox is built into our fundamental modes of thought? Or there is the well-known statement by Epimenides the Cretan to the effect that all Cretans are liars. If the statement is true, then the statement is false, since it is uttered by a Cretan. If the statement is false, then Cretans can indeed tell the truth, but then the statement becomes an instance of a lie. What are we to believe? There is also Bertrand Russell's paradox, which strikes at the heart of mathematical set theory and not just at the idea of truth and falsity. Divide all classes into those that do not contain themselves as members (e.g., the class of mathematicians) and those that do (e.g., the class of all thinkable concepts). Now, let us call the first type of class "normal" and the second "nonnormal," and let N stand for the class of all normal classes. Is N a normal class? N is normal if—according to the definition of normal —it does not contain itself as a member. But if it does not, then N is indeed nonnormal, for it is a member of the class of all normal classes, that is, it is a member of itself. From the opposite perspective, if N is nonnormal, then it is a member of itself, but that means that—as a member of the class of all normal classes—it is not a member of itself.

Gödel's paper is quite involved, containing 46 preliminary definitions as well as important preliminary theorems, but it is possible to at least suggest its approach. Gödel began by devising a way of mapping the ideas from logic onto numbers. For example, take the principle of tautology:

$$(\quad p \quad \lor \quad p \quad) \quad \supset \quad p$$
$$8 \quad 12 \quad 2 \quad 12 \quad 9 \quad 3 \quad 12$$

Each of the elementary signs (such as $\lor$ and $\supset$) was assigned an integer from 1 to 10; each "sentential variable" (p, q, . . .) is designated by a number greater than 10 and divisible by 3 (12, 15, . . .); each individual variable (x, y, . . .) is designated by a number greater than 10 that leaves a remainder of 1 when divided by 3 (13, 16, . . .); and each predicate variable (P, Q, . . .) is designated by a number greater than 10 that leaves a remainder of 2 when divided by 3 (14, 17, . . .). These numbers are used as exponents of the prime numbers (numbers divisible only by themselves or one) taken in order of occurrence, and these are all multiplied together. The first six prime numbers are 2, 3, 5, 7, 11, 13, and 17. Thus, we may achieve the following mapping:

$$(\qquad p \qquad \lor \qquad p \qquad) \qquad \supset \quad p$$
$$2^8 \times 3^{12} \times 5^2 \times 7^{12} \times 11^9 \times 13^3 \times 17^{12}$$

This product is known as the Gödel number corresponding to the principle of tautology.

One interesting characteristic of prime numbers is that they can only be factored out in one way from products of primes, that is, we can take a number that is a product of primes and locate the original primes. Thus, we can not only create a Gödel number from a statement of logic; we can also recreate that statement of logic from the Gödel number. As a simple example, take the number 162. Let us factor it into its component primes:

2	162	We have, then:
3	81	$2^1 \times 3^4 = 162$
3	27	But these exponents correspond to the logical signs $\sim$
3	9	("not") and $\exists$ ("There is an . . .")
	3	

Thus 162 is the Gödel number for "There is not."

Here, then, is how Gödel utilized his mapping technique. He centered on this metamathematical statement: "The formula with Gödel number h is not demonstrable." Now, the statement was so constructed that the Gödel number corresponding to the statement is h. The statement—let us call it G—in effect asserts its own indemonstrability, although it is legitimate or demonstrable in the sense that it can be equated with the Gödel number h. Gödel then proceeded to show that G is demonstrable if and only if its negation, $\sim$G, also is demonstrable. This is like the barber who shaves himself only if he does not shave himself. If G is demonstrable, then it is not demonstrable. And if $\sim$G is demonstrable, then G is demonstrable. But if a formula and its negation are both derivable from a set of axioms, then the axioms are not consistent. For arithmetic to be consistent, neither G nor its negation can be demonstrable, that is, G must be an undecidable formula of arithmetic. From here, Gödel proved that the consistency of arithmetic itself is undecidable by any metamathematical reasoning that can be represented within the formulae of arithmetic. But G, according to the proof, is not only undecidable; according to metamathematical reasoning, G is also a *true* mathematical statement.

Thus, arithmetic is incomplete in the sense that there is at least one arithmetical truth that cannot be derived from the arithmetical axioms and still can be established by metamathematical reasoning. But this is not the only such truth: we can keep constructing such nonderivable truths indefinitely. There is an endless number of true arithmetical statements that cannot be formally deduced from any specified set of axioms in accordance with a closed set of rules of inference. Even if we keep adding axioms to correspond to these new truths, we will never be able to achieve a completeness that encompasses the remaining truths that cannot be derived from the existing set of axioms.

What, then, is the significance of the foregoing for our purposes? For the logician and mathematician who does not stray outside of his own discipline, the results might seem to be discouraging. Overall, they point up the limitations of language, logic, and set theory—the heart of much of mathematics—because of the paradoxes involved and the lack of completeness. He can of course try to get around all this by being careful to avoid truth-falsity statements that have reference to the statement itself, and the same for sets that refer to the statement about sets itself. But this is actually avoiding the central issues raised by the paradoxes involved.

In my view, the contradictions or paradoxes discussed above provide an opportunity for examining fundamental issues within the history of Western civilization, issues that should not be avoided. Neither are they so far removed from the discussion of Section 15.1 if our perspective is broad enough. The history of the industrial revolution in western society is also a history of the separation of self from environment. We view ourselves as passive observers of the external reality, not seeing ourselves as actively participating in that reality. So it is entirely natural that our language and thought processes should become paradoxical as we use them in reflexive ways, ways that are strange to the Western mind. It is not simply this self-reference that is involved: it is also the simplistic two-valued logic on which our thought, both logical and mathematical, is based. Thus, it is the whole formist approach, as illustrated by the distinction between the plane of truth and the plane of observation. As for multivalued logics, we have barely begun to explore them. Our quest is for certainty, for proof, for definite and irrefutable statements within the context of verification. We know little of the context of discovery. Should we then ignore a clear message to the effect that the closed logical system is incomplete, that it cannot be used to derive an infinite number of truths?

The limits of the formist paradigm also imply limits to the mechanistic paradigm that is based largely on the formist approach to truth. Neither gives us direction for moving forward within the context of discovery, although both can help us to understand our limitations via the context of verification. Somehow, we need to move in a reflexive direction to move into the context of discovery, perhaps engaging in a process of continuing socialization where we continue to step outside of ourselves and look back at ourselves. How do we move? Perhaps what is most important is to leave this question open, on the assumption that our very narrowness in sticking to one discipline or one paradigm has kept us from opening up this question and keeping it open. In their analysis of the significance of Gödel's Proof, Nagel and Newman were open enough to go beyond its discouraging aspects, as related to logic and mathematics, and to think broadly of its humanistic implications, implications that the social scientist should be at least equally aware of:

> Gödel's proof should not be construed as an invitation to despair. . . . It does mean that the resources of the human intellect have not been, and cannot be, fully formalized, and that new principles of demonstration forever await invention and discovery. . . .

. . . The theorem does indicate that the structure and power of the human mind are far more complex and subtle than any non-living machine yet envisaged. Gödel's own work is a remarkable example of such complexity and subtlety. It is an occasion not for discouragement but for a renewed appreciation of the powers of creative reason.[7]

15.3   Organizational Intelligence

The central issue here is how to achieve technological applications of scientific knowledge. But wait: when the word *technological* is put forward, do we immediately conjure up a bureaucratic division of labor, where the scientist is one person and the technologist another? Or have we learned to put the concept of paradigm to work and, thus, to monitor our own innermost thoughts? According to the pragmatist paradigm, for example, the scientist and the technologist are one and the same person: we are all scientists in that we test ideas against experience, and we are all technologists in that we put ideas to work in our efforts to solve problems. Here, we return to the relationship between Figure 1-1, where the scientific method is seen as a feedback process, and Figure 1-2, where human interaction is seen as a feedback process. Perhaps, then, at the very least we should not limit ourselves to thinking only in one paradigm or the other, since each has something to offer that the other does not have. We cannot ignore the bureaucratic division of labor, since it is all around us as well as inside of us. But neither can we ignore a less divided and more reflexive orientation, since the limitations of a division of labor with little communication—Durkheim's concept of an "abnormal division of labor"—are becoming more and more obvious. In his study of organizational intelligence, Wilensky points up some of these limitations and suggests some ways out.

Let us begin with Wilensky's overall outline of the problems involved:

From area bombing to radar, from the Bay of Pigs to the missile crisis and the test-ban treaty, from Korea to Vietnam, failures and successes alike underscore two themes in my analysis of types and functions of intelligence. First, when the problem is technical, when substantial departures from previous practices occur or unprecedented programs are launched, the facts count; but stereotypes constituting the verbal environment of an organization—captured in felicitous slogans—can for years remain impervious to evidence. Second, there is an increasing use of men who combine technical and political skills to create a more sophisticated imagery of organizations (or nations) and their external and internal environments. . . .

The knowledge explosion intensifies an old problem: how to draw good intelligence from a highly compartmentalized body of knowledge

[7] Ibid., p. 230.

and get it into the room where decisions are made. Sources of failure are legion: even if the initial message is accurate, clear, timely, and relevant, it may be translated, condensed, or completely blocked by personnel standing between the sender and the intended receiver; it may get through in distorted form. If the receiver is in a position to use the message, he may screen it out because it does not fit his preconceptions, because it has come through a suspicious or poorly-regarded channel, because it is embedded in piles of inaccurate or useless messages (excessive noise in the channel), or, simply, because too many messages are transmitted to him (information overload). . . .

Intelligence failures are rooted in structural problems that cannot be fully solved; they express universal dilemmas of organizational life that can, however, be resolved in various ways at varying costs. In all complex social systems, hierarchy, specialization, and centralization are major sources of distortion and blockage of intelligence. The quality of intelligence is also shaped by the prevailing concepts of intelligence, the problems to be confronted, the stages of growth of the organization, and the economic, political, and cultural contexts of decision.[8]

Although Wilensky is primarily concerned with the technological applications of information at national policy levels, we can view his analysis as, more generally, having implications for all technological applications of information. I would like to focus here on three issues involved in this process. The first and, I believe, the most important is one that Wilensky has little to say about: the question of how good the information is that we wish to apply, that is, the quality of our information. The second and the third are hierarchy and specialization, two structural aspects of organization that too often are seen as inherent in the nature of organizations and thus only partially solvable.

With regard to the quality of information, I am reminded here of the preceding discussion of Gödel's Proof: we are so deeply enmeshed in considerations having to do with the context of verification that we give little attention to the context of discovery. Can we, or should we, really separate the problem of applying information from the problem of further developing its quality? Should not one of the major considerations of applications be their experimental implications? All this depends on our assessment as to how good our information really is, or how high the level of water in the beaker is. If we assume—as appears eminently reasonable in the light of human failures to deal with central problems—that it is not very high, then the context of discovery becomes an urgent priority. And by centering so much on the context of verification, do we not let slip through our fingers all kinds of information that might carry our ideas further? Are we not so committed to the truths we already possess that when we

[8] Harold L. Wilensky, *Organizational Intelligence* (New York: Basic Books, 1967), pp. 40–42.

attempt to put them to work in an action context we become blind to their deficiencies and to paths for improving them? Is this not symptomatic of our over-all approach to human communication and problem-solving, where we talk but do not listen, where we act but do not monitor the effectiveness of our actions, where our attitudes are favorable or unfavorable but rarely open to new ideas and least of all to a questioning of themselves?

How do we, then, learn to approach phenomena with fewer narrow stereotypes that are impervious to evidence, with less commitment to the truths we already possess? This problem is one I have tried to address in much of this book, pointing up the complexity and dynamism of phenomena and pointing to certain linguistic and cybernetic tools as aids in moving away from narrowing and static stereotypes. Perhaps another metaphor might help at this point. Let us imagine that this book is some 100,000 pages long instead of its 400-odd pages, and that 99,600 are blank. Then this book becomes no more than a very scant introduction to a subject that is almost completely unknown. The book is yet to be written, and you, the readers, must do the writing. The Words of the Methodologists cannot carry you very far, for they have thus far produced very little effective knowledge, and we may see this in the proportion of blank to filled pages. What is important, then, is to begin again to think freshly on all the fundamental questions, for our answers have proved to be most inadequate. What is the scientific method? How do we move forward within the context of discovery and the context of verification? How do we define research problems? How do we construct data to provide effective information feedbacks relative to those problems? How do we communicate to ourselves and others? How can we bring to bear paradigmatic and theoretical considerations within the research context? How can we free ourselves from convictions of our own research inadequacies? How are our everyday life experiences related to scientific research? How can we learn to develop an experimental, gaming, cognitive, nonverbal, historical, and statistical approach?

A second topic I want to consider relating to technology has to do with hierarchy. I will start by assuming that both the basic researcher and the social technologist construct the kind of hierarchy where he himself is quite high and his opposite number is quite low. Thus, for example, the sociologist still—in this day and age—would tend to think of educators and social workers and city planners as intrinsically less creative than himself. He would grant that they are doing necessary legwork, but it is legwork and not brainwork, and after all it is only brainwork that really matters for him. And what of the social technologist's stereotypes? These, I am afraid, are no better. The social scientist is seen as hiding from the mainstream of society's problems, communicating only with other social scientists, collecting useless data, and all the while watching while society falls apart. His "brainwork" is seen as irrelevant esoteric stuff, for he has not faced up to the hard realities of life. Thus, both the social scientist and the social technologist define their opposite numbers in such a way that they are useless and have nothing to offer in the way of contributing to the solution of his problems. There is, then, no need for communication, for nothing can possibly come of it. Each sees the other as a second-class citizen, and thus proceeds to rule him out from among those worthy of communication. Of course, the foregoing is a stereotypical statement, but it seems to convey the thrust of the existing situation.

Is there an alternative to this kind of hierarchy? Must we continue to see one another in this way? Is such hierarchy a necessary component of "structural problems that cannot be fully solved"? I can only begin to answer such questions within the context of the situations discussed in this book. If, for example, the researcher begins to become more reflexive, then he will treat his interviewees or informants or subjects as people who can help him to get information about himself. But then the status barriers between researcher and researched begin to break down: each is providing the other with information about self and other, and neither assumes a godlike monopoly of creative information. Both have a great deal to learn. Now, this is admittedly only one small context, yet it is also a model of a different mode of communication than the hierarchical one. Can it be extended to encompass an ever-widening range of contexts within which social scientist and social technologist are communicating? I believe it can, but it will take a great deal of effort and a great deal of understanding about the differences between such a world and the one we live in most of the time.

Our final topic has to do with the existing abnormal division of labor, that is, with specialization accompanied by little communication among the disciplines or subdisciplines. A lot of discussion on this topic goes something like this:

> Specialization is a necessary evil. It's too bad that knowledge is now so vast that we have no choice but to split it up in little pieces and divide the pieces amongst ourselves. The day in which it was possible for one brain to encompass a significant proportion of human knowledge is long past, and we have to make the best of it. And after all, human talents are limited. There are few among us who are potential Einsteins or Rembrandts. As for the rest of us, at least we can contribute in our own small ways by becoming specialists.

How much of this is true? Is human knowledge in fact so vast, and if so, why has not this vastness revealed itself in human abilities to cope with human problems? Are human capacities in fact so unalterably limited, or have we developed the kinds of human institutions and personalities where we have learned to define our situation in that way and, thereby, have shaped that situation? It is difficult to contradict the previous paragraph without having an alternative paradigm in view. One such paradigm is the pragmatist one, where we see everything we think and do as having interdisciplinary implications: we are nonspecialists without knowing ·it. The influence of a Freud, a Marx, or a Darwin, for example, has been far greater on the consciousness of the ordinary human being—all of us—in his everyday life than its resultant corps of specialists who make a livelihood out of attempting to apply these ideas. We are all of us Freudians, Marxists, and Darwinians to a degree, whether or not we are aware of it, and we thereby shape ourselves and the world at every moment.

Yet how do we choose to put to work the theory available to us? When someone takes the position that the sociologist need not concern himself with Asimov's *Foundation* or Gödel's Proof, then he is making an assumption that it is useful to separate these pieces of knowledge. Such an assumption, I believe, places the sociologist in a narrow and static position as he confronts human phenomena, for his sociological stereotypes become closed to deep knowledge from the humanistic and physical science traditions. We learn to see human behavior as something both less creative and less systematic than we might otherwise see it because of our assumption about the separation of literature and mathematics from concerns about the nature of human behavior.

In a like manner, we might see ourselves as adopting theoretical stances bearing on all of the disciplines all of the time. The problem, then, is not our inability to deal with a wide range of disciplines but, rather, the ways in which we deal with them. Since we are specialists in only one discipline—and even there we tend to be far from the top of the hierarchy—our tendency would be to see ourselves close to the bottom of all specialized hierarchies in our attempts to cope with the interdisciplinary phenomena around us. Such a stance would lead to disagreement with the foregoing statement about the impossibility of going beyond specialization. Yet it is also within our power to reverse any given hierarchy. We can see the specialist as having written only a few pages of the book of knowledge required to solve any important problem. And we can see ourselves—to the degree that we learn to develop broader perspectives—as having a much better chance than the narrow specialist of filling those empty pages: because we are more aware of the empty pages than he is.

15.4 Conclusions

Here, then, we return to our point of origins—a reflexive, developmental, and experimental approach—only I hope that in the course of our journey we have created a spiral more than a circle, ending with a bit more understanding of what is involved. It is reflexive in its recognition of the minute beginnings that our research efforts presently represent and of the vast potential that the human being represents. It is developmental in its recognition that we are already theorists in all of the various disciplines, that by seeing ourselves remaining at the bottom of the various hierarchies we are shaping ourselves and our environment along negative or downward positive loops, and that we might alternatively adopt a stance that moves self and environment in an upward positive loop. Less technically, we might learn to renew our faith in the potential of the scientific method. And it is experimental in its insistence that to attempt to accomplish all in one fell swoop is characteristic of a formist either-or paradigm that will probably fail in the modern world, and that if time and experience are of importance, we must learn to let them work for us. We need not know at this point how to fill all the empty pages. What is required is that we make the effort here and now to fill one of them.

Exercises

Rather than a series of exercises focusing only on this chapter, here in this final chapter it is perhaps most appropriate to attempt to pull together the book as a whole in relation to the student's orientations. What are the most important ideas for a given student? How do they relate to his own ideas? How might they best be put to work in specific research contexts? How might they be used in the constructive criticism of current research efforts as illustrated by the article literature? What directions do they suggest for research efforts of the future? What implications do they have for sociological theory? What are the implications of paradigmatic analysis for sociology? What are the current prospects for a "normal" division of labor, and what can be done to improve them? What does all of the foregoing suggest about the nature of the human being? What does it imply about present and future human institutions?

Annotated References

ASIMOV, ISAAC. *Foundation*. New York: Avon Books, 1966. The discussion of *Foundation* in this chapter constitutes little more than an introduction to the insights contained in a book that may one day be assessed as one of the most important books ever written on the industrial revolution.

Mathematics in the Modern World: Readings from Scientific American. San Francisco: W. H. Freeman & Co., Publishers, 1968. Introductions by Morris Kline. This includes many of the sources for the foregoing discussion of Gödel's Proof, including Quine's article on paradox,

Pfeiffer's on symbolic logic, Cohen and Hersh's on non-Cantorian set theory, and Nagel and Newman's on Gödel's Proof. The book is also an open door to a discipline that stands waiting to be related to social science in important ways.

WILENSKY, HAROLD L. *Organizational Intelligence*. New York: Basic Books, Inc., Publishers, 1967. Perhaps the time has come for us to begin to probe into the fundamental structural problems—such as hierarchy, specialization, and centralization—that make life so difficult in the modern world. If something can be done about them, then we had best begin by understanding their nature and how they have conspired to help create the various hells—along with sundry heavens—that have been involved in the human experience.

Index of Names

A

Abbott, Edwin, 17*n*.
Almond, Gabriel A., 258, 258*n*., 259
Aquinas, St. Thomas, 59
Archimedes, 28
Aristotle, 51*t*., 59
Asimov, Isaac, 333, 333*n*., 334, 335*n*., 349–50

B

Bacon, Francis, 13, 13*n*., 59
Bell, B., 45*n*.
Berger, Peter L., 91*n*.
Berkeley, George, 27, 51*t*.
Bertalanffy, Ludwig von, 36*n*.
Blackwell, Lois, 147*n*.
Blalock, Ann B., 293*n*., 311
Blalock, Hubert M., Jr., 289*n*., 291, 293*n*., 301*n*., 308*n*., 311, 324*n*., 325, 325*n*., 326*n*.
Blau, Peter M., 80, 82, 88*n*., 99, 102*t*.
Blumer, Herbert, 80
Boole, George, 340
Bosanquet, Bernard, 36, 51*t*.
Bradley, F. H., 36, 51*t*.
Bronowski, J., 5*n*.
Bross, Irwin D., 291
Buckholdt, David, 147*n*.

C

Campbell, Donald T., 159–60, 160*n*., 161–62, 162*n*., 165, 165*n*., 166–67, 167*n*., 172, 176, 231, 231*n*., 237, 238*n*., 253, 270
Caro, Francis G., 163
Chapin, F. Stuart, 157, 160, 160*n*., 161, 163
Chave, E. J., 214*n*.
Clausen, John A., 208*n*.
Cloward, Richard, 241, 241*n*.
Cohen, Morris R., 58*n*., 150*n*., 158*n*., 171*n*.
Cohen, Paul J., 351
Cohn-Bendit, Daniel, 242
Comte, Auguste, 37, 37*n*., 38, 44, 51*t*., 90
Copernicus, 10
Coser, Lewis, 80, 102*t*.
Cronbach, Lee J., 140*n*., 141*n*.

D

Dahrendorf, Ralf, 80
Damon, A., 45*n*.
Darwin, Charles, 349
Davies, James C., 94, 94*n*., 95, 192, 201
Davies, Vernon, 315*n*.
Democritus, 27, 51*t*.
Denzin, Norman K., 221*n*., 227*n*., 236, 236*n*., 253, 270
Descartes, René, 27, 51*t*.
Dewey, John, 42, 51*t*.
Dickson, William, 14*n*., 157
Dillon, David, 73–76
Doyle, Arthur Conan, 238
Durkheim, Émile, 38, 38*n*., 41, 51*t*., 63–64, 90–91, 91*n*., 102*t*., 103, 345
Dutton, John M., 203

353

Whitehead, Alfred North, 340
Whittaker, Roger, 259–60
Wiener, Norbert, 65, 65*n*., 66, 78
Wilder, Raymond L., 146*n*.
Wilensky, Harold L., 345–46, 346*n*.,
   351
William of Ockham, 59
Williams, Robin M., Jr., 111
Wolfgang, Marvin E., 155, 217*n*.

Y

Yates, F., 158

Z

Zeitlin, Irving M., 79–80, 80*n*., 103
Znaniecki, Florian, 6, 103

Index of Subjects